Milestones – Setbacks – Sidetracks

The Path to Parliamentary Democracy
in Germany

Historical exhibition in the
Deutscher Dom in Berlin

The Path to Parliamentary Democracy in Germany

Historical exhibition in the Deutscher Dom in Berlin

MILESTONES SETBACKS SIDETRACKS

Imprint

Organizer
German Bundestag

Conceptual direction
Prof. Lothar Gall

Concept, texts and accompanying media
Prof. Lothar Gall
Jörg von Bilavsky
Dr. Jörg Judersleben

Exhibition design and production
Hans Dieter Schaal,
Attenweiler
das planungsbüro
(Martin Müller), Berlin

Graphic design
Bertron & Schwarz,
Schwäbisch Gmünd
cliff house GRAFIK DESIGN
(Alex. Weiher), Wiesbaden

Graphic production
Gigant-Foto GmbH, Berlin
Oschatz Visuelle Medien
GmbH & Co. KG, Wiesbaden

Media production
artemedia ag, Potsdam
Peito GmbH, Berlin
(also CD-ROM development)
R.C.F., Berlin
TeleFactory GmbH, Berlin

Media technology
ict GmbH, Berlin
Hörmann Kommunikations-
Technik, Stade

Lighting and electricity
Büro Steinigeweg, Berlin
Energie Torgau,
Elektroanlagenbau, Torgau
XXLight Adam/Binsert, Berlin

Restoration assistance
Ulrich Lang,
Frankfurt am Main

Exhibition construction
Schröder GmbH & Co.
Stahlbau KG, Rathenow
Studio Babelsberg GmbH,
Potsdam

Replicas and model construction
Formlos (Peter Gragert), Berlin
Manfred Jonas, Berlin

Audio guide
Antenna Audio, Berlin

Graphic design (catalogue)
Marc Mendelson;
assisted by Meike Sander,
Karen Weinert, Berlin

Printing and proofreading (catalogue)
DCM GmbH & Co. KG,
Meckenheim

The Exhibition, with the
President of the German
Bundestag, Mr Wolfgang
Thierse, as its patron,
is organized by the
German Bundestag.

Catalogue, 1st edition

© Published by:
German Bundestag
11011 Berlin

Berlin 2003
English edition

Translated by:
Language Services of the
German Bundestag
in cooperation with:
Anna Canning
Hillary Crowe
Raymond Kerr

Die Deutsche Bibliothek –
CIP Einheitsaufnahme
**Wege – Irrwege – Umwege.
Die Entwicklung der parlamen-
tarischen Demokratie in
Deutschland;**
Historische Ausstellung im
Deutschen Dom in Berlin /
Hrsg. Deutscher Bundestag,
Berlin. 1. Auflage Berlin:
Deutscher Bundestag, 2002

Englische Ausgabe unter
dem Titel:
**Milestones – Setbacks –
Sidetracks**
The path to parliamentary
democracy in Germany

Französische Ausgabe unter
dem Titel:
Cours – Contours – Détours
Histoire de la démocratie
parlamentaire en Allemagne

ISBN: 3-930341-55-7
NE: Deutschland/Bundestag

The Exhibition is open
on Tuesdays from 10 to 22 hrs,
and from Wednesday to
Sunday and on public holidays
from 10 to 18 hrs
(June – August 10 to 19 hrs).

Guided tours (including
in English and French):
Telephone
+49 (0)30 227-3 04 31
to –3 04 33
or Fax
+49 (0)30 227-3 04 38
or by e-mail:
ausstellungsbuero.pi5@bun-
destag.de
Requests should be made
well in advance.

Catalogue and CD-ROM
available from:
ausstellungsbuero2.pi5@bun-
destag.de

The nominal charge is:
Catalogue and CD-ROM
– 10 euros
Catalogue only
– 10 euros
CD-ROM only
– 10 euros

CONTENTS

FOREWORD

by Wolfgang Thierse,
President of the German Bundestag

The parliament is a focus of great interest in Germany's old-new capital city, a fact borne out by the astounding number of people – about four million – who have visited the Reichstag building since it re-opened in autumn 1999. In view of this, it was felt that a dedicated exhibition presenting the historical highs and lows of Germany's parliament was urgently called for.

The very title of the exhibition, "Milestones – Setbacks – Sidetracks: the Path to Parliamentary Democracy in Germany", is intended to highlight the fact that parliament and the free democratic basic order in our country that it stands for are by no means to be taken for granted. They had to be fought for, and we must safeguard them and continue to develop them. The first section of the exhibition opened earlier in the Deutscher Dom to mark the 50th anniversary of the German Bundestag, although at the time it was part of a bigger exhibition, "Questions on German History", subtitled "Paths to Parliamentary Democracy".

This new exhibition shows the beginnings of parliamentary democracy in 1848, the founding of the German Empire in 1871, the Weimar Republic and the demise of parliamentary democracy in the period of National Socialism. It also shows the new beginnings of political life in the western and the eastern zones of occupation, and the emergence and development of two distinct political systems up until the reunification of the two German states. The exhibition covers the period right up to the present, and also seeks to throw light on possible trends for Germany's future development.

At the same time, it is clear that Germany cannot find its way in isolation; it is embedded in a wider supranational context, and especially within the politics of an increasingly closely-knit Europe. Here too, many – and often quite distinct – paths have been discussed and rejected or embarked upon, and this is still the case. Parliamentarization of Europe has certainly not yet reached the level desired by its citizens – and that includes its elected representatives. Rather than lamenting this as a shortcoming, however, we should view it as a challenge.

I hope that visitors to the exhibition, "Milestones – Setbacks – Sidetracks: the Path to Parliamentary Democracy in Germany", will be prompted and inspired by it to look more closely at the history of German parliamentary democracy and the opportunities it presents, and to play an active part in preserving and developing it.

Wolfgang Thierse

INTRODUCTION

by Lothar Gall

Anyone seeking to examine 200 years of German history through the medium of an exhibition must begin by asking themselves a number of questions. How important is an understanding of the past for our perception of the present and our attitude towards the future? This is a widely debated and universal theme. And the related question: What should be the exhibition's practical objectives? And finally: In an increasingly interdependent world, doesn't the choice of a national frame of reference – in this case, the history of parliamentarism and the development of the political parties in Germany – narrow our perspective, thus marginalizing central aspects of today's global reality?

These are undoubtedly legitimate questions. They go to the heart of what this type of exhibition should seek to achieve. In a broader sense, they also encapsulate the underlying issue: What message should modern historiography seek to convey, especially when presenting research findings through the accessible medium of an exhibition?

One thing is clear from the outset: it is impossible to transpose the findings and interpretations of historical research into an exhibition in a "linear" way. Historical research is usually general and abstract, whereas an exhibition achieves its impact visually, through illustrations, using real-life examples and images of specific events and revealing the processes and developments as they occurred. The links between them and the factors which make apparently isolated events characteristic of an entire period are not immediately apparent: the visitor must be made aware of them through the juxtaposition of images and texts grouped around specific themes. The stories conveyed through these images – which appear on the face of it to be highly disparate and only loosely connected – must be woven into an overarching "history" to reveal their true context, meaning and significance. Yet the images do not only cast light on these broad connections; they also challenge the viewer to embark on their own voyage of historical discovery. And this is the real appeal of a (well-designed) exhibition: for the images can be viewed from many different perspectives, opening up the subject to a variety of interpretations and raising new questions. In this way, the exhibition frees itself from the constraints imposed by the organizers' chosen framework and reflects the reality of life in all its diversity and immediacy.

Anyone embarking on the task of designing and preparing an exhibition must therefore take into account – but can also build on – this dynamic quality of their chosen medium. The task of this exhibition is to present, in visual form, the two centuries of German history which followed the epoch-making events of the French Revolution and, in particular, to answer questions on the development of parliamentary democracy in Germany. At the same time, however, it was essential to avoid a superficial approach which merely reported the events, even though television has taught us that this is the easiest objective to achieve when using visual images.

This decision – to avoid superficiality – was taken at the start of the project and crucially shaped the exhibition's format. It was closely linked with other key decisions on content and focus, especially regarding the emphasis to be placed on the individual elements of the exhibition. The central theme – the development of parliamentary democracy in Germany – had to be embedded and presented within its broader historical context in order to illustrate the profound transformation of society which resulted from Germany's emergence as a modern industrial nation. At the same time, it was important to reveal the social and political effects of this process, thus providing a more accurate picture of the historical situation: its specific problems and challenges, its contradictions and thus its political agenda. And finally, from this basis, the key turning-points in Germany's political development in the nineteenth and twentieth centuries had to be presented, highlighting their causes, defining factors, and short- and long-term repercussions: the upheavals of the years between 1806 and 1815; the 1848 revolution; the major constitutional conflict in Prussia and the founding of the German Empire in 1871; the revolution of 1918 and the creation of the Weimar Republic; its collapse and the seizure of power by the National Socialists – the deadly enemies of liberal parliamentary democracy and its social, economic and governmental system; the successful restoration and modernization of this system in the western part of Germany after 1945 and the development of yet another repressive regime in East Germany during this period; and, finally, the overthrow of this regime by those subject to its depredations in an act of revolutionary self-liberation, an event which was followed by the unification of the two German states – separated since 1945 – in a democratic parliamentary process. By focussing on the major turning-points in German history, it was possible to divide the exhibition into separate and self-contained sections which can be viewed individually. The organizers were thus able to include additional material on influences which helped to shape the face and intellectual mood of the various chapters in history but which, from today's perspective, no longer tend to be regarded as directly relevant to them.

Naturally, this structure and emphasis pose a number of problems. Some aspects which the individual visitor might regard as important have received less attention, while others – primarily those which were difficult to depict visually – could only be covered in the explanatory texts. Some major causal links have only been touched upon, and a few loose ends inevitably remain. The decision to separate the exhibition into distinct historical periods – revised in terms of content and based not only on significant events but also on what are generally accepted to be periods of major transformation – is undoubtedly open to criticism for a variety of reasons. Nonetheless, it must be borne in mind that as well as fulfilling the academic agenda outlined above, the organizers also had to consider a range of practical issues, notably the "staying power" of visitors who may not be familiar with the subject matter, and, not least, the length of time they can be expected to spend in the exhibition. Here, it was important to create as clear a structure as possible, highlighting thematic links and locating events in clearly defined timeframes, so that visitors can choose for themselves what they want to see, depending on their own particular interests.

There are inevitably limits to these endeavours, especially as the exhibition is intended to focus on history from a thematic rather than an event-specific perspective. However, since the exhibition's primary objective is to raise awareness of the complex factors and conditions which determine political action, these limits can also act as an incentive for visitors to ask their own questions, make their own comparisons, and find their own answers to the issues raised. Despite all the pointers offered within the exhibition via its content and structure, this obviously still demands a great deal of the individual visitor. Nonetheless, this is no more than the demands made of every citizen who exercises political judgement and helps to shape the political will by casting their vote in a well-functioning democracy. Indeed, the two are inextricably linked – and mindful of this connection, the exhibition organizers have used it as a yardstick in deciding what can realistically be expected of visitors in terms of their concentration span and ability to form their own critical judgements.

In line with this approach, every effort has been made to draw a clear distinction and ensure that the past is not presented as a direct argument for or against a particular policy at present. This applies to the exhibition as a whole, but it naturally applies especially to the sections which are directly relevant to the present day, notably the section dealing with Germany's history since 1945. Since these events are still very recent, the sources are very fragmentary and great care must be taken when seeking to arrive at a balanced historical judgement. The organizers' clear priority was therefore to provide detailed information and documentation rather than attempt to define and evaluate the events in categorical terms.

This might appear unsatisfactory to some people and may well trigger debate and criticism. From the point of view of the individuals who are required to play their part in the political decision-making process, such criticism is of course quite legitimate and even welcome. Nonetheless, it is one thing for a person to draw on the recent past when making political judgements, thus giving these events an extra dimension – a process this exhibition seeks to facilitate – but quite another for the exhibition organizers to attempt to steer visitors towards specific political conclusions. In general, however, the visitor will find that there is no lack of clear and unequivocal judgements voiced in the exhibition whenever the findings of historical research and the academic debate permit. In line with the conceptual agenda outlined above, these opinions naturally go far beyond the naïve but well-intentioned picture-book sketches which merely celebrate the victories of the supposed forces of good and lament their defeats. Instead, they seek to explore each conflict, the various interests and ideas involved, and the genuine scope for decision-making, rather than focussing solely on what might have been desirable outcomes in individual cases. This approach will undoubtedly provoke criticism too, and such criticism is both justified and welcome. Indeed, it could be regarded as a yardstick of the exhibition's success in encouraging visitors to form their own opinions on history and politics and revitalizing the debate about major historical turning points and their impact on the present day.

As we have said, the question which the exhibition organizers would like to make the focus of this exhibition, and whose timeliness and topicality cannot be denied, is this: what were the historical conditions which fostered or impeded the development of liberal parliamentary democracy in Germany? What were the obstacles to its introduction? Which movements combated or endorsed it? What were the conditions on which it was based, and why did Germany fulfil them relatively late and often inadequately? Why was parliamentary democracy in Germany not only vulnerable to external threats but also beset, from the outset, by internal crises and self-destructive tendencies? And finally, why has the authoritarian state in whatever form – the very antithesis of democracy – continued to exert such fascination in Germany even to the present day? All these questions are explored in depth in this exhibition. The answers which it attempts to provide are set in the specific context of each historical period. Yet if we look closely and are not distracted by superficial and often misleading parallels, it is clear that they are relevant to today's political debate as well. This is especially true of one aspect which – if ignored – could pose a real threat

to the entire system of liberal parliamentary democracy: that each period crucially shapes the system's external features and organizational forms, as well as some of its functions and mechanisms which make up less of its real substance than we are sometimes led to believe. Here, too, an analysis of history can help to strengthen the ability to distinguish between form and substance, and, going a step further, to recognize when and where – under changed conditions – form and substance begin to collide. If this exhibition succeeds in prompting a move in this direction by encouraging visitors to think about the past, overcome entrenched attitudes to history, and open their minds to new developments, it will have succeeded in its objective. It will then have far greater legitimacy than many of the faddish calls, from all sides of the spectrum, for the dismantling of the supposedly false perceptions of history espoused by political opponents.

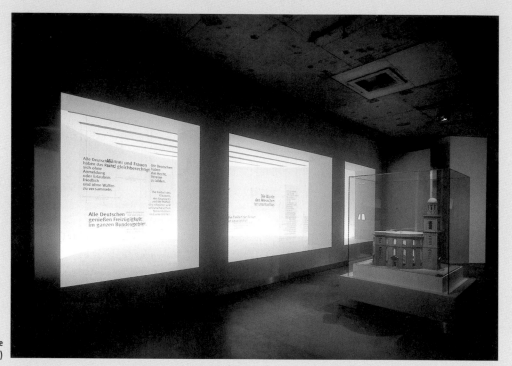

Model of
St Paul's
Church,
Frankfurt, and
installation
on the
Fundamental
Rights of the
German People
(Level 1/detail)

Replica of the
Bismarck
monument,
formerly
in Frankfurt
(Level 2/detail)

Post-war
impressions
from occupied
Germany
(Level 3/detail)

Historic
debates in
the German
Bundestag
(Level 1.1/
Central
Courtyard)

I. THE DAWN OF PARLIAMENTARISM AND THE REVOLUTION OF 1848/49

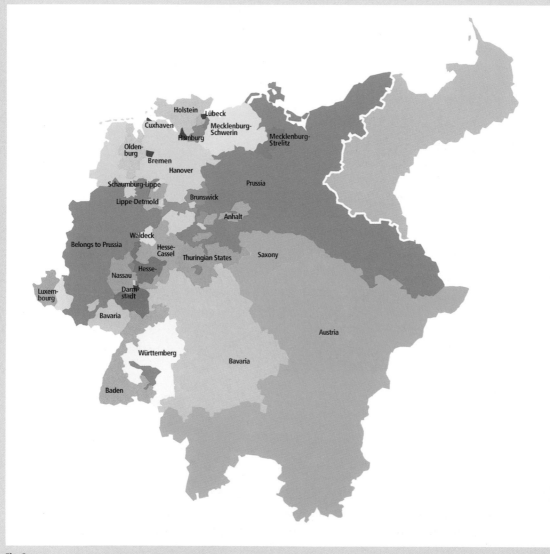

The German
Confederation
after 1815

At the turn of the nineteenth century, Germany's political and social system plunged into crisis. In France, contemporaries were witnessing the emergence of a politically self-confident nation which, under the leadership of an economically invigorated and enlightened bourgeoisie, had freed itself from the shackles of the *ancien régime*. The revolution of 1789 had swept away the divisions between classes – or "estates" – and citizens' legal equality was now enshrined in a constitution. Against this background, the political and social conditions in place in the "Holy Roman Empire of the German Nation" seemed hopelessly anachronistic. Presiding over the loose association of states comprising hundreds of autonomous fiefdoms was the German Emperor, whose political influence, however, was largely confined to his Habsburg hereditary lands. "The Holy Roman Empire would undoubtedly still be the most formidable power in the whole of Europe if its estates, especially the most powerful ones, were united and paid greater heed to the common good than to their private interests", wrote the German constitutional lawyer, Johann Jacob Moser, as early as 1745. Indeed, it was the princes' particularist interests which ultimately stifled reform of the Empire's parliamentary assembly – the Imperial Diet, or Reichstag, at Regensburg. The real power was exercised by the absolutist rulers in their individual fiefdoms, with the rivalry between the two great powers, Prussia and Austria, frequently influencing their political decisions. It was almost inevitable, under these circumstances, that the princes and their

disenfranchised subjects lacked any political consciousness of nationhood. Only in literary circles did an awareness of a nationhood which transcended social barriers begin to emerge in the eighteenth century; in Friedrich Schiller's words, "The German Empire and the German nation are two separate notions ... as the political Empire shakes, the spiritual realm becomes ever more steadfast and complete".

Due to the fragmentation of political authority and the absence of an economically strong bourgeoisie, the French Revolution, while arousing intense intellectual excitement, had little political impact in Germany. However, the onslaught of the victorious French revolutionary armies and the defeat of the two great powers, Austria and Prussia, caused major changes which culminated in the dissolution of the Empire in 1806. In this hour of defeat, it began to be recognized for the first time that the roots of this disaster lay in the deep rift between state and society, and that a bourgeois society based on the principles of liberty and equality was essential in casting off the shackles of French domination. Reforms of the institutions of state, it was argued, would lead to citizens' political emancipation and awaken their interest in state and nation. In Prussia, the reformers sought to establish a "representative system" aimed at ensuring citizens' participation in the legislative process and renewing their love for their Fatherland. However, the programme foundered on the reactionary policies pursued by the individual states and the reforms' lack of social justice, which granted privileges to persons with education and wealth while impoverishing peasants and artisans.

The reforms introduced in the Confederation of the Rhine under Napoleon also aimed to achieve economic liberalization and citizens' equality before the law. Above all, however, their purpose was to establish a centralized administration which would serve the power-political interests of France. In contrast to Prussia, where no "representative system" was in place even after 1815, political emancipation progressed more quickly in the former Confederation of the Rhine states; Austria, meanwhile, remained in thrall to its absolutist system.

Under the oppressive yoke of French occupation, the Prussian reformers' notions of nationhood gave the crucial impetus to the liberation movement. Yet the victory over Napoleon's armies did not produce the political changes sought by patriots. At the Congress of Vienna, it was the princes, yet again, who redrew the map of Germany. Hopes that a German nation-state with a representative assembly would be established were dashed: instead, the negotiations created the German Confederation with its permanent congress of ambassadors, entrenching the sovereign rights of the princes. The Confederation's main objective was to stifle liberal and national opinion and persecute those who still had the audacity to call for constitutions, national assemblies and press freedom. "Constitutions based on the traditional provincial assemblies (*landständische Verfassungen*)" – pledged in Article 13 of the Federal Act (*Bundesakte*), which was the legal basis of the Confederation – were established in only a few individual states.

In the decades between 1815 and the outbreak of revolution in March 1848, known as the *Vormärz*, or pre-March period, numerous reform movements emerged in opposition to the system embodied by the German Confederation. Despite their different social backgrounds, political objectives and methods, these movements were united in their belief that Germany's outmoded economic, social and political system could only be transformed through the creation of a nation-state based on parliamentarism.

Large sections of the bourgeoisie were mobilized by the concept of a nation-state – an idea which was inspired by the wars of liberation and flourished especially among the patriotic student fraternities, or *Burschenschaften*. At the Wartburg Festival in 1817, they staged the first public demonstration for German unity, burning reactionary symbols and writings to reassert their opposition to the traditional order. Even at this stage, the radical wing was already calling for the violent overthrow of princely authority and the creation of a republic.

The proponents of political liberalism, the most important opposition movement of this period, sought to achieve their objectives – personal and political liberty, such as freedom of expression, press freedom and freedom of association, and citizens' participation in the political process – by legal means, initially within the individual states. They favoured the system of government exemplified by the constitutional monarchies of England and France and based on the constitutions adopted in the individual states since 1815. Although the liberals had some success in implementing individual reforms, their efforts to introduce more far-reaching changes foundered on the enduring support for the principle of monarchy, the individual states' claim to sovereignty, and the attempts by governments to reduce parliament and the press to mere instruments of the executive.

The restrictions on freedom merely served to strengthen the liberals' national agenda. The most notable example was the motion tabled by Karl Theódor Welcker in the Baden lower house, calling for the creation of an all-German parliament. The "radical" minority among the liberals went even further in their calls for social and political reform. Adhering to the principle of "the nation governing itself" ("the sovereignty of the people"), their prime demand was for social equality. Against the background of mass poverty ("pauperism") caused by a dramatic increase in the population during the pre-March period, they advocated the adoption of measures to benefit the weaker groups in society.

The various political movements continued to be united by the goal of national unity. With widespread political unrest erupting throughout Europe, it was the July revolution of 1830 in France, in particular, which inspired the German national movement to take action. The political demonstrations culminated in 1832 with the Hambach Festival, when liberals and democrats alike called for unity within a nation-state, press freedom and constitutional reform, prompting a new wave of repression.

The breach within the political opposition finally occurred on the eve of the 1848 revolution, when the two main factions set forth their demands in separate manifestos: the moderate liberal faction in the Heppenheim programme, the more "radical" democratic movement in the Offenburg programme. The manifestos set out their respective approaches to a new social and political order – a contest whose outcome would ultimately be decided by revolution.

The political and social tensions were exacerbated by the economic crisis affecting all the European countries after 1846. However, what finally unleashed the uprisings in Germany was the February revolution in Paris in 1848 and the abdication of the French king. Discontent among broad sections of society triggered widespread political action, and the popular assemblies, revolts and demonstrations – initially supported by almost every group within society – constituted a mass movement which paved the way for the "civil revolution" of 1848. This political protest was channelled and articulated through the "March Demands", whose principal aims were freedom of the press, trial by jury, constitutional forms of government in the individual states, and the convening of an all-German parliament. Faced with insurrection on a massive scale, the German princes were forced to make concessions and endorsed key elements of the March Demands. Their consent to the convening of a national parliament made Frankfurt am Main, once the site of the election and coronation of German kings and emperors, the focal point of the revolution, for this was the meeting-place of the *Vorparlament*, the pre-parliament, directly convened by the revolutionary movement. Attempts by a small group of left-wing republicans to turn the pre-parliament into a revolutionary executive failed; the liberal majority prevailed and, in agreement with the individual state governments, announced free elections to a National Assembly. On 18 May 1848, the freely elected representatives of the people convened in Frankfurt's Paulskirche for the first time. No political parties existed at this stage; it was only during the course of the ensuing debates that like-minded delegates came together to form informal groupings, or factions, resembling parties. The majority of delegates were moderate liberals who showed great willingness to compromise with the governments of the individual German states and substantially shaped the policies pursued by the National Assembly.

During the following months, the Assembly's deliberations were dominated by two key tasks: to create a central government and draw up a national constitution. With regard to the former, the Assembly voted as early as June to appoint a provisional imperial government. By electing a Habsburg – Austrian Archduke John, who was known to be liberal and popular with the people – as Imperial Administrator and by forming a cabinet, the Assembly sought to drive forward the creation of a nation-state which at this stage still included Austria. However, as the newly created centralized executive had no civil service or army pledged to allegiance, the National Assembly was soon forced to recognize that it would always be reliant on the individual states' support in implementing its decisions.

The most important and passionately debated issue was the drafting of the "Fundamental Rights of the German People", which were adopted after lengthy debates on 21 December 1848. These were costly debates – for they gave the traditional powers time to rally their forces again. Nonetheless, they were necessary, as the Fundamental Rights helped to consolidate the economic, social and legal constitution of the fledgling nation-state. The Fundamental Rights were also an expression of the desire to dismantle the class-based

hierarchy of the traditional social order and thus strip the nobility of its privileges and abolish the last vestiges of the feudal system. From now on, there was to be equality before the law and equal opportunities for all citizens, based on the model established by the American and French Revolutions and enshrined in law.

In late summer 1848, while delegates were still debating the Fundamental Rights, the National Assembly faced its greatest crisis. German nationalists staged an uprising in Schleswig – which was threatened with annexation by Denmark – and were supported by Prussian troops despatched by the National Assembly. Under pressure from the other European states, however, Prussia then withdrew its troops and signed an armistice unilaterally at Malmö. As the Assembly lacked the instruments to assert its interests, it was compelled to accept the Prussian position. In Frankfurt, opponents of the armistice promptly staged a popular rebellion against the Assembly; Austrian and Prussian troops had to be deployed to protect it and quell the revolt. The crushing of secondary rebellions in south-western Germany, the Vienna uprising in October and the insurrection in Berlin in November marked the turning point in the revolution.

Repeatedly interrupted and influenced by these events, the National Assembly commenced its deliberations on the institutional part of the constitution in September. The key issues were the territorial limits of the future German nation-state and the associated problem of its head of state. At first, the majority of delegates favoured a "Greater German" solution which would only include those regions of Austria which were German-speaking, thus separating them constitutionally from the other Habsburg territories. This option was thwarted by the new Austrian Prime Minister, Prince Felix Schwarzenberg, who, after the crushing of the non-German nationalist movements, introduced a centralized constitution for the Austrian Empire as a whole, thus paving the way for a "Little German" solution.

Whether the Empire was to be headed by a dynastic imperial directorate or become a united democratic republic, Austria's "go-it-alone" approach left the National Assembly with little scope for negotiation. The liberals were now forced to make concessions to the democrats on electoral law in order to prevent the establishment of a republican government. A constitutional solution was adopted with the election of the king of Prussia as German Emperor. However, in April 1849, Frederick William IV, a passionate believer in the divine right of kings and with a romantic notion of nationhood, refused to accept an imperial crown offered by a parliament and also rejected the Imperial Constitution, despite its recognition by the governments of 28 German states.

In early 1849, fresh uprisings sought to enforce the Imperial Constitution by bringing pressure to bear on the governments, initially by peaceful means, but soon with violence. Lacking support from parliament, these regional uprisings were unsuccessful and were brutally quelled by opponents of the revolution. Following a walk-out by most of the liberals, who condemned the violence, the National Assembly was now dominated by the republican left. However, they no longer had any political influence, and soon after convening as the "rump parliament" in Stuttgart, were forcibly disbanded by the Württemberg army. The

Paulskirche project had finally failed. The "March Achievements" were repealed in all the German states with the help of the German Confederation, which was re-established in summer 1851. The Confederation not only abolished the Fundamental Rights, but also emerged yet again as an instrument of political repression. Liberals, democrats and social revolutionaries were subject to surveillance, arrested, or forced to emigrate abroad.

The German revolutionaries of 1848/49 failed in their attempt to establish a constitutional nation-state from below by liberal and democratic means as a response to the political and social demands of the time. Their efforts foundered above all on the issue of German unity. During the final stages of the revolution and in subsequent years, the national question became a power game between Prussia and Austria, who vied for dominance in Germany and stifled social and political reform. As scepticism about the ideals of the 1848 movement steadily increased, there was growing support for pragmatic policies which responded to current conditions. Only the "New Era" ushered in by Prussia's new monarch at the end of the 1850s opened up the renewed prospect of social and political reform.

Nonetheless, the revolution should not be viewed solely as a failure. It did much to promote constitutional principles and thus paved the way for a political system based on parliamentarism in the long term. The high level of political activity among the general public established the basis for a diverse party-political landscape in future. Not least, the Paulskirche Constitution became a model for the Weimar Constitution and, later, the Basic Law promulgated in Bonn.

1. The French Revolution and its influence on the German states

The storming of the Bastille on 14 July 1789 has become the symbol of the French Revolution. It marked the beginning of radical social and political transformation, not only in France but throughout Europe.

However, it was the revolutionary act by the deputies of the third estate – the commons – who proclaimed themselves the *Assemblée nationale* – the National Assembly – on 17 June 1789 which set these momentous events in motion. Three days later, having adjourned to the *jeu de paume* – an indoor tennis court – at Versailles, they took an oath not to disband until a just constitution had been established for France. With the storming of the Bastille – the state prison which symbolized the absolutism and corruption of the *ancien régime* – the smouldering resentment of the people of Paris finally erupted, reinforcing the political demands. The revolution rapidly spread throughout France and was soon irreversible. Just two months later, the French *Assemblée nationale* adopted the Declaration of the Rights of Man and Citizen, thus expressing its commitment to the principles of political liberty and equality before the law as natural and inalienable rights of the individual. It became the template for liberal constitutions throughout Europe.

News of the revolutionary events and ideas quickly spilled across the French borders and

The storming of the Bastille on 14 July 1789. Painting by Jean-Baptiste Lallemand

Meeting of the Mainz Jacobin Club in the Elector's Palace, 1792

spread among Germany's bourgeoisie, which was sympathetic to the aims of the revolution while condemning its methods. The European monarchies, on the other hand, viewed the events in France as a direct threat to their power and authority. Pres-

German hand-bill with symbols and slogans of the French Revolution

Opposite page: The Declaration of the Rights of Man and Citizen, in a German edition from 1792/93

sured into action, not least by the French emigré aristocracy who had fled from France, the princes resolved in April 1792 to take military action. However, the French revolutionary armies not only put up formidable resistance; they even invaded the territory of the Holy Roman Empire of the German Nation, seizing the cities of Speyer and Mainz on the Rhine. Following the proclamation of the First Republic in France in September 1792, a new and more radical tendency with close links to the French Jacobins now emerged here as a counterpoint to the Enlightenment movement, which tended to be more reform-minded than revolutionary. Boosted by the French occupation, "German Jacobins" – including the essayist Georg Forster, who had participated in James Cook's second voyage around the world – established the first republic on German territory in Mainz in 1792/93. Supported by only a minority of the city's population, however, it soon collapsed after French withdrawal.

The departure of the French forces was short-lived, however. With Napoleon, a statesman entered the political arena whose intention was not merely to defend the revolution

Erklärung der Rechte des Menschen und des Bürgers.

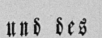

Da die Stellvertreter der französischen Nation, welche die National-Versammlung ausmachen, in Erwägung zogen, daß Unwissenheit, Vergessenheit und Verachtung der Menschenrechte die einzigen Ursachen des allgemeinen Unheils, und des Verderbnisses der Regierungen sind; so beschlossen sie, die natürlichen, unveräußerlichen und heiligen Rechte des Menschen, mittelst einer feyerlichen Erklärung, in deutliches Licht zu setzen: damit diese Erklärung allen und jeden Gliedern des Staatskörpers immer vor Augen liege, und sie an ihre Rechte und Pflichten unablässig erinnere; damit man die verschiedenen Handlungen der gesetzgebenden und der ausführenden Macht, mit dem Zweck aller und jeder Staatseinrichtungen stets vergleichen könne, und daher mit desto mehr Ehrfurcht für dieselben erfüllet werde; damit künftighin des Reichsbürgers Berufungen auf Rechte in dieser Erklärung so einfache als umstößliche Gründe finden, und demnach selbst zum Widerstand zu Erhaltung unserer Reichs-Verfassung und zu allgemeiner Wohlfahrt, gedeihen möge.

Zufolge dessen erkennt und erkläret die National-Versammlung, in Gegenwart und unter Obwaltung des Höchsten, folgende Rechte des Menschen und des Bürgers.

I.
Von ihrer Geburt an sind und bleiben die Menschen frey und an Rechten einander gleich. Bürgerliche Unterscheidungen können nur auf gemeinen Nutzen gegründet seyn.

II.
Jede Bildung politischer Gesellschaften hat die Erhaltung der natürlichen und unverjährlichen Rechte des Menschen zu ihrem Zwecke. Dieser Rechte Gegenstände sind Freyheit, Eigenthum, Sicherheit und Widerstand gegen Unterdrückung.

III.
Die höchste Machthabung jedes Staates gründet sich wesentlich auf die Nation. Weder einzelne Personen, noch Körperschaften, können je irgend eine Macht ausüben, die nicht ausdrücklich aus dieser Quelle fließe.

IV.
Die Freyheit besteht darin, daß jeder alles thun darf, was keinem andern schadet. In Ausübung natürlicher Rechte sind demnach keinem Menschen andere Grenzen gesetzt, als die, welche den Genuß gleicher Rechte anderen Gliedern der Gesellschaft sichern. Das Gesetz allein kann diese Grenzen bestimmen.

V.
Das Gesetz darf Handlungen nur in so fern verbiethen, als sie der Gesellschaft schädlich sind. Was das Gesetz nicht verbiethet, darf niemand hindern; und niemand darf gezwungen werden, zu thun, was das Gesetz nicht befiehle.

VI.
Das Gesetz ist der Ausdruck des allgemeinen Willens. Zu Bildung desselben haben alle Bürger gleiches Recht, persönlich, oder durch Stellvertreter, Theil zu nehmen. Das Gesetz muß für alle und jede, es seye zum Schutz oder zur Strafe, Ein und dasselbe Gesetz seyn. Vor ihm sind alle Bürger gleich, haben alle zu allen öffentlichen Würden, Stellen und Aemtern, nach Maaßgab ihrer Fähigkeiten, gleiche Ansprüche. Es läßt keinen andern Unterschied zu, als den, welchen Tugenden und Talente machen.

VII.
Kein Mensch darf gerichtlich angeklagt, in Verhaft genommen, oder sonst in persönlicher Freyheit gestöret werden; es seye dann in Fällen, die das Gesetz bestimmt, und nach der Form, die es vorschreibt. Alle die, welche willkührliche Befehle bewirken, ausfertigen, ausüben, oder vollstrecken lassen, sind der Strafe unterworfen. Hingegen ist jeder Bürger, der in Kraft des Gesetzes vorgeladen oder gegriffen wird, augenblicklichen Gehorsam schuldig. Durch Widerstand wird er straffällig.

VIII.
Das Gesetz soll nur Strafen verordnen, die umumgänglich und einleuchtend nothwendig sind. Niemand kann je gestraft werden, als nur in Kraft eines verordneten Gesetzes, welches vorher ausgekündet, und nachher auf das Verbrechen gesetzmäßig angewendet worden.

IX.
Da kein Mensch eher für schuldig angesehen werden kann, als bis er nach dem Gesetze dafür erkläret wird; so folget daraus, daß jeder, den man in Verhaft zu nehmen unumgänglich nöthig findet, gegen alle Strenge, die dazu nicht nöthig ist, durch das Gesetz ernstlich geschützt werden muß.

X.
Wegen Meinungen, selbst in Religionssachen, darf niemand beunruhiget werden, wenn er nur durch derselben Aeusserung öffentliche Ordnung, welche das Gesetz eingeführt hat, nicht störet.

XI.
Die freye Mittheilung der Gedanken und Meinungen ist eines der schätzbarsten Rechte des Menschen. Jeder Bürger darf demnach frey reden, schreiben und drucken lassen, was er will. Nur in den, vom Gesetze bestimmten, Fällen hat er den Mißbrauch dieser Freyheit zu verantworten.

XII.
Zur Gewährleistung der Rechte des Menschen und des Bürgers wird öffentliche Gewalt erfordert. Folglich dienet die Einführung dieser Gewalt zu gemeiner Wohlfahrt aller und jeder, und nicht zu besonderm Nutzen derer, denen sie anvertrauet wird.

XIII.
Zu Unterhaltung öffentlicher Gewalt, und zu Bestreitung der Verwaltungskosten, wird allgemeiner Beytrag unumgänglich erfodert. An diesem müssen alle Bürger, nach Maaßgab ihres Vermögens, gleichen Antheil nehmen.

XIV.
Die Bürger haben das Recht, die Nothwendigkeit des öffentlichen Beytrages zu untersuchen, und ihn durch sich selbst, oder durch ihre Stellvertreter, frey zu genehmigen, zu bestätigen, desselben Verwendung zu wissen, und die Summe, die Quellen, woraus sie bezogen wird, die Art der Erhebung und die Dauer zu bestimmen.

XV.
Die Gesellschaft hat das Recht, von jedem öffentlichen Geschäftsträger, wegen seiner Verwaltung, Rechenschaft zu fordern.

XVI.
Ein Staat, worin der Rechte Gewährleistung nicht gesichert ist, worin die Grenzen verschiedener Machthabungen nicht bestimmt sind, hat keine Verfassung.

XVII.
Da das Eigenthum ein unverletzbares und heiliges Recht ist; so kann niemand desselben beraubt werden: es seye dann, daß öffentliche und gesetzmäßig bewährte Noth solches Opfer augenscheinlich erheische. Aber auch dann darf dieß nur unter Bedingung gerechter und vorläufiger Schadloßhaltung geschehen.

In deutscher Sprache herausgegeben von Andreas Meyer, Sohn, französischen Staats-Bürger zu Straßburg; und bey ihm um 12 Sous zu haben, in der Kronenburgerstraße N°. 60.

against its external enemies, but to impose its principles throughout Europe. His wars of conquest, fought in the name of the revolution, shattered the domestic and foreign policy structures of the *ancien régime* within a matter of years. After the French victory over Austria in 1805, Prussia also sustained a crushing defeat at the twin battles of Jena and Auerstedt in October 1806.

Napoleon's victories brought about a dramatic transformation of Europe's territorial and political structures. In Germany in particular, the changes were radical and far-reaching. With the Principal Resolution of the Imperial Deputation (*Reichsdeputationshauptschluss*) of February 1803 and the peace treaties of 1805/06, ecclesiastical property was expropriated and transferred to the larger and medium-sized states. Minor imperial estates were stripped of their status as sovereign members of the Empire, and

through a process known as "mediatization", bishoprics, abbeys, petty principalities and imperial cities were absorbed into larger territories. At the same time, secularization – the removal of ecclesiastical rulers' social, political and economic power – was the first significant step in dismantling feudal society and its estates. The aristocracy lost many of its important privileges and positions, and peasants and the bourgeoisie were now able to acquire former church lands and property.

The territorial simplification of the German states by Napoleon gave rise to a shift in the power structure, especially in southern and western Germany. In particular, the newly emergent kingdoms of Bavaria and Württemberg and the Grand Duchies of Baden and Hesse-Darmstadt were indebted to France for their substantial territorial gains. Their rulers' allegiance to Napoleon found practical expression in the creation of the

Battle of Jena,
14 October
1806

Confederation of the Rhine by sixteen southern and south-western German states on 12 July 1806. Shortly afterwards, they proclaimed their secession from the Empire. On 6 August that year, under pressure from Napoleon, the Habsburg Emperor Francis II announced that he was laying down the imperial crown, an act which formally abolished the Holy Roman Empire.

In the confederated states, the political reforms were prompted, firstly, by France's power-political interests and, secondly, by the states' own interest in welding their newly acquired lands with their core territories to form a single cohesive polity. After somewhat tentative first steps, the administration was centralized and the economic and legal system unified in line with the French model. However, Napoleon's dream of creating a single federal state was shattered by the power-political aspirations of Prussia and Württemberg, the largest confederated states.

Faced with Napoleon's policies, even the Prussians were forced to acknowledge the need for a reform of government and administration. With his "Nassau Memorandum", Baron Karl vom und zum Stein was one of the first reformers to draft a comprehensive strategy "to breathe new life into the spirit of the community and create a sense of civic responsibility". His primary objective was to increase the efficiency of public administration and rationalize the financial system, but his proposed reforms also aimed to liberate society by introducing a new system of civil law. The problems associated with this measure were especially evident in the conflicts surrounding the introduction of the *Code Napoléon*, Napoleon's Civil Code of 1804, in the Confederation of the Rhine. Its anti-feudal, bourgeois and

The princes of the Confederation of the Rhine pay homage to Emperor Napoleon, July 1806

egalitarian elements were resisted with particular vigour by the former elites.

The most striking examples of the transition from traditional authoritarianism to a liberal state was the military reform, which opened the way for ordinary citizens to join the officer corps and thus removed the aristocracy's monopoly on commissions in the army. With the introduction of general conscription, military service was no longer to be regarded as a much-resented obligation but as a citizen's patriotic duty. Other key social reforms in Prussia included the emancipation of the peasantry, the legal steps to emancipate the Jews – which granted them a measure of equality and some civil rights – and the Municipal Ordinance of 1808, which conferred extensive rights of self-government on the municipalities, thus strengthening citizens' opportunities for political participation. However, the Prussian reform-

Baron Karl vom und zum Stein, Prussian minister and reformer

ers were not guided by any notion of citizenship based on equality within a national constitutional state. On the contrary, in seeking to achieve a compromise between the system of estates and a representative system of government, the Prussian reformers were inspired by a traditional concept of the state which prevented "development from within or from without" (Baron Carl August von Hardenberg) and was to be regarded as a "revolution in a positive sense". The more far-reaching objectives nurtured by Stein and Hardenberg, namely to introduce the representative and constitutional features of municipal administration in the higher tiers of government as well, foundered – along with the draft constitution – on the Prussian monarchy's pro-Restoration claim to sole representation.

The reforms in Prussia and the other states aimed above all to mobilize the nation in the struggle against Napoleon. With the introduction of Napoleon's protectionist trade policies, at the latest, the mood turned against French domination even in the Confederation of the Rhine. Poets and philosophers became mouthpieces for the general public's anti-Napoleonic sentiments, pledging their hearts and minds – as in the song "What is

Letter from the City of Berlin, dated 1841, conferring civic rights on Martin Valentin, a Jew

Opposite page: Ceremonial mass for the newly elected Berlin city councillors in St Nicholas' Church, 1808

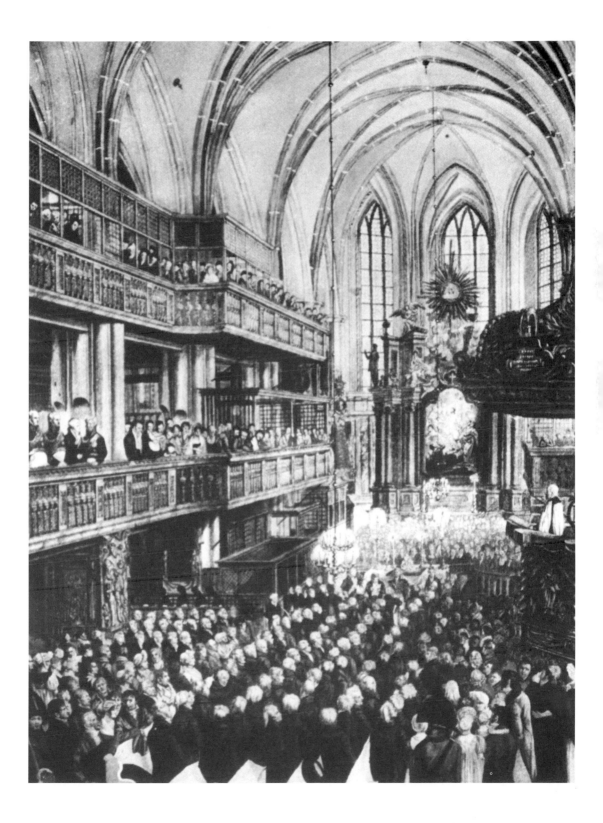

The departure of the East Prussian civil guard, 1813. Painting by Gustav Graef, around 1860/61

the Germans' fatherland?" penned by Ernst Moritz Arndt – to patriotic and national sentiments. The call for liberation from Napoleonic rule was linked with hopes for a national and liberal constitutional state. In financial and personal terms, too, the Germans were no longer willing to bear the burdens of French occupation and Napoleon's ongoing wars of conquest. In the long term, the somewhat reluctant and tactically-minded Prussian King Frederick William III was unable to withstand the growing resistance which first emerged among the ranks of the Prussian

military. This burgeoning national fervour mobilized many volunteers from all sections of the population to organize themselves into volunteer corps (*Freikorps*). In the wake of Napoleon's defeat in Russia in 1812, the time had come to join forces and finally throw off the yoke of foreign domination. At the Battle of the Nations at Leipzig on 16-19 October 1813, the Prussian, Austrian, Russian and Swedish allies secured the decisive victory. Napoleon was routed and forced to retreat across the Rhine to France; the Confederation of the Rhine collapsed.

The Battle of the Nations at Leipzig, 19 October 1813

2. The Congress of Vienna and the founding of the German Confederation

With the victory over Napoleon, peace was restored to Europe after more than 20 years of warfare. However, Europe's states – devastated by revolution and war – yearned for order and stabiliIy. From September 1814 to June 1815, princes and ministers from Russia, Great Britain, Austria and Prussia – the allied great powers – met with representatives of the other German and European states, as well as negotiators from defeated France, to redraw the map of Europe. Among the German slates, the two great powers Prussia and Austria were primarily concerned with restoring their old sphere of influence, whereas the middle-sized German states were determined to secure their sovereignty, newly established under Napoleon. The outcome of the negotiations took account of both sides' interests. In a major territorial shake-up, the great powers – largely on the basis of Napoleon's reforms – reshaped the

"The kings' cake": French cartoon satirizing contentious territorial issues, 1815

European states in line with the principle that "legitimate", i.e. pre-Napoleonic rulers, should govern everywhere, albeit without reinstating every former "legitimate" ruler. They also restored the balance between the European states. The subsequent establish-

Meeting of envoys to the Congress of Vienna in the palace on *Ballhausplatz*

The monarchs of the Holy Alliance (from left): King Frederick William III, Emperor Francis I, and Czar Alexander I

ment of the Holy Alliance between Russia, Austria and Prussia was intended, first and foremost, to consolidate and defend the dynastic orders and suppress all national liberation movements. The great powers agreed that there should be no restoration of the Empire, which had been abolished in 1806.

The prospect of national unity – a cherished principle of the liberal movement and the Freikorps during the wars of liberation – thus faded out of reach. Instead, the Federal Act (*Bundesakte*) adopted at the Congress of Vienna merely created a loose confederation of states for Germany whose aim was to preserve the independence of its members, defend the system of monarchy, and stifle the emergent social and political movements. The Confederation initially comprised 37 states and four free cities. In the case of Prussia and Austria, only their former imperial territories were included in the Confederation; West and East Prussia and the non-

First meeting of the envoys of all the member states of the German Confederation in Frankfurt am Main, 1816

Group of
nationalist
students in a
tavern in
Neuenheim,
1814/15

German territories of the Habsburg Empire were excluded. The Confederation lacked a representative assembly and joint head of state; instead, its supreme institution was the Federal Assembly (*Bundesversammlung*), later known as the Federal Diet, or *Bundestag*, which was a permanent congress of ambassadors of the German princes and free cities under Austrian chairmanship. Convening in the Thurn and Taxis Palace in Frankfurt/Main until 1866, the Federal Assembly had limited impact in terms of creating legislation, an administration or jurisprudence which applied to all states. While thus proving extremely cumbersome and hostile to reform, it nonetheless succeeded in maintaining peace at both domestic and international level for many years. The price of this success, however, was the suppression of all efforts to establish a more liberal political order.

It was only the vague promise, contained in Article 13 of the Federal Act, that constitu-

tions based on the traditional provincial assemblies (*landständische Verfassungen*) would be established in all states of the Confederation that gave the liberal movements cause for hope. In the individual states, there were highly divergent views on how and when this should be achieved. While Prussia and Austria maintained their absolutist systems of government, the southern German states seized the opportunity to introduce modern representative constitutions and thus strengthen their sovereignty vis-à-vis the German Confederation. For the first time, these constitutions guaranteed citizens basic rights and freedoms, as well as opportunities for political participation through freely elected parliamentary assemblies, known as chambers. However, as the restrictions imposed by the reactionary regimes tightened, Article 13 of the Federal Act was increasingly interpreted in the spirit of Restoration and the monarchical principle, which meant that state authority continued to be vested in the princes, and the estates were only granted rights of political participation under specific circumstances.

This interpretation was vigorously resisted by south-western German liberals, who expressed their views at parliamentary level in "cameral disputes".

For the radical national groups, the constitutions and declarations of intent were not enough. Against the background of the wars of liberation, patriotic student fraternities (*Burschenschaften*) at the universities voiced criticism of the German Confederation's political system. On 18 October 1817, at the behest of the Jena patriotic student fraternity, some five hundred students gathered at Wartburg Castle in Thuringia. The Wartburg Festival, which celebrated the tercentenary of the Reformation and the fourth anniver-

sary of the Battle of the Nations at Leipzig, marked the beginning of the political demonstrations in Germany. In his celebratory address, a student named Riemann from Jena voiced sharp criticism of the German Federation and expressed hopes which linked the patriotic student fraternities with national unity. Yet it was a small group of students from the circle of *"Turnvater"* Friedrich Ludwig Jahn – self-styled apostle of German physical culture – which incensed political opponents by staging a ceremonial burning of "un-German" books and symbols of absolutism. The *"Code Napoléon"*, works by August von Kotzebue, including his history of Germany, and *"Die Restauration der Staatswissenschaften"* by the ultra-conservative lawyer Karl Ludwig von Haller were thrown into the flames, along with symbols of the standing army – a wig, a Prussian lancer's corset and a corporal's

Procession by students and gymnasts to the Wartburg near Eisenach, 18 October 1817

Cartoon satirizing the suppression of intellectual freedom and freedom of expression after the adoption of the Karlsbad Decrees in 1819

swagger-stick. The selection of items reveals the ambivalence of the student movement, in which liberalism and nostalgia were often intertwined.

The murder of August von Kotzebue, a writer in the employ of the Russian legation, by the student fanatic Karl Ludwig Sand on 23 March 1819 – intended as a signal against the Restoration and in favour of the German nation-state – heralded a period of more intense repression and political persecution. The Karlsbad Decrees of 20 September 1819, primarily the work of Prince Klemens Lothar von Metternich and which remained in force until 1848, established a police state and a comprehensive system of surveillance designed to clamp down on the liberal and national movements. The impact of press censorship on the opposition was particularly severe: all printed material comprising less than twenty leaves (320 pages) had to be submitted to the censor prior to publication. Many leading figures and supporters of the liberal and democratic opposition were persecuted and in some cases sentenced to lengthy terms of imprisonment.

Murder of August von Kotzebue, a writer in the employ of the Russian legation, in Mannheim on 23 March 1819

Prince Clemens Wenzel Lothar von Metternich, Austrian Chancellor and a key figure in the reaction during the *Vormärz* period. Portrait by Thomas Lawrence, around 1815

3. *Vormärz* and the liberal movement

The family of the master locksmith Hauschild. Painting by Eduard Gärtner, 1843

At first glance, the decades known as the *Vormärz*, or "pre-March" period – also termed "Biedermeier" in German social and cultural history – which preceded the revolution of 1848/49 appear to be a time of stagnation and introspection. Yet in reality, these decades were marked by the rise of the bourgeoisie as the leading social class, its finely honed political skills paving the way for the steady expansion of its influence. Not only in Germany but elsewhere in Europe too, the liberal and national movements worked tirelessly to achieve fundamental rights, freedoms and national unity.

Opportunities for political participation arose primarily in the parliaments which had been established in more than half the German states. Parliamentary life was particularly vibrant in the southern German states, where constitutions had been introduced after the Congress of Vienna. After the July revolution in 1830 in Paris, constitutionalism spread to north and central Germany as well. Everywhere, however, the parliamentary assemblies were established within the framework of a constitutional monarchy which generally provided for a bicameral system. The upper house was drawn from the nobility, the churches, the universities and other institutions, while the lower house – the freely elected assembly – formed the modern element of parliament. The individual states' electoral law limited the number

Laying the foundation stone of the Constitution Column in Gaibach, near Würzburg, in May 1821 to commemorate the Bavarian constitution, adopted three years earlier

parliaments was influenced not only by electoral law, i.e. the granting of the right to vote and the right to stand for election on the basis of property qualifications, but also by education and available free time. A new political elite therefore emerged, mainly consisting of lawyers, academics, government officials, and some members of the commercial bourgeoisie. The cities thus formed the social bedrock of parliamentarism during the *Vormärz* period.

During the elections to the state parliaments, or *Landtage*, and in the work of the parliamentary bodies, separate groupings began to emerge, based on political objectives, which soon coalesced into parliamentary groupings, the forerunners of the political parties. Here, members developed the skills and knowledge which enabled them to challenge governmental and bureaucratic claims to power. However, the new parliaments' powers were still fairly limited: they

of voters through a highly restricted property franchise. The electoral law of the Grand Duchy of Baden was most progressive in this respect, for it granted all citizens of the municipality, as well as government officials, the right to vote. The composition of the

Interior view of the hemicycle of the Stuttgart *Landtag*, 1833

could not bring forward legislation or have a say in the formation of the government. Their most effective weapon in the political debate proved to be their right to be involved in matters of public finance, their right to deliberate draft laws introduced by the government, and their general right of petition, which enabled them to exert considerable pressure, also in public, on the monarchist governments. Throughout the *Vormärz* period, vociferous "cameral disputes" frequently broke out, focussing on the expansion of the two chambers' powers but also the exercise of fundamental political rights. Large sections of the bourgeoisie were also active outside parliament and organized themselves into associations in opposition to the reactionary politics of the German Confederation.

After the Wartburg Festival and the murder of Kotzebue, the forces of reaction initially quelled all moves towards greater liberty, but the opposition drew fresh inspiration from the frequent political uprisings occurring throughout Europe. The first sign of hope came from the Greek revolt against Ottoman rule in 1821, which unleashed a broad wave of sympathy and support throughout Germany. The establishment of a Greek state in 1833, with the election of a king (Otto of Bavaria), strengthened Germany's national movement in its political objectives and the liberal concepts of reforms with which it was associated. But it was the July revolution in Paris in 1830 against the reactionary policies of Bourbon king Charles X, who sought to reverse many aspects of the revolution, which had a far greater impact on Germany and the other European states. In Great Britain and Switzerland, on the other hand, the governments tried to stave off revolution by introducing electoral and constitutional reform.

In Germany, the northern and central states in particular, which had not yet adopted a

"Liberty Leading the People". Painting by Eugène Delacroix, 1830

Scenes from
the revolution-
ary events of
1830

The Cassel deputation presenting a petition requesting the convening of the estates to Elector William II, 15 September 1830.

constitution, now found themselves in the grip of revolution. In Brunswick, the young Duke Charles II, having refused to convene the estates, was driven off his lands overnight and his castle was plundered and set alight. His brother's appointment as regent and the adoption of a constitution fulfilled the bourgeois opposition's key demands. Events led to a similar outcome, albeit less violently, in the Kingdom of Saxony, where the unrest centred on Dresden and Leipzig. Here, the conservative King Anton voluntarily abdicated in favour of his more reform-minded nephew Frederick August who – by appointing a liberal ministry and adopting a constitution based on the south German model a year later – acceded to the bourgeoisie's political demands. In other parts of Germany, too, the unrest triggered a wave of constitutional reform. For example, in the Electorate of Hesse-Cassel, with its absolutist and despotic system of rule, vigorous pressure from the bourgeoisie led to the adoption in January 1831 of the most liberal and progressive of the new constitutions. Among other things, it established a unicameral system with a bourgeois/peasant majority and the right to bring forward legislation.

Although there were very few places in Germany and Europe where the national and liberal opposition achieved its goals, it nonetheless fostered a general mobilization of political forces. So too did the Polish uprising which was crushed by the Russians in 1831. Patriotic Polish emigrés who fled to Germany were fêted as champions of Germany's own liberation, and some sections of the liberal opposition formed solidarity groups, known as Polish associations.

The activities of the liberal opposition culminated in a mass meeting at Hambach Castle on 27 May 1832, when between 20,000 and 30,000 people from all over Germany gathered to call for constitutional reform, press freedom and national unity. The Hambach Festival was a vivid demonstration to the monarchs of the movement's popularity beyond the borders of their own individual fiefdoms. Yet again, the princes saw this as a threat to their power and responded once more with arrests and bans on associations. The desperate attempt by a small group of radical intellectuals to incite general revolution by storming the main guard house in Frankfurt/Main met with

Demonstrators marching to Hambach Castle near Neustadt in the Palatinate, 27 May 1832

little popular support and collapsed. The more radical opposition forces emigrated, primarily to liberal Switzerland, where almost 40,000 emigrants joined to form artisans' associations and similar organizations which aroused no suspicion. In Paris, emigrants formed the "League of Outcasts" in 1834; their "Declaration of the Rights of Man and Citizen" declared war on social inequality and became the model for the socialist organizations which were founded in the 1840s.

The struggle for political liberty and national unity was not only waged on the streets, in associations, and in parliament. Men of letters and academics were also swept along by the general politicization of society. Members of the "Young Germany" group, such as Karl Gutzkow, or authors linked with it, such as

Ludwig Börne or Heinrich Heine, sharply criticized the social and political conditions in their novels, poems and especially in literary journals. They saw themselves as a counter-movement to the classical and Romantic eras, which they regarded as having no relevance to politics, and their polemical, provocative and witty criticism of the existing system aimed to achieve freedom of thought and political opinion in a democratically constituted republic.

The liberal movement's political programme during the *Vormärz* period was devised by the Freiburg constitutional lawyers Karl Rotteck and Karl Theodor von Welcker in their "*Staatslexikon*" published between 1834 and 1843. In it, they set forth the intellectual and constitutional bases of liberalism, which were rooted in the tradition of the Enlightenment.

Radical students and artisans storming the main guard house in Frankfurt am Main, 3 April 1833

Heinrich Heine. Portrait by Isidor Popper, around 1843

Karl von Rotteck and Karl Theodor Welcker, leading liberals in Baden and authors of the *Staatslexikon*

In 1837, however, political interest centred on the fate of seven professors from Göttingen University who protested publicly against the annulment by the new Hanoverian king Ernst August of the 1833 constitution and the oath of allegiance sworn on it by government officials. As a result of their protest, the "Göttingen Seven" – who included the Brothers Grimm, the historian Friedrich Christoph Dahlmann and the literary historian Georg Gottfried Gervinus – were dismissed from their university posts and instantly became national symbols of liberal resistance.

A turning point came in 1840, when Frederick William IV ascended the Prussian throne, reawakening the hopes of the politically aware public. Widely regarded as an opponent of the bureaucratic authoritarian state and an enlightened monarch, he began his reign by pardoning political prisoners and appointing three of the Göttingen professors to Prussian universities. He also curbed political persecution within the Confederation and appointed moderates to ministerial posts. In a bid to court popularity, he satisfied the desire – prevalent among much of the

Banquet in Berlin's royal palace after the coronation of King Frederick William IV, 1840

The "Göttingen Seven": top: Georg Gottfried Gervinus, Wilhelm Eduard Albrecht. Centre: Heinrich Ewald, Friedrich Christoph Dahlmann, Wilhelm Weber. Bottom: Wilhelm and Jakob Grimm

bourgeoisie – for a demonstration of national unity by staging symbolic and populist events, such as the festival to mark the resumption of building work at Cologne Cathedral in 1842. Yet in the long term, the hopes proved to be a "long chain of misunderstandings" (Heinrich von Treitschke), as the Prussian king blocked the repeated calls for the completion of the constitution by referring to the universal applicability of his divine right as king. By 1847, however, the financial difficulties faced by the state left him no choice but to comply with the growing demands for a parliamentary assembly, and the United Diet, or *Vereinigter Landtag*, was convened. Yet this attempt at conciliation between the king and his subjects collapsed following a fierce dispute over the United Diet's powers between members and the Crown, and it was dissolved after just two months.

The political awakening of the 1840s was also marked by a schism within the liberal opposition. Liberals and democrats pursued a common goal, i.e. the creation of a nation-state, but their views on the type of constitutional system to be established in future differed radically. In their Offenburg programme of 12 September 1847, the democrats called for a republic, universal suffrage and effective social policies to benefit the lower classes. The liberals responded on 10 October 1847 with the Heppenheim declaration, in which they presented the case for constitutional monarchy, the expansion

Die Forderungen des Volkes.

Unsere Versammlung von entschiedenen Freunden der Verfassung hat stattgefunden. Niemand kann derselben beigewohnt haben, ohne auf das Tiefste ergriffen und angeregt worden zu sein. Es war ein Fest männlicher Entschlossenheit, eine Versammlung, welche zu Resultaten führen muß. Jedes Wort, was gesprochen wurde, enthält den Vorsatz und die Aufforderung zu thatkräftigem Handeln. Wir nennen keine Namen und keine Zahlen. Diese thun wenig zur Sache. Genug, die Versammlung, welche den zweiten Festsaal füllte, eignete sich einstimmig die in folgenden Worten zusammengefaßten Besprechungen des Tages an:

Die Forderungen des Volkes in Baden:

I. Wiederherstellung unserer verletzten Verfassung.

Art. 1. Wir verlangen, daß sich unsere Staatsregierung lossage von den Karlsbader Beschlüssen vom Jahr 1819, von den Frankfurter Beschlüssen von 1831 und 1832 und von den Wiener Beschlüssen von 1834. Diese Beschlüsse verletzen gleichmäßig unsere unveräußerlichen Menschenrechte wie die deutsche Bundesakte und unsere Landesverfassung.

Art. 2. Wir verlangen Preßfreiheit; das unveräußerliche Recht des menschlichen Geistes, seine Gedanken unverhüllt mitzutheilen, darf uns nicht länger vorenthalten werden.

Art. 3. Wir verlangen Gewissens- und Lehrfreiheit. Die Beziehungen des Menschen zu seinem Gotte gehören seinem innersten Wesen an, und keine äußere Gewalt darf sich anmaßen, sie nach ihrem Gutdünken zu bestimmen. Jedes Glaubensbekenntniß hat daher Anspruch auf gleiche Berechtigung im Staate.

Keine Gewalt dränge sich mehr zwischen Lehrer und Lernende. Den Unterricht scheide keine Confession.

Art. 4. Wir verlangen Vereidigung des Militärs auf die Verfassung.

Der Bürger, welchem der Staat die Waffen in die Hand gibt, bekräftige gleich den übrigen Bürgern durch einen Eid seine Verfassungstreue.

Art. 5. Wir verlangen persönliche Freiheit.

Die Polizei höre auf, den Bürger zu bevormunden und zu quälen. Das Vereinsrecht, ein frisches Gemeindeleben, das Recht des Volkes sich zu versammeln und zu reden, das Recht des Einzelnen sich zu ernähren, sich zu bewegen und auf dem Boden des deutschen Vaterlandes frei zu verkehren — seien hinfüro ungestört.

II. Entwickelung unserer Verfassung.

Art. 6. Wir verlangen Vertretung des Volks beim deutschen Bunde.

Dem Deutschen werde ein Vaterland und eine Stimme in dessen Angelegenheiten. Gerechtigkeit und Freiheit im Innern, eine feste Stellung dem Auslande gegenüber gebühren uns als Nation.

Art. 7. Wir verlangen eine volksthümliche Wehrverfassung. Der waffengeübte und bewaffnete Bürger kann allein den Staat schützen.

Man gebe dem Volke Waffen und nehme von ihm die unerschwingliche Last, welche die stehenden Heere ihm auferlegen.

Art. 8. Wir verlangen eine gerechte Besteuerung.

Jeder trage zu den Lasten des Staates nach Kräften bei. An die Stelle der bisherigen Besteuerung trete eine progressive Einkommensteuer.

Art. 9. Wir verlangen, daß die Bildung durch Unterricht allen gleich zugänglich werde. Die Mittel dazu hat die Gesammtheit in gerechter Vertheilung aufzubringen.

Art. 10. Wir verlangen Ausgleichung des Mißverhältnisses zwischen Arbeit und Capital. Die Gesellschaft ist schuldig die Arbeit zu heben und zu schützen.

Art. 11. Wir verlangen Gesetze, welche freier Bürger würdig sind und deren Anwendung durch Geschwornengerichte.

Der Bürger werde von dem Bürger gerichtet. Die Gerechtigkeitspflege sei Sache des Volkes.

Art. 12. Wir verlangen eine volksthümliche Staatsverwaltung.

Das frische Leben eines Volkes bedarf freier Organe. Nicht aus der Schreibstube lassen sich seine Kräfte regeln und bestimmen. An die Stelle der Vielregierung der Beamten trete die Selbstregierung des Volkes.

Art. 13. Wir verlangen Abschaffung aller Vorrechte.

Jedem sei die Achtung freier Mitbürger einziger Vorzug und Lohn.

Offenburg, 12. September 1847.

The democrats' Offenburg Programme of 12 September 1847

of the Customs Union into a confederation, and reform policies which were agreed with the existing authorities. At this point, only a small group of radical liberals considered revolution an option.

The political developments were accompanied by growing social and economic crisis. In 1844, Silesian weavers revolted in protest at the competition from industrial production and cheap imports. Two years before the outbreak of revolution, Europe was gripped by an economic crisis which led to hunger riots in the less well-provisioned cities. A combination of political, social and economic factors thus formed the backdrop to the revolution which broke out in spring 1848.

A bakery being looted in Stettin, 1847

4. The March revolution of 1848

Storming of the *Palais Royal* in Paris, 24 February 1848

Despite the fraught political and social situation in late 1847 and early 1848, very few people in Germany anticipated revolutionary uprisings. The problems and expectations of the various social groups in the individual German states seemed far too disparate. It was the February revolution of 1848 in France which triggered the upheavals in Germany and across Europe. As elsewhere in Europe, the general economic crisis, with its rising prices and falling wages, had led to famine in France which hit the increasingly radical urban proletariat and rural population especially hard. In Paris, the workers and petty bourgeoisie, led by the socialist Louis Blanc, called for the establishment of national workshops to put an end to unemployment and starvation. The attempt by democratic elements of the middle classes to defuse the situation through the adoption of reforms failed. Workers, citizens and the national guard – who came down on the side of the revolutionaries – initially fought side by side against the traditional political order and the vested interests of the upper middle classes. On 24 February, they stormed the Palais Royal, burned the throne on the *Place de la Bastille* and forced the abdication of the "Citizen King" Louis Philippe. The Second French Republic was proclaimed. By now, however, the revolutionaries' disparate political objectives were becoming increasingly obvious. Violent clashes occurred between the bourgeois majority and the radical socialists, ending in June with the crushing of a workers' uprising by the military.

It was only a matter of days before the spark of the February revolution ignited in the German states as well. Often accompanied by violent unrest in the countryside, the people voiced their criticism of prevailing social and political conditions in popular

Die Volks-Kommission in Hanau an den Kurfürsten von Hessen, königl. Hoheit.

Durch die Proklamation Eurer königl. Hoheit vom 7. d. sind die Wünsche des Volkes nicht erfüllt und seine Bitten unvollständig gewährt worden. — Das Volk ist mißtrauisch gegen Eure königl. Hoheit selbst, und sieht in der unvollständigen Gewährung seiner Bitten eine Unaufrichtigkeit. Das Volk hat in der unvollständigen Gewährung seiner Bitten nichts gesehen, als die dringendste Aufforderung, sich noch enger zusammenzuschaaren und eine noch festere Haltung Eurer königl. Hoheit gegenüber einzunehmen.

Das Volk, welches wir meinen, ist nicht der vage Begriff mehr von ehedem, nein es sind Alle — Alle! Ja, königl. Hoheit, Alle! Auch das Militär hat sich für einstimmig erklärt!

Das Volk verlangt, was ihm gebührt. Es spricht den Willen aus, daß seine Zukunft besser seyn solle, als seine Vergangenheit, und dieser Wille ist unwiderstehlich. — Das Volk hat sich eine Kommission erwählt, und diese verlangt nun für es und Namens seiner:

1) Besetzung aller Ministerien, soweit diese nicht neuerdings geschehen ist, mit Männern, welche das Vertrauen des Volkes genießen.
2) Auflösung der wieder einberufenen Ständeversammlung und alsbaldige Berufung neu zu erwählender Stände.
3) Bewilligung vollständiger Preßfreiheit auf Grund der hierzu im §. 95 der Verfassungsurkunde gewährten Zuständigkeit.
4) Vollständige Amnestie für alle seit dem Jahre 1830 begangenen politischen Vergehen.
5) Gewährung vollständiger Religions- und Gewissensfreiheit und deren Ausübung.
6) Hinwirkung bei dem deutschen Bund auf Bildung einer deutschen Volkskammer. Zurücknahme aller den Genuß verfassungsmäßiger Rechte, ganz insbesondere das Petitions-, Einigungs- und Versammlungsrecht beschränkenden Beschlüsse.
7) Die bestimmte Zusage, daß die bereits durch die Proklamation vom 7. d. zugesicherten und in Beziehung auf die ausgesprochenen Desiderien weiter erforderlichen Gesetzentwürfe der nächsten Ständeversammlung vorgelegt werden.
8) Entschließung Eurer königl. Hoheit, binnen drei Tagen von heute an, deren Verstreichen ohne Antwort als Ablehnung angesehen werden soll.

Jetzt ist die Stunde gekommen, wo Sie zu zeigen haben, königl. Hoheit, wie Sie es mit dem Volke meinen. Zögern Sie nicht einen Augenblick, zu gewähren, vollständig zu gewähren!

Besonnene Männer, königl. Hoheit, sagen Ihnen hier, daß die Aufregung einen furchtbaren Charakter angenommen hat.

Bewaffneter Zuzug aus den Nachbarstädten ist bereits vorhanden, schon wird man mit dem Gedanken einer Lostrennung vertraut, und kennt recht wohl das Gewicht der vollendeten Thatsachen.

Königl. Hoheit! gewähren Sie! Lenke Gott Ihr Herz.

Hanau, den 9. März 1848.

Die Volkskommission.

Pelissier. Ziegler. Pflüger. Eberhard. Braun. Nauh. Weidmann. Schreer. Heydt jun. Rommel. Braubach, Adv. Rollenberger. Springmühl. Nöttelberg. Renaud. Preffel, Dr. Mauns, Adv. Chr. Lautenschläger. Schärttner. H. Jung. Graf. W. Wagner. August Gonze. Aug. Rühl.

Catalogue of demands presented by the Hanau people's commission to the Elector of Hesse-Cassel, 9 March 1848

assemblies, demonstrations and petitions. In southern Germany (Mannheim), this criticism found expression in the "March Demands", whose principal aims were press freedom, trial by jury, the arming of civil guards, and the convening of a national parliament. These aims were soon adopted and articulated in other states as well.

The bourgeois movement drew considerable support from the sometimes violent uprisings among the rural population, whose political demands focussed primarily on the abolition of feudal burdens. They left the ranks of the revolutionaries soon after their goals were achieved. There was initially a strong pro-revolutionary platform among the urban population: citizens and workers, master craftsmen and journeymen, urban middle and lower classes joined forces to fight on the barricades. Yet the social differences continued to exist. With the fulfilment of the March Demands, the majority of the bourgeoisie had no further interest in the revolution being continued, as demanded by the radical left. Indeed, they even hindered the lower social classes from asserting their radical social and political agenda by violence. The liberal bourgeoisie, which relied on constructive cooperation with the existing authorities, retained the upper hand and soon took over the political leadership.

Caught unawares by the scale and dynamic of the events, the governments did not dare to respond with violence. On the contrary: in an attempt to defuse the situation, they complied with the political and social demands by appointing liberal ministers. What ultimately decided the fate of the revolution, however, was the turn of events in the two largest German states, Austria and Prussia.

Austria's ultra-conservative Chancellor of State, Prince Metternich, was convinced that he could quell the unrest unleashed in Austria by the February revolution. Yet as the economic crisis deepened, and with the Czechs, Hungarians and Italians rising up in rebellion, the people of Vienna showed a growing willingness to revolt. On 7 March, Viennese liberals circulated a petition setting forth the key political demands, which were later formulated in rather more trenchant terms by the students. Without waiting for these demands to be debated in the Lower Austrian Diet (*Ständehaus*) on 13 March, a mass demonstration took place which culminated in the storming of the Provincial Diet (*Landhaus*). The military was reluctant to intervene, and tensions mounted throughout Vienna. Workers and students – later joined by the civil guard – defended themselves vigorously. In order to prevent the situation from escalating further, the government decided not to crush the rebellion by military force. Prince Metternich – the symbol of reaction – was ousted and fled to England. The Imperial Government was forced to allow the civil guard to carry arms and pledged to grant a constitution, which was enacted in April.

Chancellor
Metternich is
deposed in
Vienna,
13 March 1848

Weapons being
distributed
to Viennese
students,
13 March 1848

In the Prussian capital Berlin, too, political unrest had been increasing since early March. A number of smaller gatherings and demonstrations in Tiergarten, including voices protesting about social conditions, prompted the government to deploy Prussian troops at key strategic points around the city. On 13 March, clashes occurred between soldiers and the Berlin crowds, resulting in the first fatalities. Five days later, the Prussian king appeared before the crowds who had gathered on Schlossplatz to assert their demands, and proclaimed the abolition of censorship and the reconvening of the *Landtag*, which had been dissolved just a year earlier. Shouts of applause were intermingled with calls for the withdrawal of the troops. When the order was given for the troops to withdraw, shots were fired, prompting cries of "treason!" Barricades were quickly erected around the city, which were defended by workers and citizens against the advancing troops. "Now, the cry 'The citizens are coming!' appears to us to be the epitome of all that is amusing; but at that time, for just twenty-four hours, it embodied a genuine force",

Cavalry attack on demonstrators in front of Berlin's royal palace, 18 March 1848

Fighting on the barricades in Neue Königstrasse, Berlin, 19 March 1848

The Prussian king Frederick William IV riding through the streets of Berlin, 21 March 1848

recalled the elderly Theodor Fontane. More than 230 people died before the king capitulated and ordered the withdrawal of the troops. On 21 March, draped in the revolutionary colours of black, red and gold, he rode through Berlin and, with the words "Prussia will henceforth be part of Germany!", acquiesced to the demand for national unity. A ministry was established under the Rhenish liberals Ludolf Camphausen and Gustav Mevissen, and a Prussian national assembly convened in May. The conditions were in place for Prussia to become a constitutional monarchy.

Fighting on the barricades in Berlin during the night of 19 March 1848

"The lying in state of the March victims", 22 March 1848. Painting by Adolph Menzel, 1848

5. The road to the Paulskirche

In order to defend and consolidate the successes achieved in street battles, meetings and petitions, the bourgeois-liberal majority in the *Landtage*, as well as many democrats, opted to achieve their objectives through reforms which had parliamentary legitimacy. The first task was therefore to convene a national parliament to draw up an all-German constitution and establish a central authority capable of governing Germany as a whole.

The pre-parliament

The political movement was spearheaded by 51 liberals and democrats from south-west Germany. On 5 March 1848, they met in Heidelberg and announced that the convening of a national assembly could no longer be postponed. Beyond this simple proclamation, and without any constitutional legitimacy, they formed a "Committee of Seven" whose aim was to convene "a more complete assembly of men who enjoy the confidence of all the German tribes": the pre-parliament. The seven-man body placed its trust in leading political and legal figures and invited "all

former or present members of the estates and legislative assemblies in all German states" to Frankfurt.

On 30 May 1848, 574 men who had responded to this call met in the Paulskirche to the acclaim of the Frankfurt populace. Yet the harmony was deceptive, for the conflicts within the bourgeoisie which had been simmering in Heidelberg now broke to the surface. While the political left, led by Gustav von Struve, called for the immediate establishment of a federal republic and the assumption of executive revolutionary powers by the pre-parliament, the majority of delegates were in favour of establishing a new political order by peaceful means and on the basis of an accord with the traditional powers. With this compromise, which was later endorsed by a majority in the National Assembly, the revolution entered a phase in which the emphasis was on legal means to achieve political goals. Violence as a means to change political conditions was rejected outright. After the radicals' motion to set up a republic was rejected by a majority in the pre-parliament, 40 delegates led by Friedrich Hecker left the assembly and sought to

Invitation to the delegate Dr Jucho to attend the deliberations of the pre-parliament in Frankfurt on 31 March 1848

Members
entering the
pre-parliament
in St. Paul's
Church, Frank-
furt, on
31 March 1848

Voters.
Painting by
Adolph
Menzel, 1848

overthrow the existing political system by force. Their attempt to unleash a national uprising with the support of volunteer forces in Baden found little popular support, and was crushed within a matter of days by the superior force of regular troops from Hesse and Baden.

The elections

Against the background of the revolutionary intermezzo in south-western Germany, the pre-parliament took just four days to establish the general principles for the elections to the future national assembly. It appointed a parliamentary "Committee of Fifty", which worked with the Federal Diet – now consisting of liberal members – and the state governments to lay down the conditions governing eligibility to vote. In essence, the right to vote was granted to male persons who had attained their majority and were able to prove their "independent" status. The definition of "independence", which in the view of the liberal bourgeoisie consisted of intellectual and financial independence, was open to highly divergent interpretation in the individual states. In extreme cases, workers and servants in dependent employment were excluded from the elections, whereas small traders who barely earned enough to survive were entitled to vote everywhere. Women were still disenfranchised; even the progressive left did not yet support the notion of women's suffrage. Overall, the number of enfranchised males – almost 80 per cent – was very high, even by comparison with other European states. Voting took place either directly or indirectly, depending on the region and electoral traditions; in most cases, however, indirect voting prevailed, with voters (all enfranchised persons) voting for electoral colleges which then decided on the granting of the mandate in a further round of elections. As there were still no party organizations in the modern sense, candidates included local dignitaries and persons renowned in the wider region for their activities during the *Vormärz*, and who were nominated by the political clubs or at public meetings. The turnout varied between 40 and 75 percent from region to region, not least because no

Verzeichniß der Wahlmänner,

welche in den 5 Urwahl-Bezirken der Vorstadt Au zur Wahl der Abgeordneten für die allgemeine Volks-Vertretung am teutschen Bunde mit absoluter Stimmen-Mehrheit erwählt worden sind.

1. Herr Alexander Moser, rechtsk. Stadtschreiber.
2.   „   Dr. Franz X. König, praktischer Arzt.
3.   „   Joseph Simmet, Pelzwaarenhändler.
4.   „   Joseph Hopf, Magistrats-Offiziant.
5.   „   Franz X. Keller, Landarzt.
6.   „   Martin Pögl, Tafernwirth.
7.   „   Sebastian Witt, Apotheker.
8.   „   Johann Köpel, Kupferschmiedmeister.
9.   „   Joseph Vizthum, Schneidermeister.
10.   „   Johann Nepomuck Ertl, Zimmermeister.
11.   „   van Mecheln, kgl. Landrichter.
12.   „   Dr. Fürst, praktischer Arzt.
13.   „   Matthäus Kluftinger, Mannheimerkoch.
14.   „   von Stegmayr, Leibhausinhaber.
15.   „   Jakob Erlinger, Bierwirth.
16.   „   Johann Schoder, Schuhmachermeister.
17.   „   Leonhard Rippolt, Glasermeister.
18.   „   Georg Reis, Schullehrer.
19.   „   Sebastian Erhardt, Krämer.
20.   „   Michael Wagmiller, Spießmüller.

Au, den 26. April 1848.

Die Wahl-Commission.

van Mecheln, k. Landrichter.   Moser, rechtsk. Stadtschreiber.
Ertl, Magistrats-Rath.   Betz, Magistrats-Rath.   Köpel, Magistrats-Rath.

previous elections had ever taken place in two-thirds of the electoral area. In the majority of cases, liberals and conservatives led the field, with left-wing and left-liberal candidates only coming to the fore in the constitutional states with a parliamentary tradition.

The National Assembly

On 18 May 1848, 330 out of 649 elected members convened for the constituent meeting of the National Assembly in the Paulskirche. In his inaugural speech, Heinrich von Gagern, who had just been elected president of the Assembly, emphasized the newly acquired "sovereignty of the nation" and its right to grant itself a constitution. However, he also left no doubt that this could only take place in agreement with the governments of the individual states.

In the following weeks and months, in addition to deliberating the new constitution, parliament focussed primarily on establishing a provisional executive. The debate about the provisional central authority revealed the differences in the various groupings' political principles. Whereas the left wing favoured the election by the National Assembly of one individual who would assume executive powers and be accountable to parliament, the right wing supported the concept of a collegiate body – with no accountability to parliament – in a process involving the princes. In the quest for a compromise acceptable to all sides, Heinrich von Gagern played a "bold stroke": he proposed to the National Assembly that an Imperial Administrator be elected who enjoyed the confidence of parliament and the princes alike. Parliament, by a large majority, elected Archduke John of Austria, a figure known for his liberal views and German nationalist sympathies, who was chosen "not because but although he is a prince". While the conservative liberals believed that his election would safeguard cooperation with the princes, the democrats prided themselves on having elected him on the basis of full parliamentary authority. In constitutional terms, however, the Imperial Administrator remained independent of parliament and, by virtue of his recognition by the princes, became the "legitimate" successor of the Federal Assembly, which transferred its powers to him. In effect, he was thus equivalent in status to a constitutional monarch, subject only to scrutiny by a ministry which he himself had appointed. For this reason, not least, great hopes were invested in the Imperial Administrator who – in his first declaration "To the German People" – pledged "after years of coercion ... full and unrestricted freedom" and the completion of a constitution for Germany. Nonetheless, the democratic associations never tired of exhorting him to respect the sovereignty of the people and to be mindful of his responsibility as head of state.

The Imperial Ministry, appointed by Archduke John under the liberal-minded aristo-

List of deputies elected in a Bavarian constituency, 1848

crat Charles Prince of Leiningen, was the only link between parliament and the Imperial Administrator. Unlike the Imperial Administrator himself, the cabinet was fully accountable to parliament. This constitutional arrangement anticipated – perhaps unwittingly – the form of parliamentary government favoured by most members of the National Assembly, which still envisaged a role for a monarch, albeit as a sovereign with limited rights. However, the weaknesses of the system soon became apparent during the practical business of government. Organizational shortcomings and disputes over competencies with the individual states soon began to restrict the freedom of action of the Imperial Administrator and his ministry. The individual states retained their powers in both the military and civilian fields, and the Imperial Administrator and his ministry were reliant on the individual states' bureaucratic and military apparatus to implement decisions. The question of diplomatic repre-

Archduke John of Austria, the Imperial Administrator, entering Frankfurt am Main on 11 July 1848

sentation remained contentious, but a particularly serious problem was the refusal of some states to place their armies under a centralized supreme command. On 6 August 1848, an appeal was issued to the armies of all the states to swear allegiance to the Imperial Administrator. Some refused outright, and it was only with reservations that two major states, Prussia and Austria, agreed to do so.

The debate about fundamental rights

After the provisional central government formally commenced its work on 3 July, the National Assembly turned its attention to its main task and began to deliberate a future constitution for Germany. The aim was to seize the opportunity afforded by the obvious impotence of the traditional powers in summer 1848 and draft a constitution designed "to establish a lasting foundation for the unity and freedom of Germany and for the wellbeing of the nation". Hard-won freedoms were to be safeguarded in a German nation-state endowed with a new social order and democratic constitution. In light, not least, of many members' experiences of the repressive system of the *Vormärz*, the National Assembly declared that it would "embark on the establishment of general rights which the constitution should grant the German people ...". The human and civil rights enshrined in the American and French constitutions were upheld as a model during the debates on fundamental rights. The primary focus of the catalogue of fundamental rights was to safeguard political and personal freedoms. For the first time in Germany's history, uniform rights for all citizens of the Reich (Article 2) were established. The special rights hitherto enjoyed by the privileged classes – the aristocracy and the clergy – were abolished and replaced by equality for all citizens before the law: "The aristocracy as an estate is hereby abolished ... All Germans are equal before the law" (Article 7). At the same time, the fundamental rights also formed the basis on which to guarantee the individual's rights vis-à-vis the state. These rights included, in particular, the inviolability of the freedom of the individual (Article 8), and unrestricted freedom of expression and religion, as well as freedom of association and assembly, which had so often been curtailed. The decisions to abolish supervision of schools by ecclesiastical authorities and to separate civil and religious marriage law were further steps towards the secularization of the German state.

The social dimension of the fundamental rights – and its implicit consequence, namely social reform – proved to be a particularly contentious philosophical issue in the debate. Although the liberal majority in the National Assembly accepted the inclusion of the principle of inviolability of property, the removal of existing aristocratic privileges and the abolition of all bonds based on subservience or thraldom in the catalogue of rights, it rejected demands for social reform. There was therefore little support for a motion tabled by one member of the National Assembly, Carl Nauwerck, who sought to enshrine the right to work in the catalogue of rights; the calls for provisions governing the social obligations of property-owners or a right to social security also found little favour. It was the social reform issue above all which cast the divergent interests of those who were in favour of a self-regulating social order, and the forces which favoured social revolution, into sharp relief.

Despite the many contentious passages, the catalogue of fundamental rights – based on the American and French models – was finally adopted in December, and proved to be a balanced compromise.

The National Assembly in session in St Paul's Church, Frankfurt, 1848

The Fundamental Rights of the German People. Coloured lithograph by Adolf Schroedter, 1849

6. The emergence of political parties

Political meeting in Trier, 1848. Painting by Johann Velten, 1848

It was the revolution of 1848/49 which prompted the emergence of political parties in the modern sense, notwithstanding the existence of various precursor parties in the south and west of Germany. At the start of the revolution, popular assemblies, demonstrations and proclamations were still the primary channels for the articulation of the political will, but the abolition of censorship and the granting of freedom of assembly and freedom of association during the "March days" in 1848 created favourable conditions for the establishment of political parties. In liberal constitutional circles, however, the terms "party" and "party ethos" continued to have negative connotations, conflicting with the liberal principle that every member of parliament must champion the common good to an equal extent. Nonetheless, by the time the elections to the National Assembly took place in April 1848, it had become increasingly apparent to political activists that their interests could be mobilized, channelled and organized more quickly and effectively through political parties. Even conservative-minded liberals such as Heinrich von Gagern soon recognized, in their daily work in parliament, that "an isolated position ... is always a weak position", and that "political influence is secured and retained only at the head of a political party".

The political associations which sprang up primarily in the towns and cities can be regarded as the birthplace of the political parties. They formulated policy programmes

"Politicians in print": cartoon satirizing the political battles being waged in the press

Democrats holding a meeting in Berlin, 1848

which they promoted in their own publications, and quickly developed their own clear political identity. Five groupings, akin to political parties, can be identified: the democrats, the liberals, the conservatives, politically active Catholics, and the fledgling workers' movement. There were also clubs and associations which articulated regional and social interests, especially at their congresses, which generally lasted several days.

The democrats

The first political movement to establish a centralized, party-type organization were the democrats, who built up an extensive network of "popular associations" at regional level. Indeed, the policy course and programme of the fledgling democratic party were formulated as early as June 1848 at the Congress of Democrats in Frankfurt. The democrats – drawn mainly from the liberal professions (lawyers, doctors, editors etc.) – were in favour of a republican system based on the principles of popular sovereignty and general, equal and direct suffrage. This was underpinned by a commitment to the notion of social reform and an open society of citizens which was to include the lower classes from the outset. Radical democrats had no qualms about resorting to violence to assert their demands.

The liberals

The liberals were more hesitant in forming groups and associations at first, generally doing so only in response to the activities of their democrat rivals. Unlike the democrats, the liberals did not manage to establish a central umbrella organization. Despite this lack of organization, the liberals – who were valued especially for their legal expertise and experience in administration – became the strongest force in the National Assembly. Their aim was progressive democratization based on a liberal economic and social order. On the issue of Germany's future system of

government, most liberals supported constitutional principles, embodied in a monarchy regulated by parliament and a constitution. Their chief publication was the "Deutsche Zeitung", which first appeared in 1847.

Title page of the *Deutsche Zeitung*, the liberals' newspaper

The conservatives

Having adopted a hesitant and somewhat defensive stance at first, the counter-revolutionary forces also began to exploit the new forms of political organization and media. In Bavaria and Prussia in particular, a conservative class comprising the aristocracy, civil servants and clergy emerged, with the aim of working towards the restitution of the monarchy's traditional rights. Their first major association was established after the victory of the counter-revolutionary forces in Berlin in November 1848. According to its statutes, the "Faithful Confederacy for King and Fatherland", or *Treubund für König und*

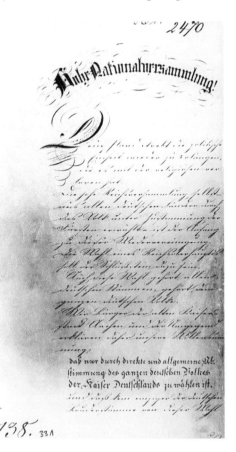

An das Volk!

Die Gefahr, die seit Monaten über uns schwebte, droht nun endlich hereinzubrechen, und uns das Heiligste, das Theuerste zu nehmen, was wir haben.

Nicht fürchten wir Anarchie, Republik, Reaction zu Gunsten des Absolutismus, diese werden ohnmächtig zerschellen an dem gesunden Geist des Volkes und an seinem kräftigen Willen. Was wir fürchten, ist der Untergang unseres Vaterlandes „Preußen".

Alles, was je in unserm Vaterlande Großes gethan und geschaffen ist, soll ungeschehen sein, aller Ruhm unserer Voreltern in ewige Vergessenheit begraben werden und der Name Preußen auf immer verlöschen! Das ist es, was unsere Feinde wollen, was sie unter den Worten „Preußen geht fortan in Deutschland auf" verstehen.

Um unsere herrliche Monarchie zu gründen, bedurfte es der ganzen Kraft des größten Mannes aller Zeiten, des Einzigen Friedrich, und als diese Monarchie in fürchtbare Bedrängniß gerieth, da erhob sich das ganze Volk und sagte: es soll nicht untergehen das Kleinod, das uns der große Mann hinterlassen, — und es ging nicht unter!

Und jetzt, wo unser Land mächtig, groß und schön ist, jetzt, wo es selbstständig der Welt gegenüber bestehen und stolz auf sich selbst das Haupt erheben kann, jetzt soll es zu Grunde gehen ohne allen Anlaß, ja sogar ohne allen Kampf? Was dem gewaltigen Kaiser Napoleon selbst nicht gelang, das sollen Phrasen und Phrasenhelden möglich machen? Und dies alles zur Ehre und Kräftigung Deutschlands, wie die politischen Intriganten sagen, obgleich die ganze Welt weiß, daß Deutschland ohne ein sehr kräftiges Preußen gar nicht bestehen kann!

Aber es ist abgesehen auf ganz Deutschland, denn ist erst Preußen zerstückelt und einer Chimäre zu Liebe aufgegangen, oder vielmehr untergegangen, dann folgt Deutschland rasch nach.

Und wir sind unserm Untergange näher als wir glauben!

O wem erbebt nicht das Herz vor Grimm und Zorn, wer fühlt nicht tief die Scham über diese Schmach, größer als das Jahr 1806 sie brachte, größer als man je sie träumen konnte!

Aber noch lebt das preußische Volk, noch sind in ihm die Erinnerungen des Ruhms nicht erloschen, und noch ist die Hoffnung nicht verloren, es werde dieses tapfere, ehrliebende Volk in der Stunde der Gefahr sich wieder wie Ein Mann erheben, und Denen sein Donnerwort zurufen, Die seine Ehre verpfänden, und seine Unabhängigkeit antasten wollen!

Berlin, den 23 Juli 1848.

Der Preußen-Verein für constitutionelles Königthum.

Handbill issued by the conservative "Prussia Association" calling for a constitutional monarchy

Vaterland, was committed to the "revival of genuinely constitutional principles" and the "affirmation of faithful love and devotion to King and Fatherland". The first conservative party organ to be published was the "*Neue Preussische Zeitung*", better known as the "*Kreuzzeitung*" [The Cross] due to the iron cross on its masthead.

Political Catholicism

From spring 1848 onwards, the campaign to assert the rights of the Church vis-à-vis the state increasingly gave rise to an organized political Catholic movement. Organizational and political backing was provided by the Pius Associations, which initiated a dynamic programme of extra-parliamentary activity. Countless newspapers, petitions and assemblies, including the first all-German Catholic Congress held in Mainz from 3-6 October

Petition submitted by the Catholic movement to the National Assembly in Frankfurt

1848, were the instruments wielded by this broad-based movement – which had virtually no parliamentary representation at first – in pursuit of its goals. It encompassed a wealth of Catholic opinion, from advocates of a "Christian" democracy to the ultra-conservative forces which featured prominently in the movement's rank and file.

The fledgling workers' movement

In 1848, working people were only just beginning to organize themselves as an independent political force. In many cases, the workers' associations were virtually indistinguishable from the democratic movement, while the social divisions between journeymen, early urban proletariat and the property-less lower classes continued to impede the formation of a single organiza-

Left: Title page of the *Deutsche Arbeiterzeitung*, 8 April 1848

Right: Call to attend a general assembly by Berlin tailors, 1848

tion. Workers still had a long way to go before they were united by the "common condition of their class", whose emergence Karl Marx predicted in his Communist Manifesto before the revolution. As well as the reactionary groups which advocated a conservative approach to social policy and were united in the craftsmen's and trades' congresses, others – which later established the "General German Fraternity of Workers" – were proponents of social reforms, while the League of Communists – a union of German emigrés based in London – fervently championed social revolution.

The interest groups

Not only the major political movements but also the social and economic forces created a public platform for themselves by establishing interest-based organizations. Associations which represented the interests of specific trades and occupations were especially keen to influence the political direction of the National Assembly through public addresses, the submission of petitions, and

manifestos. The Congress of German Crafts and Trades was particularly successful at mobilizing public support with its denunciation of liberal trade policies and calls for the introduction of protective tariffs.

The political groupings in the National Assembly

After its inaugural session in Frankfurt on 18 May 1848, little time elapsed before more stable political groups formed in the National Assembly as well, based on shared political beliefs and voting habits. They drew on the experience gained in the parliaments (*Landtage*) of the southern German states and sought to organize parliamentary work effectively. The majority of members belonged to these groupings, which were named after the inns and taverns of Frankfurt where they regularly held their informal meetings. The groupings elected executive committees, drew up membership lists, and adopted policy programmes. From now on, they would dominate parliamentary procedure and were already referred to as "parties" in some quarters.

"The ladies' political club": cartoon satirizing women's political activities, 1848/49

STATUTEN DER GESELLSCHAFT
IN MILANI'S CAFÉ-HAUS.

1. Die Mitglieder verpflichten sich, beabsichtigte selbstständige oder Verbesserungs-Anträge, sowie Interpellationen an die Minister, vor deren Einbringung in die National-Versammlung, einer Verhandlung in der Gesellschaft zu unterwerfen, und von denselben abzustehen, wenn sie nicht die Unterstützung der Majorität der Gesellschaft in gemeinschaftlicher Versammlung finden.

Eine Ausnahme hiervon ist nur mit Genehmigung der Gesellschaft zulässig, und wird ausserdem nur in unvorhergesehenen dringenden Fällen, und im Verlaufe der Verhandlungen während der Sitzungen der National-Versammlung, mit Genehmigung des Vorstandes, für gerechtfertigt angesehen.

2. Die Gesellschaft sucht sich für die Abstimmungen in der National-Versammlung über die vorkommenden einzelnen Fragen möglichst zu einigen.

Wenn in einer eigens berufenen, oder aus wenigstens der Hälfte der Mitglieder bestehenden Versammlung zwei Drittel der Anwesenden eine Frage für eine Parteifrage erklären, darf kein Mitglied der Minderheit gegen die von der Mehrheit angenommene Ansicht in der National-Versammlung sprechen oder stimmen.

Jeder in einer solchen Parteifrage von einer Versammlung der Gesellschaft gefasste Beschluss ist auch den Abwesenden mitzutheilen.

3. Für die Vertretung der Ansichten und Beschlüsse der Mehrheit der Gesellschaft in der National-Versammlung, sowohl bei offenen als bei Parteifragen, versichert sich die Gesellschaft in der Regel zum Voraus bestimmter Redner aus ihrer Mitte.

4. Die Sitzungen der Versammlung finden Sonntag, Montag, Mittwoch und Donnerstag, jedesmal Abends 7 Uhr, Statt.

5. Die Gesellschaft wählt für je 4 Wochen einen Vorstand von 3 Mitgliedern.

6. Die Mitglieder des Vorstandes haben abwechselnd die Verhandlungen der Gesellschaft zu leiten, für Ordnung und Ruhe, insbesondere für das Unterbleiben von Privat-Unterhaltung während der Berathungen zu sorgen.

Statutes of the conservative "Milani" grouping

In the National Assembly, the ultra-conservative right was represented by the grouping which met in the aristocratic surroundings of the Café Milani. Most of the deputies who met here were Prussian, and some of them maintained close contacts with Frederick William IV. Their primary goal was to preserve the monarchy while protecting the interests of the individual states. As the parliamentary arm of the counter-revolution, the ultra-right was loathed by the lower classes, a sentiment which culminated in the assassination of two conservative deputies during the September unrest.

The predominant force in parliament was the centre right, mainly comprising deputies from the Casino Party, which determined the progress of the Assembly's deliberations to a significant extent. Most of its members favoured a constitutional monarchy with restricted suffrage. One of the most promi-

nent deputies from the liberals' constitutional wing was the president of the National Assembly, Heinrich von Gagern.

Most of the left-wing liberals joined either the *Württemberger Hof* or the *Westendhall* groupings. These deputies were committed unconditionally to parliamentary democracy and rejected any deals with the princes. During the September crisis, however, many deputies abandoned their allegiance to the *Württemberger Hof* and joined the centre-right grouping at the *Augsburger Hof*.

The "left" in the National Assembly met at the *Deutscher Hof*. Its members were committed to popular sovereignty, a unicameral system, general, equal and direct elections, and parliamentary control of the Government, with the aim of radically transforming the social order. Although they played a pioneering role in the formation of the

Members of the "Casino" grouping of constitutional liberals in the National Assembly

Members of the "Augsburger Hof" left-liberal grouping

political groupings, there was little unanimity within their ranks on how to achieve their goals. Whereas the moderates who met at the *Deutscher Hof* had no desire to use anything other than legal means to achieve their objectives, the radical *Donnersberg* group did not rule out the option of revolution. Extremist groupings, either conservative or socialist, were not represented in parliament.

The left in the National Assembly, Frankfurt

7. Turning points of the Revolution

Prussian troops marching into Schleswig, spring 1848

By summer 1848, there were growing signs of a turn in the tides of the revolution throughout Europe as the established powers crushed uprisings in Poland, Hungary, France and Italy. Against this background, the military and political wrangling over possession of Schleswig and Holstein was the crisis which sealed the National Assembly's fate. The duchies of Schleswig and Holstein, which had joined the revolution in April, rose up against their ruler, the Danish king, in protest at his plans to annex Schleswig, which – unlike Holstein – was not part of the German Confederation. The duchies' provisional revolutionary governments appealed for military assistance from the federal troops, which was duly provided under Prussian command. The focus of public interest now shifted to the problem of national unity, which increasingly dominated the debates in parliament as well. Even though the German troops conducted a successful campaign against Denmark, the Prussian king – under diplomatic pressure from England and Russia – signed an armistice. This action by Prussia not only weakened the position of the two duchies, but also bypassed the provisional central government in whose name the campaign had been fought. Prussia's high-handed approach to the Schleswig-Holstein issue forced the National Assembly to take a vote which would affect the future not only of the two duchies but also of the German nation-state as a whole. Endorsement of the armistice by a majority in the National Assembly would mean that Prussia had crucially undermined not only the nationalist movement but the credibility of parliament itself. Rejection of Prussia's methods by the National Assembly meant risking a war in Europe and abandoning the path of consensus with the German princes.

The National Assembly debating whether to accept the armistice, 16 September 1848

Street fighting outside St Paul's Church, 18 September 1848

Faced with this situation, heated disputes on how to proceed flared up between the various political groups. In its first vote, the National Assembly narrowly rejected the armistice by 238 votes to 221. It was the first victory for the left in the National Assembly, and was secured only with the support of patriotic liberals, including the historian Friedrich Christoph Dahlmann, who believed that any surrender of Schleswig and Holstein was a betrayal of the cause of German unity. The cabinet under Charles Prince of Leiningen, who had pressed for an end to the war, now resigned over the issue. When an attempt by Dahlmann to form a new administration failed, parliament's decision appeared increasingly fragile. Yet calls from the radical left for the struggle against Prussia to commence also failed to secure a parliamentary majority. The National Assembly remained mired in a state of powerlessness and passivity until it finally reversed its original decision and accepted the armistice by 257 votes to 236. Many liberals who had previously opposed the armistice now voted in favour, having recognized the political and military risks associated with its rejection. For the republicans, parliament's impotence and failure to assert itself against the established powers further reinforced their feelings of scepticism towards the moderate liberal policy course supported by the parliamentary majority. The likelihood that the princes would renounce their sovereign rights in favour of a German nation-state within a parliamentary system of government now appeared increasingly remote.

Frankfurt

Parliament's endorsement of the armistice contained in the Treaty of Malmö was exploited by some republicans and democrats to incite the population against the liberal majority in the National Assembly. On 17 September, one day after the vote, more than 15,000 people heeded the call from the Democratic Association and the Workers' Association and gathered at a demonstration at Frankfurt's *Pfingstweide*. In a proclamation, the parliamentarians who had voted for the armistice were branded as "traitors to the German people, German freedom and honour". Workers and democrats now also demanded a left-wing walk-out from parliament and even the dissolution of the National Assembly. The same night, the Imperial Minister of the Interior, Anton von Schmerling, marshalled troops from neighbouring Mainz to protect the National Assembly. When the enraged mob tried to assert its demands more vigorously the following morning at the Paulskirche, they found themselves confronted by Prussian and Austrian troops. The situation escalated as the military barred the way to some demonstrators seeking to enter the church. Soon afterwards, the square was cleared as running battles were fought in the narrow streets and alleys in Frankfurt's city centre. More than a thousand insurgents set up barricades to defend themselves from the hated military. The revolt culminated in the murder of two conservative parliamenta-

The murder of the two conservative deputies, Prince Felix von Lichnowsky and Hans von Auerswald, at the gates of the City of Frankfurt, 18 September 1848

rians, Hans von Auerswald and Prince Felix von Lichnowsky. The imposition of a state of siege and the unconditional use of military force were now the only options, in the National Assembly's view, to take control of the situation. In all, the street battles claimed 80 lives. Fearing further unrest, the central government now resorted to repressive measures akin to those used during the *Vormärz*, banning associations and hunting down the insurgents. It devised plans to impose punishments for "press offences" committed by civil servants and public authorities, and requested the states to submit "precise statistics on existing democratic associations, and their branches, in Germany". Parliament's safety and protection were secure, but the price was high. The September crisis reinforced the established powers and deepened the rift between constitutional and democratic parliamentarians.

The Grand Duchy of Baden

Despite the crushing of the insurrection led by Friedrich Hecker in April and the ban on popular committees in south-west Germany, the democratic republicans could still count on strong support here, especially among the petty bourgeoisie and the rural population. The Grand Duchy of Baden remained in a state of "cosy anarchy", with democratic popular associations still tolerated. The radical democrat Gustav von Struve, who had emigrated to Switzerland, reawakened memories in Baden with his call for "revolution and a republic" in Germany. By late summer, the time seemed ripe once more for a revolutionary uprising in Baden, especially as the mood among the lower classes was becoming increasingly ugly as a result of repressive new finance laws and a petty-minded judiciary.

The endorsement of the armistice finally gave Struve the opportunity he was looking for to incite the population against the National Assembly in handbills in which he proclaimed: "Triumph! The Frankfurt parliament is exposed! There is no longer a German parliament – just an enraged population face to face with a handful of scoundrels .... The whole of Germany is rebelling against the rule of the princes and is fighting for the freedom of the people!" In the mistaken belief that the Frankfurt revolutionaries had triumphed, he proclaimed the "German Social Republic" from a window of Lörrach Town Hall on 21 September, pledging that there would be "prosperity, education and freedom for all". Supporters of the monarchy were to be arrested, and the assets of the state, the Church and the monarchists were to be seized and handed over to the local

authorities. The insurrection quickly spread to the uplands of Baden, but little time was lost before the revolutionaries suffered a crushing defeat at the hands of the superior Baden troops at Staufen on 24 September.

Vienna

Not only in Frankfurt and Baden but in Austria, too, the tides of revolution seemed to be turning. Since summer, social tensions had been simmering in the Austrian capital, while national tensions heightened in other parts of the multi-ethnic Habsburg empire. The starting point for Vienna's counter-revolution and the strengthening of the Habsburg monarchy, however, was the campaign to crush the independence movement led by Lajos Kossuth. When Kossuth launched an offensive in October to achieve Hungarian independence and inflicted a devastating defeat on the Governor of Hungary, the Emperor stepped up his military measures and mobilized German and Italian troops. Mutiny by a battalion stationed in Vienna which refused to take up arms against the Hungarians finally trig-

Left:
Gustav von Struve proclaiming the German Republic from a balcony at Lörrach Town Hall, 12 September 1848

Right:
Murder of Austria's War Minister Count Baillet de Latour in Vienna, 6 October 1848

gered insurrection in the capital on 6 October, with the Democratic Associations, working men's clubs, civil guards and student leagues joining forces with the insurgents. One of the first casualties was War Minister Count Theodor Baillet de Latour, who was hanged from a lamp-post.

In the Frankfurt parliament, the events in Austria were watched with concern. While a deputation of liberal parliamentarians sought to end the civil war by diplomatic means, a handful of left-wing deputies, including Robert Blum, seized the initiative and joined the revolutionaries on the barricades, briefly taking control of the city. But the imperial troops were already mustering at the gates of the city under Field Marshall Prince Alfred von Windischgrätz. A state of siege was imposed, and within five days, the military had succeeded in recapturing the city despite bitter resistance from the revolutionaries. The triumph of the reactionary monarchist forces claimed several thousand lives. With utter disregard for his parliamentary immunity, Robert Blum was seized and summarily executed. The National Assembly's muted protests against this outrage were a further sign of its impotence against the established powers. The dissolution of the Reichstag in Vienna, the appointment of Prince Felix zu Schwarzenberg – a reactionary champion of Greater Austria – as Minister-President, and the imposition of a neo-absolutist constitution consolidated the victory of the counter-revolutionary forces in Austria.

Robert Blum, a deputy in the National Assembly, is summarily executed at Brigittenau in Vienna on 9 November 1848. Painting by Carl Constantin Heinrich Steffeck, 1848/49

Berlin

The news of the triumph of reaction in Vienna could not fail to have an impact in the Prussian capital. Since the summer, parliament and the monarch had been squabbling over the constitutional loyalty of the military, which – for no discernible reason – had opened fire on the civil guard and workers at a demonstration, killing 14 people. However, it was the appointment of the reactionary general Count Frederick William von Brandenburg, a relative of the royal house and supporter of the "camarilla", as Minister-President which finally unleashed the second wave of revolution in Prussia. The Prussian National Assembly unanimously rejected the appointment of the general, who was prepared to complete the counter-revolution. However, the king ignored parliament's decision and commenced the implementation of the "battle-plan" which he had worked out in September with the military. The Prussian king suspended the Prussian parliament and moved its seat to the nearby town of Brandenburg. He responded to democratic and left-wing protests by closing the inns they used as meeting-places. Finally, they were forcibly dispersed by the military. The revolutionary spirit of the "March days" now gave way to conflict and resignation among the bourgeoisie, which the monarchy exploited for its own ends. Although Berlin's civil guard opted to show no more than passive resistance, this itself was used as the formal justification for 40,000 troops to enter the city under General Wrangel. Only the imposition of a state of emergency and martial law on 12 and 14 November 1848 briefly triggered armed resistance by democratic groups in the city. However, the monarchy could count

on the loyalty and fire-power of its troops, which quickly brought the insurrection under control. The king was now determined to regain power. He promptly dissolved the Prussian National Assembly, now relocated in Brandenburg, and imposed a constitution which, while making a number of concessions to the liberals, granted the king sweeping emergency powers. Counter-revolution had triumphed in Prussia as well.

The Reich constitution

Although the triumph of the counter-revolutionary forces in Frankfurt, Vienna and Berlin had largely sealed the revolution's fate, the National Assembly was still in the process of debating the fundamental rights. Even though time was pressing, it was October before the National Assembly turned its attention to the key power-political and institutional elements of the constitution. In this context, two issues were of central importance: firstly, the borders of the future Reich territory, and secondly, its head of state, which would ultimately determine

Berlin workers
storming the
armoury,
14 June 1848

Forcible dissolution of the Prussian National Assembly, 15 November 1848

the form of government to be adopted. The two problems were interlinked and were crucially influenced by Prussian-Austrian dualism. Initially, a majority of deputies in the National Assembly agreed on a "Greater German" solution, which meant that the Reich should include all the territories of the German Confederation, the Duchy of Schleswig and the East Prussian provinces, but would exclude the non-German speaking regions of the Habsburg empire in order to avoid nationality conflicts. However, Austria's demand that its state unity be preserved and its rejection of a centralized constitution in March 1849 put paid to plans for a "Greater German" solution. Many of its advocates now joined the group led by Heinrich von Gagern which supported a "Little German" solution. Even the democratic left was won over by concessions on the contentious issue of electoral law.

Once a decision had been taken in favour of a "Little German" solution, the debate – under way since January 1849 – about the head of state took a new turn. The advocates

of a "Greater Germany" had already put forward a number of quite contradictory proposals, ranging from a dynastic imperial directorate to a unitary democratic republic, but the majority of deputies now endorsed the option of a hereditary Prussian emperor.

The Reich constitution, adopted on 27 March 1849 in what was ostensibly a sovereign act, was a balanced compromise which would become a template for Germany's future constitutional development. The demands of the bourgeois-liberal majority in the National Assembly, who advocated a federal state with a bicameral parliament and a hereditary head of state, prevailed. The only concessions made to the left were the acceptance of universal suffrage and the restriction of the monarch's powers.

With the adoption of the Reich constitution and the election of the Prussian king as "Emperor of the Germans", the liberal and national movement believed it was close to achieving its objectives. Placing their faith in the words uttered by the Prussian king

The Prussian king, Frederick William IV, receiving the Imperial Deputation of the National Assembly in Berlin's royal palace, 3 April 1849

Frederick William IV in the heady March days of 1848 that "Prussia will henceforth be part of Germany", the National Assembly sent a deputation to Berlin to offer him the imperial crown. Yet his guarded reply that first of all, "the assent, freely given, of the crowned heads, the princes and the free cities" must be secured, was merely a pretext for rejecting the outcome of the election. Indeed, he had already made his views plain in a letter to the Prussian envoy in England, Baron von Bunsen, in December 1848: "A legitimate King by divine right, indeed the King of Prussia, who is blessed not with the oldest but with the noblest crown, stolen from no one, is now expected to accept an imaginary coronet of mud and clay ... Let me tell you bluntly: should the crown of the German nation which, a thousand years old, has

rested now for 42 years, ever be conferred again, then it shall be by me and my peers; and woe betide anyone who presumes to claim a right to which he is not entitled." Still faithful to the romantic notion of the divine right of kings, he could not tolerate the idea of an imperial crown depending on the will of a parliament. On 28 April, in a despatch to the central government, he formally rejected both the imperial crown and the constitution. The constitutional arrangements developed by the National Assembly had failed.

The campaign for the German imperial constitution

The Prussian king's decision was received with disappointment and consternation in the National Assembly at first. Even the recognition of the imperial constitution by 28 state governments in a collective note on 14 April 1849 could do little to alter the situation, especially since the larger German states – notably Austria, Prussia, Bavaria, Saxony and Hanover – had rejected it. Even though the National Assembly had the law on its side following the adoption and promulgation of the constitution in the Imperial Law Gazette, it was forced to take action, firstly by the rejection of the constitution by the larger states and, secondly, by the emerging popular movement.

With its resolution of 4 May 1849, adopted by a narrow majority, calling upon "the governments, the legislative bodies, the communes of the individual states [and] the entire German people" to ensure the recognition and enforcement of the constitution of the German Reich, the National Assembly disregarded the sovereign rights of the individual states and conferred indirect legitimacy on extra-parliamentary action. Further resolutions, especially Gagern's government programme which endorsed this course of action in moral terms, prompted more and more deputies to turn their backs on parliament. Finally, all that remained was a "rump parliament" consisting of left-wing deputies. Fearing that parliament would be forcibly dissolved by Prussian troops stationed in Mainz, the deputies relocated to Stuttgart on 30 May. Just three weeks later, on 18 June, the government of Württemberg blockaded its meeting rooms and ordered the military to disperse the deputies.

After May 1849, however, the fate of the revolution was no longer really dependent on parliament's decisions. Workers', popular and fatherland associations were attempting to exert pressure on the governments locally through petitions, press campaigns and street assemblies. The tone of the statements grew sharper and the willingness to enforce the constitution by violence became increasingly apparent. Thus on 8 May, citizens of Heidelberg declared, "on our own initia-

tive and of our own free will, solemnly and publicly, that we are ready to protect and defend the German Imperial Constitution, drawn up and proclaimed, together with the fundamental rights and the electoral law, by the National Assembly in Frankfurt am Main, with our lives and all that belongs to us." The pro-constitution rebellion was focussed primarily on the states which had rejected the constitution. Whereas it was confined to local unrest in Prussia, and was quickly crushed by the military, there were bloody and longer-lasting conflicts in Saxony, the Palatinate and Baden.

In Saxony's capital, Dresden, the "fatherland associations" took up arms when the king dissolved the chambers which supported the constitution and summoned the Prussian

Dissolution of the rump parliament in Stuttgart by the Württemberg military, 18 June 1849

Fighting on the barricades in Dresden, May 1849. Painting by Julius Scholtz, 1849

military. With the battle-cry "Hurry swiftly with weapons and ammunition! Now is the time!" the crowd stormed the armoury. Under the command of the Russian anarchist Mikhail Bakunin and expertly directed by the architect Gottfried Semper, barricades were erected across the city. Even such prominent figures as Saxony's *Kapellmeister* Richard Wagner joined the workers and artisans who formed the main revolutionary force. As the king fled on foot to safety on a steamship on the Elbe, a provisional government was installed in Dresden. For a brief period, it seemed as if popular sovereignty would triumph. However, the provisional government's appeal to the citizens of Saxony to join the uprising met with little support. The arrival of Prussian troops sealed the fate of the uprising, which was brutally crushed within just six days.

Battle between Baden rebels and Prussian troops at Gross-Sachsen an der Bergstrasse, 16 June 1849

The Baden revolutionary army is disarmed at its Rastatt stronghold, 23 July 1849

The bloody events in Dresden did not discourage the insurgents in the Palatinate and Baden from seeking to enforce the imperial constitution by violent means. In the Palatinate, this was not the only objective; here, democrats were also fighting for separation from Bavaria. With the words "Since the government has become a rebel, the free citizens of the Palatinate will become enforcers of the law", the popular associations seized the initiative, and a provisional government was installed. Proclaiming the independence of the Palatinate as a sovereign state, it succeeded in taking over the affairs of state for a short time. However, even before Bavaria could formally request military aid, Prussian troops entered the Palatinate and restored order.

In Baden, where the government had recognized the imperial constitution, the popular associations' demands went even further. Rejecting constitutional monarchy, they demanded democratic and social reforms, the free election of army officers, the abolition of all feudal dues, protection against the dominance of capitalists, and state-funded unemployment benefits. On 13 May, a popular assembly attended by some 35,000 people declared: "The German princes have sworn to suppress freedom and have joined forces in pursuit of this end; their betrayal of the people and of the Fatherland is clear for all to see. The people of Baden will therefore support the popular movement in the Palatinate with all the means at their disposal." The popular movement even received military backing from rebel troops in Baden's own army. German democrats' hopes were revived as companies of riflemen, members of the national gymnasts' movement, and Polish and Hungarian legions also hurried to offer their support. But tenacity, courage and endurance were not enough to vanquish the Prussian military and the imperial troops under the command of the Prussian prince who was destined to become Germany's Kaiser Wilhelm. The blame for the defeat lay not only with the popular army's military and strategic inferiority, but also the timid approach adopted by Baden's provisional government. It refused to support the rebellion in the Palatinate, outlawed the radical democratic opposition in Baden, and sought to prevent the armed struggle from spilling over to other German states. The surrender of the rebels at their last remaining stronghold at Rastatt, under siege from Prussian troops, on 23 July 1849 marked the failure of the liberal and democratic movement's final attempt to enforce the imperial constitution for all the German states against the princes' resistance. The Prussian military courts were implacable, sentencing rebels to death, imprisonment and hard labour in a process of summary justice which lasted until late October.

The forces of reaction in the 1850s

The triumph of reaction in Europe, 1849. Cartoon by Ferdinand Schroeder, 1849

The failure of the revolution was due not only to the dominance of the established dynasties, the armies' loyalty to the monarchy, and the bureaucracy. The rifts between the groups within and outside the National Assembly had also impeded concerted and unified action. Even after the revolution, bourgeois-liberal ideas and radical democratic concepts remained irreconcilable, as did the interests of the propertied and propertyless classes.

The bourgeoisie's inability to unite and assert itself was exploited by the established powers to initiate a comprehensive reactionary backlash. Having intimidated the opposition with the Prussian military tribunals, the princes now embarked on the systematic reversal of the revolution's achievements. During the first phase, most liberal "March ministries" were replaced by conservative ones, and in some states, the princes had no qualms about dissolving the parliaments. The liberal constitutions were revised, progressively dismantling the bourgeois freedoms which had been achieved and substantially curbing the rights of

political participation. In place of the liberal constitutions, étatist-conservative constitutions were adopted, as in Prussia, where a three-class voting system was introduced which divided voters into three categories based on income. This system favoured the small group of high earners, who were able to elect as many electoral college members and deputies as the largest category, the low earners. The introduction of public hustings also tightened control over the individual's electoral choices.

These reactionary measures were coordinated by the re-established Federal Diet, or *Bundestag*, in Frankfurt am Main. One of its first acts was to adopt a resolution, called *Bundesreaktionsbeschluss*, on 23 August 1851, which curtailed basic rights – especially freedom of the press and freedom of association – in all the German states. The "Police Union of the Major German States" was established as an effective surveillance instrument for the reactionary forces, and was designed to seek out and crush subversive activities by liberals, democrats and socialists. All these repressive measures resulted in what has often been described as the "quiet of the graveyard" in Germany until the end of the 1850s.

While the German princes systematically rolled back the achievements of the liberal and nationalist movements, the future of Germany's system of government continued to be an unresolved problem. Plans to establish a "Little German" federal state under Prussian leadership were vetoed by Austria. The issue of national unity vanished from the political agenda for the time being, while the dualism between Prussia and Austria became entrenched.

Revolutionaries in exile

In order avoid imprisonment or even the death penalty, many persecuted revolutionaries had little choice but to emigrate abroad, despite the substantial financial and personal risks which emigration entailed. For example, almost 80,000 citizens of Baden left their home – around six percent of the Grand Duchy's population. The emigrants went to Switzerland, Great Britain and above all America, in other words, to countries with a more liberal political climate.

Most refugees left their homes for social and economic reasons, however. It was the prospect of more secure and better-paid

Meeting room of the reestablished German Confederation in the Thurn and Taxis Palace, Frankfurt

Deliberations on the reform of the German Confederation at the Dresden Conference, 1850/51

employment and the opportunity to acquire land freely in America which prompted many emigrants to seek a new life for themselves. The political émigrés, including well-known members of the pre-parliament such as Gustav von Struve and Friedrich Hecker, accounted for a relatively low proportion of the emigrants, but their influence on the host country's political life was tangible. As well as publishing newspapers and establishing associations, many emigrants aspired to a career in politics. One of the most successful was Carl Schurz, a key figure in the uprising in Baden and the Palatinate, who became a senator in the state of Missouri in 1869 and even advanced to the post of Secretary of the Interior under Republican President Rutherford B. Hayes in 1877. During the American Civil War, former German rebels and mutinous soldiers took up arms for the Northern states, which fought for the end of slavery under the Republican Abraham Lincoln. Very few emigrants returned to Germany; most made new lives for themselves abroad.

Opposite page:
Top:
Below deck on an emigrants' ship, 1849

Bottom:
Carl Schurz giving a speech at an election meeting in Cincinnati in the 1870s

**The German
Empire in
1871**

In October 1858, one year after the abdication of Frederick William IV on grounds of ill health, his brother in Prussia took over the reins of government. When the Prince Regent formed a liberal-conservative ministry and announced far-reaching reforms, many people hoped that a "New Era" was about to commence, a hope reinforced by the fact that in other German states, too, new cabinets were embarking on a moderate liberal course. In Austria, on the other hand, which until 1861 had no constitution, the imperial government held on tenaciously to its neo-absolutist style of rule despite half-hearted economic reforms. Prussia successfully resisted Austria's accession to the increasingly prosperous German Customs Union, thereby exacerbating the rivalry between the two powers as each tried to gain the upper hand.

The weakening of tsarism in Russia as a result of the Crimean War of 1853/54-1856 and, above all, the unification of Italy in 1859, gave a further boost to the optimism with which many liberals and democrats throughout Germany looked to the future. The National Association, founded in the same year, took up the idea of a "Little Germany" that had failed a decade previously – in other words, the idea of German unification based on a parliamentary system, under Prussian leadership. 1861 saw the founding of the German Progress Party, creating an alliance of committed liberals and democrats that pursued the goals of the National Association within Prussia. In the elections to the Prussian *Landtag* that same year, the Progress Party at once became the strongest party.

The Prussian government, however, unlike other state governments, did not seek to cooperate with the liberals, and a confrontation soon arose between the executive and parliament over the issue of military reform. This confrontation increasingly acquired the character of a constitutional conflict. The Progress Party saw this as a decisive trial of strength with the conservative-monarchist state. However, it was a trial it was unable to win. In September 1862, the arch-opponent of the liberal movement, Otto von Bismarck, entered the political stage following his appointment as prime minister of Prussia. He had gained a reputation as an ultra-conservative Junker as early as 1848, and he now steered a tough antiparliamentarian course, practically governing outside the framework of the constitution on the basis of a budget adopted without consulting parliament. The Progress Party was basically powerless against him. Hampered in terms of its influence by the conservative attitude of the rural population and committed to upholding the shared interests of the property-owning middle-classes and the Prussian state, its resistance was ultimately ineffectual – and this was one of the reasons that prompted the working classes to break away politically from the liberal movement. From this point on, middle-class and working-class opposition forces went their separate ways.

While opposition at home crumbled, Bismarck scored a series of foreign-policy successes. In June 1866, the conflict with Austria, which had still been an ally of Prussia in the victory over Denmark in 1864, was finally settled in Prussia's favour at the battle of Königgrätz (Sadowa). Two months later, the parliament of the German Confederation sat for the last time in Augsburg. Now that the "Little German" solution to the question of national unity under Prussian leadership was clearly on the political horizon, and Prussia's sphere of influence stretched as far as the river Main as a result of the newly founded North German Confederation, many liberals decided henceforth to support Bismarck's policies. While the left wing of the Progress Party continued to attach overriding importance to freedom, the national liberals believed that conditions in Prussia could only be liberalized after national unity had been achieved.

In fact, the constitution of the North German Confederation was already tailored to the possible accession of the southern German states. Moreover, the newly created parliament of the Customs Union, whose members were elected from all German states, was already considered a national institution. Fear of an intervention by France, however, initially made Bismarck hesitate to take the offensive and press ahead with the process of political unification.

Growing tensions between Prussia and France, exacerbated by the candidacy of a Hohenzollern prince for the Spanish crown, finally culminated in a declaration of war by France. This sparked a wave of national outrage throughout Germany. The military pacts between the German states came into effect, and these were supplemented in the course of the war by treaties between the German monarchs and governments with a binding force akin to that of international law. Following the military defeat of France and the fall of the French Empire, a ceremony held in the Hall of Mirrors at Versailles on 18 January 1871, attended by high-ranking members of the German nobility and military, marked the founding of the German Reich. It was an act accomplished from above by the conservative Prussian state and the German princes.

Although national unity was greeted with enthusiasm by the vast majority of Germans, the Empire was based on an unequal alliance between the national and liberal movements on the one hand and the conservative Prussian leadership on the other, and it was criticized by many contemporaries as being "incomplete". According to the demands of the liberals, the Reich was to be governed on a broad, parliamentary basis. In reality, however, it was governed by a single man, who, moreover, depended solely on the confidence of the Emperor. The extremely complicated Reich constitution was tailored to the personality of Bismarck who, as Reich Chancellor and prime minister of Prussia, controlled the entire apparatus of government: imperial departments, which were headed not by accountable ministers but by state secretaries bound by instructions from above, the *Bundesrat*, or Federal Council, in which Prussia held sway due to its supremacy, and the Prussian Ministry of State headed by Bismarck himself. Although the *Reichstag*, or parliament, was formed on the basis of general, secret, equal and direct elections, in which all men over the age of 25 were eligible to vote, its political influence was largely limited to the field of legislation. Whereas in 1848/49 the goal had been to create a democratic, constitutional state based on the sovereignty of the people, the Empire founded in 1871 was an authoritarian state based on a national monarchy. In it, the nation, as the sum of all social forces, had no decisive role in the political process.

The first decade of the Empire was marked by heightened social and party-political tensions. A campaign was launched against the opposition parties – the left-liberal Progress Party, but especially the Catholic Centre Party and ultimately also the Social Democrats – which were termed "enemies of the Reich". On the instigation of Bismarck, special regulations and restrictions were imposed on the Centre Party at the beginning of the 1870s and then, in 1878, on the Social Democrats. These moves inflicted lasting damage on the belief that interests could be balanced peacefully within a national community and helped to harden party-political fronts. Moreover, these restrictive measures failed to achieve their main political goal: the "*Kulturkampf*", or "cultural struggle" between church and state, and the "anti-socialist law" did not in the end weaken the Centre Party or the Social Democratic Party, but instead made them consolidate internally and helped them make political advances. They plunged the National Liberal Party, meanwhile, into an identity crisis. The National Liberals had ultimately given their approval to the anti-socialist law, thereby abandoning a fundamental principle of liberal legal thinking, and their decisive rejection of the policy of state welfare provision introduced by Bismarck did nothing to resolve matters, especially as the liberals were unable to provide a convincing answer of their own to the "social question". However, Bismarck's attempt to reconcile the working classes to the existing political and social order by raising its material well-being was also unsuccessful, even though the system of social insurance was further expanded during the Wilhelmine period. Instead, workers' organizations and the large industrial and agricultural interest groups formed during the period of economic crisis after 1873 continued to face each other across an unbridgeable divide. The nation-state became increasingly divided along class lines.

Bismarck's habit of responding to conflict situations by strengthening the conservative state and cementing the status quo ultimately led to the rupture of his alliance with the National Liberals. The change of course in domestic politics in 1878/79 was equivalent to a second founding of the Empire along conservative lines. Liberals in the civil service and public administration were largely replaced by staunch advocates of the conservative line, and the liberal ministers in Prussia resigned. The reorganization of the imperial departments strengthened the power of the Reich government and thus also of the Reich Chancellor. In the latter years of the Bismarckian era, the landowners – predominantly aristocratic Junkers – east of the Elbe, heavy industrialists and the conservative state leadership joined forces in pursuit of their common interests. The shift in economic policy from free trade to protective tariffs and the increase in indirect taxation placed a heavy burden particularly on the economically weak sections of the population who, in the major urban regions at least, turned increasingly to the social democratic movement. Middle-class liberalism was gradually eroded by the conflict of interests between the landowning Junkers and industrialists on the one hand and the working classes on the other.

Bismarck's dismissal in 1890 precipitated a crisis of government in the Empire. The young Emperor William II wanted to be "his own Chancellor", but his attempt to set up a system of "personal rule", as he called it, failed. He was unable to set a clear course in the field of domestic and foreign policy: he had neither the stature nor the ability to oversee the complex of institutional structures – the imperial offices, the Federal Council, the Ministry of State, the *Reichstag* and the Prussian parliament – let alone play them off against one another as Bismarck had often done. A "New Course" was proclaimed nonetheless: the anti-socialist law was repealed and, in the so-called February Decrees of 1890, a comprehensive package of social security legislation was announced. Despite this, the Social Democrats were able to increase their share of the vote from 763,000 in 1887 to 1.4 million in 1890, increasing it still further in the decades that followed. Following the Reichstag election of 1912, the Social Democrats became the largest party in parliament for the first time.

The shift to a policy of imperialism marked the final attempt to mask tensions at home, this time by successes abroad. However, the hopes of liberal imperialists such as Max Weber and Friedrich Naumann, who expected a dynamic foreign policy to create more internal dynamism as well, were not fulfilled. The new *Weltpolitik*, or world policy, in fact did more to strengthen the conservatives' claim to power: their national slogans and, in particular, their propaganda campaigns for a powerful German navy, won them broad popular support. William II's claim that the German Empire had become a "world empire" was rapturously received. In reality the successes were meagre, but their price was disproportionately high: rather than enhancing the Empire's prestige, the policies of the Reich leadership led the country, hitherto bound into the existing, albeit fragile, European balance of power through the alliances forged by Bismarck's policies, into a position of increasing isolation. Allied to the Dual Monarchy of Austria-Hungary, which internally had been ailing for some time, the Empire ultimately found itself facing a superior alliance composed of her international rivals: France, Russia and Great Britain. The failure of the new *Welt-*

politik ultimately prompted a calamitous push forward – into the catastrophe of the First World War.

Neither the "truce" between the political parties (even the majority of Social Democrats voted for the war credits), nor the general euphoria that greeted the outbreak of war in August 1914 lasted for long. The war aggravated the rifts on domestic policy, which now became even more closely bound up with Germany's foreign-policy objectives; some parties called for a negotiated peace settlement, others for a peace based on military victory and annexation. The radicalization of left and right was reflected in 1916/17 in the founding of the Spartacus League on the one hand and the German Fatherland Party on the other. However, the political and military collapse of the German Empire in November 1918 provided an opportunity for a return to the liberal and democratic ideals that had underpinned the national idea in the *Vormärz* preceding the Revolution of 1848/49, in the Revolution itself, and in the "New Era".

1. From the Prussian constitutional conflict to the "Little German" nation-state

In February 1860, a bill was tabled in the Prussian *Landtag*, or state parliament, that carried the potential to trigger a state crisis of dangerous proportions. The bill was based on the army reform plan devised by War Minister Albrecht von Roon and supported by the King, which envisaged extending the period of compulsory military service to three years and radically reducing the *Landwehr*, a kind of reserve militia that was one of the achievements of the reform programme implemented in the run-up to the anti-Napoleonic wars of liberation. This transparent ploy to turn the army into an instrument unconditionally obedient to the crown, in line with the Prussian state's absolutist tradition, met with resistance in the lower house, where the liberals had held a majority since 1858. Spearheading the forces that refused to approve funding for the reform of the army was the German Progress Party set up by left-wing liberals and democrats in

King William I
of Prussia,
1864

Otto von
Bismarck as
Prussian Envoy
in Paris, 1862

Bismarck at
a sitting of
the Prussian
Chamber of
Deputies, 1862

early June 1861, which advocated a resolute struggle for a parliamentary constitutional state and a new social order, but also included in its programme a call for national unity. In the elections to the lower house in December 1861 they won 106 seats, while the conservative grouping shrank to a mere 15.

The Prussian government and the King clung stubbornly to their plans. As a result, the lower house refused to pass the overall budget for 1862, which prompted the vociferously antiparliamentarian military camarilla associated with Edwin von Manteuffel to dismiss the moderate liberal ministers and contemplate plans for a *coup d'état*. In September 1862, final efforts to arrive at a compromise between crown and parliament failed. William I balked at the dire prospect of a civil war and announced his intention to abdicate in favour of the Crown Prince, who sympathized with the liberals.

Faced with this situation, the authoritarian monarchist state found a staunch defender with superior political skills in the person of Otto von Bismarck, who at that time was Prussia's envoy in Paris. Bismarck managed to persuade the King to persevere, whereupon he was appointed prime minister and invested by the King with full powers. In the opinion of Ludwig August von Rochau, Bismarck's appointment meant that, as far as the liberals were concerned, the forces of reaction had "by the grace of God, shot their last and sharpest bolt".

And indeed Bismarck showed little inclination to respect the rights of parliament. He made this quite plain when presenting his political credo to the budget committee of the lower house: "The great questions of our day cannot be solved by speeches and majority votes – that was the great mistake of 1848 and 1849 – but by iron and blood."

Then, in October 1862, the upper house, loyal to the King, approved the government's draft budget; in doing so it acted in breach of the constitution, under which the lower house had this power. An open battle between the reactionary landowning Junker and the liberal middle classes seemed imminent. Bismarck exacerbated the conflict by claiming that a "loophole in the constitution", interpreted in accordance with the wishes of the crown, provided justification for him to govern despite effectively having no budget. In May 1863, four-fifths of the deputies present in the Prussian lower house voted in favour of a parliamentary system of government, and neither political pressure nor massive efforts to influence voters in favour of the conservatives managed to prevent another clear electoral victory for the liberals. People close to the King began to fear that revolution was brewing.

However, anti-government opposition ultimately proved to be less solid than William feared. Liberals and democrats from all over Germany, bitterly disappointed by the anti-parliamentarian course steered by the Prussian government, now flocked to join the "Greater German" *Reformverein*, or Reform Association, founded in autumn 1862 in opposition to the "Little German" National Association. The majority of Prussian liberals, however, remained opposed to reform of the German Confederation, as advocated by the Viennese court, and instead continued to support the "Little German" concept of national unification that could only be based on Prussia. Remarking that Bismarck would first have to secure legitimation for the repression that everyone was feeling, right-wing liberal Rudolf Haym signalled *pars pro toto* that the liberals might be willing to compromise – in the event of successes in the foreign-policy arena.

These successes were not long in coming. When the King of Denmark abolished the special status of the Duchies of Schleswig and Holstein and incorporated Schleswig into his national territory, Bismarck seized this first opportunity to present himself as the executor of the German national movement. He prevailed upon Austria to take up arms alongside Prussia, and on 18 April 1864 the desired military success was achieved with the capture of the Danish fortifications at Dybbøl (Düppel).

"Alas – we so often come up against opposition up there". This cartoon, which appeared in *Kladderadatsch* in 1859, refers to the demands of the National Association (*Nationalverein*) for a "firm, strong and durable central government" and to the misgivings of the German princes

Prussian and
Austrian
soldiers during
the German-
Danish War,
1864

The Prussian
First Army
advancing
across the
River Bystřice
(Bistritz)
at the Battle
of Sadowa
(Königgrätz)
on 3 July 1866

Following the victory over Denmark, Schleswig was placed under Prussian and Holstein under Austrian administration – the visible expression of a fragile parity that was not destined to endure, particularly since Prussia was soon openly demanding the annexation of the duchies. In the summer of 1865, Austrian plans for a Central European customs union foundered on the resistance of Prussia, whose economic power now exceeded that of Austria, and on 9 April 1866 Karl Friedrich von Savigny, the Prussian envoy in Frankfurt, called for the establishment of a freely elected German national assembly. When the cabinet in Vienna then moved that the Federal Diet (*Bundestag*) take steps to resolve the disputed status of Schleswig and Holstein, Prussian troops occupied Holstein. The war for hegemony in Germany had begun. Twelve of the secondary states in Germany, loyal to the Confederation, fought on the Austrian side against Prussia, which was allied with Italy.

Das ganze Deutschland soll es seyn!

"The whole of Germany – that is how it should be!" is the caption of this cartoon, portraying Prussian hegemony in the North German Confederation and the exclusion of Austria from the community of German states

Within a matter of weeks, on 3 July 1866, the military conflict was decided on a battlefield to the north-west of the Bohemian fortress of Sadowa (Königgrätz). In the Treaty of Prague, the peace settlement essentially spared Austria, but she did have to cede Venetia to Italy and renounce any attempt to revive the German Confederation. In this way, Austria lost her membership of the community of German states. Besides incorporating Schleswig-Holstein, Prussia also annexed Hanover and the Electorate of Hesse as well as Nassau and Frankfurt and assumed the leading role in the newly created North German Confederation, the constitution of which was designed to facilitate the possible accession of the Southern German states.

Within Prussia, the resounding success was met with wild enthusiasm, which even spilled over into the Liberal-Democratic camp. When, in the Bill of Indemnity, the Government sought the retroactive approval of the newly elected Prussian Diet (*Landtag*) for the expenditure it had been incurring without a legal budget, the overwhelming majority of the deputies gave their consent. This was what finally split the Liberals too. While the left wing of the Progress Party upheld the primacy of freedom and rejected Prussia's claim to national hegemony "for as long as Prussia has not established freedom within its borders" (Benedikt Waldeck), other Liberals felt that, unless the national question were first resolved, "the very existence of a rational and liberal Prussian constitution" would be "an impossibility" (Maximilian von Forckenbeck). The conscience-salving formula "through unity to liberty" became the rallying cry of those Liberals who turned their back on the Progress Party in the summer and autumn of 1866 to form a new parliamentary group, the National Liberals. Resolved now to cooperate with Bismarck, the National Liberals urged the Prime Minister to complete the process of national unification as swiftly as possible.

Bismarck, however, was an astute tactician. After all, there were deep reservations about the creation of a nation state, a military power, in which Protestant Prussia would predominate, and there were strong reservations about the liberal economic policies of the North German *Reichstag*; these reservations were reflected in the success of the particularists in the elections of February

The Battle
of Sedan on
1 September
1870

Special sup-
plement on
the signing of
the peace
preliminaries
in Versailles

and March 1868 to the parliamentary assembly of the *Zollverein*. Moreover, it was to be feared that France, sensing a threat to her position as the leading continental power, might choose to intervene.

By the spring of 1870, however, Bismarck considered that the time was ripe to provoke such intervention. He supported the candidature of Prince Leopold von Hohenzollern-Sigmaringen, a relative of the Prussian King, William I, for the vacant Spanish throne, which rekindled old French fears of encirclement. These fears then led to a critical diplomatic confrontation, and Prince Leopold's candidature was renounced. Emboldened by this withdrawal, the French Government demanded guarantees from William I, as head of the House of Hohenzollern, that the candidature for the Spanish crown would never be renewed, including a sort of formal written pledge. William telegraphed Bismarck in Berlin, stating that he considered the matter closed and that he had declined to give such guarantees. Bismarck published a condensed version of the telegram, conveying the impression that the French demands had been brusquely rejected and so presenting the Government

in Paris with the choice between a humiliating diplomatic climbdown and the risk of a military trial of strength. On 19 July 1870, it declared war on Prussia. In the eyes of the Southern German states, this was the *casus foederis* that was defined in their mutual-assistance treaties, and so they entered the war on the side of Prussia.

Although Helmuth von Moltke's campaign plan, after a rapid series of early successes, threatened to go awry at Gravelotte and Saint-Privat, his troops finally succeeded in cutting off Marshal Bazaine's army in Metz and encircling Marshal MacMahon's army in Sedan. With the surrender of the fortress of Sedan and the capture of Napoleon III on 2 September 1870, the French Empire collapsed. Nevertheless, the war against what was now the French Republic continued for almost five months until the armistice was signed. In the Treaty of Frankfurt, signed on 10 May 1871, the French Government under Adolphe Thiers had to agree to pay five billion gold francs in war reparations and to cede Alsace and part of Lorraine to Germany –

a heavy burden on future relations between the two nations.

Meanwhile, a number of quasi-international treaties concluded between the monarchs and governments of German states were ratified by the *Reichstag* of the North German Confederation and the parliamentary assemblies of Southern Germany. There were no more formal barriers to German unity. By pledging considerable amounts of money from the confiscated assets of the Hanoverian Guelph dynasty, Bismarck finally overcame the persistent opposition of King Ludwig II of Bavaria to the bestowal of the title of Emperor on William I as the presiding monarch at the head of the confederation.

On 18 January 1871, the German monarchs, together with their senior officials, diplomats and generals, gathered in the Hall of Mirrors in the palace of Versailles. No elected representatives of the people were present. The proclamation of the Emperor was a piece of courtly and military pageantry in which a princely confederation assumed the mantle of statehood.

Proclamation of the Emperor in Versailles on 18 January 1871. Painting by Anton von Werner, 1885 version

2. Constitution, Imperial Diet and parties

The imperial constitution of 16 April 1871 was largely identical to the 1867 constitution of the North German Confederation. Bismarck played a decisive part in its formulation; now that he was the Imperial Chancellor (*Reichskanzler*), it guaranteed him an abundance of power, the exercise of which could be neither controlled nor restricted by Parliament. Since the Imperial Chancellor was accountable to the Emperor (*Kaiser*) alone for his political actions, a relationship of loyalty and trust between the two was the main prerequisite for the office of Imperial Chancellor. Its incumbent decided on the guidelines of government policy. It was on his proposal that the Emperor appointed and dismissed the secretaries of state who were entrusted with the administration of the various departments of the imperial civil service. It was he who chaired the Federal Council (*Bundesrat*), which was constitutionally the supreme organ of government in the Empire (*Reich*), and by virtue of customary law the Imperial Chancellor almost invariably headed the Prussian state ministry until 1918. It is not surprising that the term *Kanzlerdiktatur*, or dictatorship of the Chancellor, surfaced even in those days as a catchword to describe the system.

The Chancellor's responsibility for conducting the civil policy of the Reich contrasted with the extraconstitutional power of command in all military matters that was vested in the Emperor as King of Prussia. This created enormous potential for the exertion of political influence by the commanding generals, the general staff and the Prussian Minister of War, who had direct relations with the Emperor and who were independent of the civil authorities of the Reich. This constellation was to play a fateful

Draft of the German Imperial Constitution of 15 November 1870

part in the developments leading to the First World War.

The German Reich was a federal state which was unquestionably dominated by the Kingdom of Prussia. More than half of the population lived within its boundaries, and almost two thirds of the imperial territory was Prussian. In the Bundesrat, the legislative arm of the federal states, Prussia had the power to veto majority decisions. Bismarck succeeded in fashioning this

The Reichstag of the North German Confederation in session

A deputation from the Reichstag formally offers the title of German Emperor to William I on 18 December 1870

The Members
for Alsace-
Lorraine
making their
entrance in
the German
Bundestag on
21 March 1871

institution of federalism into a bulwark protecting the monarchy against any increase in the powers of the Imperial Parliament. Whereas Reichstag deputies could not be members of the Bundesrat and had to give up their mandate if, for example, they wished to pursue a career in government, the Imperial Chancellor, the secretaries of state and the Prussian ministers were *ex officio* members of the Reichstag as plenipotentiaries of the Bundesrat.

Large ethnic minorities lived within the borders of the Reich. These minorities were represented in Parliament, but their political integration went no further than this; the attempts to integrate them into the Reich were pursued on a purely bureaucratic level. In the face of opposition that was sometimes vehement, German was imposed as the only language of instruction in schools within the Polish-speaking areas from 1872 and in the primarily Danish-speaking region of Northern Schleswig from 1878. But even the people of Alsace and Lorraine, most of whom were German-speakers, had reason to feel discriminated against: after an initial period of direct rule from Berlin, the "new imperial territory" was placed under the authority of an imperial governor, who was assisted by a purely consultative regional

committee. Not until 1911 was Alsace-Lorraine accorded the status of a federal state. It is no wonder that most of its enfranchised population voted for anti-Reich protest groups in the first few Reichstag elections.

Along with the monarch, the imperial chancellor and executive he appointed and the Bundesrat, the Reichstag was the fourth organ of the constitution. As had already been the case in the North German Confederation, the Reichstag was elected by universal, equal and direct manhood suffrage and by secret ballot, and this was undoubtedly an advanced electoral system for its day. Elections were held at three-yearly intervals until 1888, when the full parliamentary term was extended to five years. According to the constitution, the members of the Reichstag "shall be representatives of the whole people and shall not be bound by orders and instructions"; when the Reichstag was in session, they enjoyed parliamentary immunity. All of this, however, was not ultimately of great significance, because the people's representative chamber actually possessed limited powers; in particular, it had virtually no influence on the formation of governments. Its role in the formulation of policies, especially foreign and military policy, was largely confined to non-binding statements of opinion – although, as decades went by, the importance attached to the opinion of the Reichstag did increase steadily. Although the Reichstag was empowered to use interpellations, questions and budgetary motions in order to initiate public debates on political controversies and to elicit explanatory statements from members of the Imperial Government, it had no power to compel these government members to resign by means of a motion of no confidence. The chancellor, monarch and Bundesrat, for their part, were authorized to dissolve the Reichstag in the event of conflict and call new elections.

Although this means that the Reich was not a genuine parliamentary monarchy, its Parliament was at least a real legislature. The Reichstag possessed extensive legislative powers, and the executive could not bypass or overrule it to enact a law. Moreover, Parliament adopted the imperial budget every year. This budgetary authority, however, was limited. Indirect taxes and duties, which accounted for most tax revenue, were fixed for a period of several years, as was military expenditure, while the financial contributions payable by the federal states, which were a major source of revenue for the imperial treasury, were also largely beyond the direct influence of the Reichstag.

Although secessions and the creation of new parties were still frequent occurrences, particularly in the Liberal camp, the German party system established itself quite quickly around 1871 as a relatively stable structure. Universal manhood suffrage was the main factor in the shift from loose-knit parliamentary groups and voters' associations to a parliament dominated by parties with a fairly firm organizational structure, a broad electoral base and distinct political platforms. These party platforms were based on the four main political ideologies that had

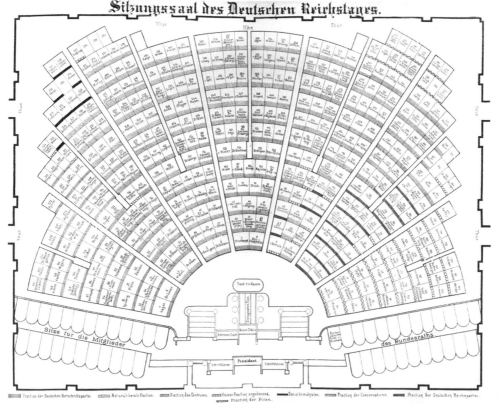

Seating plan of the German Reichstag at its temporary home in the Royal Prussian Porcelain Works

A Berlin polling station during the elections to the Reichstag for its seventh legislative term on 21 February 1887

crystallized in the middle of the century, namely Liberalism, Conservatism, political Catholicism and Socialism. Accordingly, each party primarily represented the sections of society whose interests were best reflected in its social policies. The left-wing Liberals were regarded as the arm of the merchant classes, but they also drew support from tradesmen, owners of small businesses and the educated classes. The National Liberals chiefly represented heavy industry but were also supported by large numbers of the educated classes and some small farmers. The Conservatives were first and foremost the champions of the large landowners, while the Social Democrats pursued the aims of the working classes. Along with a number of parties representing

A Berlin polling station during the elections to the Reichstag for its thirteenth legislative term on 12 January 1912

regional and ethnic minorities, the Centre, the party of political Catholicism, defied this type of categorization, for it was a religious creed that held the Centre Party together.

The constitution only gave parties the choice of loyally serving the government or opposing it, without offering the prospect of real participation in political decision-making as the reward for such loyalty. While it is true

Members of Parliament leaving the Reichstag building by the doorway at 4 Leipziger Strasse in 1889

A municipal council meeting. Wood engraving from a painting by Richard Scholz, 1898

that the Chancellor and the Imperial Government were compelled to rally the support of parliamentary majorities for their bills, they could still operate without the confidence of Parliament; this, coupled with the fact that the majorities mustered in this way did not thereby obtain any share in the exercise of governmental power, meant that the parliamentary groups ultimately had no incentive to enter into stable coalitions and develop policy guidelines to which other groups could subscribe. Instead, the parliamentary groups – and the various factions within the groups – generally clung rigidly to their ideological principles. Moreover, the gulf between the executive and the legislature was exacerbated by fundamental cross-party opposition to the Imperial Government within the Reichstag, reflected in the tendency to form majorities for the sole purpose of defeating particular government bills, an attitude that was destined to persist into the Weimar Republic, with crippling effect.

The organizational structure of the parties still differed in certain respects in the early days of the Empire. Whereas the Social Democrats, and the Centre too, led by elected quasi-official executive committees, canvassed for mass membership from an early date and used their members' subscriptions

to finance their activities, the less tightly organized Liberal and Conservative parties were initially dependent to a great extent on the financial resources of their leading politicians and of the circles with which they associated. The internal cohesion of the Centre and Social Democrats, the parties that Bismarck declared to be "enemies of the Empire", was also far stronger, at least in the early decades of the Reich, than that of other parties, particularly the Liberals, who traditionally adopted a more individualistic approach and whose history in this era was a veritable catalogue of schisms. Nevertheless, it may be said of all parties that their development had largely begun before the creation of the Reich and did not end with the revolution of 1918/19. With modified aims and, in some cases, new names, they continued to form the main bands of the German political spectrum in the Weimar Republic.

The Liberals of the Left

In Prussia, the rise of Liberalism during the "New Era" led in June 1861 to the emergence of the German Progress Party (*Deutsche Fortschrittspartei*), which counted among its members such prominent figures as Rudolf

Virchow, Theodor Mommsen and Werner Siemens. In the tradition of 1848/49, it stood for German unity and the convening of a national Parliament. Committed to the liberal ideal of the rule of law, it also campaigned for an independent judiciary, ministerial accountability and the separation of church and state.

Led by its parliamentary group in the *Landtag* and supported by local electoral committees, the German Progress Party, within months of its creation, won more seats than any other party in the elections of December 1861 to the Prussian Chamber of Deputies (*Abgeordnetenhaus*). Driven not least by the desire to defend and strengthen the rights of Parliament, it led the struggle to secure unrestricted parliamentary control of the budget, including the military budget. None the less, Bismarck's successes of 1864 and 1866, which brought a united Germany within reach, did not fail to make an impression on the Progressives. In September 1866, they voted for the Bill of Indemnity, and six months later the right wing of the party seceded to form the National Liberal Party.

After the Reichstag sitting of 24 January 1882. The figures engaged in this debate are (left to right): Albert Hänel, Eduard Lasker, Rudolf von Bennigsen and Eugen Richter

Left:
Eugen Richter, an opponent of Bismarck and an influential politician of the Liberal Left

Right:
Friedrich Naumann, founder of the National Social Union *(Natio-nalsozialer Verein)*

In imperial Germany there were always several left-wing liberal parties, and their rivalry contributed to the relatively indistinct profile and isolation of the Liberal Left. October 1881 saw its greatest electoral success, in which the following parties shared: the old Progress Party, the Württemberg-based German People's Party *(Deutsche Volkspartei)*, which followed a radical democratic line, and the Liberal Union *(Liberale Vereinigung)*, a group formed from the left wing of the National Liberals which was to unite with Eugen Richter's Progress Party three years later to form the German Liberal Party *(Deutsch-Freisinnige Partei)*. As a key force of the middle-class opposition, the Liberal Party

condemned reactionary policies, socialism, protectionism and the interventionist welfare legislation of the Imperial Government and campaigned for systematic progress towards parliamentary government in the Reich. After its defeat in the 1887 elections, however, it changed its approach to one of intransigent obstructionism.

The revival of left-wing Liberalism was primarily generated by the Liberal Alliance *(Freisinnige Vereinigung)*, associated with the former National Liberals Ludwig Bamberger und Heinrich Rickert, which grew out of another schism in 1893. In close cooperation with Friedrich Naumann's National Social Union *(Nationalsozialer Verein)*, most of whose members joined the Liberal Alliance in 1903, this former free-trade lobby now came to advocate partnership between capital and labour in pursuit of the ideal of a "Social Empire". This principle also ultimately underlay the programme of the Progressive People's Party *(Fortschrittliche Volkspartei)*, into which the vast majority of the left-wing liberals reorganized themselves in 1910 and which consolidated its position quickly enough to secure 42 seats in the Reichstag

National Social Union membership card

election of 1912. The abandonment of its advocacy of *laissez-faire* liberalism and the intensification of its quest for ways of promoting the public welfare eventually led it to cooperate with the Centre and the Social Democratic Party of Germany (SPD).

During the First World War, differences within the party concerning the foreign policy of the Reich vented themselves in fierce controversies between annexationists and supporters of a negotiated peace. In the end, the Liberal Left was not only involved in the campaigns for parliamentary government and reform of the Prussian electoral system but also subscribed to the peace resolution adopted by the Reichstag. After the revolution of 1918/19, the Liberal Left organized itself into the German Democratic Party (*Deutsche Demokratische Partei*), whose leaders had a decisive influence on the constitutional foundations of the new republic.

The National Liberals

In March 1867, the Liberals who had seceded the year before from the Progress Party and had formed their own group in the Prussian Chamber of Deputies constituted themselves as the National Liberal Party (*Nationalliberale Partei*). Supported by broad sections of the business community and the educated classes, the party distanced itself from a doctrinaire view of Liberalism in order to play an active part in the unification policy of the Prussian Government and in the creation of a Little German economic unit. The National Liberals, for example, supported the Commercial Code (*Handelsgesetzbuch*) and the Trade Act (*Gewerbeordnung*) of 1869, but also pressed successfully, under the powerful influence of Johannes von Miquel, who later became the Prussian Minister of Finance, for the adoption of a liberalized code of criminal law. In the first Reichstag of unified Germany they were by far the largest parliamentary group, and in Eduard Simson, who had presided over the Frankfurt Assembly in St Paul's Church, they provided the Reichstag with its first President (Speaker).

Until the second half of the 1870s, the National Liberals acted to all intents and purposes as the governing party on which Bismarck could rely. For example, they supported his *Kulturkampf* against perceived political meddling by clericalists, and in 1878, unlike the Liberal Left, they eventually approved Bismarck's anti-Socialist legislation.

Bismarck's switch to the Conservatives and the adoption of protectionist policies fragmented the National Liberal camp. After a

Bild ohne viele Worte.

Eine Liebe ist der anderen werth.

"One good turn deserves another": *Kladderadatsch* cartoon satirizing the Prussian Chamber of Deputies' approval of the Indemnity Bill

Parliamentary *soirée* in the Imperial Chancellor's palace in Berlin, 1878. The figures conversing in the foreground on the left of the picture are Rudolf von Bennigsen and Franz August Schenk von Stauffenberg, members of the National Liberal Group in the Reichstag

few staunch advocates of protective tariffs had split from the party, a group of equally staunch advocates of free trade, led by Maximilian von Forckenbeck, Eduard Lasker and Ludwig Bamberger and supported by commercial and banking circles, founded the Liberal Union in 1880 on the anti-protectionist side; three years later, the Union merged with the Progress Party and subsequently formed the core of the Liberal Alliance (*Freisinnige Vereinigung*), which existed as a separate entity from 1893 to 1910. The remaining National Liberals, under the leadership of Johannes von Miquel, went on to adopt the Heidelberg Declaration in 1884, in which they committed themselves to a pro-Government line on social, colonial and military policies with a view to the creation of a Liberal-Conservative reformist alliance.

This aim manifested itself in the "cartel" of 1887, an electoral pact between the National Liberals and the two Conservative parties, which produced another pro-Bismarck majority in the Reichstag; this majority, however, ultimately proved to be unstable. In the 1890s, when the Centre became a more pro-Government party and a potential member of majority coalitions, the National Liberals lost even more of their political clout. In addition, the "Young Liberals" (*Jungliberale*) within the party became increasingly critical of its affinity with the Conservatives on tariffs and social policy. The "Bülow Bloc" of 1907, in which the National Liberals and Conservatives were now joined by the *Freisinnige* (the Liberal Alliance and Liberal People's Party), pushed through progressive legislation on the right of association and assembly but was soon defeated on the reform of public finances, tax legislation and the issue of the Prussian electoral system.

The enthusiasm for imperialism and colonialism that infected the majority of the middle class in the reign of William II profoundly influenced the party's political course after 1914. The annexationists, foremost among whom were Ernst Bassermann and Gustav Stresemann, determined the profile of the party, which voted against the peace resolution in the Reichstag and ceased its occasional participation in the cross-party committee on the peace process. At the same time, however, Stresemann in particular was a consistent advocate of far-reaching democratization within Germany.

In December 1918, the Central Executive of the National Liberal Party formally dissolved the party. The bulk of its members reorganized themselves into the newly created German People's Party (*Deutsche Volkspartei*), while others joined the German Democratic Party (*Deutsche Demokratische Partei*) or the – rather insignificant – conservative Nation-

Prominent National Liberal politicians, 1878. Above (left to right): Wilhelm Wehrenpfennig, Eduard Lasker, Heinrich von Treitschke and Johannes Miquel. Below (left to right): Franz von Roggenbach, Karl Braun, Rudolf Gneist and Ludwig Bamberger

Scene outside a Berlin newspaper printing office shortly after the Reichstag elections of 27 October 1881

al Liberal Imperial Party (*Nationalliberale Reichspartei*).

The Conservatives

In the 1850s, Conservatives tended to organize themselves into agricultural associations and societies for the primary purpose of defending the interests of the large landowners. Supported by the cabinets of the Restoration period, they were the dominant parliamentary force in Prussia until the *Landtag* elections of 1858. Their pro-Government and anti-Liberal stance made them natural allies for Bismarck in the constitutional conflict, but, as supporters of the old confederation of states, most of

them were initially opposed to his policy of unifying the Reich.

In 1866, however, the secession of the Free Conservatives (*Freikonservative*) in the Prussian Chamber of Deputies created a Conservative group that supported Bismarck's line unreservedly. Five years later, the Free Conservatives joined forces nationally to form the German Imperial Party (*Deutsche Reichspartei*). Under the leadership of Wilhelm von Kardorff they advocated a strong state and sought an accommodation between the interests of heavy industry and those of the large landowners. After electoral successes in the 1870s the Imperial Party's share of the vote dwindled, and in

Members of the Reichstag from the Imperial Party (*Reichspartei*), photographed in 1889. Standing: Josef von Ellrichshausen. Seated, left to right: Heinrich von Friesen-Rötha, Wilhelm von Kardoff and Iwan Baumbach

1912 only 14 of its candidates were elected to the Reichstag.

The German Conservative Party (*Deutschkonservative Partei*), founded in 1876, made a better showing. Because of the Prussian three-class voting system, based on the tax revenue contributed by voters, the German Conservatives held sway in the Prussian *Landtag*. As the party of the upper-class estate owners, who were mainly concentrated in the part of Prussia to the east of the Elbe, the German Conservatives supported the tariff policy of the Imperial Government. The lowering of the corn tariffs in 1890 increased the influence of nationalist-inclined radical farmers, who formed the Farmers'

League (*Bund der Landwirte*) in 1893. Even before the founding of the new League, at the German Conservatives' "Tivoli Congress" in 1892, the moderate party leader, Otto von Helldorf-Bebra, was ousted, and a new programme was adopted. Besides protectionist demands, the new political programme also contained German nationalist and anti-Semitic elements. The new party line was also shaped by the Christian Social Party (*Christlich-Soziale Partei*) of the Berlin royal chaplain Adolf von Stöcker, who sought to win over the working classes to his ideology of social conservatism and opposition to large-scale capitalism. Since 1881, his organization had been formally incorporated into the German Conservative Party. By 1907,

Adolf Stoecker, Protestant minister, royal chaplain and the key figure in the Christian Social Party

Elard von Oldenburg-Januschau, one of the most popular representatives of the German Conservative Party

however, its share of the national vote had sunk below ten per cent.

After the demise of the "Bülow Bloc" in the spring of 1909, the German Conservatives adopted a stance of decidedly anti-reformist right-wing opposition to the Imperial Government. Scarcely restrained any more by the moderating influence of party leader Ernst von Heydebrand und der Lasa, radical farmers and chauvinistic agitators now completely transformed the face of the party. During the Great War, the vast majority of the German and Free Conservatives supported expansionist war aims, favoured the dictatorship to which the Army High Command aspired and rejected any steps towards democratization. As a reaction against the Reichstag's peace resolution, the Fatherland Party (*Vaterlandspartei*) was formed in 1917 by Alfred von Tirpitz and his associates; this new party demanded the continuation of the struggle until Germany achieved a "victorious peace".

In November 1918, the Conservative parties combined with the Pan-German Association (*Alldeutscher Verband*), anti-Semitic groups and a scattering of monarchists from the Centre and National Liberal parties to found the German National People's Party (*Deutschnationale Volkspartei*).

Oſtelbien

(Zeichnung von E. Thöny)

„Es iſt eine liberale Stimme abgegeben worden. Der Schulmeiſter kriegt von heute ab keine Kartoffeln mehr."

"One vote was cast for the Liberals. No more potatoes for the schoolmaster from today!" is the caption in this *Simplicissimus* cartoon by Eduard Thony, which satirizes the paternalism of the landowners and the people's dependence on them in the territory to the east of the Elbe

The Centre

In 1852, sixty Catholic parliamentarians in the Prussian Chamber of Deputies formed a confessional special-interest group. Because they sat in the middle of the chamber, they called themselves the Group of the Centre (*Fraktion des Zentrums*). Although the Centre was originally intended to represent all Christian denominations, during the founding years of the Reich it developed into the voice of political Catholicism. Accordingly, its bastions were to be found in western and southern Germany and in Upper Silesia. When the *Kulturkampf* was unleashed in all its severity by the Imperial Government in 1872/73, it helped to strengthen the cohesion of the party's socially heterogeneous constituency and to give its political platform a sharper profile. With Ludwig Windthorst as its leader, the Centre campaigned in the Reichstag for Catholic interests, both cultural and social, for adherence to the federal principle and for a protectionist economic policy, based on solidarity. This course was also subsequently supported by the Christian trade unions and the People's Association of Catholic Germany (*Volksverein für das katholische Deutschland*), an organization closely linked with the Centre.

Although the Centre scarcely had any central institutions and the annual rally of German Catholics (*Katholikentag*) fulfilled the function of a party congress to some extent, the party was able to consolidate its position in the Reichstag within a short time. Favoured by the constituency map, which was still based on the population distribution of 1864, with the result that the most populous urban areas were increasingly underrepresented as the century progressed, the Centre was generally the group with the largest membership in the years from 1881 to 1912. At the local level, the Centre was organized into committees, which comprised civic dignitaries and representatives of the clergy; the link with the voters was primarily forged through the various Catholic associations.

The broad spectrum of the party, ranging from the Catholic rural aristocracy to the middle classes with strong confessional leanings and the Christian labour move-

Kladderadatsch cartoon on the Prussian "May Laws" of 1873, which were directed against political Catholicism. The figure behind Bismarck is Adalbert Falk, Prussian Minister of Education and Cultural Affairs from 1872 to 1879

Ludwig Windt-
horst, the uni-
fying figure
who guided the
Centre Party
through the
Kulturkampf
period

Gesetz-Sammlung

für die

Königlichen Preußischen Staaten.

№ 15.

(Nr. 8292.) Gesetz, betreffend die geistlichen Orden und ordensähnlichen Kongregationen der katholischen Kirche. Vom 31. Mai 1875.

Wir Wilhelm, von Gottes Gnaden König von Preußen rc. verordnen, mit Zustimmung beider Häuser des Landtages, für den Umfang der Monarchie, was folgt:

§. 1.

Alle Orden und ordensähnlichen Kongregationen der katholischen Kirche sind vorbehaltlich der Bestimmung des §. 2. von dem Gebiete der Preußischen Monarchie ausgeschlossen.

Die Errichtung von Niederlassungen derselben ist untersagt.

Die zur Zeit bestehenden Niederlassungen dürfen vom Tage der Verkündung dieses Gesetzes ab neue Mitglieder, unbeschadet der Vorschrift des §. 2., nicht aufnehmen und sind binnen sechs Monaten aufzulösen. Der Minister der geistlichen Angelegenheiten ist ermächtigt, diese Frist für Niederlassungen, welche sich mit dem Unterricht und der Erziehung der Jugend beschäftigen, um für deren Ersatz durch anderweite Anstalten und Einrichtungen Zeit zu lassen, bis auf vier Jahre zu verlängern. Zu gleichem Behufe kann derselbe auch nach Ablauf dieses Zeitraums einzelnen Mitgliedern von Orden und ordensähnlichen Kongregationen die Befugniß gewähren, Unterricht zu ertheilen.

§. 2.

Niederlassungen der Orden oder ordensähnlichen Kongregationen, welche sich ausschließlich der Krankenpflege widmen, bleiben fortbestehen; sie können jedoch jederzeit durch Königliche Verordnung aufgehoben werden; bis dahin sind die Minister des Innern und der geistlichen Angelegenheiten ermächtigt, ihnen die Aufnahme neuer Mitglieder zu gestatten.

Jahrgang 1875. (Nr. 8292.)   31   §. 3.

Ausgegeben zu Berlin den 3. Juni 1875.

J. KARLINGER   Die Fraktion des Centrums im deutschen Reichstage 1882.   MÜNCHEN, DEP.

ment, compelled it to engage in constant efforts to reconcile opposing interests. Moreover, its political options also tended to change with shifts in the internal or external balance of power. In 1878 the group voted for Bismarck's protectionist tariff policy but rejected his anti-Socialist legislation. In the 1890s, when the party, under Ernst Liebers, sometimes steered a pro-Government course, it supported the Imperial Government's naval shipbuilding programme, but after the turn of the century it began to level fierce criticism at the Government's *Weltpolitik*, i.e. the attempt to establish Germany as a world power. After the so-called "Hottentot elections" of 1907, when public opinion was polarized between colonialism and anti-colonialism and the Centre subsequently found itself in temporary political isolation, the conservative core of the party that had set the agenda in the early days came into its own once again. This, however, did not prevent a gradual convergence with Liberalism. From 1912, cooperation between the

Centre and parts of the Liberal camp became a factor to be reckoned with in German politics.

During the Great War the Centre initially adopted annexationist positions. After 1916, however, support for a negotiated peace gained the upper hand, and the group voted for the peace resolution in the Reichstag. Vehement opposition from conservative groups within the Centre to its involvement in the Cross-Party Committee strained party unity to its limits, but in the end the supporters of a negotiated peace carried the day. In November 1918, the leading Centre politician Matthias Erzberger headed the German delegation to the armistice talks in Compiègne.

The Social Democrats

In the mid-19th century, the labour force initially organized itself into so-called

The Parliamentary Group of the Centre in the Reichstag, 1882

Opposite page: Text of the law banning Catholic religious orders and order-like congregations from Prussia, 1875

Workingmen's Educational Associations (*Arbeiterbildungsvereine*) under the umbrella of Liberalism. In 1863, Ferdinand Lassalle founded the General German Workingmen's Association (*Allgemeiner Deutscher Arbeiterverein*), which pressed for the parliamentary representation of the working classes and their participation in state-assisted production cooperatives. The Marxist-influenced Social Democratic Workers' Party (*Sozialdemokratische Arbeiterpartei*) that was founded six years later by August Bebel and Wilhelm Liebknecht, on the other hand, sought the replacement of the capitalist production system and took a more sceptical view of the prospects of parliamentary reform. The increasing number of government measures against the organized labour movement resulted in the unification of the two parties in Gotha in 1875 on the basis of a compromise programme in which the ending of exploitation and of political and social injustice was declared as the supreme goal.

At the instigation of the Imperial Government, the National Liberal and Conservative majority in the Reichstag proscribed the Social Democratic organizations and the related trade unions. However, these anti-Socialist laws, under which the Social Democrats were still permitted to take part in elections and therefore continued to enjoy parliamentary representation, only served ultimately to consolidate the internal unity of the Socialist Workers' Party (*Sozialistische Arbeiterpartei*) and to boost its support, which increased still further after the legislation expired in 1890. In the Reichstag that was elected in 1878, there were only twelve Social Democrats; twelve years later there were already 35 Social Democrats among the 397 Reichstag deputies, and in 1912 the party, now known as the Social Democratic Party of Germany (*Sozialdemokratische Partei Deutschlands – SPD*), became the largest parliamentary group for the first time.

As the political weight of Social Democracy increased, the strife within the party over the best way to achieve a Socialist state became fiercer. A revisionist group, whose most prominent members were Eduard Bernstein and Georg von Vollmar, declared that the Marxist predictions contained in the first part of the party's Erfurt Programme of 1891 were now outdated. The group called for a policy of political and social reforms designed to achieve real improvements in the living standards of working people. The centre of the party, led by August Bebel and Karl Kautsky, regarded the struggle for parliamentary supremacy as merely the first step on the way to a Socialist society, which would inexorably follow the equally predestined demise of the capitalist system. A radical group advocated a politically motivated

general strike, clinging uncompromisingly to the philosophy of the class struggle and the concept of the Socialist International. In 1914, the group's spokesman, Karl Liebknecht, became the first Reichstag deputy to vote against the approval of war credits.

Two and a half years later came a split in the SPD. The Independent Social Democratic Party (*Unabhängige Sozialdemokratische Partei*) rejected the majority policy of observing a parliamentary truce for the duration of the war and cooperating with the other parties. The Spartacus League (*Spartakusbund*) led by Liebknecht and Rosa Luxemburg was funda-

mentally opposed to the prevailing system, and in the autumn of 1918 it called for the establishment of a German Republic based on Soviet-style workers' and soldiers' councils. The majority Social Democrats, however, whilst participating in the general strike of January 1918, stepped up their efforts to cooperate with other parties. Together with the Centre and the Progressive People's Party, they worked on proposals for a conciliatory peace settlement. The transformation of the Reich into a parliamentary democracy in October 1918 fulfilled one of the key aims of the SPD, and there were even two Social Democrats in the last Imperial Government.

Meeting of a Workingmen's Educational Association, 1868

Social Demo-
crats August
Bebel and
Friedrich Wil-
helm Fritzsche
during the
Reichstag
debate on the
anti-Socialist
laws on
17 September
1878

Meeting of
Social Demo-
cratic women
in Berlin, 1891

Der rote Siegfried

nach der Wahlschlacht 1912.

Aus der Tiefe stieg das Volk empor und rechnete ab.

Die Sozialdemokratie erhielt:

1871	113 048 St. u. 2 Abg.	1890	1 427 298 St. u. 35 Abg.
1898	2 113 536 St. u. 56 Abg.	1903	3 010 756 St. u. 81 Abg.
1912	4 250 329 St. u. 110 Abg.		

Colour post-
card printed
to mark the
Social Demo-
crats' victory
in the Reichs-
tag elections
of 12 January
1912

3. Cooperation between the monarchy and National Liberalism

The alliance that was forged in 1866/67 between the Conservative Prussian Government and the National Liberal Party survived beyond the proclamation of the Empire in January 1871. While the creation of the North German Confederation had already established a single economic area in April 1867, the legal structure of which was rapidly developed by the National Liberal Group in the Reichstag in an informal alliance with Free Conservatives and Liberals of the Left, the need to base internal development on a sound legal footing became even more acute with the creation of the Empire in 1871. The first elections to the national Reichstag in March 1871 saw the National Liberals obtain more votes than any other party; the parliamentary group of the National Liberals initially comprised 125 out of 382 deputies and cooperated closely with the Free Conservatives of the Imperial Party (*Reichspartei*). The requirements of practical day-to-day politics – or, to use Bismarck's term, *Realpolitik* –

meant that the National Liberals did not throw their full weight behind the traditional primary concern of the liberal party, namely the introduction of a parliamentary system of government, although they never entirely lost sight of that aim but rather deferred its achievement indefinitely.

The contribution to the integration of the nation state that was rendered by the National Liberals as allies of the Imperial Government, particularly through their cooperation in the unification process, should not be underestimated. The Coinage Act (*Münzgesetz*) of 1871 established the mark as the currency unit for the whole of Germany, and in 1872 a uniform Penal Code was introduced, followed in the next five years by codifications of extensive areas of civil law. Freedom of trade and establishment were enshrined in law, partly through extensions of the reform acts that had been adopted for the North German Confedera-

The Berlin
Stock
Exchange,
c. 1875

tion. The regulation of poor relief was another of the priority areas in this daunting legislative workload, as was the reform of the Prussian administration. And the Imperial Press Act (*Reichspressegesetz*) of 1874 fulfilled – albeit with certain restrictions – one of the basic demands made by the revolutionaries of 1848/49, namely freedom of public expression.

These relatively rapid successes were largely due to the fact that the National Liberals – unlike the pro-government parliamentary majorities of later years, which were mostly driven by short-term tactical considerations – regarded themselves as cooperative and active partners of the Imperial Government. In this constellation, the groundwork for the implementation of legislative bills was often done in pre-parliamentary deliberations. Rudolf von Delbrück, head of the Federal Chancellery from 1867 and then head of the Imperial Chancellery until 1876, was a staunch and powerful ally of the National Liberals within the Executive, while they themselves were represented in the Prussian Cabinet, where two of their members, Otto Camphausen, the Minister of Finance, and Adalbert Falk, the Minister of Education and Culture, were influential politicians who guaranteed prompt consultation with the parliamentary group in the Reichstag.

Although Bismarck's alliance with the National Liberals imparted the necessary impetus to the process of national integration in legal and economic terms, when it came to social policy the alliance had quite the opposite effect. Bismarck's *Kulturkampf* against the Catholic Church in Germany and its staunch adherents in the political sphere, who were suspected of maintaining "international links" and conspiring with separatist minorities, was unreservedly supported by all Liberals. This conflict, which began with disputes between the Government and the Catholic Church on the supervision of schools and on civil marriage, soon escalated into a bitter confrontation in which the Government resorted to overt repression. Through the "pulpit clause" adopted by the Reichstag

Rudolf von Bennigsen, respected National Liberal politician and advocate of cooperation between the Crown and Parliament

Rudolf von Delbrück, President of the Federal Chancellery from 1867 to 1871 and of the Imperial Chancellery from 1871 to 1876

back in 1871, which barred the clergy from commenting on affairs of state from the pulpit "in any manner likely to endanger public order", the proscription of the Jesuit order throughout the Reich and the Prussian "May laws" of 1873, the Church and its clergy were subjected to state supervision; by 1876, all the Prussian bishops had been imprisoned or deported, and a quarter of Catholic parishes had no incumbent priest. This was the first emergency legislation against alleged "enemies of the Reich", a practice that would come back to haunt Germany, that poisoned the domestic climate and undermined belief in tolerance and peaceful accommodation of interests within the national community, without achieving the desired result. On the contrary, in the second Reichstag elections in January 1874, 83% of the Catholic electorate voted for the Centre, increasing its parliamentary representation from 61 to 91 seats.

Finally, when the limitations of state power and the display of solidarity by the Catholic faithful could no longer be ignored, the laws enacted in the course of the *Kulturkampf* were gradually repealed. The legacy of these laws, however, was a more deeply entrenched distrust of the Reich among many Catholics.

The internal structure of the young nation state was even more violently shaken by the struggle against Social Democracy. Fearing political and social revolution and "red anarchy", Bismarck forced the issue in the spring of 1878, when he blamed the Social Democrats for two attempts to assassinate the Kaiser that were actually perpetrated by people acting alone. The Reichstag was dissolved, and the elections that followed in July were conducted against the background of the Congress of Berlin, convened to revise the recent peace settlement in the Balkans,

Zwischen Berlin und Rom.

Der letzte Zug war mir allerdings unangenehm; aber die Partie ist deshalb noch nicht verloren. Ich habe noch einen sehr schönen Zug in petto!

Das wird auch der letzte sein, und dann sind Sie in wenigen Zügen matt — — wenigstens für Deutschland.

Der Pfeil ist auf die Socialdemokraten gerichtet; wie aber, wenn er über das Ziel hinausfliegt?

"The arrow is aimed at the Social Democrats, but what if it overshoots the target?" – cartoon from *Kladderadatsch* on the ambivalent attitude of the Liberals to the anti-Socialist laws, 1878

at which Bismarck's stock rose even higher than before. This contributed to a marked increase in the Conservative vote. The anti-Socialist laws, the second version of which was adopted less than three months later by an amenable majority in the Reichstag, were intended to eliminate Social Democracy as a political force once and for all.

All Socialist and Communist associations and assemblies were dissolved, their publications were proscribed and Social Democratic agitators were imprisoned or deported by the police authorities. The fact that the increasingly self-assured left wing of the National Liberals had previously pressed successfully for a moderation of the laws and the specification of an expiry date does not alter the fact that the National Liberals' eventual approval of the legislation was tantamount to a betrayal of the Liberal principle of the rule of law. The decision of the Left to vote with the party and the party's decision to let its principles be overridden by a perceived *raison d'état* ultimately dissolved the cement of common convictions that still held the National Liberal camp together at that time. Its disintegration was only a matter of time.

There were other reasons, in point of fact, for the break between Bismarck and the National Liberals. In 1873, the economic boom of the unification period was followed by a sustained economic crisis, arousing all types of fears and provoking fierce criticism of the Liberal economic order, which was dismissed as unbridled "Manchester-style" *laissez-faire* Liberalism. Towards the end of the seventies, this continuing depression coincided with a structural crisis in the agricultural sector. This brought the large landowners of Eastern Germany into the ranks of the opponents of free trade, the landowners whom Bismarck called "a patient people, loyal to the state and conservative, minded to preserve". The Union of Fiscal and Economic Reformers (*Vereinigung der Steuer- und Wirtschaftsreformer*), founded in 1876, became their lobbyists for the imposition of agricultural tariffs, campaigning alongside the Central Association of German Industrialists (*Centralverband Deutscher Industrieller*), which was established in the same year as the first powerful umbrella organization for the pro-tariff industries. In the struggle against the economic precepts of Liberalism, the landowning *Junkers* and the big industrialists found a

Steel-rolling mill. Painting by Adolph von Menzel, 1875

common cause, which was quite quickly transfigured into a "corn and steel alliance". Bismarck's unmistakable preference for this alliance, which manifested itself in a switch to an interventionist economic policy, meant the end of his alliance with the National Liberals. The strengthened left wing of Eduard Lasker and his associates was not prepared to go along with this new conservative course at any price and, in the words of Maximilian von Forckenbeck, Lasker called "the free and vigorous citizenry back to the barricades". In May 1879, Forckenbeck demonstratively resigned the presidency of the Reichstag.

The Tariffs Bill finally broke up the parliamentary group of the National Liberals, with only a minority of them remaining in Bismarck's camp. Thus the Conservative elites achieved a success that far outreached the domain of economic policy. The long-cherished hope of the Liberals and Democrats that the Reich would become a parliamentary democracy, that the elected representatives of the people would be able to exercise real control over the Executive, was now dead and buried. In many respects, the Reich had assumed the character of a class society. It was not without justification that this domestic sea change of 1878/79 was described by some as the "second founding of the Reich".

Inspection of the new potato spinner. Wood engraving from a painting by Konrad Ahrends, 1887

Left:
Maximilian von Forckenbeck, leading representative of the left wing of the National Liberals

Right:
Otto Theodor von Seydewitz, Conservative politician; succeeded Forckenbeck as President (Speaker) of the Reichstag in 1879

"The dragon slays St George" – cartoon from the *Berliner Wespen* on the Government's switch to political co-operation with the Conservatives, 1879

4. Tariffs, Conservatism and the welfare state

"Don't be too presumptuous," said the Liberal spoke, "as soon as the wind changes, I shall be back up there" – cartoon satirizing the shifting domestic alliances of the Imperial Government in the late Bismarck era, before 1887

The dramatic decisions of the late 1870s set the course that domestic politics was to follow throughout the next decade. The Social Democrats were marginalized, but the abandonment of the *Kulturkampf* meant that the exponents of political Catholicism were at least sufficiently integrated now for the Centre to eschew a position of outright opposition to the system. The protective tariffs and an increase in tobacco duty brought the Reich new revenue that stabilized its finances for a time but also increased the cost of living, causing hardship to the population in the lower income brackets.

Towards the end of the Bismarck era, the Imperial Government no longer commanded a parliamentary majority that was stable enough to support its policies with anything more than *ad hoc* case-by-case decisions. Until 1884 the remaining National Liberals were not prepared to cooperate with the Conservatives on the basis of a substantive platform, and an alliance between the Conservatives and the Centre, whose federalist principles had recently led them to block sweeping tax and financial reforms that would have freed the Reich from financial dependence on the federal states, was even more of a non-starter in view of the *Kulturkampf*. The Reichstag election of 1881 was won by a coalition of opposition parties, comprising the Centre and the Liberal Left, reinforced by the National Liberal Secessionists. It was not until six years later, after the Heidelberg Declaration, from which the National Liberals emerged again as acceptable allies for the Imperial Government, that the fiction of an acute external threat to Germany, which was heightened by massive government propaganda, led to the return of a pro-Government parliamentary majority of Conservatives and the National Liberals, who had now embraced centralism. Although this majority voted for the *Septennat*, the military budget which was to run for seven years and which provided for a 26,000-man increase in the size of the armed forces, and for further tightening of the tariff laws, the "cartel" as a whole was not sufficiently stable to form a sound basis for Bismarck's policy in the longer term.

It is no wonder that such constellations strongly encouraged the tendency to govern over the heads of the parties, and indeed the roots of this practice lay in the imperial constitution itself. Bismarck's persistent attempts to base his economic policy on corporations and associations – though torpedoed by the Reichstag – were entirely consistent with this approach to government, as were the occasional hatching of plans for a *coup d'état* and the short-lived restoration of the old Prussian State Council (*Staatsrat*). The social welfare legislation of the eighties, however, also initiated by the Chancellor, was supported by the Centre and the National Liberals once they had overcome their initial mistrust. The Sickness Insurance

Report in the *Illustrierte Zeitung* of 9 June 1883 concerning the Reichstag vote on the Sickness Insurance Funds Act (*Krankenkassengesetz*)

Wochenschau.

Der deutsche Reichstag erledigte im Lauf der vergangenen Woche zwei Vorlagen von besonderer Wichtigkeit: das Krankenkassengesetz und die Gewerbeordnungsnovelle. Die entscheidende Abstimmung über das Krankenkassengesetz erfolgte in der Sitzung vom 31. Mai, und zwar wurde das Gesetz bei namentlicher Abstimmung mit 216 gegen 99 Stimmen angenommen. Geschlossen dafür stimmten die beiden conservativen Fractionen, das Centrum, mit Ausnahme des Abgeordneten v. Alten-Linden, die Polen, die Nationalliberalen und die Volkspartei; die Minderheit wurde gebildet durch die Fortschrittspartei, die Mehrzahl der Secessionisten und die Socialdemokraten. Mit „Ja" stimmten die Secessionisten v. Bunsen, Grieninger, Jegel, Kochhann (Landsberg), Lasker, v. Löw, Lüders (Görlitz), Pflüger, Schlutow, Schröder, Schröter und Thomsen. Außerdem erklärten sich für das Gesetz die Abgeordneten v. Bockum-Dolffs, Treitschke, v. Ludwig und die Elsässer Grad und Zorn v. Bulach; dagegen die Elsässer Kablé, Winterer und Dollfus, der Welfe Langwerth v. Simmern, der Däne Lassen und der Abgeordnete v. Bühler-Oehringen. Damit hat der erste der socialpolitischen Gesetzentwürfe die Zustimmung von mehr als Zweidrittheilen der deutschen Volksvertretung erlangt. Vor der Abstimmung erklärte der Abgeordnete Dietz im Namen der socialdemokratischen Partei: das Gesetz entspreche weder im ganzen noch in seinen einzelnen Theilen den berechtigten Anforderungen der arbeitenden Klassen. Nach vielen Richtungen bezeichne das Gesetz sogar eine Verschlechterung des gegenwärtigen Zustands, insbesondere durch die Ausschließung der ländlichen Arbeiter, die Beibehaltung der Fabrikkassen, die ihrer Natur nach nur ein Mittel zur Unterdrückung der Arbeiter durch die Kapitalisten seien, durch die Beschränkung des Verfügungsrechts der Mitglieder, endlich durch den polizeilichen Charakter des ganzen Gesetzes.

The last order issued by Kaiser William I, dated 8 March 1888, in which he authorizes the Imperial Chancellor to close the Reichstag

Abonnements
werden beim Verlag und dessen bekannten Agenten entgegengenommen, und zwar zum voraus zahlbaren Vierteljahrspreis von:
Mt. 4,10 für Deutschland (direkt per Brief-Convert)
Schil. 2,75 für Oesterreich (direkt per Brief-Couvert)
Schil. 2.— für die übrigen Länder des Weltpostvereins (Kreuzband).

Inserate
die berigespaltene Petitzeile 5 Pence = 25 Pfg. — 50 Cts.

Der Sozialdemokrat
Organ der Sozialdemokratie deutscher Zunge.

Erscheint wöchentlich einmal in London.
Verlag der German Cooperative Publishing Co. L. Barotstein & Co., London N. W. 114 Kentish Town Road.

Postsendungen franco gegen franco. Eingeschriebene Briefe nach England kosten Doppelporto.

No. 10.   Briefe an die Redaktion und Expedition des in Deutschland und Oesterreich verbotenen „Sozialdemokrat" wolle man unter Beobachtung äußerster Vorsicht abgeben lassen. In der Regel schicke man uns die Briefe nicht direkt, sondern an die bekannten Dedadressen. In zweifelhaften Fällen eingeschrieben.   8. März 1890.

20 Mandate im ersten Wahlgang, 17 in der Stichwahl.
1,341,587 sozialdemokratische Wähler — 567,405 Zuwachs

Im ersten Wahlgang:

Glauchau-Meerane:
J. Auer, Sattler (Schriftsteller) in München.
Hamburg I.:
A. Bebel, Drechslermeister (Schriftsteller) in Dresden.
Hamburg II.:
J. H. W. Dietz, Buchdrucker in Stuttgart.
Greiz:
C. Förster, Zigarrenarbeiter in Hamburg.
Altona:
Karl Frohme, Schlosser (Schriftsteller) in Hannover.
Leipzig-Land:
F. Geyer, Zigarrenarbeiter in Großenhain.
Nürnberg:
K. Grillenberger, Schlosser (Korrektor) in Nürnberg.
Barmen-Elberfeld:
F. Harm, Weber (Gastwirth) in Barmen.
Mülhausen i. Elsaß:
F. Hickel, Schreiner in Mühlhausen.
Berlin VI.:
W. Liebknecht, Schriftsteller in Borsdorf.
Hamburg III.:
Wilhelm Metzger, Spengler (Journalist) in Hamburg.
Chemnitz:
Max Schippel, Schriftsteller in Berlin.
Mittweida-Limbach:
A. Schmidt, Buchdrucker in Berlin.
Solingen:
Hg. Schuhmacher, Gerber in Solingen.
Schneeberg-Stollberg:
J. Seifert, Schuhmacher in Zwickau.
Berlin IV.:
P. Singer, Kaufmann in Dresden.
Zwickau-Crimmitschau:
W. Stolle, Gärtner (Gastwirth) in Gesau.
München II. und Magdeburg:
G. Vollmar, Schriftsteller in München.
Gera:
E. Wurm, Schriftsteller in Dresden.

In der Stichwahl wurden gewählt:

München I.:
J. Birk, Gastwirth in München.
Braunschweig:
W. Blos, Schriftsteller in Stuttgart.
Bremen:
J. Bruhns, Zigarrenarbeiter in Bremen.
Mannheim:
A. Dreesbach, (Kaufm.) Mannheim.
Calbe-Aschersleben:
Aug. Heine, Hutfabrikant in Halberstadt.
Naumburg a./Saale:
W. Hoffmann, Zigarrenarbeiter in Chemnitz.
Mainz:
Franz Jöst, Tischler in Mainz.
Halle a./Saale:
Fritz Kunert, Lehrer (Redakteur) in Breslau.
Hannover:
H. Meister, Zigarren-Arbeiter in Hannover.
Ottensen-Pinneberg:
H. Molkenbuhr, Zig.-Arbeiter in Kellinghusen.
Frankfurt a./M.:
Wilh. Schmidt, Lithograph in Frankfurt.
Sonneberg:
P. Reißhaus, Schneider in Erfurt.
Königsberg i./Pr.:
Carl Schulze, Zigarrenarbeiter in Königsberg.
Lübeck:
Th. Schwarh, Koch (Gastwirth) in Lübeck.
Nieder-Barnim:
Arth. Stadthagen, Rechtsanwalt in Berlin.
Breslau-Ost:
Franz Exhauer, Tischler in Berlin.
Offenbach-Dieburg:
Carl Ulrich, Schlosser (Redakteur) in Offenbach.

Siegreiche Stichwahlen:

	1890	1887	Stichwahl
München I	7,570	4,563	14,432
Braunschweig	13,621	10,656	15,000
Bremen	14,843	7,743	16,404
Mannheim	8,701	5,128	12,601
Calbe-Aschersleben	12,514	4,857	16,373
Naumburg	10,563	5,591	13,000
Mainz	8,000	5,526	10,000
Halle a. S.	12,618	6,590	14,500
Hannover	16,570	12,210	19,000
Ottensen	10,820	6,820	13,010
Königsberg	12,327	7,987	13,138
Frankfurt a. M.	12,654	8,640	18,090
Lübeck	6,389	4,254	7,316
Nieder-Barnim	13,628	5,680	15,400
Breslau-Ost	9,996	7,781	12,337
Offenbach	10,331	8,024	13,000
Sonneberg	7,215	4,659	10,000

In the illustration: "Unser die Welt, trotz alledem!", "1890", "20. Febr."

Der erste Akt.

Das war vor der Entscheidungsschlacht
In eurem Lager wüstes Lärmen!
Die Becher klangen durch die Nacht,
Musik, Geschwirr und trunkes Schwärmen.
Wir sahen euch im Tanze drehn
Durch eurer Lagerfeuer Qualmen
Und ließen uns herüberwehn
Vom Wind die Melodie von Psalmen.

Da ward gebetet und geseufzt,
Denn abseits von der tollen Rotte
Hat zitternd Trost und Schutz gesucht
Das Muckerthum bei seinem Gotte;
Und während auf den Knien lag
Mit Angstgeplärr der Troß der Pfaffen,
Schärft pfeifend für den „Ehrentag"
Der Uebermuth sich seine Waffen.

So habt ihr, prahlend und verzagt
Und mit geheucheltem Vertrauen,
Die Nacht verjubelt und verklagt,
Statt ernst auf's gute Recht zu bauen;
Und während still das Dunkel wich
Dem Tag und seiner Strahlenkrone
Vollzog in finsterm Schweigen sich
Der Aufmarsch unsrer Bataillone.

Vernehmlich liefen durch die Reih'n
Geflüsterte Kommandoworte;
Ein Jeder stand im Morgenschein
Geschlossen am bestimmten Orte.
Wir wußten, wo der Gegner stand,
Und konnten nicht im Wege irren,
Und wenn ein schwacher Laut entschwand,
So war's der Waffen leises Klirren.

Wohl krampfte zornig sich die Hand,
Wohl schlug das Herz im heißen Grimme,
Doch selbst die tiefste Wallung fand
In diesen Stunden keine Stimme.
Und kaum ein Lächeln ward getauscht
Von Freunden, wie ein erstes Wahnen,
Wenn leicht im Morgenwind gerauscht
Die ehrenreichen rothen Fahnen.

Ein Wink, dann ein Trompetenstoß,
Ein Schrei des Hasses tausendstimmig —
Und furchtbar brach das Wetter los,
Bildschön, erhaben, aber grimmig!
Das war kein zierlich Lanzenspiel,
Das war ein Kampf auf Tod und Leben,
Und wer von unsern Hieben fiel,
Dem wurde kein Pardon gegeben.

Und wie sie fielen! Links und rechts
Brach's wie der Sturm in ihre Glieder,
Warf rauh die derbe Faust des Knechts
Die zarten, schlanken Herrlein nieder.
Der Sturm zerblies ihr Heer wie Schaum —
Sie suchten sich umsonst zu sammeln,
Und selbst die Frömmsten fanden kaum
Die Zeit, ihr Stoßgebet zu stammeln.

Ward deines Gleichen je gesehn,
Gewaltigster der Niederlagen?
Um ihr die Armada war's geschehn,
Bevor sie sich noch recht geschlagen,
Und mancher prahlerische Held
Geziert mit Federn und mit Orden,
Irrt jammernd flüchtig über's Feld
Und sucht verzweifelnd sich zu retten.

Die sich gebrüstet und gebläht,
Als ob sie Keiner jemals schlage —
Wie Garben liegen sie gemäht
Nach diesem großen Ehrentage.
Und die voll Hochmuth uns gedroht,
Daß sie uns festeten und bänden —
Kein Hund nimmt einen Bissen Brot
Nach diesem Tag aus ihren Händen.

Nach ihren stolzen Fahnen greift
Die Hand des Niedrigsten und Letzten;
Durch Blut und Koth der Wahlstatt schleift
Er spöttisch singend die zerfetzten;
Und was nur splitterte, nicht brach,
Untrann mit rächenden Geschicken,
Denn unter dieser Last von Schmach
Wird es wie Rohr zusammenknicken.

Wir aber stehen stumm und dicht
In Massen wieder und Kolonnen,
Wir sind die blöden Narren nicht,
Zu glauben, Alles sei gewonnen.
Das große Schauspiel hat gepackt —
Es fehlt mit einem Eisenbiß!
Doch is's, ihr Herr's, der erste Akt
Des Riesendramas nur gemeiret!

R. L.

Act (*Krankenversicherungsgesetz*) of 1883 was followed the next year by the Accident Insurance Act (*Unfallversicherungsgesetz*), and then old-age and invalidity insurance schemes were introduced in 1889. This legislation created a system of social security that was far ahead of its time and undoubtedly constitutes an outstanding political achievement. Nevertheless, it was not enough to lure the working classes away from the criminalized Social Democrats. Bismarck's hope that the creation of the welfare system would win the hearts and minds of workers for the imperial political order was never fulfilled.

On 9 March 1888, Emperor William I died. After the brief 100-day reign of his terminally ill son, Frederick III, William's grandson mounted the throne as William II in June. In the field of foreign policy, the new Kaiser's aim was to establish Germany as a world power. In domestic policy, his initial aim was to effect a reconciliation with the Social Democrats. Both of these aims were at odds with Bismarck's basic political tenets. The

outcome of the elections in February 1890 exacerbated this rift into a governmental crisis. The "cartel" suffered a heavy defeat and fell apart. The Social Democrats won the largest share of the vote for the first time, trebling the number of seats it held in the Reichstag. The anti-Socialist laws, which the Reichstag had upheld throughout the eighties, were finally allowed to expire. Bismarck's attempt, which smacked of sheer desperation, to put the Centre at the heart of a centre-right coalition, provoked this comment from the party leader, Ludwig Windthorst: "I have just come from the political deathbed of a great man". In fact, Bismarck's unpredictable tactical manoeuvring was ultimately seen by his contemporaries as nothing more than an unprincipled bid to cling to power. Under pressure from the parties and large sections of public opinion, the Kaiser finally decided to end his power struggle with the Chancellor by dismissing him. A few days later, on 29 March 1890, Bismarck withdrew to his Friedrichsruh estate. A new era – the Wilhelminian era – had dawned.

Opposite page: Front page of *Der Sozialdemokrat* of 8 March 1890. The newspaper, published in London, reports the huge increase in the Social Democratic vote in the recent Reichstag elections

Bismarck's departure from Berlin on 29 March 1890, following his dismissal

5. Changing alliances and personal rule

In the 1890s, the Reich developed into the leading industrial nation in Europe. Industrial expansion, particularly in the chemical and electrical-engineering industries but also in shipbuilding and heavy-machinery construction, heralded a period of economic boom in which powerful groups of companies such as Krupp, Siemens and AEG achieved dominant market positions. Politics in the Reich was now marked, even more strongly than in the late Bismarck era, by a parallelogram of forces formed by conflicting individual interests and reflected in the heterogeneous and indeed disparate nature of each parliamentary majority that was put together.

At court, in the army and in the administration, the Conservative elites consolidated their power bases. Associations of imperialist agitators, such as the Pan-German League (*All-deutscher Verband*) and the Navy League (*Flottenverein*) soon crossed the line between extraparliamentary lobbying and the exertion of direct political influence. The same applies to the powerful special-interest groups into which growing numbers of industrialists and owners of large farms were organizing themselves. From 1893 onwards, the Farmers' League (*Bund der Landwirte*) fought to prevent any repeat of the cut in corn tariffs that had been made in 1890, successfully mobilizing widespread support with their nationalistic and increasingly anti-Semitic propaganda. After the mass strike by textile workers in Crimmitschau in 1904, associations of employers began to join together in confederations, primarily the Central Bureau of German Employers' Associations (*Hauptstelle Deutscher Arbeitgeberverbände*) and the Federation of German Employers' Associations

Official opening of the Kiel Canal (*Kaiser-Wilhelm-Kanal*) on 21 June 1895

Opposite page: Ceremony marking the centenary of the Krupp company on 8 August 1912. The figure at the lectern is Kaiser William II

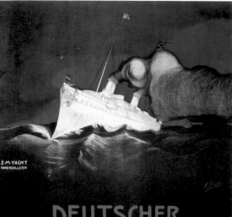

The Kaiser's yacht *Hohenzollern* depicted on a Navy League poster, 1901

atives and chiefly represented smaller export-orientated industrial companies. The Conservative organizations of big industrialists faced far stiffer competition, however, from the Hanseatic Federation (*Hansa-Bund*), which was formed in 1909 and of which 90 per cent of all the Progressive People's Party deputies became members. The Federation, however, was unable to prevail against the "Cartel of the Productive Classes" (*Kartell der schaffenden Stände*), in which a large percentage of the Central Association eventually combined with associations of farmers and of small and medium-sized businesses.

(*Verein Deutscher Arbeitgeberverbände*). Both confederations were closely linked with the Central Association of German Industrialists (*Centralverband Deutscher Industrieller*), which had long been active both inside and outside the political domain. There had already been a split in this organization back in 1894; the breakaway group, the Industrialists' League (*Bund der Industriellen*), was associated with the National Liberals rather than the Conserv-

The labour force was also organizing itself into powerful lobbies at this time. While the influence of the Christian trade unions and the Liberal trade association founded by Max Hirsch and Franz Duncker (*Hirsch-Dunckerscher Gewerksverein*) remained relatively weak, the membership of the Socialist-orientated free trade unions (*Freie Gewerkschaften*) increased fiftyfold between 1890 and 1913, when it reached two and a half million; by 1911, the German Metalworkers' Association alone had 500,000 members. The General Commission (*Generalkommission*) under Karl Legien, which was the umbrella organization of the free trade unions, became the largest workingmen's organization in Europe.

Under the heading "Through darkest Germany", *Simplicissimus* published this cartoon by Thomas Theodor Heine on the mass strike by textile workers in Crimmitschau, 1904

Against this background, the task of controlling or at least stabilizing the political power struggle proved impossible for Bismarck's successor. As Imperial Chancellor, Count Leo von Caprivi was committed to the development of government social policy and to greater tolerance towards the Poles and towards the Hanoverian Guelphists; in a spirit of "enlightened Conservatism", he tried to secure the political cooperation of the Centre and the Liberal Left. After he had been forced onto the defensive by the electoral victory of the old "cartel" parties in June 1893, a conflict with the Conservative Prime Minister of Prussia, Count Botho zu Eulenburg, compelled him to resign the following year. Chlodwig, Prince of Hohenlohe-Schillingsfürst, Imperial Chancellor from 1894 to 1900, was easily outmanoeuvred by the initiators of a new right-wing *Sammlungspolitik*, whose chief exponent was Johannes von Miquel; the aim of this policy was to concentrate the power of the landowning aristocracy and the entrepreneurial class with a view to defending their interests, especially against the working classes; Hohenlohe-Schillingsfürst did, however, succeed in persuading a reluctant Kaiser to consent to the lifting of the ban on assemblies of associations. In October 1900, by which time the *Sammlungspolitik* had reached its limits in the Reichstag and the domestic political situation had begun to change, the Kaiser's favourite, Prince Bernhard von Bülow, was appointed Chancellor. For the time being, however, responsibility for home affairs was largely in the hands of Count Arthur von Posadowsky-Wehner, Secretary of State in the Imperial Ministry of the Interior, who put an end to the policy of active repression that had been targeted at the Social Democrats and reactivated the welfare state. His reform of the system of invalidity insurance was the first piece of welfare legislation to be supported by the votes of the Social Democrats. Once again, however, a concession failed to steal the Social Democrats' thunder and reduce their vote as it had been intended to

By 1911, the German Metalworkers' Association had already amassed half a million members

Count Leo von Caprivi (top right), Imperial Chancellor from 1890 to 1894, addressing the Reichstag

Chancellor Bülow
giving a speech.
Painting by
Georg Walten-
berger, about
1902

Johannes von Miquel, leader of the National Liberals and Prussian Minister of Finance from 1890 to 1901

Count Arthur von Posadowsky-Wehner, Secretary of State in the Imperial Ministry of the Interior from 1897 to 1907

do, particularly because the increase in the customs tariff in December 1902 presented the workingmen's party with the opportunity to lead a campaign against "bread profiteering" and the unbroken influence of the Prussian "*Junker* regime". The ultimate reason for Posadowsky's dismissal, however, was his cooperation with the Centre, whose key parliamentary position filled the Conservatives, the Liberals and, above all, the Kaiser with growing apprehension.

The electoral campaign of 1906/07 was focused on the perceived need to pursue a more active colonial policy, and so the pro-colonial Conservative-Liberal "Bülow Bloc" targeted its attacks on the disintegrative inclinations of the Centre and SPD and their unreliability on "national questions". Even the Liberals of the Left had only recently approved the amended Navy Act (*Flottengesetz*) of 1906, thereby signalling their agreement in principle with the foreign policy of the Imperial Government and their willingness to cooperate with it. Nevertheless, precisely because it was such a broad coalition, the Bülow Bloc lacked internal cohesion. Since it was impossible to create a sustainable balance of interests in such a rainbow coalition, the Chancellor tried to circumvent the problem by making concessions to the various party wings, instantly attracting accusations of unprincipled scheming. This approach resulted, for example, in the adoption in 1908, after long and arduous wrangling, of positively liberal legislation on the right of association, which allowed women and young persons to take part in public political life for the first time. In the same year, however, a new law also gave the Prussian Government the right to confiscate Polish estates for the benefit of German settlers. Although the provisions of this special legislation were seldom applied in practice, it provoked understandable responses from the Polish minority, especially since the Eastern Marches Association (*Ostmarkenverein*) in particular was becoming more and more vociferous at that time in its calls for a campaign against all things Polish.

The Bülow Bloc was finally brought down by the Chancellor's cautious – and unsuccessful – efforts to reform the three-class voting system in Prussia and by the problem of the imperial finances. The repeal of the "Franckenstein clause", which had limited imperial revenue from customs duties until 1904, only temporarily improved a financial situation which had again become precarious. When Bülow then considered the introduction of a tax on inheritance and on ownership of real estate, the Conservatives, together with the Centre, whose period on the political sidelines had only just ended, blocked the planned reforms. For the first time, parliamentary defeat had forced a chancellor to resign: in June 1909, Bülow tendered his resignation, the *ad hoc* alliance of Conservatives and Centrists pushed through legislation for the taxation of movable capital and for increases in indirect taxation and the introduction of new indirect taxes, and the new Chancellor, Theobald von Bethmann Hollweg, was faced with a political constellation of almost unprecedented complexity. The much-maligned practice of governing over the heads of the parties now seemed to be not so much a result of the continuing failure to establish parliamentary government as the inevitable consequence of the fact that the Chancellor could not count on even a reasonably reliable combination of parties in the Reichstag.

Be that as it may, Bethmann Hollweg did achieve certain early successes. In 1911, Alsace-Lorraine was finally accorded the same constitutional status as the German federal states. In the following year the system of social insurance was extended with the adoption of the Imperial Insurance Code (*Reichsversicherungsordnung*) and the Salaried Employees Insurance Act (*Angestelltenversicherungsgesetz*). In January 1912, however, the electoral triumph of the SPD, combined with a stabilization of the Liberal Left, which was also reflected by an increase in its vote, sharply polarized domestic politics once again. The signs of an imminent alliance between the strong Social Democrats and the Liberal Left, which had reformed itself into a social-liberal movement, was met by

Nationalist postcard, about 1905

the Conservatives in particular, supported by their main bastion in Prussia, with a complete blockade on further reforms. In this way the domestic political fronts had been clearly drawn on the eve of the First World War, but they had also become so firmly entrenched that Bethmann Hollweg's "diagonal" approach was doomed to failure.

In general terms, the Reichstag must undoubtedly take a share of responsibility for the paralysis of German domestic politics during the Wilhelmenian era. Majorities assembled for the sole purpose of opposing particular legislation all too quickly became the norm, special-interest cartels pursued all-too-narrow political goals, and these phenomena all too often prevented constructive policymaking. None the less, such manoeuvring also reflects the growing self-assurance of a parliament that the Imperial Government could scarcely continue to disregard, even – ultimately – on foreign-policy issues. Anti-parliamentary plans for *coups d'état*, which latterly stemmed

Prince
Bernhard von
Bülow after
his resignation
in June 1909,
photographed
in conversa-
tion with his
successor,
Theobald von
Bethmann
Hollweg

Reichstag debate on the *Daily Telegraph* affair, 10-11 November 1908

primarily from the General Staff under Count Alfred von Waldersee, now stood little genuine chance of succeeding. The growing reputation of the Reichstag was manifested by its increasing public prestige as well as by the introduction of deputies' remuneration in 1905/06. Moreover, with a few exceptions, a parliamentary majority could now be expected to oppose restrictive laws in specific areas. Both the Sedition Bill (*Umsturzvorlage*) of 1894 and the Prisons Bill (*Zuchthausvorlage*) of 1899 were voted down by the Reichstag. On increasingly frequent occasions, even the Kaiser felt compelled to justify his political measures, or to have them justified, to Parliament. In October 1908, when an interview given by William to the British *Daily Telegraph* placed further strain on Germany's foreign relations, which were already under a heavy cloud, every one of the parliamentary groups in the Reichstag was appalled by the monarch's high-handed behaviour, and Bülow was unwilling to accept responsibility for the Kaiser's statements. William had no option but to give an undertaking to confine himself in future to the discharge of his "constitutional responsibility" – another boost to the prestige of the Reichstag, though it was not followed

by any moves in the direction of parliamentary government.

While the "*Daily Telegraph* affair" is symbolic of the enhanced self-assurance of the Reichstag, it also illustrates the unpredictability of the monarch. The "personal rule" that William II sought to impose, his martial posturing and interference in everyday politics, had dire repercussions on the international stage in particular. Whereas Bismarck had repeatedly emphasized that the Reich did not seek to annex new territories but to secure its position within the balance of forces in Europe and had only reluctantly bowed to pressure from the Colonial League (*Kolonialverein*) and the Society for German Colonization (*Gesellschaft für deutsche Kolonisation*) for the conversion of a few areas of land in Africa and the South Pacific into German colonies, William II, by contrast, was unmistakably proclaiming a "new course": *Weltpolitik* as the mission, global power as the goal, and the navy as the instrument – that was his slogan. The Kaiser's aim, which he stressed in provocative speeches, of obtaining a "place in the sun" for Germany led the Reich into isolation, with

Demonstration against the Prussian three-class voting system in Brandenburg on 6 March 1910

only minimal gains in the form of colonial possessions in China and the Pacific; more-over, the often brutal conduct of the expedition corps and colonial forces damaged Germany's international reputation. The decision not to extend the Reinsurance Treaty that Bismarck had concluded with Russia encouraged Franco-Russian rapprochement, while the expansion of the German fleet overseen by Alfred von Tirpitz, Secretary of State in the Imperial Naval Department, even more than the construction of the Berlin-Baghdad railway, intensified Anglo-German rivalry, which escalated into an open naval arms race in 1906. Two years previously, France and Great Britain had settled their colonial differences and concluded the *Entente Cordiale*, and their joint opposition would thwart the first German attempt to become involved in Morocco. And then in 1907 came the Anglo-Russian convention on spheres of influence in the Balkans. Germany had a feeling that she was being encircled, and there was growing nervousness within the Imperial Government.

The blame for this perilous increase in international tension on the German side cannot, however, be assigned solely to the Kaiser and the generals who were requesting more and more armaments appropriations. After all, large parliamentary majorities, which were not accountable for foreign policy, had approved the measures to expand and modernize the army and navy. The decision in favour of the amended Navy Act, which was adopted in 1912 in the wake of the German defeat in the third Moroccan crisis, was backed by the votes of the Liberal Left and even of the Centre. While progress down this slippery slope did represent an advance towards the generally desired aim of national cohesion, the cost of this advance was an unprecedented militarization of the whole of public life.

Largely isolated abroad, paralysed and incapable of constructive renewal at home, the Reich drifted inexorably towards the European political crisis of 1914.

Colour post-card from the German colony of Kiao-chau in China

William II with generals and foreign guests observing the Fifth and Sixth Army Corps on manoeuvres, 1913

6. From truce to constitutional reform

The heir to the Austrian throne, Franz Ferdinand (right), and his wife Sophie, photographed in Sarajevo shortly before their assassination on 28 June 1914

In the summer of 1914, the escalation of tensions between France and Germany, the naval rivalry between Germany and the British Empire, Russia's aggressive policy in the Balkans and the fulfilment of Austro-German treaty obligations culminated in the outbreak of the First World War.

When a Serbian nationalist assassinated the heir to the Austrian throne and his wife in Sarajevo on 28 June, the Cabinet in Austria made preparations for the occupation of Serbia, and Russia responded with general mobilization on 31 July. For Berlin, the die was cast: this conflict would have to be resolved by force of arms. Although the aim of German diplomacy, unlike that of the High Command, was to avoid a major war if at all possible, and although the British Government in particular

still made occasional attempts to mediate, the automatic sequence of mobilizations now destroyed any prospect of a political settlement of the international crisis. In order to defeat France before the armies of her Russian ally could be deployed on the Eastern Front, three German armies circumvented the French border fortifications and advanced through neutral Belgium, prompting Britain to declare war on the Reich on 4 August. Germany and Austria-Hungary, the Central Powers, on whose side the Ottoman Empire and Bulgaria soon joined the war, now faced the armies of the Triple Entente of France, Britain and Russia, which were joined by countries such as Japan, Italy, Romania, China and, finally, the United States. In spite of considerable early successes, the Central Powers' prospects of winning the war were poor.

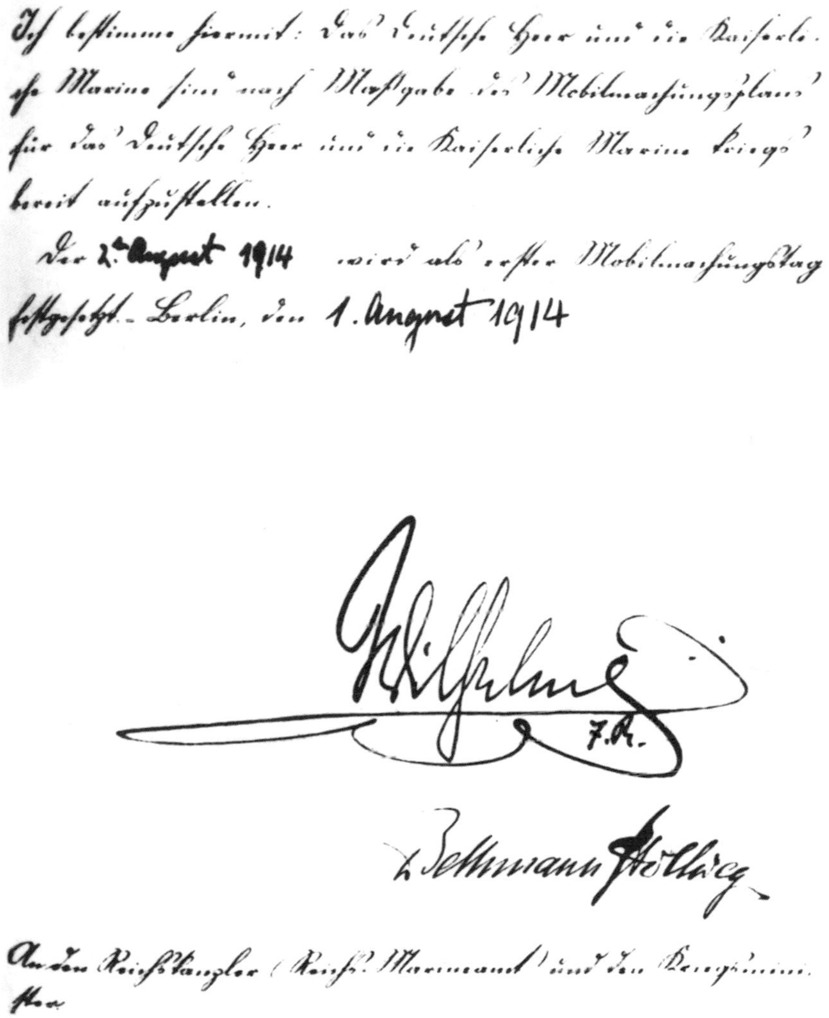

[handwritten mobilization order in German]

Ich bestimme hiermit: Das deutsche Heer und die Kaiserliche Marine sind nach Maßgabe des Mobilmachungsplans für das deutsche Heer und die Kaiserliche Marine kriegsbereit aufzustellen.

Der 2. August 1914 wird als erster Mobilmachungstag festgesetzt. Berlin, den 1. August 1914

Wilhelm I.R.

Bethmann Hollweg

An den Reichskanzler

Mobilization order signed by the Kaiser on 1 August 1914

The German population reacted to the outbreak of war with a mixture of euphoria and hysteria, black humour and panic. The prevailing mood in these circumstances, however, was one of determination to set aside internal disputes and differences. The nation was apparently united in its perception of the conflict as a just war of self-defence. The parliamentary groups made a truce, which the Kaiser, as the commander-in-chief, also embraced in the words suggested to him by Bethmann Hollweg: "I no longer know any parties; I only know Germans." By approving the war credits, even the Social Democratic Group in the Reichstag decided to put national solidarity before party politics. Left-wing intellectuals within the party, however, such as Karl Liebknecht and Rosa Luxemburg, who would subsequently form the *Gruppe Internationale*, which was the forerunner of the Spartacus League and hence of the Communist Party, in 1915 were quick to call for a struggle against the "imperialistic war".

The German victories in the first months of the war led to a more intensive discussion of war aims, a discussion in which the political parties also engaged. The National Liberals, the Conservatives and, initially, a great majority of the Centre supported the plans of

Military parade
with captured
artillery in
Berlin on
2 October 1914

the Army High Command and argued for annexations, particularly in Belgium and Russian Poland, whereas the bulk of the Social Democrats and most of the Progressive People's Party, and even the Imperial Chancellor, looked for ways to negotiate a peace settlement.

The course of the war up to 1916 fuelled the arguments of both sides. On the one hand, the danger of a Russian attack on Berlin had been averted in the late summer of 1914 and in February 1915 by the Battle of Tannenberg, where the Russian forces were encircled, and the winter battle of the Masurian Lakes; apart from occasional Russian successes in Galicia in 1914/15 and Aleksei Brusilov's advance in the Carpathians in 1916, the Central Powers remained constantly on the offensive in the east and in the Balkans, where first Serbia in 1915 and then Montenegro and Romania in the following year were forced to capitulate. On the other hand, the German advance in the west had quickly ground to a halt in the Battle of the Marne in September 1914; tactical efforts to outflank opposing

forces ended with deadlocked fronts all the way from the Flemish coast down to the Swiss border. From then on, bitter trench warfare raged on the Western Front, in which both sides sought to achieve the crucial breakthrough that would turn the war in their favour, engaging their forces in battles in which appalling numbers of lives were lost. This misguided strategy was typified in the case of the Western Allies by months of fruitless assaults in the Champagne region in 1915 and on the German side by the "hellhole of Verdun", the unsuccessful attempt by the German High Command to "bleed the French armies dry" in 1916 by deploying an unprecedented concentration of troops and firepower in a massive bombardment of the French fortifications around Verdun.

With the passage of time, the Central Powers' lack of resources became ever more apparent. Back home in Germany, disillusionment was spreading. The predominance of the war economy and the British naval blockade were leading to increasingly serious supply problems; in the "turnip winter" of 1916/17,

Opposite page:
Crowds outside the
Imperial
Palace in
Berlin during
the Kaiser's
address on
1 August 1914

The battlefield
of Verdun,
1916

Germany was hit by widespread famine. In urban regions, not even horse meat could be bought without ration tokens. By January 1918 – and before then in some cases – protest strikes against the "unjust" distribution of foodstuffs had turned into political strikes. The shadow of revolution was falling on Germany.

Against this background, the power structure in the Reich was changing. Caught between an Army High Command which, under Field Marshal General Paul von Hindenburg

and Major General Erich Ludendorff, had laid claim to dictatorial powers since 1916, and a Parliament that was increasingly insistent in its demands for a more decisive role in the political process, the Kaiser and the civilian Imperial Government saw their influence dwindle rapidly. Two events in 1917 illustrate this shift. As an opponent of the unrestricted submarine warfare with which the German navy had been trying to bring Britain to her knees since February 1917 and which had brought the United States into the war in April, Bethmann Hollweg had long been a

Striking munition workers in front of the Berlin Trades Union Headquarters in January 1918

Major General Erich Ludendorff, leading strategist of the German High Command

thorn in the flesh of the military staff and the parliamentary Right. On 12 July, Hindenburg and Ludendorff forced the Imperial Chancellor to resign; his successors were to remain politically insignificant to a great extent. A week later, the majority in the Reichstag risked open confrontation with the Army High Command. On the basis of previous deliberations held by the Cross-Party Committee, in which deputies from the SPD, the Centre, the Progressive People's Party and, at times, the National Liberals, had been working since the beginning of the month to formulate guidelines for the introduction of parliamentary government in the Reich and principles for a peace settlement which, they believed, could be acceptable to all parties, the Reichstag adopted a resolution calling for a negotiated peace in which there would be no winners or losers

Internationally, however, this peace resolution had no more effect than the half-hearted diplomatic efforts of previous years. Now that the United States had entered the war, the political and military leaders of the Western Allies were more determined than ever to secure an outright victory over the

Grand Admiral Alfred von Tirpitz, advocate of unrestricted submarine warfare and chairman of the Fatherland Party from 1917 to 1918

The plenary chamber of the Reichstag on 19 July 1917, during the inaugural address by the new Imperial Chancellor, Georg Michaelis

Central Powers. Within Germany, the peace resolution led to a further widening of the political spectrum. In April 1917, left-wing Social Democrats had already broken away from the SPD to form the Independendent Social Democratic Party of Germany (USPD) and wage a more uncompromising struggle against the continuation of the war. When numerous representatives of the mother party also took up this struggle, the extraparliamentary Right, on the initiative of Wolfgang Kapp and with the active support of Ludendorff, organized itself into the extreme nationalist Fatherland Party, with Admiral Tirpitz as its first chairman. It demanded the shelving of all internal reforms and the continuation of the war until victory was achieved on all fronts.

In actual fact, the course of the war in 1917 had made a victory for the Central Powers appear possible again. In Russia, the Czarist regime had been overthrown in the February Revolution, the "Kerensky offensive" that had

been launched on the orders of the new Provisional Government had collapsed with huge losses, and with the Bolsheviks' October Revolution the surrender of Germany's Russian adversary appeared to be imminent. On the River Isonzo (Sočo) front near the Austro-Italian border, German and Austrian troops achieved a breakthrough at Karfreit (now Kobarid, Slovenia), although its significance was overestimated at the time. The unrestricted submarine warfare created severe difficulties for the British war economy for a time, and mutinies had broken out in the French army after the failure of offensives at Arras and on the Aisne, showing the hapless commander-in-chief Robert-Georges Nivelle the limits of his troops' resilience. Finally, in March 1918, when the new Russian Bolshevik Government had to accept the terms dictated to it in the peace treaty of Brest-Litovsk, including the loss of Russia's western provinces, recognition of Ukrainian independence and the obligation to pay reparations, the German

zum Protokoll vom ...
... Februar 19..

Entwurf eines Gesetzes
zur Abänderung der Reichsverfassung.

—

Wir **Wilhelm,** von Gottes Gnaden Deutscher Kaiser, König von Preußen usw.

verordnen im Namen des Reichs, nach erfolgter Zustimmung des Bundesrats und des Reichstags, was folgt:

Die Reichsverfassung wird wie folgt abgeändert:

1. Im Artikel 11 werden die Absätze 2 und 3 durch folgende Bestimmungen ersetzt:

   Zur Erklärung des Krieges im Namen des Reichs ist die Zustimmung des Bundesrats und des Reichstags erforderlich.

   Friedensverträge sowie diejenigen Verträge mit fremden Staaten, welche sich auf Gegenstände der Reichsgesetzgebung beziehen, bedürfen der Zustimmung des Bundesrats und des Reichstags.

2. Im Artikel 15 werden folgende Absätze hinzugefügt:

   Der Reichskanzler bedarf zu seiner Amtsführung des Vertrauens des Reichstags.

   Der Reichskanzler trägt die Verantwortung für alle Handlungen von politischer Bedeutung, die der Kaiser in Ausübung der ihm nach der Reichsverfassung zustehenden Befugnisse vornimmt.

   Der Reichskanzler und seine Stellvertreter sind für ihre Amtsführung dem Bundesrat und dem Reichstag verantwortlich.

3. Im Artikel 17 werden die Worte gestrichen:

   „welcher dadurch die Verantwortlichkeit übernimmt".

4. Im Artikel 53 Abs. 1 wird folgender Satz hinzugefügt:

   Die Ernennung, Versetzung, Beförderung und Verabschiedung der Offiziere und Beamten der Marine erfolgt unter Gegenzeichnung des Reichskanzlers.

5. Im Artikel 64 Abs. 2 werden im ersten Satz hinter dem Worte „Kaiser" die Worte eingeschaltet:

   „unter Gegenzeichnung des Reichskanzlers".

6. Im Artikel 66 werden folgende Absätze 3 und 4 hinzugefügt:

   Die Ernennung, Versetzung, Beförderung und Verabschiedung der Offiziere und Militärbeamten eines Kontingents erfolgt unter Gegenzeichnung des Kriegsministers des Kontingents.

   Die Kriegsminister sind dem Bundesrat und dem Reichstag für die Verwaltung ihres Kontingents verantwortlich.

Urkundlich usw.
Gegeben usw.

Beglaubigt:
Berlin, den 26. Oktober 1918.
Der Präsident des Reichstags.
Fehrenbach

Constitutional Reform Bill, countersigned by the President of the Reichstag on 26 October 1918

Pictured at Eysden station in the Netherlands, the figure in the fur cloak is William II on his flight from Germany

High Command believed that the time was ripe for the decisive push in the West. In four massive waves of attack, the German armies drove back the Western Allies' front; the booming of guns could be heard as far away as Paris. The intended breakthrough, however, was not achieved, as the Allies, who were now finally under a unified command, held their nerve. They counterattacked with a force consisting mainly of fresh troops against an adversary whose strength had been sapped by years of static trench warfare. The eighth of August, 1918, was to go down in history as the German army's darkest day as Allied tanks broke through the German lines by Amiens.

Now, when it was too late, the political restructuring of the Reich that had been blocked for decades finally got under way. In October 1918, the Kaiser, who, in the Easter message he delivered as King of Prussia back in 1917, had held out the prospect of abolishing the three-class voting system in Prussia, accepted an Imperial Government in which representatives of the majority parties in Parliament assumed responsibility for governing the country. The Conservative camp was aghast to learn of the appointment of Philipp Scheidemann, the leader of the Social Democratic Party, as a cabinet minister. The Reichstag, the Bundesrat and the Kaiser then adopted the long-awaited constitutional reform, which even the High Command was now advocating – albeit for purely tactical reasons in view of Germany's imminent defeat. Henceforth the consent of the Reichstag and Bundesrat would be required for declarations of war and the conclusion of ceasefires and peace treaties; the Imperial Chancellor could no longer govern without the confidence of Parliament. And so Germany became a parliamentary monarchy – for all of two weeks.

In fact, revolution could no longer be averted. On 28 October, the day on which the constitutional reforms were adopted, a mutiny broke out on ships of the German Fleet. Within a few days, the disturbances had spread from Kiel to other Northern German towns; on 7 November, the Bavarian Wittels-

bach dynasty was overthrown in Munich. The monarchy's days were numbered. Under pressure from the insurgents, the Imperial Chancellor, Prince Max von Baden, felt compelled to announce the abdication of the Kaiser on his own authority. On 10 November, the day after the German Republic had been proclaimed in Berlin and the day before a German delegation headed by Matthias Erzberger accepted the Western Allies' ceasefire conditions and signed the armistice in Compiègne, William II fled to the neutral Netherlands. On 28 November 1918, he formally renounced the throne. The German Empire had ceased to exist.

III. THE WEIMAR REPUBLIC

Memelland ceded
to Lithuania

Northern Schleswig
ceded to Denmark

Remained part
of Germany
following a plebiscite

Königsberg

Free City
of Danzig

Remained part
of Germany
following a plebiscite

Hamburg

Posen and large parts
of West Prussia
ceded to Poland

Berlin

Occupied Ruhr District

Eupen-Malmédy
and Morosnet
ceded to Belgium

Cologne

Breslau

Remained part
of Germany
following a plebiscite

Eastern Upper Silesia ceded
to Poland

Occupied
Rhineland

Frankfurt

Hultschin Land ceded
to Czechoslovakia

Saarland administered
by the League of Nations
and occupied by France

Alsace-Lorraine
ceded to France

Munich

The German
Reich after
1918

After four hard years of war, the Germans' national fervour of August 1914 had given way to a sense of disillusionment and exhaustion. In view of their material prob lems, the population hardly noticed the parliamentarization of the Reich that had been initiated by a cross-party committee while fighting was still going on. The German people were finally awakened to the reality of defeat by the Kiel Mutiny in early November, which unleashed a wave of revolution that swept Germany, bringing about the collapse of the authoritarian monarchist regime. Under pressure from mass demonstrations, the Reich Chancellor, Prince Max of Baden, had little option but to announce William II's abdication without the Emperor's consent. On 9 November 1918, power was handed over to Friedrich Ebert, the leader of the majority Social Democrats, and Germany was proclaimed a republic by Philipp Scheidemann (SPD), bringing Hohenzollern rule over the German Reich to an end.

The Majority Social Democratic Party (MSPD) became the leading political force in Germany at this time, calling for the introduction of parliamentary democracy, proportional representation, women's suffrage and improvements to the workers' economic and legal situation. The party wanted at all costs to avoid a radicalization of the revolution and prevent the establishment of a Soviet-style republic. This was the avowed aim of the Spartacists, who, under the leadership of Karl Liebknecht, distanced themselves from the Social Democrats. Initially, however, workers' and soldiers' councils took control of many towns, led from the outset by Majority Social Democrats, but also by members of the Independent Social Democratic Party (USPD), which had split from the SPD in 1917.

On 10 November, the Berlin Workers' and Soldiers' Council recognized the Council of People's Representatives, which consisted of equal numbers of Majority Social Democrats and Independent Social Democrats, as Germany's provisional government. Within this body, the Majority Social Democrats continued to steer a staunchly anti-revolutionary course, calling for elections to set up a constituent National Assembly, which they expected to establish a parliamentary system of government. In order to find quick solutions to the country's pressing social and political problems, the new government fell back on the old military and bureaucratic elites, which to a large extent remained in their positions of leadership. The workers' and soldiers' councils, now dominated by MSPD supporters, finally cleared the way for elections to take place in early January. The results confirmed the Majority Social Democrats as the strongest political party. Together with the Centre Party and the German Democratic Party (DDP), they formed what was known as the "Weimar Coalition", which held a two-thirds majority in the constituent National Assembly. The first Reich President to be elected by parliament, Friedrich Ebert, was also drawn from the ranks of the Majority Social Democrats.

The Constitution drafted by Hugo Preuss, a left-liberal constitutional lawyer, was adopted with some modifications by the National Assembly on 11 August 1919. It satisfied the old liberal demand for parliamentary democracy, thereby guaranteeing direct popular influence over the political process. Extensive powers were conferred on the President, whose position was initially conceived as a counterweight to parliament. In the Republic's years of crisis, however, he became the central political figure in the country.

During the deliberations on the Constitution, decisions were made that severely disrupted efforts to stabilize the political system and poisoned public opinion in Germany for many years. At Versailles, the victorious powers demanded that Germany cede territory, accept restrictions on its sovereignty and pay reparations, which placed a lasting strain on the Republic in the economic and domestic policy fields. More than anything else, the declaration that Germany bore the sole guilt for the outbreak of the war was rejected with indignation by all sections of society and political camps. However, as the consequences of resuming military action would have been catastrophic, both domestically and in foreign policy terms, the National Assembly had little choice but to accept the peace treaty.

The extreme right, which was neither willing to admit that the country had been defeated in the war nor accept the parliamentary system of government, accused the parties that had worked for a negotiated peace in 1917 of having betrayed an "undefeated army", dealing it a fatal "stab in the back". The far right's activities culminated in attempted putsches and political assassinations. In turn, the equally anti-republican far-left forces resorted to protests and acts of violence in their attempts to rekindle the revolution, which they perceived to have "stalled". The first elections to the Reichstag took place in June 1920 under sustained internal and external pressure, and it soon became apparent how difficult it would be to form strong coalitions in future. The Weimar Coalition suffered a devastating defeat, losing its parliamentary majority, which it never regained in the years that followed. It was now impossible for the parties committed to democracy and loyal to the constitution to form a stable government. Eventually, the Centre Party, the German People's Party (DVP) and the DDP formed a minority administration tolerated by the SPD.

The financial burden imposed by the reparations demands rapidly became a permanent problem for both domestic and foreign policy. From the German government's perspective, the reparations placed excessive demands on the country's economy and threatened the solvency of the state. Endeavouring to bring inflation and the national debt under control, the government asked for a deferral of payments and permission to convert the reparations from cash transfers into consignments of goods. Germany's coalition governments repeatedly foundered on the reparations issue and proved unable to distribute the costs of the war in a socially equitable fashion. Ultimately, reparations payments, coupled with the occupation of the Ruhr by French and Belgian troops, pushed inflation to its peak in 1923. The redistribution of the nation's wealth shattered the fabric of German society and reinforced the widespread rejection of the Republic.

It was only the introduction of a new currency, the rentenmark, replaced shortly afterwards by the gold-backed reichsmark, that stabilized monetary conditions. This made the resumption of constructive reparations negotiations possible. The victorious powers now recognized that Germany was not economically in a position to meet their reparations claims. Despite severe difficulties, many enterprises managed to modernize their production facilities by taking out foreign capital investment loans. Real wages, production and export figures regained their pre-war levels around 1926, depending on the sector in question. As the economy recovered, the country's social and political development also entered calmer waters. Gustav Stresemann's achievements in the field of foreign policy were another factor that helped to ease political tensions. He succeeded in strenglhening the position of the Reich, mitigating the consequences of the war and re-establishing Germany as an equal negotiating partner in the international arena, lhereby making progress towards a revision of the Treaty of Versailles.

However, these developments were repeatedly jeopardized by other, conflicting tendencies and events. On the domestic front, the belief in the authoritarian state remained undiminished. Indications of this included the controversy over the expropriation of the territorial princes' assets, the attitude of the judiciary towards enemies of the Republic, and the tendency of the German armed forces, the *Reichswehr*, to form a state within the state. The hopes of anti-republicans loyal to the Emperor now centred on retired Field Marshal Paul von Hindenburg, who was elected Reich President in 1925 following the death of Friedrich Ebert, and who interpreted and applied the letter rather than the spirit of the Constitution.

The world economic crisis in the winter of 1929/30 brought this period of relative economic and political stability to an abrupt end. Many enterprises had financed their development with short-term loans from foreign investors, which were now being called in. In an effort to remain competitive, almost all sectors of the economy reacted by cutting wages and laying off staff. The consequence was a rapid rise in the numbers of unemployed, who suffered not just materially but psychologically as well, and became ever more receptive to the anti-republican slogans and promises of the right and left. The general feeling of insecurity also affected the middle classes, and they too paid increasing heed to the radical groups who continued and slepped up their agitation, further undermining the German people's dwindling confidence in the institutions of democracy and the ruling parties. The weaknesses of Weimar democracy and its institutions now became all too apparent, as did the lack of support for them among socially and politically influential groups, as well as broad sections of the population.

The Grand Coalition between the SPD and the bourgeois parties broke up in March 1930, ostensibly over the question of how the financial burdens of unemployment insurance should be distributed. At this moment, the Reich President, to whom the constitution granted considerable powers over parliament, became the key actor in German politics. Invoking Article 48 of the Weimar Constitution, he appointed the Reich Chancellor without consulting parliament – officially in order to avert a temporary state of emergency. On taking office, Heinrich Brüning (Centre Party), the man Hindenburg had chosen, stated bluntly that in future he would not feel himself "bound to any coalition" and, if necessary, would seek to govern on the basis of a system of emergency decrees that – since he could threaten to dissolve the Reichstag at any time – would make him independent of parliament. Not least on account of these events, many voters turned away from parliamentary democracy in disappointment and, at the elections held in September 1930, began voting for extremist parties, most notably the rising National Socialist German Workers' Party (NSDAP).

The inability of parliament to assemble a constructive majority, and the Chancellor's dependence on the personal and political trust of the Reich President steadily eroded the parliamentary system, revealing the unbridgeable ideological barriers and, above all, structural faults with which the Republic had been burdened from the very beginning. The centre of political power now shifted gradually from parliament and the parties to a small circle of anti-republicans who sought to win over the elderly Reich President to their ideas. Ultimately, various right-wing groups entered into a political alliance of convenience that, with the support of the Reich President, worked actively for the permanent establishment of an authoritarian, anti-parliamentarian, presidential regime. Hindenburg's re-election as Reich President in spring 1932 opened the way for this solution to the crisis.

Whereas the first presidential cabinet under Brüning accepted the principles of the rule of law when it took office and was tolerated by a majority in the Reichstag, the governments formed by Papen and Schleicher in 1932 were completely dependent on the favour of the Reich President and his advisers. However, the maintenance of presidential rule for purely tactical, power-political reasons contributed little to the solution of the country's urgent social and economic problems. In the end, despite serious reservations, the Reich President entrusted the formation of a presidential government to the man who had been making a name for himself for years as the most radical anti-republican opponent of parliament and who, by contrast with Papen and Schleicher, enjoyed mass support: Adolf Hitler, the leader of the National Socialist German Workers' Party.

1. The Revolution of 1918/19 and the birth of the Republic

The parliamentarization of the Reich was not achieved as a result of long-term planning and struggle by a broad republican movement, but was a consequence of the military defeat for which the armed forces and the monarchy were responsible, a defeat that led to the Revolution and made the establishment of the Republic possible.

Following the victory over Russia in March 1918, the military and political leadership believed they could decide the war in Germany's favour with a major offensive on the Western Front. After a few days, however, the German troops' advance had ground to a halt, and in the summer the Allied troops succeeded in making the decisive breakthrough at Amiens that turned the course of the war. The German Military High Command now had to admit to the country's political leaders that the war was lost and that com-

plete military collapse could only be avoided by offering the American President Woodrow Wilson a cease-fire and pleading for peace. In order to avoid defeat and save face, the military commanders, the monarchy and the existing Reich government were prepared to place the peace negotiations in the hands of a new administration enjoying parliamentary support. Shortly afterwards, Erich Ludendorff, the Military High Command's "secret" leader, explained the – purely tactical – calculation behind this move to his staff officers: "I asked His Majesty to involve those circles in the government whom we have principally to thank that we have come this far. Consequently, we will now see these gentlemen moving into the ministries. Let them conclude the peace that has to be concluded. Let them clear up the mess they have got us into."

Field Marshall Paul von Hindenburg (left) and Quarter-Master General Erich Ludendorff (right) discussing the military situation with William II at Central Headquarters in Spa (Belgium)

The Main Committee of the Reichstag, October 1918

The Parliamentarization Decree signed by the Emperor on 30 September 1918 paved the way from a constitutional to a parliamentary monarchy. In early October, the new Reich Chancellor, Prince Max of Baden, formed a cabinet made up of members of the Majority Social Democratic Party, the Progressive People's Party and the Centre Party, which held a joint majority in the Reichstag and had already been working together in the cross-party committee since 1917. The Committee had made repeated demands for the parliamentarization of the Reich executive, and this was also anchored in the constitution in late October.

However, the new government took office in the most unfavourable circumstances conceiv-

able. Under pressure from the Military High Command, and faced with a disastrous military situation, it sent a peace note to the American President, an admission of defeat that shocked the public by revealing the true nature of the situation. Wilson's conditions were understood by the population of Germany as a call for the Emperor's abdication. Many members of the governing parties believed that Germany would not gain fair terms for the cessation of hostilities unless this demand was satisfied.

William II and the military leadership were on no account ready to acknowledge the authority of the Reich government and submit to the American peace conditions. The situation came to a dramatic head when the Admiralty began making preparations for the High Seas Fleet to put to sea. The sailors saw their commanders' move as an attempt to sacrifice them senselessly in a final battle and deliberately sabotage government policy. Beginning with mutinies in the northern seaports, a revolutionary movement spread throughout Germany in a matter of days, also attracting the support of large numbers of factory workers. Spontaneously formed workers' and soldiers' councils assumed political and military control in many towns

Mutinying sailors of the German High Seas Fleet in Kiel, early November 1918

Armoured car on patrol in Berlin, November 1918

and cities. On 8 November 1918, the Bavarian House of Wittelsbach became the first German dynasty to be toppled.

On 9 November, a few days after the outbreak of the Kiel Mutiny, the wave of revolution reached Berlin. Here, by contrast with other cities, the political future of the Reich was at stake. The Reich Chancellor, Prince Max of Baden, believed that the new parliamentary monarchy could only survive if the Emperor abdicated. When William II refused to give up the throne completely, the Chan-cellor announced the abdication on his own authority and handed over the chancellorship to the leader of the Majority Social Democrats, Friedrich Ebert, from whom the revolutionary masses expected a new political beginning. Ebert's fellow Social Democrat Philipp Scheidemann proclaimed the "German Republic" from a window of the Reichstag, while a little later the same day the leader of the Spartacus League, Karl Liebknecht, speaking on the balcony of the Berlin City Palace, declared Germany a "Free Socialist Republic". From this point on, the conflicting

Left: Philipp Scheidemann proclaiming the "German Republic" from a window of the Reichstag Building, 9 November 1918

Right: Karl Liebknecht proclaiming the "Free Socialist Republic" from the balcony of the Berlin City Palace. Painting by Erhard Schlicht, 1954

ideas represented by the two men were to dominate the debates between reformist and revolutionary forces within the Social Democratic movement about the internal structures of the new Republic.

As in many other German towns and cities, real power in Berlin lay in the hands of the spontaneously elected workers' and soldiers' councils, which overwhelmingly supported the reformist policies of the Majority Social Democrats. In order to avoid "fraternal infighting", they transferred the provisional exercise of governmental power to the Council of People's Representatives, which consisted of equal numbers of Majority Social Democrats and Independent Social Democrats. Initially, this body had to ensure fuel and food supplies for the population, reintegrate returning soldiers into society, and maintain external and domestic security. The representatives of the MSDP, in particular, were convinced that it would only be possible to manage the consequences of the lost war by cooperating with the imperial bureaucracy, the military establishment and the business community. This cooperative approach, however, stood in the way of decisive political, social and economic reforms along democratic lines, which were delayed by the government on account of its immediate problems.

The question of the date for elections to the constituent National Assembly was politically more controversial in the Council of People's Representatives and of greater significance for the reorganization of the state. The left wanted fundamental socialist demands to be satisfied first. The radicals in the Spartacus League even called for the dissolution of the Council of People's Representatives and the establishment of a dictatorship of the proletariat. However, the Majority Social Democrats on the Council of People's Representatives insisted resolutely on the principle of parliamentary democracy and argued for a freely elected National Assembly to be convened that would decide on the future shape of the state and German society. They won a clear majority for this course in mid-December 1918 at the Reich Congress of Workers' and Soldiers' Councils. A motion calling for the prior establishment of a "system of councils as the basis for the constitution of the Socialist Republic" was rejected by the delegates. Due to the rapid pace of events, the proposals for the immediate "democratization" of the army, administration and economy tabled by the Independent Social Democratic Party and adopted by the Congress never came to fruition.

At the end of December, the Independent Social Democratic members on the Council

The Council of People's Representatives, November 1918. From left: Emil Barth, Otto Landsberg, Friedrich Ebert, Hugo Haase, Wilhelm Dittman and Philipp Scheidemann

Spartacists behind a barricade of paper rolls in Berlin's newspaper quarter, January 1919

of People's Representatives resigned, mainly due to fundamental differences over military policy, in particular with the Military High Command, and were replaced with two Majority Social Democrats. Their resignation was triggered by Ebert's order to deploy troops against a rebellious navy division with left-wing sympathies. The break between the two left-wing parties introduced a second, much more radical phase of the Revolution, which was unleashed spontaneously in January 1919 by extremists in the Communist Party of Germany (KPD), the Independent Social Democrats and the Revolutionary Shop Stewards. The attempt to topple Ebert and Scheidemann by means of an uprising was frustrated by the Free Corps, whom the government called upon for assistance. However, the troops with which the Majority Social Democrats wanted to protect the Republic were themselves anti-republican and felt no obligation to support the revolutionary executive. Although the restoration of security and order in Berlin had been announced, the Communist leaders Rosa Luxemburg and Karl Liebknecht were captured and brutally murdered by Free Corps officers. The progressive radicalization of the groupings on the left and right strengthened the MSPD leadership's readiness to

cooperate with the military and the bureaucracy. An alliance with the bourgeois parties to maintain order and stabilize the domestic situation was becoming increasingly likely.

In this heated political climate the elections to the National Assembly on 19 January, in which women were able to vote for the first time, ended with a clear victory for the moderate democratic parties. With a turnout of 83 percent, the Majority Social Democrats won the most seats and, in view of the tense political situation, decided not to join forces with the Independent Social Democrats but cooperate with the bourgeois parties that had been re-establishing themselves since November 1918. Together with the Centre Party and the German Democratic Party, the SPD formed what was known as the "Weimar Coalition", which was able to rely on the support of a three-quarters majority in the National Assembly. So as to be able to meet without disruption following the disturbances that had taken place in Berlin in January, the National Assembly convened at the National Theatre in Weimar on 6 February 1919. It elected Friedrich Ebert as the first President of the Republic, and shortly afterwards he swore in the first German government, led by the new Reich Minister President Phillip Scheidemann, to enjoy democratic, parliamentary legitimation.

The Weimar Constitution

Many aspects of the draft constitution presented in February by the new State Secretary of the Ministry of the Interior, the left-liberal professor of constitutional law Hugo Preuss, drew on the liberal, democratic tradition of 1848. The central political organ was now the Reichstag, which was responsible for legislation and the control of the executive. As regards their involvement in the legislative process, the constituent states, the *Länder*, which were represented in the Reichsrat, merely had an advisory function. In order to avoid "parliamentary absolutism" – something that conservatives were not alone in fearing – the Reich President was vested with extensive political powers. Elected directly by the people, the President also remained constitutionally independent of parliament.

His power to appoint governments, dissolve the Reichstag and even, on the basis of Article 48, temporarily suspend the most important fundamental rights in exceptional situations not only allowed him to act as a counterweight to parliament but, in conjunction with his function as Supreme Commander of the Armed Forces, effectively made him a kind of "substitute Emperor". Trusting that the Reich President would stand above party politics and remain faithful to the constitution, the National Assembly did not provide for any body to scrutinize his actions. Parliament's authority as the legislature was limited, not only by the Reich President's extraordinary powers, but also by the plebiscitary elements included in the constitution, such as the right of veto by referendum. The proportional system that replaced first-past-the-post voting was more democratic since it reflected the will of the electorate with greater accuracy; however, it encouraged a fragmentation of the party system that had the potential to paralyse parliamentarianism in times of crisis.

The National Theatre in Weimar on the day of the swearing-in of the Reich President, 11 February 1919

Reich President Friedrich Ebert at his desk in the Weimar Palace, February 1919

However – contrary to Preuss's rigidly centralist plans for the new order – Germany continued to have a federal constitution and Prussia still enjoyed a strong position, though the central Reich government gained greater power, particularly as a result of Erzberger's financial reforms in 1920. Nor was the basic form of the state created in 1871 questioned by any of the parties following the military defeat.

By contrast, the section of the Constitution setting out fundamental rights was the subject of long debates between the various political and social groups in parliament. For instance, the Centre Party was able to draft numerous provisions concerning ecclesiastical matters and education in line with its convictions, while the SPD gained acceptance for particular ideas about the state's role in welfare provision. Unlike the Basic Law of 1949, the Weimar Constitution did not make these fundamental rights directly enforceable in law.

The Weimar Constitution was adopted in late July and signed by the Reich President on 11 August. As a whole, it represented a compromise between the moderate Social Democrats and the liberal bourgeoisie. Despite its structural weaknesses, the constitution created, for the first time, the

Die Verfassung des Deutschen Reichs. Vom 11.August 1919.

Das Deutsche Volk,

einig in seinen Stämmen und von dem Willen beseelt, sein Reich in Freiheit und Gerechtigkeit zu erneuen und zu festigen, dem inneren und dem äußeren Frieden zu dienen und den gesellschaftlichen Fortschritt zu fördern, hat sich diese Verfassung gegeben.

foundations for the development of a democratic social order in Germany. However, it was confronted with a social reality that lagged far behind its ambitious goals and placed a heavy burden on the young Republic.

The German delegation during the negotiation of the peace conditions at Versailles, 1919

Removal of agricultural machinery to France, 1920

The Treaty of Versailles and its domestic consequences

The National Assembly had to discuss the final peace treaty even before it had adopted the Constitution. In early May, the peace conference which had been meeting in Paris since 18 January – without any involvement of the defeated parties – presented the German delegation with the final conditions for the acceptance of the Treaty of Versailles. The territories to be ceded, limitations on German sovereignty and reparations set out in the Treaty represented massive demands. Yet it was the fact that these demands were justified by Germany's sole guilt for the war that triggered a storm of outrage, uniting all political camps. As the Treaty was accompanied by an ultimatum and any rejection of it would have had catastrophic consequences, the National Assembly voted by a large majority to accept it. Regardless of the constraints under which the Treaty had been signed, those who had been involved in the political negotiations found themselves subjected to a vicious campaign of defamation from the extreme right. Matthias Erzberger, a Centre Party politician who had signed the Armistice, was particularly targeted by these attacks, which culminated in his assassination in 1921.

The signing of the Treaty of Versailles and the adoption of the Constitution by no means signalled the start of a phase of domestic political stabilization. With its agitation against the Treaty of Versailles, the politicians who favoured compliance with its conditions and the "November criminals" responsible for the Armistice in 1918, the extreme right sought to mobilize the masses in order to bring down the Republic. The Weimar Republic's first major crisis came when Wolfgang Kapp, the director of an East Prussian agricultural credit cooperative, and General Walther von Lüttwitz staged a putsch in Berlin on 13 March 1920. The leaders of the coup wanted to destroy the democratic, parliamentary state and replace it with an authoritarian regime. By refusing to use

Demonstration in Berlin against the Versailles Treaty, March 1919

Soldiers of
the Ehrhardt
Brigade raising
the Imperial
Navy Flag in
Berlin during
the Kapp
Putsch,
13 March 1920

Wolfgang
Kapp fleeing
to Sweden,
spring 1920

USDP demonstration in Berlin, 1920

armed force to put down the putsch, which was primarily supported by right-wing Free Corps, the country's military leaders were consciously accepting the government's potential downfall. Most of the cabinet and Reich President Ebert left the capital for Dresden. It was only the mobilization of social forces that prevented the coup from succeeding. Apart from a small number of conservatives, the putsch had no active support and collapsed in the face of a general strike called by the unions and the SPD, and the wait-and-see attitude of the ministerial bureaucracy. Nevertheless, having returned to Berlin, the government failed to exploit this defeat as an opportunity to replace personnel in government institutions and the military apparatus, and take firm action to stabilize the democratic system.

The radicalization of domestic politics, the difficult economic and social problems resulting from the war, and Germany's almost hopeless situation in the field of foreign policy were reflected in the results of the Reichstag elections held on 6 June 1920. The far-right and far-left parties were able to increase their vote considerably, while the Weimar Coalition lost almost 40 percent of its seats and with them its majority in parliament, which it was never able to regain. This was the beginning of years of political instability, during which minority cabinets replaced each other in rapid succession.

2. The parties of the Weimar Republic

By contrast to Imperial Germany, the Revolution of 1918/19 and the adoption of the Weimar Constitution made the parties the real bearers of political power. Although new parties were founded, particularly on the left and right margins of the political spectrum, the old pre-war party system remained largely in place. The parties had been shaped by Imperial Germany and, although they had been renamed, superficially taking account of the conditions of the new age, there were barely any major changes of personnel and little was done to adapt to the requirements of a democratic parliamentary order. The larger parties still regarded themselves as representing relatively clearly defined social groups and ideologies. In order not to disappoint their potential voters, they were reluctant to assume the responsibility of government, which often involved taking unpopular decisions. With this approach, they were hardly capable of resolving political problems through compromise or building stable majorities in the Reichstag. The controversies about policies and objectives also led to splits and factionalism within the parties, creating insecurity among both party members and the wider electorate over the long term.

The elections to the constituent National Assembly resulted in the formation of the "Weimar Coalition", a viable governing alliance consisting of the SPD, the Centre Party and the DDP, which were all committed to the new state. However, from June 1920 onward, the responsibility for government lay for the most part in the hands of politically unstable minority cabinets. Furthermore, the conflicts that repeatedly broke out between the parliamentary groups and the Reich governments that depended on their support hindered constructive, consistent policy-making.

Long before the profound crisis of the state in the 1930s, the parties and parliament were failing to exercise constructively the responsibility for governing and scrutinizing the actions of the executive that fell to them following the collapse of Imperial Germany. The structural weaknesses of the party-based parliamentary system ultimately made the Reich President the decisive political figure in times of crisis and supplied authoritarian, anti-democratic groups with powerful arguments, helping them to agitate against the "irresponsible", "incompetent" rule of the parties and parliament.

The lasting polarization of politics was also reflected in the range of parties active in the Weimar Republic, which extended from advocates of a Soviet-style state to supporters of the Republic and proponents of an authoritarian military dictatorship.

Reichstagswahl
Wahlkreis Potsdam II

1	Sozialdemokratische Partei Deutschlands Zubeil — Bernstein — Künstler — Ryneck	1	○
2	Deutschnationale Volkspartei Graf von Westarp — Geisler — Ohler — Mueller-Otfried	2	○
3	Deutsche Zentrumspartei Dr. Beufch — Schönborn — Dr. Salzgeber — Frohn	3	○
4	Kommunisten Geschke — Bierath — Nebe — Roth	4	○
5	Deutsche Volkspartei von Kardorff — Dr. Luther — Schwarz — Margis	5	○
6	Nationalsozialistische Freiheitsbewegung Groß-Deutschlands Wulle — Kube — Dr. v. Brehmer — Dr. Malguth	6	○
7	Deutsche Demokratische Partei Dr. Dernburg — Nuschke — Dr. von Hülsen — Emmeluth	7	○
9	Wirtschaftspartei des deutschen Mittelstandes Drewitz — Cloffer — Bernhäufer — Simon	9	○
11	Deutsch-Hannoversche Partei Alpers — Nölte	11	○
13	Freiwirtschaftsbund F.F.F. (Freiland-Freigeld) Beckmann — Lugzat — Webermann — Dr. Großheide	13	○
14	Haeuffer-Bund Louis Haeuffer — Olga Haeuffer — Juels — Kappbahn	14	○
15	Polnische Volkspartei Karolczat — Grzesiat — Ledwolorz — Wierzoret	15	○
16	Unabhängige Sozialdemokratische Partei Deutschlands Liebknecht — Wiegmann — Kiefel — Gronwald	16	○
17	Aufwertungs- und Wiederaufbaupartei Brenneisen — Marschner — Große — Schubert	17	○
18	Deutsch-Soziale Partei und Reichsbund für Aufwertung Kunze — Drewin — Schäffer — Hach	18	○
19	Deutsche Aufwertungs- und Aufbaupartei Noll — von Herwitz — Ginschel — Dr. Heine	19	○

Opposite page: Demonstration supporting the elections to the National Assembly on 19 January 1919

Ballot paper for the Reichstag elections, 1920

The Communist Party of Germany

In the Weimar system, the extreme left was represented by the Communist Party of Germany (KPD), which was founded in Berlin on 1 January 1919 by members of the radical wing of the USPD (the Spartacus League) and left radicals from Bremen. Its political programme was based on a pamphlet written by Rosa Luxemburg, *What Does the Spartacus League Want?*, which defined the group's aims as the formation of a socialist republic and the replacement of the parliamentary system with a constitution on the Soviet model.

The KPD became a mass party in late 1920 when it merged with the left wing of the Independent Social Democrats. In the early years of the Weimar Republic it sought to use violence to realize its social and economic ideas, which were based on a dogmatic interpretation of Marxism. Following its abandonment of putsch tactics in 1923/24, the KPD modelled itself ever more closely on the Soviet Communist Party, both organizationally and in policy terms. Following the economic and political crisis of 1929/30, the Communists enjoyed increasing popularity and again adopted an uncompromising stance, opposing and undermining the

Poster advertising *The Red Flag*, the central organ of the Spartacus League

Weimar Republic. Completely misjudging the policies of the National Socialists, the Communists concentrated on campaigning against the Social Democrats, whom they denounced as "social fascists". By doing so, they did much to facilitate Hitler's seizure of power.

KPD electoral propaganda for the Reichstag elections on 14 September 1930

The Social Democratic Party of Germany and the Independent Social Democratic Party of Germany

Even during the Imperial period, there were fundamental internal disagreements within the Social Democratic Party of Germany (SPD) between the political pragmatists who supported parliamentary methods and revolutionaries who believed in a democracy based on workers' and soldiers' councils. In 1917, differences over war credits and the general conduct of the war led the Independent Social Democratic Party of Germany (USPD) to break away from the SPD, which then came to be known as the Majority Social Democratic Party (MSPD). However, there continued to be major conflicts between moderates and radicals within the new organization. While the majority of the party favoured socialist reforms, its left wing tended to support the radical programme of the Spartacus League. The November Revolution finally forced the party to decide where it stood. The majority of the USPD were in favour of cooperation with the MSPD in the Council of People's Representatives. However, the party was unable to overcome the MSPD's resistance to its ideas about greater political involvement for the working classes and left the coalition after a few weeks. This acceler-

SPD electoral poster, 1920s

ated the radicalization of the USPD's members, leading to the party's ultimate disintegration in 1922.

Following the 1918/19 Revolution, the SPD, as the strongest party in the Reichstag, found itself playing a leading political role. Under Friedrich Ebert's leadership, the party very

Cyclists carrying USPD placards and flags in Berlin, 1921

Wählt verfassungstreu

SPD electoral
poster, 1932

consciously took a pragmatic, anti-revolutionary political approach that enabled it
to cooperate with the bourgeois parties.
However, it also turned to anti-democratic
forces in the military and the administration
for support in stabilizing the democratic
parliamentary Republic, which lost the party
a considerable number of votes in the
Reichstag elections of June 1920. The leadership's attempts to extend its core electorate
beyond its traditionally proletarian supporters and transform the SPD into a "left-wing
mass party" (Heinrich August Winkler) were
frustrated by internal disputes. Despite this,
the SPD remained the strongest parliamentary group in the Reichstag until 1932 and
therefore continued to bear a great deal of
parliamentary responsibility. However, it
refused to join governments during the
relatively stable phase of the Republic because working with the bourgeois parties
would have forced it to make concessions
that could have compromised it in the eyes
of its supporters. In consequence, the Social
Democrats repeatedly found themselves
torn between their loyalty to their ideological principles and the requirements of government responsibility. These conflicts often
forced the SPD onto the defensive and –
despite the significant role played by the
party in decision-making on domestic and
foreign policy – not infrequently prevented it
BVP electoral　from actively influencing the political course
poster, 1919　taken by the Republic.

The Centre Party and the Bavarian People's Party

Following the failure of initial attempts to
form an inter-denominational party, the
Centre Party was re-established in 1918/19
and again became a key political force
within the Catholic electorate. The social
spectrum of its supporters extended from
large landowners and heavy industrialists to
small farmers and Christian trade unionists,
which forced the party to struggle continually to balance widely diverging interests and
pushed it into the political middle ground.
While the Bavarian People's Party (BVP) was
formed in 1918 by Bavarian conservatives
who advocated the restoration of the monarchy and the federal principle, the majority
of the Centre Party – albeit with reservations
– supported the democratic parliamentary
Republic. The Centre Party played an important mediating role between 1919 and 1932,
taking part in all the Reich governments
during this period and providing the Reich
Chancellor on several occasions. Only under
the leadership of Ludwig Kaas, who was

rettet · die · heimat

wählt
Bayerische Volkspartei

DDP poster for the Reichstag elections in 1924

elected party chairman in 1928, and in particular during the chancellorship of Heinrich Brüning, did the party's authoritarian, anti-parliamentary elements gradually gain the upper hand. It became less and less willing to support the Republic by entering into viable governing coalitions with the Social Democrats at national level.

The German Democratic Party and the German People's Party

In the last months of the war, nationalists and left-wing liberals were already considering a merger between their parties that would enable them to represent the interests of the bourgeoisie more effectively. However, the plans for the merger collapsed in November 1918 as a result of differing economic and social policy ideas, as well as political reservations about particular leading individuals in their predecessor parties.

The initially stronger left-liberal forces gathered in the German Democratic Party

(DDP), the majority of whose members had belonged to the now dissolved Progressive People's Party and the left wing of the National Liberal Party. With its professed belief in the sovereignty of the people, the DDP wished to gain a following among the pro-republican Protestant bourgeoisie, and act as both a counterweight and bridge to the strong socialist forces. The DDP emerged from the elections to the National Assembly as the third-strongest party and, as part of the Weimar Coalition, made a major contribution to the drafting of the Constitution. However, it lost almost half its seats in the ensuing Reichstag elections. This trend accelerated in 1923 as a result of the inflation crisis and the fact that middle-class businesspeople, above all, turned away from the party. In the end, despite a reorganization in 1930, this reduced the DDP to a splinter party that had failed to convert its theoretical ideals into pragmatic, modern economic and social policies or balance the various interests it represented.

Left:
Centre Party electoral poster, 1930s

The DDP lost votes mainly to the German People's Party (DVP), which was founded with parallel aims in December 1918 and drew supporters above all from the right wing of the national liberals. Above all, the DVP represented the interests of big business and sections of the educated middle classes, initially emphasizing its distance from the Social Democrats, calling for the

Wählt meine Partei
die Deutsche
Volkspartei

DVP electoral poster, 1932

The German National People's Party

The German National People's Party (DNVP) was formed in December 1918 overwhelmingly by supporters of the conservative parties of Imperial Germany, as well as *völkisch* (racist nationalist) associations and other anti-Semitic groups whose long-term aim was the restoration of the monarchy. The party was dominated by large landowners and heavy industrialists, but also attracted a broad range of voters with its patriotic slogans, including officers, civil servants, academics, office workers and small farmers. Although the party initially saw its role as fighting the parliamentary system, as well as socialist and communist tendencies, this approach threatened to lose it votes as long as the Republic remained superficially stable. The DNVP joined governments formed in 1925 and 1927 in order to gain greater political influence and effectively promote the essentially economic interests of its supporters. The internal discrepancy between principled

establishment of a strong central power and secretly refusing to rule out the restoration of the monarchy. However, the party's chairman, Gustav Stresemann, used the years that followed to mould it into a party able to assume the responsibilities of government on several occasions and win over broad sections of the population by pursuing a successful foreign policy that genuinely served the national interest. Stresemann's conciliatory approach to foreign affairs and his mediating role, both within his own party and between the governing parties, were strong assets in the struggle to mobilize voters, but were lost after he died in 1929. Nevertheless, it was not just the death of its impressive leader, but also the wider crisis of liberalism that reduced the DVP to a splinter party after 1930.

Frei von Versailles!
Los von jüdisch-sozialistischer Front!
für Freiheit u. Vaterland!
Deine Losung
Deutschnational!

DNVP electoral poster, 1920s

The DNVP's Berlin campaign headquarters

opposition and active cooperation continued to burden the DNVP and, in 1928, led to a power struggle won by the right wing of the party around Alfred Hugenberg. Under his leadership, the DNVP again became a purely oppositional party and also sought to cooperate with the National Socialists in order to achieve its anti-republican aims.

The National Socialist German Workers' Party

In the spring of 1920 the German Workers' Party was renamed as the National Socialist German Workers' Party (NSDAP). In the early years of the Republic it was just one of many organizations on the extreme nationalist right that formed rallying points for the members of older anti-Semitic, *völkisch* groupings and the Free Corps of the revolutionary period. These groups, most of which were regionally based, sought to bring about the rapid downfall of the parliamentary

Republic, resorting to political murders, attempted coups and aggressive protests to achieve their aims. During its early years, the NSDAP's activities, mainly organized from Bavaria, were also directed at bringing about

NSDAP electoral poster, 1933

NSDAP
election rally
at the Berlin
Sport Palace,
September
1930

Hitler giving a
speech during
electoral cam-
paigning, April
1932

a political coup. The 1923 November Putsch led by Hitler in Munich was a dismal failure and resulted in the fragmentation of the National Socialist movement. However, by early 1925 Hitler, acting as party chairman, had begun to rebuild the NSDAP, establishing a disciplined organization throughout the Reich. The intention was now to distinguish the party more clearly from other extremist groupings and undermine parliamentary democracy by legal means – though without completely abandoning the use of violence. In the years that followed, Hitler successfully eliminated his internal opponents, subordinating the party and its organization to himself both personally and in policy terms. However, it was only during the severe economic, social and political crisis after 1929 that the NSDAP actually gained greater electoral support, becoming a political home for opponents of the parliamentary system from all social backgrounds, as well as victims of the catastrophic economic and social situation.

3. 1923: A year of crisis

Four years after the November Revolution, the Weimar Republic had still not achieved stability. Within a year, it was to face its hardest test thus far on both the foreign and domestic policy fronts.

The German Government's request to be granted a reprieve on its reparations liabilities, which was rejected by the Reparations Commission, triggered a series of crises. When, at the beginning of the year, the deliveries of wood and coal which Germany was obliged to make failed to materialize, French and Belgian troops marched into the Ruhr, aiming to use the German coal-mining region as an economic and political pawn. The French were not merely intending to underline their claims to reparations through this occupation. Secretly, they were aiming to shift the Franco-German border.

In Germany, the occupation of the Ruhr set in motion a national wave of protest, supported by all sections of society. The Reich Government, devoid of any means of exerting diplomatic or military pressure, called on the population of the Ruhr to put up passive resistance. The aim was to show the French and Belgians that their policy of using Germany's industrial heartland as a political pawn would not pay off. Despite appeals by the Reich Government, this passive resistance soon gave way to acts of sabotage by right-wing extremists. These acts were tacitly tolerated by the Government, and punished severely by the occupying forces.

But time was running out for both the population of the Ruhr, whose suffering was growing, and the German Government. The costs of the resistance campaigns, together

French "bicycle brigade", Essen, 1923

Hände weg vom Ruhrgebiet!

German propaganda postcard, 1923

regions. Reich Chancellor Wilhelm Cuno (independent) and his cabinet were unable to find a way out of their policy, which was no longer tenable either financially or diplomatically. On 13 August 1923, the Government was replaced by a "Grand Coalition" comprising the SPD, DDP, Centre and DVP and led by the new Reich Chancellor and DVP Chairman Gustav Stresemann. In the face of resistance from the left wing of the SPD and the right wing of his own party, Stresemann succeeded in gaining parliamentary support for the unconditional cessation of the struggle in the Ruhr. In the Reichstag, he countered the nationalist Right's accusations that he was a traitor by arguing: "The courage to assume responsibility for abandoning passive resistance is perhaps more nationalist than the slogans with which the decision was opposed." At the same time, Stresemann's Government took financial policy measures to halt the

with the shortfalls in tax revenue and the drop in industrial production, created state debt on an unforeseen scale. From April onwards, it became impossible to finance the resistance from regular revenues alone; most of the costs were covered by loans provided by the Reichsbank and by printing extra money.

Inflation, already rampant as a result of the reparations liabilities and war debts, now developed into hyperinflation. The Mark became completely worthless, leading to a further deterioration in the social and economic situation throughout the Reich. There were looting and hunger strikes in some

French soldier on a requisitioned coal train, 1923

Kaufe:
Stampfpapier: 20,000
Lumpen: 50,000 Mark.
Knochen: 5,000 Mark.

downward slide of the German currency. The introduction of the Rentenmark in November 1923 soon helped to stabilize the economic and social situation.

Coup attempts from left and right

The domestic and economic crisis in autumn 1923 also provided the extreme left and right with an ideal breeding ground for coup attempts outside the Ruhr. Supported by the French and Belgian occupying powers, separatist groups had been carrying out violent attacks in the Rhineland and the Palatinate since August, hoping to secure economic and political advantages by declaring independent republics. But the separatists were defeated due to public

resistance, not least as a result of their brutal excesses, and were promptly abandoned by the French as well.

But the coup attempts in central Germany, Hamburg and Bavaria proved even more of a threat to the Republic's existence. From summer onwards, the KPD, with Moscow's backing, had been preparing for revolutionary action in Saxony and Thuringia. Boosted by its government alliances with the SPD in Dresden and Weimar, the KPD now sought to bring about the violent overthrow of the state with the help of the "proletariat masses". But its plans were thwarted by the Reich Government, which forced the departure of the KPD from the two *Land* governments, invoking Article 48 of the Constitution, the so-called emergency clause, and

Trading worthless money following the introduction of the *Rentenmark* on 15 November 1923

sent in the Reichswehr to disarm the paramilitary combat units. Parallel to this, an unsuccessful uprising unleashed by the Communists in Hamburg also proved unsuccessful.

In Southern Germany, by contrast, the Republic was under threat from the right. Following the November Revolution and the forcible removal of the Munich soviet republic, Bavaria had emerged as a hotbed of reactionary conservatism and extreme right-wing activity. The Bavarian State Government used the cessation of passive resistance in the Ruhr as an opportunity to impose a state of emergency and forge plans to establish a dictatorship. The attempt by the Reich President to reverse this unauthorized action by the State Chancellery by invoking Article 48 failed due to the refusal of the Reichswehr command to fire on its own people. From 8 to 9 November, Hitler exploited this political and military state of

emergency to attempt a coup. He compelled the Bavarian State Government to resign by force of arms and demanded that its political and military leaders join the "National Revolution" and the "March on Berlin". By agreeing under duress to these demands, the Government regained room for manoeuvre, which it was then able to exploit in order to put down the NSDAP's amateurish coup attempt. The failure of Hitler's attempted coup also foiled the Bavarian State Government's plans to establish a national dictatorship. The NSDAP, German *völkische* Freedom Party and KPD were temporarily outlawed throughout the Reich.

Thus, by the end of 1923, the Republic had withstood its most difficult test so far and thwarted the attempted coups from the left and the right. With its prompt action to end the struggle in the Ruhr and the introduction of the currency reform, the Republic had once again gained room for manoeuvre in

The Reichswehr marching into Dresden at the end of October 1923

SA troop carrier, 9 November 1923

The defendants in the "Hitler Trial", 1924

The initiators of the currency reform: Gustav Stresemann (right) and Hans Luther, Finance Minister from 1923 to 1925

the foreign policy arena and laid the foundations for a phase of relative economic and social calm.

Yet the surmounting of the crisis did not banish the doubts about the Republic which existed within the bureaucracy, the military and judiciary, as well as among large sections of the population. Among the middle classes in particular, who were hit hard by inflation, there was widespread disaffection, which governments in the years to come were unable to dispel.

4. Domestic stabilization and ongoing conflicts

In the five years between 1924 and 1929, relative stability was achieved for the first time on the domestic, foreign policy and economic fronts. Yet even during this period of comparative calm, the Parliament and the political parties were unable to consolidate the political and socio economic system over the long term. As the Weimar coalition still had no parliamentary majority during this period, the coalitions or minority governments produced were extremely volatile. Government policies generally failed due to the uncompromising stance of coalition partners, especially with regard to economic and social policy. A further problem for the parliamentary system was the parliamentary groups' attitude towards the Reich governments which they formally supported. As the opinion-forming process within the parliamentary groups was shaped by frequently shifting alliances within the parties, cabinet ministers could never be fully confident of the support of their party colleagues.

The parties' inability to make compromises – and thus to assume genuine government responsibility – led, in this phase too, to frequent intervention by the Reich President, on whom the governments became increasingly dependent. The associated erosion of Parliament's power was evident from the ongoing conflicts, resulting in the ousting of the coalition government in question or at least a government crisis.

At the end of 1923, following a vote of no confidence in Stresemann tabled by the SPD, a minority government of the bourgeois parties, led by Reich Chancellor Wilhelm Marx (Centre Party) was established. This government, which was not dependent on a parliamentary majority, was able, on the

Friedrichstrasse in Berlin, a favourite place for shopping and strolling, in the mid-1920s

Constitution Day ceremony in the plenary chamber of the Reichstag, 11 August 1927

basis of a temporary Enabling Act, to adopt a number of measures designed to bring about domestic and economic stability. Following the lifting of the state of emergency in February 1924, the Marx cabinet realized that the chances of the Enabling Act being extended by the Reichstag were slim. In order to prevent the amendment or repeal of ordinances which had already been agreed, the Reich President, at the request of the cabinet, dissolved Parliament and called an early election. There was a sharp drop in

Delegates at the London Reparations Conference in the summer of 1924; in the front row, fourth from left, the American banker and chief negotiator Charles Gates Dawes

Propaganda for the Reichstag elections on 7 December 1924

the votes received by the governing parties loyal to the Republic in particular, as voters blamed them for the economic and social effects of the crisis. Once again, problems surfaced in seeking to form a coalition, as the SPD refused to take on government responsibility and there was little chance that a government majority in Parliament could be achieved without the DNVP as the second strongest parliamentary group.

The DNVP's stance on the Dawes Plan now became the central issue in the coalition negotiations. The Dawes Plan aimed to link the level and type of reparations to how the German economy was actually performing and provided for closer economic cooperation with the Americans. Although the nationalist DNVP had reservations about the Dawes Plan and whipped up public support against its acceptance, the majority of its Members gave way under pressure from the influential industrial lobbies. But the coalition negotiations failed all the same, this time because of the negative stance of the Centre Party and sections of the DDP. In the Reichstag elections which followed in December 1924, the gradual stabilization of the economic and political situation was

reflected in a fall in the number of seats won by the extreme left and right. But the right-wing "Citizens' Bloc" Government formed by the Centre Party, BVP, DVP and DVNP, led by the independent Hans Luther, who had close links with the DVP, was also short-lived. By October 1925, the coalition had collapsed due to the differences of opinion between the DNVP parliamentary group and the coalition on a key foreign policy issue, which led to the loss of its parliamentary majority.

The 1925 Reich President elections

Not long after the formation of the first right-wing government, the political conflicts in the Reichstag were overshadowed by the death of Reich President Friedrich Ebert at the end of February 1925. The head of state's powerful position in relation to the Reichstag had already become evident during Ebert's tenure. Thus it was clear that the election of the new Reich President would send out a signal either for or against the parliamentary system. Following a first round of elections in which none of the candidates won an absolute majority, the parties of the Weimar coalition nominated

State funeral for Reich President Friedrich Ebert, 1925

Opposite page:
Top:
Propaganda in support of Paul von Hindenburg for the presidential elections on 26 April 1925

Bottom:
Paul von Hindenburg being sworn in as Reich President in the Reichstag, 12 May 1925

Wilhelm Marx, a committed defender of the Republic, as their contender. The right wing also identified a suitable challenger, the "victor of Tannenberg", 77-year-old Paul von Hindenburg, who had retained his popular appeal. Hindenburg was politically inexperienced, but he was astutely advised and presented himself in the election campaign as a defender of the Fatherland and a constitutional loyalist. The votes of the BVP supporters enabled him to secure a surprise victory and become the new Reich President.

Initially, however, Hindenburg neither confirmed the fears of the left nor fulfilled the expectations of the right. A monarchist at heart, he regarded himself as bound by his oath of allegiance to the constitution, although he followed its letter rather than its spirit. Nevertheless, a covert constitutional shift took place during his time in office, evident from the attempt to strengthen the Reich President's position in relation to Parliament. When, at the end of 1926 for example, an implementing law for Article 48 of the Weimar Constitution was brought forward which would have restricted his powers, he made clear in no uncertain terms to the Reich Chancellor that the Reich President must be given "a free hand in taking defensive measures to avert threats". Regardless of the changing political alliances and imperatives, he backed participation by the DNVP during government crises and spoke out against social democracy. While Ebert had demonstrated his unconditional support for parliamentary democracy through his non-partisan leadership, the same can hardly be said of Hindenburg.

The "flag dispute" and the expropriation of the princes' assets

In 1926, a series of domestic crises occurred which served to boost the conservative trend which began with the election of

Reichspräsident von Hindenburg bei der Eidesleistung am 12. 5. 25.

Reich President Hindenburg at the inauguration of a memorial commemorating his August 1914 victory at the Battle of Tannenberg

Hindenburg and prevented a long-term stabilization of the domestic situation.

Just four months after the formation of the second Luther cabinet in January 1926 following lengthy negotiations, disagreement erupted over the Flags Regulation. In 1919, the National Assembly had made a concession to the supporters of the Kaiserreich, allowing its black, white and red flag to be displayed alongside the official black, red and gold Reich flag on merchant vessels. But many Germans living abroad wanted the old colours to be granted some kind of formal status. Hindenburg took up their cause, pressurizing the cabinet into enacting a Flags Regulation which allowed the black, white and red flag to be flown at diplomatic and consular missions abroad. This amendment, whose constitutionality was questionable, proved domestically explosive, triggering unruly protest demonstrations and a two-day battle of words in the Reichstag. The opponents of the Regulation saw it as an attempt to undermine the Republic and its symbols. Finally, a motion of no confidence tabled by the Social Democrats led to the resignation of the Luther cabinet, although the Regulation itself was not repealed.

The continuing influence of the conservative forces soon became evident on a further contentious issue. In contrast to the situation in Austria, the property of the German princes was not expropriated in 1918/1919, but merely confiscated. In the years which followed, negotiations took place in which the former landowners were able to win concessions, which meant that either their assets would be returned, or substantial compensation paid. In view of the high levels of unemployment, the KPD, SPD and the unions supported a bill providing for the expropriation of the princes' assets "for the public good", without payment of compensation. As the bourgeois parties in the Reichstag opposed the law, it was decided to bypass Parliament and hold a referendum on 20 June 1926 to endorse the

Cartoon illustrating the dispute over the Flags Regulation, from the *Kladderadatsch* magazine, May 1926

SPD propaganda procession by the SPD, campaigning for the expropriation of the princes' assets in summer 1926

bill. However, the Government, at Hindenburg's request, classified the bill as a law amending the constitution. This meant that it could only be adopted with an absolute majority of those eligible to vote. Although there was a great deal of support for expropriation, even outside SPD and KPD circles, the first referendum in the Weimar Republic's history failed. At the same time, this SPD-initiated plebiscite nurtured the mistrust within the bourgeois parties; as a result, despite several attempts to reach agreement, no coalition had been formed between these parties by the time the Reichstag elections took place in May 1928.

The 1928 Reichstag elections

The Citizens' Bloc, led by Reich Chancellor Marx, broke up as the result of controversy over the reintroduction of strictly separate Catholic and Protestant elementary schools. The left-wing parties made significant gains in the elections in May 1928, while the bourgeois centre parties and the DNVP saw the number of their seats decline. This meant that government participation by the SPD once again became likely. However, the fragmentation of the moderate bourgeois parties, reflected in particular in gains by the smaller parties, and the shift to the right by the Centre Party and DNVP, triggered by the election of new party chairmen, demonstrated that it was becoming increasingly difficult to form stable majority governments.

At this point, only a Grand Coalition could have secured a parliamentary majority, and although the SPD abandoned its opposition to this, strong reservations remained within the Centre Party and the DVP. However, after intervention by Stresemann, a government was finally formed. This cabinet initially lacked support from its own parliamentary groups and thus became known as the "cabinet of personalities". Although the Grand Coalition formed under Reich Chancellor and SPD Chairman Hermann Müller was to be the Republic's most enduring government, differences on social and economic policy

The Chairman of the DNVP, Alfred Hugenberg (centre) at a ceremony commemorating the founding of the Reich, 1931

Reich Chancellor Hermann Müller (SPD), delivering his government policy statement in the Reichstag, 3 July 1928

threatened to erode the cohesion of the coalition.

Within only a few weeks of being formed, the coalition faced a major test. The building of the Armoured Cruiser A, which had been agreed by the Citizens' Bloc, had initially been postponed due to lack of funds. The new government now voted to begin construction. But the SPD, which – as the opposition party – had spoken out against the project during the election campaign, refused to back its government members on the project. The Reich Chancellor and his SPD ministers were thus forced to vote against the cabinet decision in the Reichstag, which not only made the work of the coalition

more difficult, but also shook the voters' faith in the cabinet's ability to govern.

Initially, however, the generally successful cooperation on foreign policy issues distracted attention from the domestic policy disagreements within the coalition. But in 1929, a furious dispute erupted both in the public arena and within the Reichstag over the acceptance of the Young Plan, which was intended to establish permanent arrangements regarding reparations and the settlement of claims. The new DNVP Chairman, Alfred Hugenberg, initiated a referendum against the Young Plan, which was exploited by Hitler for propaganda purposes. The referendum failed, but it brought the DNVP

KPD demon-
stration in
Berlin against
the production
of Armoured
Cruiser A,
August 1928

Poster promot-
ing the
referendum
against the
Young Plan

and NSDAP closer together in the Reichstag and fuelled the aggressive and revisionist mood within the Reich. Although the extremist parties voted against the Young Plan, it was adopted by a majority of parliamentarians. Yet, in light of the increasing social and economic problems caused by the worldwide depression, this foreign policy success went virtually unnoticed by the German people. The left and right wings of the coalition now began to pursue their own divergent interests when tackling the problems at hand. The common ground within the coalition soon disappeared.

5. The Great Depression of 1929 and its consequences

With the onset of the worldwide depression, hopes of stabilizing the parliamentary system in Germany on a more enduring basis were dashed. From 24 October 1929, stocks on New York's Wall Street had been in free fall. As a result of years of over-investment, a surplus of goods had been created for which there was no demand. Shareholders and speculators reacted by panic-selling. In order to retain their liquidity, the US banks withdrew the funds which they had used to make short-term investments in Europe. The intermeshed international financial systems and economies meant the American slump spread rapidly, developing into the greatest economic crisis of the 20th century. Germany's economy was hit hardest of all, as around three-quarters of the short and medium-

term foreign loans granted both to industry and to local and municipal authorities had been used for long-term investments. The consequences were a decline in investment, factory closures, wage cuts, mass unemployment and a protectionist tariff policy. These, in turn, led to an economic slump which developed into a structural crisis in both Germany and the other industrialized countries.

In particular, the costs resulting from the rapid increase in unemployment presented the Parliament and government with seemingly intractable problems. Finally, the grand coalition collapsed as the result of the dispute over the financing of unemployment insurance, which prompted the SPD to walk

Crowd on Wall Street in New York following the October 1929 stock market crash

Dole queues in Berlin, 1930

Unemployed people scanning the newspapers for jobs, around 1930

A crowd of worried savers outside the closed doors of the Berliner Bank, 1931

Slum tenement in Hanover, 1930

People queuing at a Berlin slaughterhouse for scraps of substandard meat, 1931

out. Believing that their interests were now too divergent to be reconciled, the parties failed to take advantage of their last opportunity to form a government majority in Parliament. Without parliamentary involvement, the Reich President now set up a government led by Reich Chancellor Heinrich Brüning (Centre Party) equipped with special powers. This government tried to defuse the crisis by pursuing a stringent anti-inflationary policy. Government spending was slashed, taxes raised, civil servants' salaries cut and incomes reduced. But Brüning's economic and financial policy simply reinforced the economic slump, which he believed to be only temporary. By 1932, industrial production had dropped to just over half its 1928 level, and shares lost two-thirds of their value. A further worsening of the crisis in 1931 led to the collapse of several banks, which brought down a number of leading companies. Unemployment, which had already been high during the years of relative prosperity, soared in the early 1930s.

Whereas only 1.3 million people had been without work in September 1929, by the start of 1932, over six million people were registered unemployed, compared with just 12 million in work. This meant that one in every three members of the workforce was jobless. Despite numerous attempts by the national and local authorities to ease the suffering through job creation measures, the depression caused impoverishment in broad sections of society. The voters increasingly lost confidence in the governing parties' ability to solve their problems and turned their backs on parliamentarianism. Faced with this social and economic crisis and increasing political radicalization, the foundations of the parliamentary system, which had never been particularly solid, began to reveal deep cracks.

6. The disintegration of the Republic

München, 5. Oktober 1931   36. Jahrgang Nr. 27

SIMPLICISSIMUS

Der letzte Demokrat   *(Karl Arnold)*

HIER RUHEN
DIE DEMOKRATIE
UND DER
PARLAMENTARISMUS
GEB· IM JAHRE 1848
GEST· AN ARTIKEL 48

„Der liebste Platz, den ich auf Erden hab', das ist die Rasenbank am Elterngrab."

Cartoon mocking the excessive use of Article 48 of the Weimar Constitution permitting emergency decrees

forging plans to break up the grand coalition, deprive Parliament of its power and marginalize social democracy as a political force. Their aim was to form a right-wing bourgeois and authoritarian government made up of the old elites, which would be able to govern without, and if necessary against, Parliament.

After the collapse of the grand coalition led by Hermann Müller, no further attempts were made to establish a parliamentary government. Instead, Hindenburg and his advisors exploited the crisis situation and charged the Centre Party politician, Heinrich Brüning, with the task of forming a cabinet. The instructions given by the Reich President were unambiguous: Brüning should not "form the government on the basis of coalition-type commitments". Bolstered by the powers which Hindenburg intended to grant him, if need be, on the basis of emergency decrees, Brüning threatened in his government policy statement that this would be the "last attempt" to "implement the solution with this Reichstag".

Meeting of the Brüning cabinet in the Chancellery gardens, August 1930

During the final three years of the Weimar Republic, the erosion of the system of parliamentary democracy steadily continued. In view of the difficulties in forming a viable cabinet, the political centre of gravity shifted away from Parliament and the parties to the Reich President and his advisors. Behind the scenes, Hindenburg's inner circle was already

Election propaganda of some of the 28 different parties for the Reichstag elections on 14 September 1930

Berlin metalworkers demonstrating against wage cuts, October 1930

With his targeted anti-inflation policy to combat the economic crisis and achieve budgetary consolidation, Brüning's long-term aim was to bring about the demise of the Versailles Treaty. However, he was unable to gain support from the DNVP, which had close links with employers, for the unpopular austerity measures which this entailed and even more effectively wrecked any chance of reaching a compromise with the SPD. When, on 16 July 1930, a majority in the Reichstag rejected the radical austerity programme, Brüning ordered the necessary measures to be enacted by the Reich President via an emergency decree. When a majority of the SPD, KPD, NSDAP and large sections of the DNVP forced the emergency decree to be revoked, Brüning took the ultimate step, asking Hindenburg to dissolve the Reichstag. From this point onwards, until the new elections on 14 September 1930, the Reich President issued the emergency decrees demanded by Brüning, in effect completing the transition from a covert presidential system of government to an overt one.

The NSDAP made clear gains in the Reichstag elections, becoming the second-strongest parliamentary group, and henceforth, in cooperation with the KPD, had a blocking minority in the Reichstag. The losers included the bourgeois centre parties, and in particular the DNVP, which lost just over half its votes. At this point, none of the parties were thinking of reviving the grand coalition. Although Brüning's minority cabinet was tolerated in Parliament by the SPD out of regard for the governing coalition of SPD, DDP and Centre in Prussia and in order to avoid a right-wing dictatorship, policy-making independent of the Reich President and constructive cooperation with the parties in the Reichstag had now become impossible. The drop in the number of Reichstag sessions, from 94 in 1930 to 13 in 1932, and the increase in the number of laws enacted by emergency decree, from five in 1930 to 66 in 1932, illustrate the extent to which the Reichstag's power and status had been eroded.

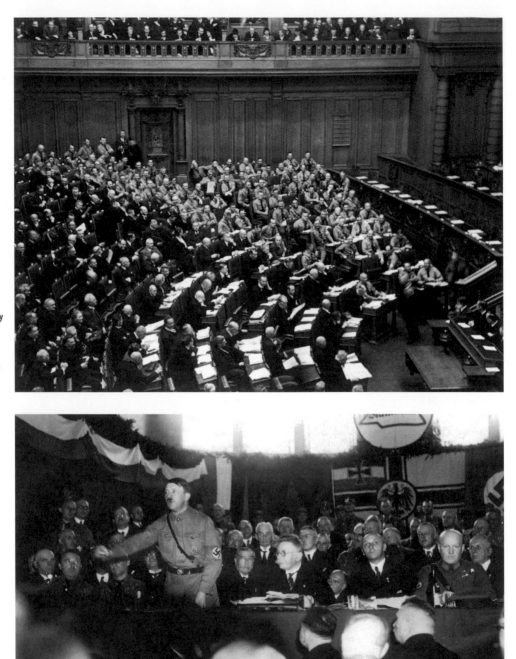

The NSDAP parliamentary group in the Reichstag, dressed in brown shirts, 30 October 1930

Adolf Hitler and Alfred Hugenberg in Bad Harzburg, 11 October 1931

Meanwhile, Brüning's anti-inflation policies were further exacerbating the economic crisis, causing mass unemployment and thus impoverishing broad sections of society. As economic and social decline accelerated, the number of those prepared to fight the Republic at any cost increased. The right-wing extremist "Harzburg Front", formed by the DNVP, NSDAP and various other paramilitary organizations in October 1931 with the express purpose of bringing down the Brüning Government, gained a particularly high profile. Brüning had already responded to the challenge from the right by reshuffling his cabinet, which now contained few party politicians and would henceforth govern even more independently of Parliament. He narrowly survived a no-confidence motion tabled jointly by the right-wing parties and the KPD, but the continuing economic crisis and the fact that Brüning's policies were tolerated by the SPD meant that he soon lost the confidence of the Reich President and his inner circle. The situation came to a head when Hindenburg was forced to rely in the presidential elections on votes from SPD voters, which he saw as a "reversal of fronts". At this point, Brüning's fall from grace was complete. In the end, Hindenburg's cabal, with the cooperation of its occasional ally, General Kurt von Schleicher, engineered his downfall, following his decision – under pressure from the interior ministers of the *Länder* – to endorse a ban on the SA (Storm Troopers) and the SS Defence Corps.

Brüning had already reduced the role of the Reichstag and its parliamentary groups to creating majorities and tolerating governments. His successors, Franz von Papen and General Kurt von Schleicher, now went even further, making a radical break with parliamentarianism. Schleicher, who wished to see the emerging National Socialist movement participate in an authoritarian anti-parliamentary presidential regime under conservative leadership, took on a key position in Hindenburg's inner circle. By giving Hitler government responsibility, he hoped to bring the NSDAP to heel in the long run.

SA groups, dressed in white shirts, after uniforms had been banned, 1931

The Papen cabinet, shortly after the swearing-in ceremony in June 1932

the grounds that it no longer reflected "the political will of the German people".

The election campaign which took place in the summer of 1932 was the bloodiest so far, leaving over 300 dead and more than a thousand injured. When riots broke out in Hamburg, Reich Chancellor Papen, at that point still in office, took the opportunity to oust the government of Prussia by emergency decree and take over the duties of the Minister-President himself in the interim. In view of the Reichswehr army's superior strength and the workers' unwillingness to fight, resistance against Papen's overt coup appeared, to the trade unions and the SPD executive, to be futile. Instead, they hoped for a swing in favour of the republican forces in the Reichstag elections of 31 July 1932. But instead, the election results served to endorse the anti-parliamentarian forces in Germany. Although Hitler's party failed to achieve an absolute majority, it was now in a position, in cooperation with the KPD, to paralyse the Reichstag completely. Hitler was no longer

But the "barons' cabinet" initiated by von Schleicher and led by Reich Chancellor Papen (now without party affiliation) was supported by very few deputies from the bourgeois parties. Before a no-confidence motion could be tabled, Hindenburg, citing the National Socialists' electoral successes in the last *Landtag* elections, dissolved the Reichstag on

Brawl between Communists and National Socialists in the run-up to the Reichstag elections of 31 July 1932

prepared to tolerate a new cabinet under Papen; he called uncompromisingly for full political power. As Hindenburg refused to abandon Papen and was not prepared to allow the NSDAP leader to take power without a fight, he once again dissolved the Reichstag, without immediately scheduling new elections, as laid down in the constitution. But Papen and the majority of his ministers were unwilling to infringe the constitution in this way and set 6 November 1932 as the date for new elections. Although the NSDAP's clear losses in the Reichstag elections gave fresh hope to the democratic parties, the distribution of seats made it impossible to form a viable coalition. Since no parliamentary solution for the crisis was in sight, Hindenburg once again charged Papen with forming a government. Papen was prepared to run the risk of civil war to implement his radical anti-republican "battle programme", but the minister in charge of the armed forces, Schleicher, refused to support it. Within a matter of days, the Papen

cabinet had resigned, clearing the way for Schleicher to become the new chancellor.

But Schleicher's final attempt to end the government crisis with the help of the unions and Gregor Strasser's moderate wing of the NSDAP, and thus prevent Hitler becoming chancellor, was in vain. When Hindenburg refused to allow him to implement an emergency plan, he resigned. At this point, the plan for government participation by the National Socialists, which Papen had been presenting to leading industrialists and in the Reichstag President's Palace since the beginning of January, was implemented. On 30 January 1933, Hindenburg appointed Hitler as Reich Chancellor. Within a few weeks, Papen's hopes of surrounding Hitler with conservative ministers, and thus controlling him, had been dashed.

Reich Chancellor Schleicher delivering his government policy statement on the radio, 15 December 1932

IV. THE THIRD REICH

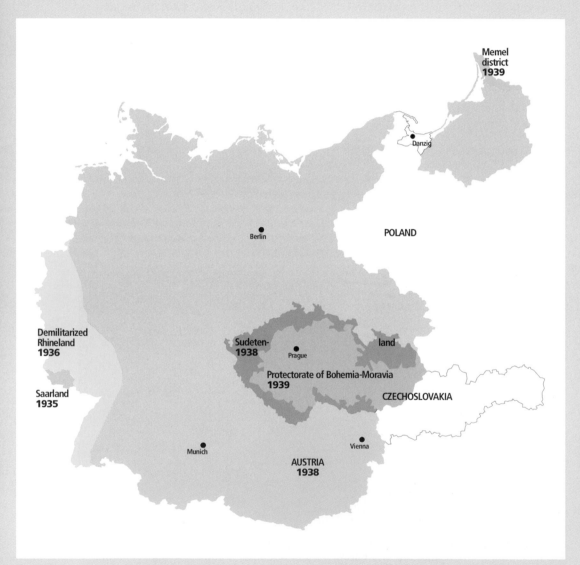

Memel
district
1939

Danzig

POLAND

Berlin

Demilitarized
Rhineland
1936

Sudeten-
1938   land

Prague

Protectorate of Bohemia-Moravia
1939

Saarland
1935

CZECHOSLOVAKIA

Munich

Vienna

AUSTRIA
1938

The German
Empire in 1939

In many ways, the transfer of power to Adolf Hitler on 30 January 1933 marked the culmination of attempts to find an authoritarian answer to the economic, social and political crisis that had afflicted the Weimar Republic persistently since 1929. At the same time, however, it marked the beginning of a development that immediately went far beyond previous attempts. The democratic constitutional order and system of government had already been undermined by the presidential system of emergency decrees in operation since 1930; now, within a short space of time, it was eliminated completely. The National Socialists took advantage both of their mass popular support and of the fact that the idea of a conservative renewal of state and society led by a strong national government initially enjoyed widespread support among the parliamentary right wing and their middle-class sympathizers. But it soon became clear who was using whom for their own ends. Although at first the National Socialists were distinctly a minority in Hitler's cabinet of "national concentration", the illusion that the new Chancellor could be deployed to drum up the support of the masses, steered as desired and then simply discarded, very soon evaporated.

One week after the Reichstag fire, on 5 March 1933, new elections to the Reichstag took place in a highly charged political atmosphere marked by deep legal uncertainty and overt terror. The NSDAP again failed to win an absolute majority, but now, together with its German Nationalist coalition partners, it held 340 of the 647 seats in parliament. With the arrest of the vast majority of KPD deputies and several Social Democrat parliamentarians, the National Socialist rulers violated the law of parliamentary immunity. It also meant that in terms of its composition, the Reichstag that passed the "Enabling Act" on 23 March with only the remaining Social Democrats voting against it, was technically no longer legal. The new Act freed Hitler from all constitutional restraints and parliamentary control. After it was passed, the National Socialist regime proceeded swiftly to liquidate the German party system entirely, using terror on a massive scale. Following the banning of the KPD and the SPD, the middle-class parties disbanded and on 14 July 1933, a Law Prohibiting the Re-establishment of Political Parties was passed. The process of creating a National Socialist one-party state was complete. From this point on, the NSDAP and its organizations controlled all aspects of political, economic and cultural life in Germany. The SA, which at first competed with the party, was eliminated as a power factor in June 1934. The Reichstag, meanwhile, was "coordinated", reducing its role to that of acclamation for the dictatorship.

The remaining institutions of the constitutional system were also deprived of power in this process referred to by the National Socialists as "*Gleichschaltung*", or "coordination", or "*Verreichlichung*" (bringing into line with the Reich system). Germany's federal structure was dismantled, turning the Reich into a unitary state, and in February

1934, just a year after the abolition of the *Länder*, or federal states, the Reichsrat that represented them was formally dissolved. The first concentration camps for political prisoners were set up as early as February 1933. Special courts based on the ground-work of the *Gestapo*, the secret police, con-trolled or took charge of the administra-tion of justice, and proved to be reliable props of the Nazi terror regime; one such court was the *Volksgerichtshof*, or People's Court, set up in April 1934. On 2 August 1934, following the death of Hindenburg, the offices of Reich President and Reich Chancellor were merged. Designating him-self "Führer and Reich Chancellor", Hitler ordered all soldiers and civil servants from then on to swear a personal oath of alle-giance to him. The construction of the "Führer state" had reached completion.

The process of "coordination" did not just affect the Reich's political structure, but the whole of society. Society was to be reshaped in accordance with the ostensibly egalitarian but decidedly racist ideology of the *Volksgemeinschaft*, or "people's com-munity". Mass organizations such as the Hitler Youth and the Reich Labour Service, but also the organized leisure movement, "Strength through Joy", and the campaign to collect donations for the "*Winterhilfs-werk*", or winter aid scheme, were intended to act as social levellers. Their primary objective, however, was to loosen people's traditional personal and social bonds and thereby make it easier for the regime to tighten its all-encompassing ideological grip. The economy too, was reorganized on a command basis. Trade unions were smashed, and the two sides of industry were incorporated into a single, centrally-run organization, the German Labour Front. Employers, whose position was strengthened by the transfer of the Führer

principle to industry, nevertheless had only limited scope in shaping company busi-ness. Although the principle of capitalist private enterprise was left untouched by the National Socialist rulers, production was largely steered by the state in accord-ance with the political objectives dictated by it.

Aided in some measure by the internation-al economic upturn, the German economy gradually began to recover from 1933 onwards. The job creation programme initi-ated by the National Socialists focused mainly on public works and at first it did little to boost industrial production. An ini-tially covert programme of rearmament, however, led to a visible drop in the num-bers of unemployed and thereby consider-ably increased popular support for the regime. The National Socialists financed their job creation and armaments pro-grammes by issuing government bonds and, ultimately, by printing money. Hitler was relatively unconcerned by the fact that, as a result, public debt reached unprecedented levels. Economic policy pri-marily served the plans nurtured by Hitler for a war of conquest in eastern Europe aimed at "extending our people's living space and enlarging its supply of food and raw materials". In 1936 the "Führer and Reich Chancellor" set out his demands: "Firstly, in four years the German army must be op-erational. Secondly, in four years German industry must be ready for war."

The National Socialist regime's foreign poli-cy, which initially appeared to be simply a continuation of the revisionist policy of the Weimar governments, secretly included in its tactics from the very beginning the idea of military confrontation as a precondition for the comprehensive reorganization of Europe along National Socialist lines. For fear of war, the western powers reacted cautiously to the German Reich's expansionist policy for a long time. Even as late as September 1938, they tried to preserve peace in Europe by giving in to Hitler on the "Sudetenland issue". When German troops occupied the rest of Czechoslovakia in spring 1939, France and Britain at last opted for a more resolute stance and pledged their assistance to Poland and other countries in eastern and south-eastern Europe in the event of a German attack. It was now clear that the next aggressive move by Germany was bound to lead to all-out war. That war began on 1 September 1939, with Germany's invasion of Poland.

Anti-Semitism, the centrepiece of the National Socialist racial ideology, was already rife in imperial Germany, but it became particularly virulent in the latter days of the Weimar Republic. Amidst the deep uncertainties of the economic crisis, a feeling of being at the mercy of anonymous social forces had gripped broad sections of the population; Nazi propaganda now succeeded in transforming this into aggression towards the "world conspiracy of Jews and bolshevists". Hitler systematically implemented a programme to eliminate these "enemies of the people". Acts of violence against Jewish citizens and their property increased and special laws were passed, each more brutal than the last, discriminating against them and ultimately depriving them of any form of livelihood. Hundreds of thousands of German Jews emigrated. The pogrom staged on 9 November 1938 was followed by numerous arrests. Since the curbing of the SA's power, the SS had become the most powerful organization in the National Socialist state and soon demonstrated that it was a body that could be relied on to execute the "will of the Führer" in this respect too. It was in

the context of the racial war being waged in the east, particularly against the Soviet Union, that the racial madness of the Nazis took on its most extreme form: with the utmost brutality and unprecedented efficiency, millions of Jews from all the occupied European countries were systematically murdered in Auschwitz and other extermination camps.

Chances for political opposition groups to mount any effective resistance to the National Socialist regime were slim from the beginning. The political left, along with sections of the middle-class, conservative camp and numerous church and military representatives, were united in rejecting Hitler. They did not form a united front to oppose him, however, due to differences of opinion regarding political alternatives, and especially due to the watertight surveillance and systematic persecution practised by the state apparatus. Not until 20 November 1944, prompted by military set-backs and the unspeakable crimes of the National Socialist regime, did a few high-ranking military figures in the nationalist-conservative camp try to trigger a *coup d'état* by attempting – unsuccessfully – to assassinate Hitler. The attack failed to topple the regime or to bring an end to the war on the western front as planned. Instead, virtually the whole of the German resistance movement was physically annihilated as a result.

In the end, the National Socialist dictatorship was overthrown by external forces, namely the advancing armies of the anti-Hitler coalition. The successful Soviet counter-offensive at Stalingrad in the winter of 1942/43 marked the turning point in the war; on 6 June 1944, Anglo-American troops successfully invaded German-occupied north-western France and opened a second major front. American and British units reached the German border in September 1944, followed by Soviet troops a month later. The unconditional surrender of the German army on 7 May 1945 in Reims, and one day later in Berlin-Karlshorst, brought the Second World War to an end in Europe. In Germany, it put an end to a criminal regime, but it also brought to an end the unity of the sovereign nation-state established in 1871.

1. The imposition of National Socialist dictatorship

When Adolf Hitler was appointed Reich Chancellor by Hindenburg on 30 January 1933, he headed a presidential coalition government. In terms of numbers, the majority of ministers in it were independent conservatives, members of the German National People's Party (DNVP) and representatives of the *Stahlhelm*, a conservative ex-servicemen's organization. Opposite Hitler and his men – Minister of the Interior Wilhelm Frick, and Hermann Göring, initially minister without portfolio but from 28 April, Minister for Air Transport – stood Vice-Chancellor Papen and the Minister of Economics and Agriculture, Hugenberg, and only four other members of the "cabinet of barons" that had lost power the previous year. They, together with the Reich Defence Minister, Werner von Blomberg, and *Stahlhelm* leader, Franz Seldte, who had been appointed Labour Minister, were expected to tame the National Socialist "movement" and hold it in check. Papen self-

confidently asserted "we have engaged him for our purposes", expressing the expectation that Hitler and the mass following of the National Socialists could serve as an instrument to bring about – this time successfully, it was hoped – an authoritarian-conservative renewal of the ailing economy and politically discredited state.

In fact, this constellation presented the National Socialists with a great opportunity. They were now able to combine the vast power concentrated in the hands of the Reich President and the presidential cabinets since 1930 with the tremendous dynamism and energy of an antidemocratic mass movement. It was this combination, and the skilful exploitation of each source of power in turn, that was at the root of the rapid establishment of the National Socialist dictatorship. Even before the new cabinet was sworn in, Hindenburg had

Hitler's cabinet on 30 January 1933. Beside Hitler, left: Wilhelm Frick (standing) and Hermann Göring

SA men burning the black, red and gold flag in the streets of Berlin

agreed to Hitler's demand to dissolve the Reichstag and hold new elections. Now, during the election campaign, the NSDAP's "combat and protection" units began systematically to terrorize their political opponents. In Prussia, where Göring, soon to be appointed prime minister, was now temporarily in charge of the Ministry of the Interior, units of the SA and SS were assigned the role of auxiliary police for this purpose.

The Reichstag building in flames in the night of 27-28 February, 1933

In the night of 27 to 28 February 1933, the Reichstag building went up in flames. The plenary chamber and the dome above it were almost completely gutted by the fire. Nazi propaganda immediately laid the blame for the arson attack, which to this day has never been satisfactorily explained, at the feet of the Communists. A Dutchman, Marinus van der Lubbe, arrested at the scene of the crime was charged with arson along with three Bulgarian communists and Ernst Torgler, chairman of the KPD deputies in the Reichstag. The latter, however, was acquitted by the Reich court in Leipzig on 23 December 1933. The Reichstag fire fitted so neatly into the National Socialists' plans to eliminate all opposition forces that they soon came under suspicion of having started the fire themselves. In actual fact, the arson attack gave the regime the pretext to step up the ruthless oppression of its opponents that was already under way. An emergency decree "to protect the people and the State" was issued by the Reich President on 28 February. It suspended key basic rights and all constitutional guarantees provided under the Weimar Constitution without formally suspending the constitution itself. In doing so, it effectively legalized the persecution and terrorization of the opposition. The deputies and leading functionaries of the KPD were arrested, Communist and Social Democrat newspapers outlawed, and the election campaign activities of all other political parties, especially those on the left, were violently disrupted. By mid-March around 10,000 people had been arrested on political grounds in Prussia alone.

Despite massive intimidation of the public and the political parties, the NSDAP won only 43.9 per cent of the votes. Its coalition partner, the DNVP (People's Party), mustered 8 per cent, and together this gave them a sufficient majority in the Reichstag. But Hitler wanted to free himself of all constitutional constraints and every conceivable form of parliamentary control. With a view to this, on 23 March he tabled a bill in the Reichstag to "Remove the distress of people and State", which has come to be known as the Enabling Act. This Act allowed the govern-

ment to pass laws – even laws contravening the constitution – without parliamentary approval. Since a two thirds majority was required to pass the Enabling Act, it was theoretically possible for the opposition to thwart it. However, the 81 Communist deputies were no longer present in the Reichstag, while the deputies from the Centre and middle-class liberal parties had been terrorized into submission. At the same time, however, they were also led by the tacit hope that they might be able to retain some degree of political influence, or at least salvage their own party apparatus, if they cooperated. Moreover, the Enabling Act did not affect the rights of the Reich President. This fact nurtured the illusion that Hindenburg – already virtually paralysed – would adopt the same stance he had taken towards Chancellors of earlier presidential cabinets

and assert his ultimate presidential authority over Hitler, whom he had so recently inaugurated into Prussia's military-aristocratic traditions in a symbolically laden ceremony in the Garrison Church in Potsdam. So, in the end, only the 94 Social Democrats present under their chairman, Otto Wels, voted against this Act that deprived parliament of all its powers and abolished the system of parliamentary democracy.

Meanwhile, the institutions of democracy fell victim to the emerging National Socialist dictatorship with breathtaking speed. Step by step, all organs of state and public institutions were subjugated to the will of the regime or abolished entirely. Political opponents were eliminated and their organizations either compelled to cease their political activity or forcibly dissolved. Pressure from above by the state machinery alternated with pressure from below on the streets; flagrant acts of violence alternated with persistent efforts by the regime to give its activities a veneer of legality by passing laws and ordinances.

Immediately after the elections in March, the process of *Gleichschaltung*, or "coordination" of the *Länder*, the constituent states of the Reich, began. Wherever there was resistance, the SA and SS were sent in to create unrest, and the "unstable situation" was then taken as a pretext by the National Socialists to appoint a *Reichskommissar*, or Commissioner. On 9 March, the last of the *Länder*, Bavaria, was forced to capitulate.

National Socialist propaganda for the Reichstag elections of 5 March 1933

Left: First sitting of the newly-elected Reichstag in the Kroll Opera House on 21 March 1933

Right: SA and SS men marching into parliament to intimidate the opposition ahead of the Reichstag sitting on 23 March 1933

Hindenburg with Hitler and Reich Defence Minister Werner von Blomberg (centre) on 21 March 1933, in front of the Garrison Church in Potsdam

A law was enacted by the government, without parliamentary involvement, on 31 March, decreeing that the *Länder* parliaments, whose composition reflected the results of democratically held elections, were to be re-constituted according to the results of the Reichstag elections. Votes for the Communist Party, however, were not to be taken into account. Following the passing of a second

"coordination law" a week later, each of the *Länder* was to be headed by a *Reichsstatthalter*, or governor, appointed by the Reich Chancellor. Finally, on 31 January 1934, under the "Act on the Reorganization of the Reich", the *Länder* were abolished, their sovereign jurisdiction was transferred to the central government, *Länder* governments subordinated to the Reich and *Länder* governors to

Right: Election of the Hamburg city parliament on 8 March 1933, without SPD and KPD deputies

The judiciary brought into line with the NSDAP regime in the new criminal court in Berlin

the Reich Minister of the Interior. Under German law, this meant that the *Länder* effectively ceased to exist. Accordingly, their representative body at Reich level, the Reichsrat, was dissolved on 14 February 1934.

At the same time as dismantling the federal structures, the National Socialists also set about "purging" the civil service and the judiciary. Under the "Act on the Re-establishment of the Permanent Civil Service", any civil servant or judge who did not pledge unconditional loyalty to the National Socialist state could be dismissed from office. An "Aryan clause", which was to feature in later laws, ordinances and statutes, appeared for the first time in this law. It stated that civil servants with "non-Aryan, and especially Jewish parents or grandparents" were to be sent into retirement. A special rule exempting Jewish civil servants who had fought in the First World War, or whose fathers or sons had died in that war, was revoked in 1935.

Having lost all political influence as a result of the Enabling Act, the democratic parties

A unit of the SA in front of trade union headquarters in Munich, spring 1933

were closed down completely by the National Socialists early in the summer of 1933. The SPD, already in a state of internal collapse with most of its leaders having fled to Prague following the occupation of the party offices on 10 May, was banned on 22 June. The other democratic parties also found that they no longer had any political room for manoeuvre and decided to opt for voluntary dissolution – the last two to do so were the Catholic Centre party and its Bavarian sister, the Bavarian People's Party (BVP), on 4 and 5 July. On 14 July, the NSDAP was made Germany's only party by law.

The trade unions' days were also numbered. Initially, anxious to preserve their own organizational structures, the numerically strong Free Trade Unions turned away from the SPD and sought to cooperate with the new rulers. The latter appeared to comply: 1 May, the day that traditionally symbolized the workers' struggle, was even declared a public holiday by the National Socialist regime. Hundreds of thousands of workers, including many leading trade union representatives, followed the call to mass rallies. But the very next day SA and SS units occupied the trade unions' offices, arrested their officials and seized their assets. On 10 May 1933, the old trade unions, representing a broad range of ideological positions, were replaced by the *Deutsche Arbeitsfront* (DAF), or German Labour Front. In the words of Robert Ley, the party's Reich Organizations

Design for a postcard for "National Labour Day"

Hitler with Protestant "Reich Bishop" Ludwig Müller and Abbot Alban Schachleiter (left) at the NSDAP national rally in Nuremberg in 1934

Leader, who was in charge of the DAF, the founding of the Labour Front "knocked the Marxist riff-raff's main weapon right out of their hands". In actual fact, the DAF was not an organization protecting workers and campaigning on their behalf, but a monolithic organization encompassing not only workers, white-collar employees, artisans and self-employed businesspeople, but also employers. Later on it even included the *Reichsnährstand*, or Reich Food Organization, into which organizations representing the interests of the agricultural sector were marshalled on 13 September 1933.

Some two weeks later the Hereditary Farm Law was passed. With it, National Socialist agricultural policy was definitively tailored to the basic premises of the "blood and soil" ideology personified chiefly by Walter Darré, who was now Reich Minister for Food and Agriculture. From now on, farms of between 7.5 and 125 hectares, whose owners were able to prove their forefathers' "blood purity" going back to 1800, were considered indivisible and inalienable hereditary farms.

The churches did not challenge the National Socialists' claim to absolute power either. The Protestant Lutheran church in particular willingly submitted to the National Socialist state – in line with its tradition as the church closest to the state in Germany. Only a minority of Protestant pastors openly opposed National Socialism, joining the synods of the *Bekennende Kirche*, or Confessing Church, that emerged out of Martin Niemöller's *Pfarrer-Notbund*, or Pastors' Emergency League. The Catholic Church proved more resilient and succeeded in particular in preserving its unity as a religious community. The price it paid for this was almost total political abstinence. Indeed, with the Concordat concluded between the Vatican and the German Reich on 20 July 1933, the Catholic Church helped significantly to enhance the standing of the National Socialist regime among the Catholic population and on the international stage. Nevertheless, it was largely due to protests on the part of Catholic and Lutheran clerics that, eight years later, the National Socialist state officially halted its by then widely known policy of killing the mentally ill, whom it regarded as "unfit for life". Criminal charges brought publicly against the regime by the Bishop of Münster, Clemens August Graf von Galen on 3 August 1941, were a decisive factor in ending these killings, which had been instigated on the Führer's orders in 1939.

So successful was the regime in "coordinating" the organs and institutions of the constitutional system that by the end of 1933 the only groups still retaining a modicum of independence, besides the churches, were large industrial enterprises and the Reichswehr, on whose cooperation the National Socialists depended. In this first year of the National Socialist dictatorship, however, the question of the balance of power within the National Socialist camp had not yet been definitively resolved. In particular the SA, led by Ernst Röhm, refused to accept that the "national revolution" had indeed come to an end, as Hitler frequently asserted. They demanded the establishment of a people's militia, with the SA as its revolutionary nucleus. Hitler hesitated for some time before finally deciding to exploit the putsch rumours that had been stirred up by the Reichswehr, afraid of losing its influence, and by an ambitious SS, to strip the SA completely of its powers. This duly took place in the form of a raid at the dead of night on 30 June 1934, and cost the lives of Röhm and his closest comrades. Later, this purge was declared to be an "act of self-defence by the state". Göring and Himmler's murder squads also seized the opportunity to eliminate a number of conservative opponents of the regime, such as former Reich Chancellor Schleicher and Edgar Jung, the unpopular confidant of the Vice-Chancellor. Papen, who had initially agreed to Hitler's action, was shunted off to Vienna as German envoy in July 1934; Hugenberg, meanwhile, had left the cabinet in June 1933.

Special edition of the newspaper *BZ am Mittag* of 30 June 1934, informing readers about Röhm's removal from office

On 2 August 1934, one month after the feigned "Röhm putsch", Reich President Hindenburg died. Hitler now merged the offices of Reich Chancellor and Reich President and assumed both himself. Reich War Minister Blomberg lost no time in demonstrating his obedience by ordering the Reichswehr to swear a personal oath of allegiance to the "Führer and Reich Chancellor", Adolf Hitler, instead of to the Constitution. Construction of the totalitarian "Führer state" was complete.

„Ich schwöre bei Gott diesen heiligen Eid, daß ich dem Führer des Deutschen Reiches und Volkes, Adolf Hitler, dem obersten Befehlshaber der Wehrmacht, unbedingten Gehorsam leisten und als tapferer Soldat bereit sein will, jederzeit für diesen Eid mein Leben einzusetzen."

Text of oath sworn by Reichswehr members, introduced on 4 August 1934

2. The ideology of the "people's community"

The National Socialist ideology was becoming increasingly widely accepted, and not only due to the incipient economic upturn. One of the decisive reasons why it was so effective with the masses was the notion of the "people's community". In this appealing element of National Socialist propaganda, an egalitarian and, at root, pre-modern ideal of society is set against the discredited, "western" concept of society associated with social hierarchies. The policy based on this may thus be seen as an attempt to mask the deep divisions within modern society and bridge the social fault-lines that continued to exist by means of a plethora of special campaigns, institutions and regulations. The German Labour Front, the Hitler Youth, the six-month Reich Labour Service that was made obligatory in 1935 for all young people over the age of 18, and conscription, also reintroduced in 1935 – all of these were

intended to break down social barriers and train people to "serve the German people as a whole". The *Winterhilfswerk*, or winter aid campaign, which took place every year by order of the National Socialist People's Welfare organization, was set up to foster solidarity with all "national comrades genuinely in need". An organization called "Strength through Joy", affiliated to the DAF, was set up to provide low-income sections of the population in particular with excursions, holidays and opportunities to participate in cultural life. A subsidiary division, "Beauty of Labour", organized works libraries and arranged for modernization of a large number of factory yards, canteens, offices and workshops, the cost of which had to be borne by the employers. Point 24 of the NSDAP's party programme, "the common good takes precedence over that of the individual", seemed to have become reality

Left:
Propaganda
poster for
*Deutsches
Jungvolk*, the
youth section
of the Hitler
Youth

Right:
Pamphlet
advertising
the first
Volkswagen

Berlin ißt heute sein Eintopfgericht

Event organized by the *Winterhilfswerk*, or winter aid scheme, in Berlin

for a great many people who expected the "people's community" to bring them security and protection. However, a genuine balance of interests cannot be imposed by state pressure, and this was not in any case the aim of the National Socialists. In the face of tangible social improvements, however, this seemed as irrelevant as the fact that the National Socialists' vague notion of a corporative state was in no way compatible with the image painted of the "people's community" as a "united society of German people irrespective of their status or origins".

Large sections of the population at least had good reason to perceive the early years of the National Socialist regime as a kind of return to normality, despite the relentless demands made on them by the National Socialist campaigns and institutions. On the surface, life in many ways seemed more peaceful than it had been during the final, turbulent days of the Weimar Republic. The immense political tensions appeared overcome and the economic and social problems that in many cases had threatened people's very livelihoods were gradually being solved

through an employment policy that was closely bound up with the carefully disguised objective of building up arms. In January 1933, over six million people were registered as unemployed. A year later, however, the number had already fallen to 2.7 million; in 1937 it fell below the one million mark. At the same time, the share of public expenditure on arms steadily increased from around 4 per cent in 1933 to more than 50 per cent in 1938. A highly diverse set of policy instruments had been developed since 1930 to boost the economy. But it was only because, combined with these, the regime was absolutely determined to expand its military capacity, and was willing to invest the increasing amounts of money required for this, that Germany ultimately managed to overcome the economic crisis more swiftly than other countries.

The boundaries of the "people's community" were clearly defined from the outset. Only those who showed unequivocal support for the National Socialist regime, and who were considered "Germans" according to its racial criteria, could belong to it. In this spirit, the

A tank leaving the production line in a German armaments factory

"Act on Reich Citizenship", the first of the "Nuremberg Laws" promulgated in 1935, stated: "Citizens of the Reich shall be only those persons of German or related blood who by their conduct show that they are able and willing loyally to serve the German people and the German Reich." Anyone else was, in a certain sense, a natural enemy of the "people's community" and, as such, at the mercy of the National Socialists and their reign of terror. Under the National Socialist regime, it was enough to have a Jewish spouse, belong to an unauthorized organization, or criticize the government's actions, for a person to be denounced, taken into "protective custody" without a court order, and ultimately interned in a concentration camp.

A key instrument in disseminating the ideology of the "people's community" and manipulating public opinion was the Reich Ministry for Public Enlightenment and Propaganda. Created on 13 March 1933, and

"Certificate of descent", issued by the Office for Genealogical Research, Vienna *Gau* (district), 13 October 1938

NSDAP – Gau Wien
Amt für Sippenforschung
Wien, 1., Am Hof 3 und 4

Bezahlt
Zahl: 10614 /38

Herr
Frau
Frl.   Plasser Viktor Josef Quirin
        (Zuname)   (Vorname)

Wohnort: Wien IV Kettenbrückengasse 16 Stand (led., verh., verw., gesch.): ledig
hat im Sinne der §§ 2 Abs. 2, und 5 der Ersten Verordnung zum Reichsbürgergesetz vom 14. 11. 1935 (Reichsgesetzbl. I S. 1333) den

kleinen Abstammungsnachweis

nach überprüften umseitig ersichtlichen Urkunden erbracht und gilt daher als

Arier – Mischling 2. Grades – Mischling 1. Grades – Jude.

Wien, am   13. OCt 1938

f. d. R.

Unterschrift. Amtssiegel

Undeutlich ausgefüllte Formblätter werden zurückgewiesen!

R 4, Vorde. kH 1/38 – 31.—100. Tausend

Books being burned on the Opernplatz in Berlin on 10 May 1933

directed by the NSDAP's Reich Propaganda Leader, Joseph Goebbels, it managed and controlled all reporting in the mass media and censored all printed publications of any significance, as well as films and theatre performances. Goebbels moved deftly between blatant repression and carefully calculated tolerance. On the one hand, there were orchestrated barbarities, like the public burnings of "subversive" books and publications held in many places on 10 May 1933, and dirigiste measures such as the founding of the "Reich Chamber of Culture" four months later, whose offices decided on the professional suitability of artists and journalists. At the same time, he deliberately promoted light entertainment in the form of ostensibly non-political radio broadcasts and films. The intention of the regime was to distract "national comrades" both from the criminal aspects of National Socialist policies and from the huge demands placed on them in their daily lives, which were organized down to the last detail. From 1939, of course, this increasingly became eclipsed by the demands of Hitler's ever more extreme military strategy. It was entirely logical, therefore, that it should be none other than Goebbels who called upon the German people, stunned by the disaster of Stalingrad, to wage "total war". And it fitted the regime's legitimizing strategy perfectly that the Reich Propaganda minister should interpret the frantic jubilation of the claque assembled in the Sports Palace in Berlin on 18 February 1943, as the agreement of the "people's community" that the war must go on, and no effort spared: "I asked you a question, and you have given me your answer. You are part of the people and thus, through your lips, the stance of the German people has made itself manifest."

3. The "coordinated" Reichstag and the National Socialist regime

"The Führer", painting by Conrad Hommel, 1933/39

direct impact on Germany's image and developments there under the National Socialist regime. Neither the regime's racial policy nor its plans for a war of conquest and annihilation in the east were conceivable in this form without Hitler.

On the other hand, National Socialist rule saw the emergence of a confusing array of parallel and competing authorities, special bodies, party organizations and offices of the SS and the *Gestapo*, the secret police. Government in the Third Reich was characterized by power struggles, conflicts of jurisdiction, the incipient breakdown of a structured system of public administration and growing frictions and inefficiency in an institutional maze. Time and again, the administrative chaos gave leading party functionaries a chance to pursue their own personal goals, and created a vacuum in which extreme National Socialist policies could evolve without hindrance. Hitler himself refused to be bound by any clear delimitation of powers or rational criteria of efficient government. This very refusal safeguarded his personal position and power, and ensured him unlimited decision-making power in situations of conflict between institutions competing in the same field. The administrative chaos that characterized the National Socialist regime by no means contradicted the dictatorship of the Führer. Rather, it was a prerequisite for it.

Germany under National Socialism is often described as the "Führer state", and with good reason. After all, from 2 August 1934, Hitler was not only head of state and leader of the government rolled into one; he was also supreme commander of the armed forces, supreme head of the judiciary and leader of the ruling party, the NSDAP. Accordingly, National Socialist propaganda stressed the Führer's omnipotence and attributed every political success to him personally. And indeed in retrospect, too, it cannot be overlooked that Hitler's *Weltanschauung*, or world-view, and the political programme he based upon it, did have a

The "coordinated" Reichstag was not one of the regime's politically active elements. With the passing of the Enabling Act, the Reichstag had effectively transformed itself from a legislative body into an organ of acclamation for the regime. After 23 March 1933, the Reichstag convened on only 19 more occasions and passed a mere seven laws. In contrast, over 900 laws were issued by the government. By the Reichstag election of 12 November 1933, the system of voting had been changed;

Wilhelm Frick, Reich Interior Minister and chairman of the NSDAP parliamentary group in the Reichstag

machinations; he set great store by the legality of the National Socialist regime's actions and conceived the parliament as a foundation stone in his plans for a reorganized and completely centralized Reich. In the end, this brought him conspicuously into conflict with Hitler. On 24 August 1943, Frick was replaced as Minister of the Interior by Reich SS Leader Heinrich Himmler; following Frick's removal from power, attempts to table legislation in the Reichstag ceased altogether. However, in the latter years of the National Socialist dictatorship, there was a marked decline even in government legislation. Under the conditions of "total war", the extreme totality of the Führer state too became apparent: political decisions were now made almost exclusively by decree of the Führer.

The paralysing of the Reichstag was also clearly evidenced in the abolition of its most important bodies and statutes. In December 1933, Göring, as President of the Reichstag, was still careful to abide by the obligation laid down in Article 35 of the Constitution to

now, unified lists offered voters only the option of unqualified acceptance or rejection of the NSDAP-nominated candidate. A few representatives of former right-wing conservative parties who – unlike KPD, SPD and state party deputies – had not been deprived of their seats, now joined the NSDAP. Others sat in as "guests" on the National Socialist parliamentary group, enabling them to continue as full members of parliament – some right up until 1945. However, from November 1933, there were only 22 such "guests" compared to 639 National Socialists in the Reichstag. Moreover, they were required to submit to National Socialist party discipline and were replaced, if they left, by party members who were above suspicion. Ultimately, therefore, the Reichstag operated completely untrammelled as a single-party parliament.

As members of the NSDAP, virtually all parliamentarians were sworn to unconditional allegiance. Any thought of keeping a check on the government was therefore ruled out from the start. The leader of the one and only parliamentary party was Wilhelm Frick, returning officer for Reich elections, who was also in charge of the Reich Ministry of the Interior. Frick used the Reichstag as an asset in his own power

Propaganda poster for the elections to the "Reichstag of Greater Germany" and plebiscite on the "anschluss" of Austria, held on 10 April 1938

Reichstag sitting on 18 March 1938. Hitler reports that "the anschluss of Austria has been achieved"

appoint select committees – a Committee for the Preservation of the Rights of Parliament and a Foreign Affairs Committee. The committees were never convened, however, and they were no longer even appointed for the parliaments elected on 29 March 1936 and 10 April 1938. In September 1935, the Reichstag rules of procedure were abolished. A process of thinning out the Reichstag staff began, culminating significantly in the summer of 1942: most of the now virtually redundant parliamentary shorthand writers were summoned to the Ukrainian town of Vinnitsa. From now on they were to be answerable to Hitler's secretary, Martin Bormann, given specially designed uniforms and assigned the task of keeping verbatim records of situation briefings and extraordinary meetings held there, as the "Shorthand Writers' Service of the Führer's Field Headquarters".

In view of the Reichstag's loss of significance, one might ask why it was not abolished altogether, like the *Länder* parliaments and the other key political institutions of the Weimar Republic. One might also ask why,

in 1937, Hitler himself drew up plans for the reconstruction of the Reichstag building, and why the draft budget for 1939 envisaged nine million reichsmarks for essential construction work. Why, indeed, did new deputies continue to take up seats in the Reichstag until well into December 1944? The reasons were multifarious. On the one hand, a seat in the Reichstag was considered a prestigious sinecure for "deserving" party members up to the very end. At the same time, the NSDAP profited considerably by keeping parliament going: by counting the parliamentary allowance towards the salaries of full-time party officials, they were able to pass party costs on to the state. Hitler for a long time was noncommittal regarding Frick's vision of a centralized state that included the Reichstag, as indeed he was about all issues concerning the definitive structure of the Reich. The idea did find support, however, among National Socialist functionaries who feared that the *Gauleiter*, or District Leaders, might become excessively independent. The main reason, however, for the continued existence of parliament was the fact that Hitler set great store by having an institution that had a semblance of plebiscitary legitimation to provide a solemn backdrop for his policy statements, and pass them unanimously. This was especially useful for presenting the outside world, and notorious sceptics within Germany, with a clear image of the much-vaunted "unity of people and Führer".

How this happened can be seen from the constituent meeting of parliament – now designated "Reichstag of Greater Germany" – held at Hitler's request on 30 January 1939. This sitting took place nearly ten months after he had been elected in the combined plebiscite on the annexation of Austria – already a *fait accompli*. Hitler thought it would be expedient to extend the electoral term of parliament, which by then was well under way, and the validity of the Enabling Act, until 30 January 1943. On Frick's command, in the guise of a request, the Reichstag gave its unanimous assent. In his subsequent policy statement, Hitler extolled the parliament as "representative of the German people, and having every right to be considered a genuine consti-

Two SS sentries standing guard outside Hitler's office in the New Reich Chancellery

tuent body". Of course, the Reichstag of Greater Germany never passed a constitution, or for that matter any other relevant legislation, although in 1943 its legislative

Telephone switchboard in the *Wolfsschanze* (wolf's lair), the Führer's field headquarters in East Prussia

Reichstag sitting on 19 July 1940, following the victory over France

crises of the previous winter of war had given rise to supply and transport bottlenecks within Germany, various Reich ministries were at loggerheads and the judiciary had made some unpopular decisions. As a result, Hitler thought it advisable once again to obtain parliamentary confirmation that the will of the Führer held absolute sway. Hans Heinrich Lammers, Chief of the Reich Chancellery, suggested having the "absolute power assumed by the Führer" sanctioned once and for all by a Reichstag resolution drafted by him and presented to parliament by Göring. The resolution stated "Therefore – without being bound by existing legal regulations – in his capacity as Leader of the Nation, Supreme Commander of the Armed Forces, head of government and supreme holder of executive power, chief of the judiciary and leader of the Party, the Führer must be in a position, if necessary, to oblige every German ... by any means he deems appropriate, to fulfil his duties." The deputies approved the resolution by rising from their seats.

period was again extended for a further four years. After the onset of war, it only sat if Hitler had a victorious campaign to report; even the declaration of war on the USA was embedded in reports of German victories.

The Reichstag of Greater Germany sat for the last time on 26 April 1942. The military

Hans Heinrich Lammers, chief of the Reich Chancellery and Hitler's legal adviser

The NSDAP

In stark contrast to the Reichstag, confined to purely decorative functions, the one and only party represented in parliament, with all its organizations – SA, SS, Hitler Youth, National Socialist Students' League, National Socialist Women's Organizations and the National Socialist Motor Corps – and associated groups, was a, indeed *the* core political organization of the Third Reich. From July 1933, the NSDAP had no political competitors, and from December 1933, it became a corporation under public law. Officially, the party was supposed to articulate the will of the "national comrades" who were more or less closely associated with it, so that the state could execute their will through the administration. The NSDAP handbook defined as a political objective a situation where "party and state are one and the same".

The primary method chosen to achieve this objective was to interlock the various institutions of party and state. Not only Hitler himself, but other high-ranking NSDAP officials like Himmler, Goebbels and Darré, too, held senior positions in public office. Analogously to his position in the party apparatus, Rudolf Hess, Hitler's deputy as party leader, deputized Hitler the Reich Chancellor as Reich minister without portfolio, and had the right to be involved in all aspects of decision-making. The National Socialist *Gauleiter*, or District Leaders, were in fact more powerful than the officials acting in a ministerial capacity, the Reich Leaders (*Reichsleiter*), as they also in many cases held key posts in the state apparatus as Reich ministers, Reich governors, or administrative heads (*Oberpräsidenten*) of Prussian provinces.

Obviously, the continuous introduction of new areas of authority frequently gave rise to power struggles within the party. It also created rivalries with state bodies that had been carried over into the National Socialist regime. The NSDAP's "Foreign Division" and Alfred Rosenberg's Foreign Policy Office competed with the ministry officially responsible for foreign policy, the Reich Foreign Office, which since 1932 had been headed by Constantin von Neurath. True to his style of leadership, Hitler presented himself as the supreme arbitrating authority in constella-

Left:
NSDAP manifesto, 41st-50th edition, 1931

Right:
Propaganda poster for the National Socialist Women's Organizations

"From Hitler Youth to Wehrmacht member", propaganda poster, 1941

tions of this sort. When Neurath lost his ministry to Joachim von Ribbentrop in 1938, he nevertheless continued as minister without portfolio and was also invested with the post of Chairman of the "Secret Cabinet Council" – an organization that existed only on paper.

While institutional expansion of the NSDAP fitted in with Hitler's calculated efforts to secure power, rapidly rising membership numbers certainly did not. After all, a mass party that was increasingly riddled with politically inactive people who had merely jumped on the bandwagon could hardly claim to embody the ideologically unshakeable elite of the National Socialist movement. Joining the state party, however, was seen – quite rightly – as a means of promoting one's career. As a result, party membership, which stood at around 850,000 on the date the National Socialists assumed power, trebled by 1 May 1933. So the party leadership issued a ban on new memberships that remained in force until 1939, although it was watered down by special

Hitler saluting units of the Reich Labour Service at the NSDAP national rally in Nuremberg in 1934

exceptions. At the end of the Second World War, the NSDAP had more than eight million members.

During the war yet more state duties were assigned to the party. From 1942, all party *Gauleiter* acted as Commissioners for Defence of the Reich at the same time, and from 1944 the party was put in charge of anti-aircraft defence and raising the *Volkssturm*, or People's Army. Especially in the latter stages of the National Socialist regime, the fact that the Führer principle was the sole basis of government was patently clear; the same was true of the NSDAP: it was obvious to the very end that the whole of this vast organization was dedicated to the same principle.

In October 1945, the victorious allied powers banned the NSDAP and its associated organizations and sub-organizations, and other bodies under its control. At the Nuremberg Trial the NSDAP was declared a criminal organization, including even the lowest-ranking party officials, the Cell and Block Leaders – a verdict that affected around 700,000 people.

The SA, SS and Gestapo

Within the National Socialist regime, the SA, SS and Gestapo were extremely important as executive organs of the National Socialist reign of state terrorism. The SA, or *Sturmab-*

teilung, founded in 1921 as a paramilitary force to fight for and defend the National Socialist party, played a crucial role in the National Socialists' struggle to win power. Invested with some police powers, it continued to act in this capacity even after Hitler's takeover. Its main task, however, was to carry out the early terror campaigns against Jewish people and intimidate or violently eliminate political opponents. Some groups also acted on their own initiative, for example during the Köpenick "Bloody Week" of June 1933, while the SA leadership under Ernst Röhm sought greater political influence, calling for continuation of the "national revolution". The SA was eliminated as a power factor in the "night of the long knives", from 30 June to 1 July 1934, and the organization thereafter confined itself mainly to providing its members with pre- and post-military training.

The attacks that deprived the SA of its power were carried out mainly by special commandos of the SS, or *Schutzstaffel*, the elite guard that grew out of Hitler's personal bodyguard. Three weeks later, Hitler made the SS, hitherto part of the SA, an independent organization.

SA terror in the run-up to the March elections of 1933

WAFFEN-SS

EINTRITT NACH VOLLENDETEM 17. LEBENSJAHR

Top:
SS formation
at the NSDAP
national rally
in Nuremberg
in 1937

Bottom:
propaganda
poster for the
Waffen-SS

special executive, responsible only to the "Führer and Reich Chancellor". It ran the concentration camps, which were guarded principally by *SS-Totenkopfverbände*, or Death's Head Formations, and it had its own commercial enterprise, in which thousands of prisoners were forced to work in inhuman conditions. After the war broke out, it even had its own army, the *Waffen-SS*, which ultimately numbered nearly a million soldiers. In the latter years of the war, as Reich Leader of the SS from 1936, and at the same time "Chief of German Police in the Reich Ministry of the Interior", and therefore State Secretary, Himmler also assumed the offices of Reich Minister of the Interior and Commander of the relief army. This definitively promoted him to the rank of second most powerful, and most feared, official of the Third Reich. Invested with wide-ranging powers, his mobile *Einsatzgruppen*, or Task Forces, "selected" the population in the conquered territories according to racial criteria and carried off "people of alien races", especially Poles and Russians, as forced labour to German territory. The decision by National Socialist leaders on the "final solution to the Jewish question" was now implemented by the SS in purpose-built extermination camps.

The Gestapo (*Geheime Staatspolizei*), or secret police, established in 1933, grew out of the political police of Prussia. It was authorized to conduct house searches without a warrant and arrest "suspicious" persons and have them interned in concentration camps at its own discretion. As the regime's principal instrument for systematically eliminating political opponents, a law passed in February 1936 assigned to the Gestapo the task of "investigating and combating all activities that pose a danger to the state throughout German territory", stating that it was to cooperate closely with the other authorities to this end. Within the concentration camps, the Gestapo was given control of the political departments that included the police records department, which had free rein to interrogate and torture prisoners and put them to death without trial. Himmler at first was only chief of the

At the head of the SS were Heinrich Himmler and his deputy, Reinhard Heydrich, who from 1932 was officially in charge of the party's internal Security Service and later also head of the Reich Central Security Office, established in 1939. Under their leadership, in the years that followed, the SS not only became the most powerful organization in the National Socialist state; it developed into a sort of

30,000 in 1944 – participated in the deportation of the Jews or were actively involved elsewhere in SS killer units.

The judiciary

The scope of authority of the judiciary was considerably reduced very early on in the Third Reich by party and military jurisdiction, but most of all by the jurisdiction of the police and the SS, which were in direct competition with it. A great many people who, in the Gestapo's eyes, had been given too soft a sentence for political, and sometimes non-political offences, were summarily taken into "protective custody" after serving their prison term. People who had just been acquitted were re-arrested by the police, sometimes before they could leave the courthouse. The conservative Reich Minister of Justice, Franz Gürtner, who had also served in the Papen and Schleicher cabinets, protested against such acts of despotism, officially declared to be "preventive measures by the state police". But his successor, Franz Schlegelberger, went along with Hitler's desire to control the administration of justice and curtailed judges' independence by ordering consultations in problematic cases. Ultimately, with National Socialist Georg Thierack in the post of Minister of Justice from August 1942, the relinquishing of authority to the police no longer met with any resistance. From July 1943, for example, offences by German Jews were punishable only by the police.

The Gestapo offices at Prinz-Albrecht-Strasse 8 in Berlin

Left. Reich SS Leader Heinrich Himmler, Minister of the Interior from 1943 and Commander of the relief army from 1944

Bottom: Ceremony marking the assumption of supreme judicial power by the Reich, 2 April 1935. The speaker is Hermann Göring

political police at *Länder* level, but following his appointment as chief of police for the whole of Germany, he brought all divisions of the police apparatus under the control of the SS, and put SS leaders at the helm of its various organs. The Gestapo and the Criminal Police together formed the *Sicherheitspolizei*, or Security Police. Soon after the start of the war, this in turn was brought under the umbrella of the Reich Central Security Office of the SS, along with the Security Service. During the war, a large number of Gestapo officers – of whom there were more than

Hans Kerrl (centre), Prussian Minister of Justice, on a visit to the elite camp for legal trainees at Jüterbog, 1934

state, such as "danger to public security". Such measures provided the finishing stroke: every conventional notion of legal certainty had now been effectively destroyed.

For political offences, the Third Reich had special courts, staffed primarily with proven National Socialists. These courts had the power to sentence suspects without preliminary legal investigation, and there was no possibility to appeal against the verdict. The offences of high treason, treason and – later – "seditious undermining of the military power" were prosecuted through the *Volksgerichthof*, or "People's Court", established in April 1934. From 1942 until his death in February 1945, this body was presided over by the infamous "hanging judge", Roland Freisler. The role the People's Court was intended to play within the regime was stated quite plainly by senior public prosecutor Parisius: "Its role is not to pronounce justice, but to annihilate opponents of National Socialism." And the People's Court applied itself to this task with considerable vigour: out of approximately 16,000 death

There was no such thing as an independent judiciary under the National Socialist regime. When the presidential statutes of the courts were abolished, their chambers and panels came under the direct control of the judicial administration. The upcoming generation of lawyers had to swear an oath to National Socialist principles at special trainee camps. In 1936, at the *"Thing des Rechts"*, or Law Assembly (whose title harked back to ancient Germanic traditions), Hans Frank, leader of the National Socialist Jurists' League, declared that before delivering their verdict all lawyers must ask themselves "How would the Führer decide in my place?" As the discretionary powers of the courts were severely curbed by being tied to the legislation of the totalitarian state, the verdict was usually the one the regime wanted. Despite this, Hitler repeatedly reproached the judiciary for not being strict enough. In the Weimar Republic there were only three offences that carried the death penalty; under the Third Reich this number rose to 45. Criminal laws were introduced with retrospective effect; categories of offender were devised that bordered on the metaphorical, such as *"Volksschädling"*, or enemy of the people, and it was made obligatory to include a clause justifying a verdict for reasons of

Roland Freisler, President of the *Volksgerichtshof*, or "People's Court", from 1942-1945

After the coup attempt of 20 July 1944: Captain Friedrich Carl Klausing being led away after being sentenced to death by the *Volksgerichtshof*

sentences imposed by German courts other than Wehrmacht courts between 1933 and 1945, more than 5,000 were delivered by judges of the People's Court.

Civil service and administration

The "Act on the Re-establishment of the Permanent Civil Service", and the detailed regulations that followed concerning its implementation, definitively excluded Communists and registered Social Democrats from continuing to work in the civil service and public administration. *Gleichschaltung* of the civil service and public administration was thus effectively complete. In line with the party motto "It is not the state that commands us, we command the state", around two per cent of the 1.5 million or so civil servants were dismissed or sent into retirement – some having to accept a cut in pension – on the basis of the "Act on the Re-establishment of the Permanent Civil Service" or the Aryan clause. Others had to be content with a "lower-ranking office". In the Interior Administration of Prussia, for a long time a bastion

Civil servants being introduced to directives for administrative officials, at the Palais Czernin in Prague, 1939

of the rule of law, the proportion of higher-grade civil servants who were dismissed or subjected to financial sanctions stood at around 28 per cent.

The old, established state bureaucracy may not have been in the least inclined to switch from its cherished "silent reserve" to open disobedience towards the new rulers, but it did attach importance to ensuring legally correct administration within the scope of its jurisdiction, even though this was increasing-

A function in Hamburg, held by the Reich Civil Service League, 3 July 1933

ly curtailed by competing authorities. It was not in the interests of independent ministers like Neurath and Schacht, or even National Socialist ministers like Göring and Goebbels, to let full-time party functionaries meddle in the management of their areas of jurisdiction. So these areas systematically closed ranks, especially against the advances of party minister Hess, who was in charge of them. This had the rather paradoxical consequence that even as late as 1938, in the Reich Labour Ministry, for example, only 5 out of 38 ministerial counsellors were party members. The Civil Service Act of 1937, which broadened the criteria for compulsory retirement even further, rarely had to be applied, however. For that, the loyalty of the civil service as a whole was too great.

Gauleiter (district leader) Arthur Greiser (2nd from right) welcoming the one-millionth resettler to the new Reich District of Wartheland, 1944

The second phase of the National Socialist regime saw the burgeoning of specialist and extraordinary administrative departments connected with the war, and the traditional Reich authorities were now definitively marginalized. In the occupied eastern territories, civil administrations comprising a *Reichskommissariat*, or Reich Commission, and general administrative offices subordinate to them, were quickly set up to replace the military administrations, which were mis-

trusted by Hitler. Here especially, the new authorities were able to act with a considerable degree of autonomy. Administrative officials of the old school were not expected to be sufficiently committed to implement plans for the ruthless Germanization of the local population, and so "battle-tried" party functionaries with no administrative experience were moved into leading posts. From here – often in fierce competition with the local SS and police leadership – they set about building their own, self-governing territorial fiefdoms with special privileges. Officials dispatched by the Reich Ministry of the Interior were often sent straight back. The resulting conflicts of jurisdiction persisted right up until the collapse of the dictatorship. In October 1941, Frick and Arthur Greiser, leader of the new Reich district of Wartheland (western Poland), ended a dispute with the Regional Commissioner over who had authority to issue directives when they came to the conclusion that the matter could only be resolved after the Reich reform had been carried out. This, of course, never happened.

In the final stages of the "Führer state", when the government lost virtually all significance, the influence of the Reich Chancellery also dwindled. Instead, the people at the Führer's field headquarters, in direct and constant contact with Hitler, became more important. This was particularly true of Hitler's confidant, Martin Bormann, who was officially in charge of the party chancellery from 1941, and from 1943 bore the title of "Secretary to the Führer". Latterly, when Hitler was completely preoccupied with the affairs of war, Bormann took care of party matters in his first role, while in

Martin Bormann, head of the NSDAP chancellery, and "Secretary to the Führer" from 1943

his second he attended to government business – although this was now largely irrelevant. Lammers, nominally still head of the Reich government, was reduced to Bormann's puppet. Towards the end of the Third Reich the "Secretary to the Führer" was one of the most powerful political figures.

The Wehrmacht

The seizure of power by the National Socialists, sloganized as a "national uprising", was by and large welcomed by the leadership and troops of the *Reichswehr*, or Reich Armed Forces. After all, by establishing a new order in Germany's internal affairs, mercilessly combating communism, and building up arms with a view to restoring Germany's position as a great power, the regime was pursuing objectives that found broad resonance within the armed forces. Reich Defence Minister Blomberg thought it would be fortuitous "if this movement soon achieves the totality it is striving for". Meanwhile, Walter von Reichenau, head of the ministerial office, demanded that commanders agree to the National Socialists' repressive measures: "All that is rotten in the state must go, and this can only be achieved by means of terror. The party will deal ruthless-

Hitler conversing with Reich Defence Minister Blomberg (left) and Werner Freiherr von Fritsch (3rd from left), Commander in Chief of the Army, 1936

ly with Marxism. The job of the Wehrmacht is to be at the ready." After the SA had been deprived of power, Hitler declared the Wehrmacht to be the military pillar of the state, the sole "carrier of arms" in Germany, while the party was the sole "carrier of the people's will". From February 1934, NSDAP insignia appeared on the uniforms of German armed forces' personnel; the oath of allegiance to Hitler

Recruits being sworn in, Potsdam, 7 November 1935

Left:
Colonel General Franz Halder, Chief of the General Staff until 1942, interned from 1944-45

Right:
Admiral Wilhelm Canaris, head of Counterintelligence until 1944, arrested following the coup attempt of 20 July 1944, and executed on 9 April 1945

they were required to swear after the death of Hindenburg went further than earlier formulations, pledging "unconditional obedience".

A law was passed on 21 May 1935, reintroducing conscription; with it, the *Reichswehr* officially became the *Wehrmacht*. Military service was made compulsory for all men between the age of 18 and 45; Jews, however, were excluded from active military service. In the period that followed, a good many officers suspected of being politically unreliable lost their posts in the military leadership. After Blomberg's dismissal, Hitler assumed supreme command of the armed forces himself and filled the newly created Wehrmacht High Command exclusively with military men who submitted completely to his will.

Nonetheless, many high-ranking officers in the Wehrmacht drew the line with regard to the military oath of obedience when the political leadership took what they considered to be an irresponsible gamble. For example, Ludwig Beck, the chief of the General Staff, resigned from active service in September 1938 because he saw that Hitler's planned military occupation of Czechoslovakia could trigger a European war, with devastating consequences for Germany. His successor, Franz Halder, together with Admiral Wilhelm Canaris, head of the foreign counterintelligence unit, or *Abwehr*, in the Wehrmacht High Command, and numerous other military and civilian opponents of the regime, in the end made plans to overthrow Hitler. This plan seemed on the point of being put into effect in the autumn of 1939. However, military successes in the early years of the war, particularly the astonishingly rapid subjugation of France – attributable to Hitler's campaign plan – coupled with serious conflicts of loyalty among the conspirators, repeatedly delayed implementation of such plans. On 20 July 1944, an attempt was finally made to topple Hitler, but it ended in disaster. A resolution passed the previous year to bring the armed forces completely under the control of the party – primarily by installing National Socialist political officers, so-called "operations officers" – was now rigorously implemented.

The conduct of the armed forces in the occupied territories and their attitude to the systematic terror practised by SS and police units varied enormously. One report from the campaign in Poland expressed "abhorrence and loathing" concerning the crimes being perpetrated, and declared it beyond the comprehension of any soldier "how such things can go unpunished, especially if they happen, as it were, under his protection". In the racial war of annihilation against the Soviet Union, on the other hand, in which both sides violated fundamental conventions of war and principles of international law, it was more common to find the armed forces and the SS operating side by side. Suspension of the rule of law for civilians meant that persons suspected of helping partisans could be summarily executed; Hitler's "Commissar Order", in which he ordered the immediate shooting of any Red Army commissar taken in battle or resistance, was carried out in a great many cases. Although criticism of such acts of terror never entirely ceased in some sections of the army, units generally covered up for, and sometimes even provided technical support for the murder of hundreds of thousands of civilians – most of them Jewish. The Wehrmacht thus became directly enmeshed in the crimes of the National Socialist leadership. On 16 October 1946, the heads of the Wehrmacht High Command, General Field Marshall Wilhelm Keitel and Colonel General Alfred Jodl, were executed in Nuremberg as major war criminals.

Shooting of
hostages
following a
drumhead
court martial
by SS and
Wehrmacht
officials in the
Yugoslavian
town of
Pančevo,
April 1941

4. Persecution and resistance

Prisoners being taken into "protective custody" at Oranienburg concentration camp on 10 April 1933. On left of row: Ernst Heilmann, leader of the SPD parliamentary group in the Prussian *Landtag*; next to him, Friedrich Ebert (SPD), son of the first Reich President

In the Third Reich, there was no centrally managed resistance movement taking co-ordinated action. To begin with, resistance was organized mainly by the Communists and the Social Democrats, who were also the primary targets of National Socialist persecution. Their conspiratorial organizations had to contend not only with the growing public support the National Socialist regime enjoyed due to its political successes, but also with internal disputes of their own. Communist party resistance groups at first made almost no attempt to conceal their operations and were quickly uncovered by

271/46.

Reichskriegsgericht   21 Abdrucke
  2. Senat
StPL (HLS) II 129/42
StPL (RKA) III 495/42   Geheime Kommandofache!   6. Jan. 1943
        III 496/42
        III 497/42

           Im Namen

des Deutschen Volkes!

Feldurteil.

In der Strafsache gegen
       1.) den Oberleutnant Harro S c h u l z e - B o y s e n ,
       2.) die Ehefrau Libertas S c h u l z e - B o y s e n ,
       3.) den Oberregierungsrat Dr. Arwid H a r n a c k ,
       4.) die Ehefrau Mildred H a r n a c k ,
       5.) den Oberleutnant Herbert G o l l n o w ,
       6.) den Funker Horst H e i l m a n n ,
       7.) den Soldat Kurt S c h u m a c h e r ,
       8.) die Ehefrau Elisabeth S c h u m a c h e r ,
       9.) den Dreher Hans C o p p i ,
      10.) den Kraftfahrer Kurt S c h u l z e ,
      11.) die Gräfin Erika von B r o c k d o r f f ,
      12.) den Handelsvertreter Johannes G r a u d e n z
wegen Hochverrats u.a.
hat das Reichskriegsgericht, 2. Senat, in der Sitzung vom 19. Dezember
1942 auf Grund der mündlichen Hauptverhandlung vom 15. - 19. Dezember 1942
an der teilgenommen haben
   als Richter:
       Senatspräsident Dr. Kraell, Verhandlungsleiter,
       General Mußhoff,
       Vizeadmiral Arps,
       Generalmajor Stutzer,
       Reichskriegsgerichtsrat Dr. Schmitt,
   als Vertreter der Anklage:
       Oberstkriegsgerichtsrat Dr. Roeder,
   als Urkundsbeamter:

                                Heeresjustizinspektor

the Gestapo. For many years the KPD continued to view the Social Democrats, or "social fascists", as they disparagingly called them, as the main enemy. Not until October 1935, did the new leadership caucus centred around Wilhelm Pieck decide to adjust the party's course. At the "Brussels Conference", the cover name for a meeting of leading Communist Party officials near Moscow, it was decided that the KPD should take "united action" with the SPD to establish an "antifascist people's front" that included all opponents of the regime. In practice, however, it proved almost impossible to realize such an ambitious plan, not least because many exiled German communists were soon caught up in the Stalinist net of terror. Within Germany, new resistance groups began to form in 1938/39, particularly around communists recently released from prison, such as Theodor Neubauer and Anton Saefkow. These groups soon transcended party boundaries, but were barely able to operate effectively due to the long-since perfected surveillance system. This was not the case, however, with the inner circle of the *Rote Kapelle*, the communist resistance organization with the most extensive network, and whose members included not only communists. Its espionage activities for the Soviet Union, coordinated by Harro Schulze-Boysen and Arvid Harnack, remained undetected until 1942, when the group was smashed as a result of betrayal. On 28 August 1944, Ernst Thälmann, longstanding chairman of the KPD, was murdered in the Buchenwald concentration

"Field sentence" issued by the Reich Court-Martial in respect of members of the resistance organization, *Rote Kapelle*

Left: Journalist Carl von Ossietzky in the Papenburg-Esterwegen concentration camp, 1934

Members of the "White Rose", a student resistance group, in Munich on 23 July 1942. From left: Hans Scholl, Sophie Scholl, Christoph Probst

camp – one of over 100 former Reichstag deputies who fell victim to the National Socialist reign of terror.

Social Democrat resistance was deeply divided. The *Deutsche Volksfront*, or German People's Front, formed in 1935 by Social Democrats within Germany associated with Hermann Brill, accused both the KPD and their own party leaders of political failure, and broke off contact with the SPD executive in exile in Prague. *Neu Beginnen*, or New Beginning, a resistance group closely connected with it, was crushed in 1938; the death sentence was meted out to more than 30 of its leaders. Although the SPD executive in exile (known as *SoPaDe*) made contact with communist officials, it rejected the KPD's goal of establishing a "dictatorship of the proletariat" and soon became embroiled in heated disputes on the political goals of Social Democracy. Largely unaffected by the strife within the party in exile over its future political direction, Social Democrats remaining in Germany stepped up their efforts to find effective ways of cooperating with

opposition groups in the armed forces and the administration from the late 1930s. The Kreisau Circle, a loose association of people opposed to the regime, was led by Helmuth James Graf von Moltke. It encompassed a wide variety of political views, including Catholic and Lutheran clerics, conservative experts from the administration, ministry officials, high-ranking Wehrmacht officers, and Social Democrats such as Julius Leber and Carlo Mierendorff. The group drafted documents containing basic principles for a future new democratic order in Germany, within a system of European states. However, it was only rather late in the day that they could bring themselves to contemplate the idea of overthrowing the National Socialist regime by force.

As well as organized resistance by conspiratorial networks operating over a more or less extensive area, there were also actions – often spontaneous and usually tied to a specific situation – by individuals acting alone or small groups. On 8 November 1939, a carpenter named Georg Elser made an attempt on Hitler's life by planting a bomb in the Bürgerbräu beer-hall in Munich. It was only by coincidence that he escaped unharmed. International attention was caught by the flyer campaigns of the *Weisse Rose*, or White Rose, a student-led resistance group at the University of Munich. They staged public political demonstrations – a unique phenomenon in the Third Reich – against the National Socialist regime. Sophie and Hans Scholl and Christoph Probst, three of the group's organizers, were put to death three days after their arrest on 18 February 1943. Their mentor, philosophy professor Kurt Huber, also later sentenced to death, fearlessly defended his actions before the People's Court: "A return to clear, moral principles, to the rule of law, and to mutual trust between one person and another, is not illegal. Quite the contrary: it is the restoration of legality."

Colonel Claus Graf Schenk von Stauffenberg, chief of staff to the commander of the relief army

Resistance only became a serious threat to the National Socialist dictatorship when nationalist-conservative groups, who held key positions in the military and civil service, also set their sights on overthrowing the regime of terror, abandoning the loyal stance they had maintained – albeit with scepticism – for so long. While there had been reservations in these circles from the beginning with regard to some of the regime's prac-

Hitler and Benito Mussolini inspecting the conference room of the *Wolfsschanze* (wolf's lair), the Führer's field headquarters, following the coup attempt by Stauffenberg

tices, pamphlets such as the "freedom letters", of the *Deutsche Freiheitspartei*, or German Freedom Party, founded in London in 1937 by liberal politicians in exile, certainly attracted attention. Within the Wehrmacht, however, actual preparations for a *coup d'état* aimed at bringing down the whole regime were only made when Germany's military situation began to worsen rapidly and the war crimes being committed became too much to bear, even for many officers trained in the spirit of military subordination and sworn to loyalty to Hitler. Most of the plotters were aware that they could no longer avert Germany's defeat. For them the true significance of their act was, in the words of Henning von Tresckow, to show "before the world and before history" that there had been resistance in Germany to the National Socialist regime. They devised a plan to kill Hitler at his East Prussian field headquarters using an explosive device, and then send in armed forces commandos to arrest all SS, Gestapo and party leaders. Available units of the relief army would be ordered to occupy all administrative authorities, ministries, and command, propaganda and transport centres.

The attack was carried out by Colonel Claus Schenk Graf von Stauffenberg on 20 July 1944, but it failed. Stauffenberg and four of his fellow conspirators were put straight before a firing squad that same evening. Others, like Beck and Tresckow, took their own lives. Around 200 resistance fighters, including many members of the Kreisau Circle, who had collaborated with the rebel military officers, were sentenced to death by the People's Court. The defendants were subjected to every sort of humiliation, culminating in the manner in which their sentence was carried out: they were hung from meat hooks. The Gestapo mercilessly unleashed the full force of its brutality on the families of those condemned, on those presumed to have been in the know, and on any remaining resistance groups, most of which were now swiftly exposed. While the situation on the war fronts was gradually becoming hopeless, the National Socialist regime notched up a last victory at home.

Foreign Office counsellor Adam von Trott zu Solz, one of the conspirators in the 20 July coup attempt, standing before the *Volksgerichtshof* on 15 August 1944

5. Persecution and extermination of the Jews

From the early 1920s a racialist world-view and anti-Semitism were central elements of National Socialist ideology. Hitler was a fanatical racist and anti-Semite. The NSDAP absorbed many prejudices long prevalent among broad sections of German society. These had been a decisive influence even before 1919 on the likes of the Pan-German League and the 400 or more *völkisch*, or nationalist-patriotic, organizations related to it. But only the crisis-ridden years of the Weimar Republic created the conditions that enabled widespread resentment towards the Jews to be translated into a radical pro-gramme of action against what was claimed to be a Jewish-Bolshevist "world conspiracy".

After the National Socialists assumed power, the grass roots of the party and its leaders in the regime, in a process of mutual radicali-zation, began to put their anti-Semitic ideas into practice. In early March 1933, hostility towards Jews began to vent itself in a series of attacks, mostly initiated by local NSDAP politicians or the SA. With a three-day boycott of Jewish shopkeepers, lawyers and doctors beginning on 1 April, the party leadership sought to gain control of this anti-Semitic movement. At the same time, a number of laws and decrees marked the beginning of a phase during which Jewish citizens were systematically deprived of their rights. This process reached its provisional climax on 15 September 1935: the so-called Nuremberg l aws, hastily drafted on Hitler's orders, quashed any last hope that Jewish people might be able to continue living within German society with even a modicum of security. Of these, the "Act on Reich Citizen-ship" established a distinction between "citizens of the Reich ... of German or related blood", and mere subjects without rights of citizenship. The "Act on the Protection of German Blood" imposed a ban on marriages and extramarital relations between Jews and

Propaganda inciting a boy-cott of Jewish shopkeepers in Berlin, 1 April 1933

non-Jews. "Racial defilement" now became a punishable offence. Subsequent ordinances pertaining to the Act's implementation stated quite clearly that "a Jew ... cannot be a citizen of the Reich", glibly defining the Jewish race on the basis of the religious affiliation of a person's close forebears.

In the first year following the assumption of power by the National Socialist regime, some 37,000 Jewish people fled Germany. This number had risen tenfold by the start of the war, with wave after wave of emigration. As many of the refugees remained in Europe, their flight by no means guaranteed them lasting protection from the National Socialist onslaught. Subjected to innumerable forms of everyday harassment, the Jewish com-munity that stayed on in Germany became more tightly knit. Self-help organizations were established, such as the Central Com-mittee for Relief and Reconstruction, di-rected by Leo Baeck, which coordinated

From 1935, identity cards of Jewish citizens were marked with a "J"

Jewish emigrants embarking in Hamburg, 1937

and financed vocational retraining and resettlement of fellow Jews who had lost their livelihoods.

In 1938, persecution of the Jews escalated to a new level. On the initiative of the Reich Ministry of Economics, temporarily headed by Göring following the dismissal of Hjalmar Schacht, some 4,000 businesses were "Aryanized" between April and October alone. Jewish doctors were henceforth to be designated *Krankenbehandler*, or medical attendants, and Jewish lawyers *Konsulenten*, or legal advisors, and only Jewish people could use their services. As "Plenipotentiary for the Four-Year Plan", Göring was given the formal right of disposal over Jewish assets with a value of 5,000 reichsmarks or more. In October, around 17,000 Polish Jews long resident in Germany were deported. When a 17-year-old Jew, Herschel Grynszpan, then assassinated a legation secretary at the German Embassy in Paris, the National Socialist regime staged a massive pogrom throughout the Reich, claiming it to be in retaliation. In the night of 9-10 November, the so-called *Kristallnacht*, or crystal night, thus named because of the broken glass left strewn on the streets, and in the days that followed, SA and SS troops and their fanaticized party comrades went on the rampage. They ransacked a vast number of Jewish businesses and homes; almost all Germany's synagogues went up in flames. Many Jewish people were murdered and more than 26,000 were detained in concentration camps at Dachau, Buchenwald and Sachsenhausen.

The intimidated population responded for the most part passively.

After the onset of war, a new flood of official decrees finalized the degradation and marginalization of those Jews still remaining in Germany. They were deprived of radios and telephone lines, subjected to a nightly curfew, forced to work in armaments factories for a pittance and, from September 1941, they were made to wear the star of David. From autumn 1940, their names were held in a "Jewish register" at the local Gestapo office. All this heralded the final stage of the National Socialists' policy on the Jews.

From the start of the Russian campaign in June 1941, resolute action was taken to carry out Hitler's threat of January 1939 that a future war would result in the annihilation of the Jewish race in Europe. This year marked the shift from persecution to systematic physical annihilation of Jewish people. Previous forms of repression and provisional plans to intern Jews outside Europe were

The synagogue on Börneplatz in Frankfurt am Main in flames on 10 November 1938

now superseded by the "final solution of the Jewish question", the term used in the minutes of the "Wannsee Conference" held on 20 January 1942, to denote the plans for genocide. Mass shootings, initially in the areas conquered by Germany, were carried out by special SS units, or *Einsatzgruppen*, and the Gestapo. Then followed the systematic deportation of all Jewish people remaining in the occupied countries of Europe and the German Reich to specially equipped extermination camps. The main camps were located at Auschwitz-Birkenau, Treblinka and Lublin-Maidanek. There, a hydrogen cyanide compound called Zyklon-B, previously tested on prisoners of war and sick detainees, was deployed for the purpose of genocide. Most of the Jews taken to the camps, usually in cattle-wagons – notably women, children and older men – were "selected" for death in the gas chambers on arrival; a slow and agonizing death through forced labour awaited the rest. The extermination camps continued to operate, and their capacity increase, until late 1944, virtually right up

Incinerator at Bergen-Belsen concentration camp

until they were captured by the Red Army. According to credible estimates, well over five million Jews fell victim to the National Socialists' racial madness.

Selection for the gas chambers at the gates of the extermination camp at Auschwitz-Birkenau, 1944

6. The Second World War

The first Wehrmacht tanks on training manoeuvres in Döberitz, 1936

From the outset, the objective of National Socialist foreign policy was expansion. In *Mein Kampf*, the blueprint of Hitler's programme, published in 1925/27, Hitler had already stated categorically that in the foreign policy field he would not be content merely to re-establish Germany's pre-1914 borders and its position as a great power. Instead, he was willing to stake everything on conquering "living space" in eastern Europe for the "Germanic master race". He reaffirmed this intention in a secret address to high-ranking German army officers on 3 February 1933.

Nevertheless, the impression originally prevailing among the German public and abroad was that Hitler was merely continuing the efforts of earlier governments to achieve a revision of the Versailles Treaty. At first, pursuing a relatively restrained foreign policy,

the National Socialist regime attempted to stabilize its initially insecure situation, as long as there was a risk of foreign intervention while it was not yet adequately armed for a military conflict. The staff of the diplomatic service, still headed by Foreign Minister Constantin von Neurath, were retained. The concordat of 20 July 1933 concluded between the German Reich and the Vatican was highly effective in counteracting potential moves to isolate Germany, as indeed was the non-aggression pact signed with Poland six months later. Neither Germany's withdrawal from the League of Nations in October 1933, nor its military build-up, in violation of the Versailles Treaty, but carried on quite openly from 1935, prevented the western powers from allowing themselves to be deceived as to Hitler's true intentions. They were even willing to seek a

Guernica.
Painting by
Pablo Picasso,
1937

new *modus vivendi* with the National Socialists. The signing of a naval convention between Germany and Great Britain in June 1935 ultimately placed Hitler's policy of rearmament on a firm diplomatic footing. It also pointed in the direction of the constellation or alliance envisaged by Hitler for his planned war of conquest in eastern Europe: after dividing up spheres of influence, the new continental power, Germany, would take its place alongside the old colonial power, Great Britain.

Instead, the regime's unbending determination to destroy the existing international order and arrive at a position of hegemony for Germany, almost inevitably encouraged it to join forces with the two other countries likewise seeking aggressively to expand their respective spheres of influence: Italy and Japan. Initially, German-Italian relations were marred by conflicts of interests concerning Austria. The colonial war of conquest waged by Italy from 1935 against the Abyssinian Empire, however, heightened tensions with Great Britain and France and led Italy to seek closer relations with Germany. From 1936, this closing of ranks was reinforced in the Spanish Civil War, in which Germany and Italy intervened on the side of the – ultimately victorious – Falangists and their *Caudillo*, Francisco Franco Bahamonte. In November 1936, Italy's fascist dictator, Benito Mussolini, for the first time referred to an "axis" between Berlin and Rome. This was now extended to Asia: the basic outlines of the system of alliances for the forthcoming war were drawn on 25 November 1936, when Germany and Japan signed the Anti-Comintern Pact, to which Italy acceded a year later.

The Munich conference of 29 September 1938. Front row, from left: British prime minister Chamberlain, French Premier Daladier, Hitler, Italy's *Duce*, Mussolini, and his foreign minister, Ciano

Following the *Anschluss*, or annexation, of Austria on 12 March 1938, which took place amidst great jubilation on the part of the local population despite the involvement of the German army, the National Socialist regime set its expansionist sights on Czechoslovakia. Hitler had plans drawn up for military action; the Sudeten Germans were to operate as a kind of "fifth column".

In September 1938, with the situation on the verge of war, the western powers still clung to the idea of being able to bind Germany into a new, pan-European order. Their compliant policy of "appeasement" reached its pinnacle at the Munich conference of 28 September 1938, at which Mussolini acted as moderator: the British and French governments again acquiesced to Hitler's demands,

Opposite page, bottom: Jubilant crowds on the Heldenplatz in Vienna during Hitler's speech on 15 March 1938

This page: German tanks in the Moravian town of Brno in March 1939

German troops advancing in Poland in September 1939

Hitler and Göring with field marshals appointed following the victory over France in September 1940

and territorial gains in the east. When the Polish government rejected this offer, Hitler – unperturbed by the British-French guarantees given to Poland – resolved to seek a military solution. At the same time, he now sought an understanding with the Soviet Union; this was sealed by the signing of a German-Soviet non-aggression pact on 23 August 1939. In an additional, secret protocol, the two dictators, Hitler and Stalin, agreed on the re-partitioning of Poland and on the boundaries of their respective spheres of influence along the Narev-Vistula-San line. On 1 September 1939, German army units crossed the border into Poland; two days later, France and Britain declared war on the German Reich. The Second World War had begun.

Germany's *Blitzkrieg* victories in the first few months of the war were due in no small measure to the failure of the western powers to establish a second front. Poland only succeeded in stemming the tide of superior German forces for a few weeks, especially when the Red Army occupied the territories of eastern Poland, as agreed, in autumn 1939. In April 1940, Hitler ordered the occupation of Norway and Denmark with a view to ensuring supplies of iron ore from Sweden, while at the same time securing a key base for Atlantic operations. On 10 May 1940, a German offensive was launched against France, Belgium and the Netherlands; it ended, surprisingly quickly, in a triumphant victory for the Wehrmacht. British troops were repulsed from mainland Europe; on 22 June, a ceasefire was imposed on a vanquished France that effectively partitioned the country: the north remained under German occupation, while in the south an authoritarian regime was established under Philippe Pétain, although the last vestiges of any scope for action it had were lost in November 1942, when German troops marched in. However, Hitler's intentions vis-à-vis Great Britain to free his hands for a war in the east failed to come to fruition; he succeeded neither in coming to an arrangement with Great Britain, as he had originally planned, nor in subjugating it militarily – primarily

and Czechoslovakia lost the Sudetenland to the German Reich. But soon afterwards, on 15 March 1939, in a flagrant breach of the Munich Agreement, German troops marched into Prague to establish the "Protectorate of Bohemia and Moravia"; Slovakia was reduced to a satellite state of Germany. For the western powers, Hitler had now gone one step too far.

Meanwhile, German foreign policy focused increasingly on Poland, its neighbour to the east. In return for concessions on bilateral issues, the National Socialist regime offered Poland an alliance against the Soviet Union

with the air offensive launched against Britain in August 1940. The American President, Franklin D. Roosevelt had meanwhile realized that armed conflict with Japan and Germany was unavoidable; with his support, the British Empire, under the leadership of Prime Minister Winston Churchill since May 1940, put up staunch resistance.

In the ensuing months, however, the military situation developed in such a way that Hitler thought he would be able to solve this problem at a later stage. In late March 1941, the *Afrika Korps* led by Erwin Rommel beat the Western Desert Force at Mersa el Brega and was advancing successfully against British positions in Egypt. In April 1941, in order to secure the southern flank for the forthcoming campaign in Russia and prevent an Allied front from being established in south-eastern Europe, German troops intervened in the war in the Balkans on the side of the Italians. They conquered Yugoslavia and Greece and took possession of Crete. Campaign "Barbarossa", too, was planned as another *Blitzkrieg*, or lightning war. Prompted by their initial successes, the bulk of the German

armed forces' leadership, like Franz Halder, chief of the General Staff, assumed that "the campaign against Russia" would be "won within a fortnight". Thereafter, they could once again focus on "the outstanding strategic tasks in the war against England".

Advancing German infantry in Soviet Russia in July 1941

The campaign began on 22 June 1941, with Germany's surprise attack on the Soviet Union. 145 German divisions and a number of contingents from Germany's allies, mainly

Starving Russian prisoners of war

Collecting
point for
Germans who
fell at Stalin-
grad in
February 1943

Romania and Hungary, faced 158 Soviet divisions and 55 tank brigades that had been deployed at the border. Some of these were virtually wiped out in the first battles of encirclement. In contrast to the war in the west, Germany's strategic objective here was not only to defeat the enemy in military terms, but to annihilate them physically: the communist leaders were to be murdered, the population decimated and the country's industrial and agricultural base destroyed. The consequence was a brutal partisan war, which nevertheless did nothing to prevent the advance of the Wehrmacht; in late autumn 1941, advance units of the German army were just 25 kilometres from Moscow. But here the German offensive ground to a halt; the German units were ill-equipped to cope with the harsh Russian winter, and they had to fend off tactical counteroffensives by the Red Army. In this situation, with Germany suffering its first serious setbacks, Hitler declared war on the United States of America on 11 December, four days after the Japanese attack on the US naval base at Pearl Harbor. It was a step only a megalomaniac would take, but one which tied in perfectly with the logic of escalation that was part of Hitler's hegemonic ambitions.

The following year, German troops launched a large-scale offensive with the aim of reaching the oil-fields of central Asia. Although at first they made significant territorial gains, bringing German dominion over foreign territory to its peak in the summer of 1942, there were already signs that a turning point in the war was imminent. Extended front lines and the capabilities of the opposing forces imposed demands that exceeded the capacity of Germany's army, its supply of raw materials and its arms industry. In November 1942, units led by Marshall Georgi Chuikov encircled 18 German and Romanian divisions at Stalingrad. The last remnants of these surrendered on 31 January and 2 February 1943. The Red Army advanced as far as the Dnieper Bend, and repulsed a counter-attack in the Kursk Salient. In North Africa, the forces of the Axis had been on the defensive since their defeat at El Alamein in autumn 1942, and they capitulated on 13 May 1943, in Tunisia. At this point France's African dominions controlled by the Vichy regime joined Charles de Gaulle's liberation army, which was later to form a "provisional government of the French Republic", on 3 June 1944. On 24 July 1943, a few weeks after the launch of the Anglo-American offensive on Sicily, Mussolini was ousted from power. After being freed by German paratroopers, the dictator's sphere of control was limited to the "Republic of Saló" in northern Italy. Meanwhile, on 3 September, the new Italian government concluded a ceasefire agreement. In the Pacific, Germany's principal ally, Japan, was no longer able to make good the losses sustained on 4 June 1942, in the air-sea battle of Midway. Allied bombing offensives on Germany intensified in autumn 1943, costing the lives of countless civilians, but in the end also striking at the nerve centre of the German arms industry. The defeat of the Wehrmacht was now only a matter of time.

As early as January 1943, Churchill and Roosevelt declared in Casablanca that their strategic goal was the "unconditional surrender" of the enemy. In the months that followed, the powers that had joined together to form an "anti-Hitler coalition" – Great Britain, the Soviet Union and the USA – coordinated their military operations with

increasing precision. At the Conference of Teheran in late November 1943, they agreed to combine the establishment of a second front in western Europe, as demanded by Stalin, with a large-scale offensive by the Red Army in the central-eastern European theatre of war. This provided support for the western Allies' landings in Normandy in June 1944, which ushered in the final phase of the war. While the forces of the coalition broke through the fortifications of the "Atlantic Wall" and the eastern Prussian defence positions, Allied bombing reduced the majority of German cities to ash and rubble. After some temporary set-backs, Soviet and United States troops reached Torgau on the river Elbe on 25 April 1945.

The fanatical resistance put up by the National Socialist regime in the battle for Berlin bore the traits of a stage-managed apocalypse. Poorly trained units of the People's Army, the German home guard, were sent to a certain death; refugees died in under-

American troops shortly after the Normandy landing on 6 June 1944

Hitler's last reserves: divisions of the *Volkssturm*, or home guard, being sworn in on 12 November 1944 in Berlin

Field Marshal Wilhelm Keitel signing the unconditional surrender of the Wehrmacht at 00.16 on 9 May 1945, in Berlin-Karlshorst

ground railway tunnels that were flooded for tactical reasons; SS commandos terrorized the war-weary population. When it was no longer conceivable that the city would be relieved militarily or that the anti-Hitler coalition could be split up – although efforts to achieve this continued in vain up to the very end – Hitler, Goebbels and other Nazi leaders took their own lives in the bunker of the Reich Chancellery. Berlin's military governor formally surrendered on 2 May 1945, followed by the Wehrmacht High Command on 7 and 8 May; the last National Socialist government, headed by Grand Admiral Karl Dönitz, was arrested in Flensburg by the occupying forces on 23 May. The war in Europe had come to an end, but the scale of the devastation was unprecedented. The Second World War is estimated to have claimed the lives of around 55 million people. The exact number, however, will never be known.

GEBT MIR FUNF JAHRE
UND IHR WERDET
DEUTSCHLAND NICHT
WIEDER ERKENNEN
ADOLF HITLER

GIVE ME FIVE YEARS &
YOU WILL NOT
RECOGNIZE GERMANY
AGAIN

Sign erected by American soldiers in Aachen, bearing a slogan of Hitler's dating back to February 1933

Under Soviet administration
in accordance with the
Potsdam Agreement

Kaliningrad

Gdansk

Flensburg

Rostock

Lübeck

Bremer-
haven   Hamburg

Soviet zone
of occupation

Szczecin

Bremen

Under Polish administration
in accordance with the
Potsdam Agreement

Hanover

Berlin

British zone
of occupation

Magdeburg

Kassel

Leipzig

Cologne

Erfurt   Dresden

Wroclaw

French zone
of occupation   Frankfurt

Saarland

Saarbrücken

Nuremberg

Stuttgart

American zone
of occupation

Freiburg   Munich

Germany
after 1945

The unconditional surrender of the German Wehrmacht on 7 and 8 May 1945, which brought the Second World War to an end in Europe, set the seal on the greatest catastrophe the German people had ever experienced in their history. Unlike at the end of the First World War, the whole of Germany was occupied by the forces of the four victorious powers and deprived of all state power. Above all, however, this defeat meant the end of the German nation-state in the form established in 1871: Prussia, the heartland of the empire, was dissolved, the eastern provinces were detached from Germany, and, for over four decades, national unity was lost.

Under the rule of the occupying powers, a number of decisions were taken which, in many ways, set the course for Germany's development after 1945. These decisions were primarily the result of the victorious powers' differing views concerning Germany's future political and social order, which quickly proved incompatible. With the onset of the Cold War in 1946/47, Germany became the showground for the conflict of ideology and power politics between East and West and its two main antagonists, the Soviet Union and the USA. This conflict led, in several stages, to the division of Germany and ultimately determined which political and social systems would be established on either side of the intra-German border. The Western powers, in their zones of occupation, took steps to promote the establishment of a parliamentary democracy based on the liberal ideal of a constitutional state and orga-

nized along federal lines. This process culminated in the promulgation of the constitution (Basic Law) of the Federal Republic of Germany on 23 May 1949. While these developments were under way, the German political parties were engaged in a heated debate concerning the nature of the future economic system in the Federal Republic. Following the currency reform of 1948 and the introduction of the Marshall Plan, the argument was won by the advocates of a market economy, who envisaged a system largely free from state intervention and based on private property, but also with an emphasis on social responsibility. Initial plans to nationalize industry were scrapped. In the Soviet zone, on the other hand, following a short phase in which all the parties were united in their pursuit of anti-fascist and democratic goals, a political system was established which came to be dominated more and more by the communists alone; the economy was completely restructured, with the expropriation of large land-holdings and the nationalization of banks and key industries. These developments ultimately led to the establishment of an East German state, the German Democratic Republic (GDR), on 7 October 1949.

During the 1950s, the division of Germany steadily deepened, putting an end to initially widespread hopes that national unity might soon be restored. In the Federal Republic, a fierce battle over the country's political orientation ensued. Under the leadership of Chancellor Konrad Adenauer – heading a governing coalition made up of the CDU and CSU, the Free Democratic Party (FDP) and the German Party – those who favoured a Federal Republic firmly oriented towards the West finally prevailed and in 1955 the Federal Republic was accepted into the Western community of states as an equal partner. In a series of countermoves, the GDR was gradually incorporated into the Soviet-dominated Eastern bloc and ultimately became a full member of the Warsaw Pact in 1955. The intra-German border marked the dividing line between the military might of the Eastern and Western blocs. And it was also German soldiers deployed on both sides of the border who were involved in maintaining the status quo and thus contributed to the divergent development of the Federal Republic and the GDR.

Once initial difficulties had been overcome, the West German economy, boosted by the urgent need for reconstruction after the devastation of the war years and by a sustained economic upturn, entered a period of tangible growth, which continued into the 1960s and benefited all sections of the population, who soon experienced a steady improvement in their standard of living. The "economic miracle" enabled solutions to be found to the massive social problems which were the legacy of National Socialism and the war, but also provided the material conditions under which a comprehensive social welfare system could be established. Above all, however, the continuing economic boom and the absence of serious social tensions gave West Germany's post-war democracy the domestic stability which the Weimar Republic had so grievously lacked.

In the East, by contrast, a Soviet-style dictatorship emerged, sometimes requiring the massive use of force to sustain it and intended to prepare the ground for a communist order. Initially, East Germany's leading state party, the Socialist Unity Party (SED), as it was officially known from 1952 onwards, sought to "build socialism" within the framework of a planned economy. Agriculture was progressively collectivized and industrial enterprises and trading concerns converted into state-owned companies. Although the efforts to build up the new system were successful to some degree, living conditions improved only gradually. Popular discontent began to grow, culminating in an uprising on 17 June 1953. Soviet tanks were deployed, and the insurrection was crushed. At this time, more than 210,000 people were leaving the GDR for the West each year. It was not until the Berlin Wall was built on 13 August 1961, and the intra-German border effectively sealed, that the GDR achieved stability as a state. Nevertheless, the East German economy increasingly lagged behind that of West Germany as time went on.

While the SED leadership was at great pains to promote the GDR as a state in its own right, there was growing support in West Germany for the Federal Republic's claim to be the sole legitimate representative of Germany to be tempered and for a change of policy on Germany.

The 1960s were a time of transition for the Federal Republic in other respects as well. The first sharp economic downturn and the ensuing crisis which faced the Erhard government in the autumn of 1966 were considered so serious that the CDU/CSU and the SPD agreed to form a grand coalition for a limited period in order to overcome the difficulties. There was also a desire within the population for a change of course in foreign and social policy, which manifested itself in two ways: on the one hand, in the student-led protest movement of the late 1960s, and, on the other, in the government changeover of 1969 when a Social Democrat became Federal Chancellor for the first time.

In the foreign policy field, the main priority of Willy Brandt's Social-Liberal government was now to improve relations with the Federal Republic's Eastern European neighbours. The treaties which were concluded with the Soviet Union, Poland, the GDR and Czechoslovakia provided for mutual renunciation of force and led to a political *modus vivendi* based on recognition of the realities which had resulted from the Second World War. The signing in 1972 of the Treaty on the Basis of Relations between the Federal Republic of Germany and the German Democratic Republic, with the aim of establishing "normal good-neighbourly relations with each other on the basis of equal rights", marked the beginning of a new era of regulated co-existence for the Federal Republic and the GDR.

After a short burst of enthusiastic domestic reform, the effects of the first oil crisis in the autumn of 1973 began to impact strongly on the Federal Republic's development. The Social-Liberal coalition under Helmut Schmidt, who became Chancellor in 1974, sought to cushion the effects of the worldwide recession on the Federal Republic. It introduced programmes to stimulate the economy and create jobs and endeavoured to pursue an internationally coordinated economic policy. However, a renewed economic downturn finally led to the disintegration of the Social-Liberal coalition. In 1982, a coalition government was formed by the CDU/CSU and the FDP under Chancellor Helmut Kohl. It set about radically reorganizing economic and social policy. Thanks in part to the global eco-

nomic upturn, the new government succeeded in bringing about a return to real growth through the implementation of policies to boost recovery. It was unable, however, to overcome the problems of persistent high unemployment and the emerging structural crisis caused by technological change and growing international competition in certain traditional sectors of industry.

In 1971, Erich Honecker took over from Walter Ulbricht as First Secretary of the SED's Central Committee and, at the VIII SED party congress in June, announced a policy away from the strictly dirigiste modernization course towards "unity of economic and social policy". Under his leadership, there was initially a tangible revival in East Germany's political and economic fortunes. With growing international recognition of the GDR as a state, the SED for a time adopted a more open and flexible stance. Although there were improvements in the supply of goods and services, they soon proved almost impossible to finance. From the end of the 1970s onwards, it became increasingly clear that the Eastern bloc states were unable to keep pace with structural changes in the economic and technological fields without exhausting their resources entirely; increased spending on arms also helped drive the economies of these countries to the brink of ruin. At the same time, the opposition movement in the GDR steadily gained strength in terms of its organization and membership, despite all the measures aimed at repression. Yet while the Soviet leadership under Mikhail Gorbachev, together with the governments of other Eastern bloc states, gradually began from the mid-eighties onwards to demonstrate a willingness to implement far-reaching political and later economic reforms, the SED leadership stubbornly refused to contemplate political liberalization in the GDR. In the autumn of 1989, the GDR was thus plunged into political crisis. This enabled the increasingly powerful pro-democracy movement to bring about the downfall of the communist one-party system and force free elections to the People's Chamber within a short period of time. Following the electoral victory of the "Alliance for Germany" on 18 March, a series of bilateral and international treaties was rapidly concluded. They formed the basis for the unification of the two German states on 3 October 1990, desired by the majority of people in the eastern and the western parts of the country.

The German Democratic Republic

1. The founding of the GDR

Unlike the situation in 1918, the collapse of the Nazi regime led to the division of the German nation-state. With the surrender of the German Wehrmacht on 7 and 8 May 1945 and the assumption of supreme authority by the Allies, German sovereignty was lost. In the years to come, Germany's destiny would be shaped by the political objectives pursued by the occupying powers which controlled the different zones, in particular the two superpowers, the USA and the Soviet Union.

Although there was a consensus in the "anti-Hitler coalition" that Germany must be democratized, denazified, and demilitarized, the two superpowers pursued very different long-term objectives in their respective zones. While the USA aimed to establish a liberal constitutional state based on parliamentary democracy, the Soviet Union's ultimate goal was to extend the communist system to the entire territory of the former Reich. Its main

The four Allied Commanders. From left: Bernard Law Montgomery (Britain), Dwight David Eisenhower (USA), Georgi Zhukov (USSR), and Jean de Lattre de Tassigny (France), 1945

priority was therefore to expand its own sphere of influence westwards and gain compensation for the losses it had suffered during the war.

Adopting the slogan "anti-fascist democratic restructuring", the Soviet Union introduced a

Soviet soldiers after capturing the Reichstag building, April 1945

Postcard showing the building where the "Ulbricht Group" lived and worked in May 1945

Factory equipment being loaded for transportation to the Soviet Union

series of reforms which created the basis for a communist system of government and society. The Moscow leadership used formerly exiled German communists to help it impose its ideas. They included a group close to Walter Ulbricht, a former Communist member of the Reichstag. In line with his maxim:

"It must look democratic, but we must have complete control", key positions – not only in the party apparatus, but also in the administration and the economy – were allocated to communists. However, it was the head of the Soviet Military Administration in Germany (SMAD) who exercised the real power in the eastern occupied zone and directed the reconstruction of the economy and administration.

The establishment of political parties

In June 1945, the SMAD became the first occupying power to permit democratic parties and mass organizations once more. The pluralist party system which it created and controlled was intended to serve as a model for the whole of Germany. The first party to be authorized by the SMAD was the Communist Party of Germany (KPD), which, for tactical reasons, originally stated as its objective "the establishment ... of a parliamentary and democratic form of government with all rights and freedoms for the people", without, however, losing sight of the aim of creating a communist system of rule. The SPD was also relaunched; it sought to unify the workers' movement in organizational terms and, at first, was keen to cooperate with the KPD. The newly founded Christian Democratic Union of Germany (CDU), which saw itself as the party of the middle classes, was committed to Christian and democratic values as well as to partial nationalization of industry. At first, the new Liberal Democratic Party of Germany (LDPD) was the only party calling unreservedly for the retention of private property and emphasizing its "non-socialist" credentials. In view of the massive challenges they faced and the experiences with the party system in the Weimar Republic, the parties agreed to work together to organize the new political start. However, once they had merged within the "Anti-Fascist Democratic Bloc", pressure from the Soviet occupying powers and the KPD gradually forced them to come into line.

When, despite its policy of "throwing the party's doors wide open", the KPD failed to secure the expected support among the population, it forced the SPD into an unequal alliance. In April 1946, under massive pressure from the SMAD and following lengthy internal

debates, the SPD leadership agreed to a merger with the KPD and thus the formation of the Socialist Unity Party of Germany (SED). At first, the party leadership was made up of an equal number of members of the two parties. Its objective, set out in its first manifesto, was to seek "the special German path to socialism".

Jakob Kaiser (at the microphone) opening the CDU party conference, 16 June 1946

Wilhelm Pieck (KPD) and Otto Grotewohl (SPD) shaking hands on the merger of their two parties into the Socialist Unity Party of Germany (SED) on 21 April 1946

Economic restructuring

By autumn 1945, the SMAD had begun to pave the way for the introduction of a socialist planned economy with a land reform which expropriated all major land-owners with holdings of more than 100 hectares. The beneficiaries of these expro-priations, for which no compensation was granted, were agricultural workers, small-holders and expellees, who were settled on this land as farmers. Industrial concerns in the hands of former "war criminals and Nazi activists" were also transferred to state

ownership by August 1946 and formed the basis for the socialist restructuring of the economy.

Right: Propaganda for the referendum on the "expropriation of the assets of war criminals and Nazis" at the SED headquarters in Leipzig, 1946

Headquarters of the German Economic Commission, responsible for central economic planning from 1947 onwards

A Juncker estate in Mecklenburg-Western Pomerania is divided up as part of the land reform, 1945

January 1949: the SED's first party conference in Berlin

The SED as the leading party

Meanwhile, political restructuring in the Soviet zone was entering a new phase. Despite the manipulation of elections at local and *Land* level, the SED was never able to gain an absolute majority in these parliaments. In 1947, after embarrassing electoral defeats for the SED and with tensions growing between the two major powers, the occupying powers pressed ahead with political restructuring in their respective zones. While the West created conditions favourable to the establishment of a partial state (*Teilstaat*), primarily through its economic policy decisions, the USSR ultimately precipitated the division of Germany through its reorganization of the SED into a "new type of party" in the eastern zone. The SED, now openly modelled on the Communist Party of the Soviet Union, began a "purge" of its political leadership, the main victims being former SPD members. Through massive intervention in the leadership structure of

the CDU and the LDPD, the SED was able to weaken its bourgeois rivals and erode their links to their sister parties in the West. At the same time, the SED also tried to widen its power base to include agricultural and nationalist/conservative groups by establishing two affiliated parties: the Democratic Farmers' Party (DBD) and the National Democratic Party (NDPD). Gradually, with the

SED election propaganda for the Berlin local elections of 20 October 1946 posted outside the Prenzlauer Berg district office

NDPD party conference in the Congress Hall in Leipzig on 15 June 1950

restricted to the Soviet zone of occupation. Within a matter of months, the "People's Council", which was elected by the assembly and controlled by the SED, unilaterally declared itself the "body appointed to represent the whole of Germany". The German communists' objective was to establish a "people's democracy" modelled on the Eastern European satellite states under Soviet control. But it was only when the founding of the Federal Republic made Soviet domination of the whole of Germany an impossibility in the short term that Stalin gave the SED leadership the green light to establish a separate state.

support of the SMAD, it was able to assert its claim to leadership in all the key political and economic bodies. The German Economic Commission (DWK) in particular emerged as the institutional forerunner of the GDR government after being assigned legislative functions in February 1948.

The next steps towards statehood were taken at the Second People's Congress a month later, billed by the SED as an event for the whole of Germany, though actually

On 7 October 1949, the "Provisional People's Chamber" met for the first time and adopted a constitution drafted in advance by the SED-controlled People's Council. Together with the *Länderkammer*, the second legislative chamber representing the interests of the regions, or *Länder*, the Provisional People's Chamber elected the communist Wilhelm Pieck as President. Former SPD politician Otto Grotewohl was appointed

Wilhelm Pieck proclaiming the German Democratic Republic on 7 October 1949

prime minister. His deputies included Walter Ulbricht (SED) and the leaders of the other East German parties. From the outset, however, the key cabinet and ministerial posts were assigned to SED functionaries.

The GDR's constitution of 1949

Although the composition of the first GDR government in effect represented a first step towards a party dictatorship, the wording of the constitution did initially contain democratic elements. According to the constitution, the GDR was conceived as a centralist state, with its parliament, the People's Chamber, as the single constitutional and legislative organ. Its members were to be elected in general, equal, direct and secret elections on the basis of proportional representation. But the guarantee of the most important basic rights was restricted by Article 6 of the constitution. Its threat of criminal prosecution for any type of "incitement to boycott democratic institutions and organizations" emerged as the most effective instrument for the

persecution of the opposition. Although Germany was described in the constitution as an "indivisible republic", the founding of the German Democratic Republic actually deepened the division of Germany.

In reality, the principles laid down in the constitution proved to be empty promises. The SED progressively expanded its power until one-party communist rule had been achieved, and extended the Stalinist model to the GDR. Both the People's Chamber and the regional and local parliaments were merely token institutions. The state apparatus, economy, judicial system and media were all dominated to a large extent by SED functionaries, who suppressed any form of involvement in decision-making processes or freedom of expression.

It was the National Front, created by the SED, which finally eliminated the last vestiges of pluralism in the GDR. It was used by the SED as an instrument not only to control and monitor the other parties and mass organizations, but also to force them to accept a

Town council meeting in Oberhof in Thuringia, 1955

Dresden residents discussing the upcoming election to the People's Chamber on 15 October 1950

single-list system of voting and hence to abandon any policy concepts of their own. The outcome of the elections to the People's Chamber in October 1950 was to be repeated time and again in the years to come. With a 98% turnout, 99.7% of voters cast their vote for the National Front. The SED itself only won 100 of the 420 seats in the People's Chamber, in line with the formula decided before the elections, but the seats which went to its affiliated parties and the mass organizations, whose members often also belonged to the SED, meant it had an absolute majority. The real power, however, was exercised by the SED Politburo, whose decisions were binding on the Council of Ministers, where the majority of posts were held by SED functionaries.

Politburo meeting during the summer of 1950. From left: Walter Ulbricht, Otto Grotewohl and Wilhelm Pieck

2. The Ulbricht era

III SED party conference in the Werner Seelenbinder Hall in East Berlin, July 1950

Following the SED's third party congress in 1950, Walter Ulbricht, who by that time had acquired a reputation as the party's "strong man", became General Secretary of the SED, which was organized on the basis of a strict hierarchy. Both within the party's ruling bodies and the state apparatus, Ulbricht was to become a crucial figure during the two subsequent decades. Utterly committed to the "theory of Marx, Engels and Stalin", in the 1950s he promoted economic reconstruction on the basis of five-year plans and sought to cement the Stalinist party dictatorship. Although Ulbricht did achieve some initial economic success, currents of opposition nevertheless surfaced both within the SED leadership and at the grass-roots. Using tough expulsion proceedings and carefully stage-managed show trials, Ulbricht was able not only to remove his opponents within the party, but also to persuade the remaining functionaries to toe the party line.

From the 1950s onwards, the other parties merely had a token function. Their only purpose was to allow the SED to claim that a pluralist democracy existed and disguise its own hegemonic position within the state apparatus. It also used what were known as the "Bloc parties" – i.e. the groupings forming the "Anti-Fascist Democratic Bloc" – and the mass organizations as "transmission belts" to promote its policies to sections of the population which had no natural affinity with the SED itself. The initial resistance

Propaganda poster for the first Five Year Plan (1951-1955)

Training for FDJ recruits in the early 1950s

Adolf Hennecke, trade union official and SED member, at the FDGB conference in the Berlin Friedrichstadt-palast, 1949

shown by several leaders of the other parties was soon suppressed by the SED through mass demonstrations, targeted intimidation and arrests. In 1952, the CDU and LDPD party executives, together with the mass organizations, formally recognized the SED's "leading role".

Once the parties had been coordinated, the SED's domestic power base appeared, for the time being, to be firmly anchored. The building of socialism within the framework of a planned economy, announced by Ulbricht in July 1952, was based on the Stalinist model of the USSR. Priority was given not only to increased ideological indoctrination and targeted training of cadres, but also to the GDR's economic reconstruction. However, Ulbricht's ambitious economic policy goals – vigorously promoted with the slogan "Learning from the Soviet Union is a lesson in victory" – were not met, despite some successes. In particular, Ulbricht was unable to keep his promise to bring about a rapid increase in living standards. Growth was retarded, not least by the neglect of the consumer goods and service sectors in favour of

Workers, waving flags, at the Brandenburg Gate on 17 June 1953

subsidies for heavy industry. When, in 1953, the SED called for an increase in productivity at a time of rising prices, popular discontent grew. Although the SED was forced to make some concessions as part of its "new course" following Stalin's death and in response to pressure from the new leadership in Moscow, it insisted on an increase in work norms. This uncompromising stance led to a strike by Berlin labourers in Stalinallee, which triggered numerous uprisings across the GDR. The SED, which at first appeared almost paralyzed, responded to this call for political freedom by declaring a state of emergency; Soviet tanks intervened and the insurrection was crushed, leaving a number of people dead. Over 6000 people were arrested, and more than 331,000 had left the GDR by the end of the year.

The uprising, denounced by party propaganda as "fascist provocation", profoundly

Completion of the first blast furnace at the Eisenhütten Ost combine, 1951

Nikita Krushchev's secret speech at the CPSU's XX Party Congress in Moscow, on the abuse of power by his predecessor, Joseph V. Stalin, 1956

shocked the GDR's leaders. After adopting various measures to defuse the political tension, the party began to search for culprits within its own ranks. The comprehensive and targeted "purge" of the party apparatus represented a further stage in the SED's consolidation of power. Ulbricht paid lip service to the rejection of Stalin's methods by the new leader of the Communist Party of the Soviet Union, Nikita Krushchev, stating that Stalin "cannot be regarded as one of the classical proponents of Marxism", and official support was given to the pardoning of political prisoners. But this did not lead to any democratization of the party structures, let alone of the state apparatus. Even long-serving party cadres from within Ulbricht's inner circle who were keen to embark on reforms in the context of de-Stalinization were judged to be part of the opposition and pose a threat to the system, and were therefore given lengthy prison sentences.

The crushing of the opposition both in and outside the party consolidated Ulbricht's position as First Secretary of the SED. Over the next few years, he was able to stabilize the GDR in both economic and domestic policy terms. Economic policy, which was pursued under the slogan "modernization, mechanization and automation" from 1956, led to a gradual improvement in living standards. These positive economic developments allowed the party leadership temporarily to dampen criticism in the population, but it was unable to gain sustained support or acceptance of its political ideology. In particular, the Bloc parties, whose membership steadily dwindled, did not fulfil the function as

Commissioning of the first research reactor near Dresden, 1957

"transmission belts" for the party, as hoped by the SED. Instead, the mass organizations, which were geared to specific tasks and interests, gained in strength. In particular, the Free German Youth, described as the "party's fighting reserve", and the trade unions, grouped together in the Free German Trade Union Federation (FDGB), were increasingly developed as schools of socialist education. The SED's ideological offensive aimed to initiate a "far-reaching socialist restructuring of ideology and culture". In the socialist community proclaimed by Ulbricht, it was not the individual, but the collective, in the context of society's needs, which was to become the yardstick of individual action.

Launch of series production of the Trabant car at the Sachsenring car plant in Zwickau, 1959

DIE ZEHN GRUNDSÄTZE DER SOZIALISTISCHEN MORAL

1 Du sollst Dich stets für die internationale Solidarität der Arbeiterklasse und aller Werktätigen sowie für die unverbrüchliche Verbundenheit aller sozialistischen Länder einsetzen.

2 Du sollst Dein Vaterland lieben und stets bereit sein, Deine ganze Kraft und Fähigkeit für die Verteidigung der Arbeiter-und-Bauern-Macht einzusetzen.

3 Du sollst helfen, die Ausbeutung des Menschen durch den Menschen zu beseitigen.

4 Du sollst gute Taten für den Sozialismus vollbringen, denn der Sozialismus führt zu einem besseren Leben für alle Werktätigen.

5 Du sollst beim Aufbau des Sozialismus im Geiste der gegenseitigen Hilfe und der kameradschaftlichen Zusammenarbeit handeln, das Kollektiv achten und seine Kritik beherzigen.

6 Du sollst das Volkseigentum schützen und mehren.

7 Du sollst stets nach Verbesserung Deiner Leistungen streben, sparsam sein und die sozialistische Arbeits-disziplin festigen.

8 Du sollst Deine Kinder im Geiste des Friedens und des Sozialismus zu allseitig gebildeten, charakter-festen und körperlich gestalteten Menschen erziehen.

9 Du sollst sauber und anständig leben und Deine Familie achten.

10 Du sollst Solidarität mit den um ihre nationale Befreiung kämpfenden und den ihre nationale Unabhängigkeit verteidigenden Völkern üben.

The SED also continued to tighten its grip on the state institutions. In February 1960, the People's Chamber voted to set up a National Defence Council, which, like the Council of State established after the death of President Wilhelm Pieck, was placed under the control of Walter Ulbricht. This allowed Ulbricht and the SED to exert direct influence on the armed forces and, together with the legislative and government powers Ulbricht exercised as chairman of the Council of State, to dominate the state apparatus completely.

The building of the Berlin Wall

The growing tension between the major powers in the negotiations over Berlin's political status, together with setbacks in agriculture and industry, were the key factors which triggered a dramatic increase in the number of refugees in 1961. Instead of responding to the mass exodus by easing the political pressure, the SED stepped up measures to combat what it regarded as "criminal attempts" to lure people to the West. The SED leadership believed that at some stage, the flight of younger, highly-qualified citizens in particular would endanger the GDR's economic and political existence. In order to prevent the country being "bled dry", Ulbricht, with the backing of the Soviet Union, took the ultimate step: the building of the Wall. At midnight on Sunday,

The "ten principles of Socialist morality" unveiled by Ulbricht at the SED's V Party Congress in July 1958

The sealing-off of the border with West Berlin, August 1961

13 August, an operation commenced which – to quote Erich Honecker – "made the world sit up and take notice". Under the direction of Politburo member Honecker, appointed Chief of Staff by Ulbricht, the People's Police, factory militia and the National People's Army sealed off the border to the Western sectors of Berlin with barbed wire and hastily constructed concrete walls. The closure of the entire border between East and West soon followed. This temporarily halted the mass exodus, and the few protests which this measure provoked were crushed by the SED within a matter of days.

Members of the factory militia at the Brandenburg gate in August 1961

Stabilization and the new constitution

The building of the Wall represented a
watershed, not only in the relationship between the two German partial states, but
also as regards the GDR's further development in domestic policy terms. By 1961,
political and economic structures in line with
the Soviet model had been put in place and
all the major posts in politics, the economy
and society assigned to SED functionaries.
The people of the GDR, who were no longer
able to leave, now had no choice but to learn
to live with the new system.

Mindful of the political and economic developments taking place in the Federal Republic
and the progressive de-Stalinization in the
USSR, the SED leadership now began to
develop more flexible ways of retaining
power to increase the GDR's internal stability.
But the functionaries were less interested in
granting political freedom; rather, they
sought to modernize the economic system.

In order to solve the economic problems,
some senior officials were replaced by economic and academic experts. Education
reforms were carried out along similar lines
as part of an effort to achieve a "scientific
and technical revolution", and a training

Walter Ulbricht
presenting the
New Economic
System of
Planning and
Management
at the SED's VI
Party Congress,
January 1963

Fruit stall in
East Berlin run
by the Trade
Organization,
around 1965

Spring trade fair in Leipzig, 1965

system with a strong emphasis on practical skills and vocational training was established. In June 1963, the government unveiled the "New Economic System of Planning and Management" (NÖSPL), which gave the nationalized plants (VEB) a greater say in preparing the annual plans and offered material incentives to increase productivity. Although factory administrations were now openly allowed to exert influence on economic planning, which led to an improvement in living standards, this new approach soon clashed with the SED's claim to power, which Ulbricht felt was increasingly under threat. The return to centralized planning resulted in the failure not only of the SED's economic plans, but also of its attempts to enhance internal stability through economic reforms.

Yet initially, the economic reforms fostered a positive mood which was conducive to change in other fields as well. Thus the SED leadership made efforts to ensure equality for women in the socialist system and demonstrate a more open attitude towards young people. From now on, young people were to

be officially permitted to ask awkward and provocative questions to allow them to develop into "independent and self-confident citizens with steadfast characters". Critical comment in literature, film and television, such as that expressed by Wolf Biermann or Frank Beyer, was also tolerated by the SED, at least for a time.

But the rapprochement between party and people came to a rapid end following the overthrow of Krushchev and assumption of power by Leonid Brezhnev, who declared de-Stalinization to have been completed. At the eleventh plenary session of the SED Central Committee in December 1965, the hardliners introduced a radical change of course in cultural policy. In particular, Erich Honecker, former head of the Free German Youth and one of Ulbricht's closest allies, criticized the "growing evidence of American immorality and decadence", which, he claimed, led to "breaches of discipline", "criminal acts", and "bouts of drinking in the style of the West German reactionary student societies". He also accused the singer and songwriter Wolf Biermann – later expelled from the GDR – of betraying the GDR "with his cynical verses, written from opposition standpoints". After almost three years, the period of liberalization, albeit limited, ended with bans on public appearances, and censorship of films and books.

Until the end of the 1960s, the party again steered a rigid course in order further to consolidate its position in the state. A new criminal code and a new constitution were introduced to underpin these policies. The new code tightened up the criminal laws relating to political activity and was designed to protect the socialist state order and social system. The new "socialist" constitution, meanwhile, took account of the political changes since 1949. Although preceded by a "popular debate", very few provisions of the draft constitution which had been presented were actually modified. In the only referendum ever held in the history of the GDR, the SED's leading role was subsequently enshrined in the constitution, adopted on 6 April 1968. Although the constitution now reflected the real balance of power, the basic

Wolf Biermann and West German cabaret artist Wolfgang Neuss during a joint performance in Frankfurt am Main, 1965

rights enshrined in it were violated time and again. The People's Chamber, anchored in the constitution as the "supreme state organ", continued to rubber-stamp the SED's decisions.

The SED tried to prevent the building of democratic structures not only from within, but also in response to external influences,

Rally outside the Humboldt University in Berlin in support of the new Constitution, 5 April 1968

Czech demonstrators by the statue of Saint Wenceslas in Prague, August 1968

especially from Czechoslovakia, where from spring 1968 onwards, the new First Secretary of the Communist Party, Alexander Dubček, was trying to establish a democratic form of socialism less closely aligned with the Soviet model. The SED leadership was not alone in fearing that the accelerating reform process in Czechoslovakia might lead to the "social democratization" of the "brother party" and spread to the GDR. Together with its partners in the Warsaw Pact, the GDR formed an "anti-reform coalition" which was intended to exert pressure on Dubček and his supporters and shore up the opponents of reform. When the Czechoslovakian commu-

nists and the anti-reform coalition were unable to reach a consensus, Leonid Brezhnev, the Soviet leader, ordered a military invasion, in which the East German National People's Army provided support, mainly by safeguarding supply lines. The surrender of the Communist Party leadership in Czechoslovakia, and the fact that the protests against the military intervention in Czechoslovakia were rapidly crushed, strengthened the SED leadership's resolve not to abandon "socialism in favour of counter-revolution".

Tribune of honour at the 20th anniversary of the founding of the GDR. Fourth from left: Leonid Brezhnev, at his side: Walter Ulbricht

The end of the Ulbricht era

At the end of the 1960s, the GDR, despite the crises which it had endured, enjoyed a relatively high level of internal stability, which Walter Ulbricht attributed, not least, to his economic and cadre policy. In his view, this proved that socialism in the GDR now served as a model for other states. Ulbricht, previously a consistently loyal supporter of the Soviet Union, had now become noticeably high-handed and self-opinionated in his dealings with it, which from the mid-1960s increasingly angered the Soviet leader. Brezhnev later confided in Honecker that Ulbricht had listed to him all the things which were wrong with the Soviet Union and exemplary in the GDR and told him how to go about the business of governing the country. Ideologically too, Ulbricht increasingly distanced himself from the Soviet Union, whose uncompromising policy on Germany he was no longer prepared to support. In order to achieve the objectives set forth in his economic plans, he sought to engage in economic cooperation with West Germany, whereas the Moscow leadership now started to block any rapprochement. Given his aspirations to political independence, his diverging ideological ideas and the economic bottlenecks facing the country, it was only a matter of time before Ulbricht was removed from power. Ironically, it was his protégé Honecker who was determined to oust him. Honecker gradually won over the majority of the Politburo and, in confidential talks with the Kremlin, criticized Ulbricht both personally and politically. By the time Moscow agreed, at the end of April 1971, that Ulbricht should be removed from office, his successor had long been decided: Erich Honecker was elected First Secretary by the SED's Central Committee – officially at the proposal of Ulbricht, who was said to be retiring because of his age.

Politburo members congratulating Walter Ulbricht on his 78th birthday, 30 June 1971

3. The Honecker era

Leonid
Brezhnev,
leader of the
Soviet Union
and the
Communist
Party, being
welcomed to
the SED's VIII
Party Congress,
June 1971

At the beginning of his term in office, Erich Honecker reaffirmed, as expected by the Kremlin, the GDR's unswerving alliance with the Soviet Union, whose leading political role was now once again recognized unconditionally. Honecker sought to counter Ulbricht's failing economic policies by proclaiming the "unity of economic and social policy", though this principle was only declared to be the basis of state policy at the IX party congress in 1976. In line with already tried and tested principles, this policy aimed to achieve a further "improvement in the material and cultural standard of living of the people" by stepping up production and rationalizing the economy. However, the social policy measures introduced to strengthen the people's trust in the SED were a novel feature. Whereas during Ulbricht's period in office, huge sums of money had been invested in science, technology and prestigious building projects, the "working population" was now to benefit directly from state expenditure. Alongside wage and pension increases, shorter working hours and free medical care, the SED leadership made particular efforts to boost housing construction. But the economic growth spurt and the temporary improvement in living conditions were built on shaky ground. In reality, these developments were due less to an increase in "the pace of development of socialist production" and "increased efficiency", as

Construction
of prefabricat-
ed housing in
Wittenberg,
March 1974

X World
Festival of
Youth and
Students in
East Berlin,
1973

claimed, than to massive borrowing from the West.

During the first few years, the tangible increase in prosperity created an unprecedented level of support for the new leadership, which it sought to consolidate by means of a limited, controlled relaxation in the cultural policy field. The leadership therefore tolerated the reception of West German television and to a certain extent abandoned its attempts to regiment young people. Art and culture were also given greater leeway. For instance, books only published in West Germany so far were now allowed to appear in the GDR too. Yet the SED left no doubt about the objectives of its cultural policy and at no point was it prepared to make what Kurt Hager, chief ideologist in the Politbüro, described as "concessions to bourgeois ideologies and imperialist perceptions of art".

The modest successes in German-German relations also contributed to a mood of optimism in East German society. While in the eyes of the GDR population these successes indicated a national rapprochement, the SED's main purpose in concluding these intra-German treaties was to secure the

Federal Republic's recognition of the GDR under international law. The accession of the two German partial states to the UN in 1973, their participation on an equal footing in the CSCF conference in Helsinki in 1975 and the

Egon Bahr and
Michael Kohl
after the
signing of
the Treaty on
the Basis of
Relations in
East Berlin on
21 December
1972

opening of the Federal Republic's permanent mission in East Berlin were regarded by the GDR leadership as significant achievements resulting from its efforts to achieve statehood.

Despite its commitment in the social policy field and its more liberal stance on cultural affairs, the new SED leadership was, like its

Erich Honecker congratulating Erich Mielke in February 1980 on the 30th anniversary of the Ministry of State Security

suppression of opponents of the regime. The members of the Politburo not only formed the party leadership but also held the key government posts. The SED's powerful hold on the state institutions was retained, as was the hierarchical structure of the party. As under Ulbricht, decision-making power remained concentrated in the hands of the General Secretary, Erich Honecker.

The expulsion of Wolf Biermann

predecessors, primarily interested in exercising and consolidating power. The party organization was further streamlined and the specialists allocated posts in the administration by Ulbricht were replaced by experienced party politicians. The top positions in the SED were also filled with apparatchiks and party members loyal to Honecker, who were to remain in office until the demise of the GDR. In particular, the appointment of the Minister of State Security, Erich Mielke, to the Politburo enabled the party to exert direct influence on the surveillance and

From the mid-1970s onwards, the economy once again began to stagnate and the liberalization of cultural policy was replaced by open repression. Honecker did not succeed in bringing about an improvement in living standards either as quickly, or as comprehensively, as he had promised on taking office. But it was not only the economic difficulties which caused headaches for the SED functionaries. They also feared that the relaxation of cultural policy which they themselves had initiated might again threaten their claim to power. The volte-face in cultural policy was triggered by the appearance of

Wolf Biermann at a press conference, following his expulsion from the GDR on 19 November 1976

the singer and poet Wolf Biermann at a trade union event in Cologne in November 1976. The singer and songwriter, who had long been a rallying figure for the critical intelligentsia, was stripped of his GDR citizenship overnight on the grounds of his "hostile attitude" to the GDR. He was a particular target for repression since he constantly highlighted the contradictions between the reality of power politics and socialist ideals. Leading artists and authors immediately published a letter of protest, to which the SED leadership reacted with warnings, bans on publication and expulsions from the party and the GDR. Fearing that this show of solidarity might encourage

the formation of political opposition groups, the SED stepped up its efforts to deal with potential opponents to the regime through judicial measures and surveillance. Biermann's loss of citizenship not only signalled a change of climate in the cultural policy field, it also dashed the intelligentsia's hopes of political change. Many of them, including reform-minded Marxists like Rudolf Bahro, were harassed, arrested, or left the GDR.

The SED attempted to shore up the dwindling confidence in its policies with a new party manifesto which, in theory at least, was intended to be written with the active involvement of the people. But in reality, the

Parade of honour by the National People's Army in East Berlin, celebrating the GDR's 30th anniversary on 7 October 1979

SED's claims to be open to discussion – like the mobilization of the masses for special occasions – were merely intended to convey the image of a united and politically active population. In actual fact, the people were never allowed any direct say.

Economic decline and the trade union movement in Poland

Despite the relatively high standard of living compared with the other Eastern bloc countries, and the achievements in the social policy field, the domestic political climate during the last decade of the GDR was characterized by economic and social decay. From the mid-1970s, the prosperity which had been bought by means of loans and a series of export drives was stagnating. The economic targets pledged by the party were unable to keep pace with the GDR population's high expectations and it had even become almost impossible to generate the funds needed to maintain the existing standard of living. Ignoring numerous warnings from within his own ranks, Honecker continued to pursue his social policy programme, which placed an unbearable strain on the economy. Investments in new technologies and the modernization of obsolete plants, as well as efforts to keep the population supplied with highly subsidized "articles for everyday use", ran into difficulties. The SED's problems were further exacerbated when the Soviet Union, itself grappling with economic problems, drastically reduced its annual deliveries of crude oil. The instruction given by Honecker to a member of his staff to "ask comrade Leonid Ilyich Brezhnev quite openly whether it is worth destabilizing the GDR and shattering the faith of our people in the party and state leadership for the sake of two million tonnes of crude oil", illustrates the gravity of the situation. The loan of billions of deutschmarks from banks in the Federal Republic arranged between SED currency dealer Alexander Schalck-Golodkowski and Bavarian Minister-President Franz Josef Strauss finally provided the GDR leadership with a brief respite from the desolate economic situation. Further attempts by the party leadership to boost the economy failed not only due to treaty

Queue outside a butcher's shop in Karl-Marx-Stadt in the early '80s

commitments vis-à-vis other Eastern European states, but also as a result of the half-heartedness of its economic reforms.

Yet the economic crisis was not the only problem; developments in neighbouring socialist Poland also presented a threat for the party leadership. There, the independent trade union movement "Solidarity", founded in 1980, was fighting for "democratic social-ism", which increasingly called into question the leading role of the Communist state party. As in the spring of 1968, the SED feared that social protests and political unrest might spread to the GDR. Honecker's criticism of the Polish workers' leaders was thus unam-biguous, culminating in the assertion that "the class interests of the workers ... can only be expressed by ... the party equipped with scientific socialism". Finally, the SED attempt-ed to counter the threat by ending visa-free travel between Poland and the GDR. Although developments in Poland did not initially pose the immediate danger which the SED had feared, they did, together with the accelerat-ing arms race between the major powers,

mobilize the opposition which had been forming within the Churches and in the peace movement from the latter half of the 1970s onwards.

Lech Wałęsa at a press conference in Warsaw following the recognition of the Solidarity movement in November 1980

General Wojciech Jaruzelski announcing the imposition of martial law in Poland on 13 December 1981

FDJ demonstration against the deployment of medium-range missiles in the Federal Republic, 1984

Perestroika and the opening of the Wall

The attempts by the SED to reduce the tensions between party and people through new ideological and peace-policy initiatives ultimately failed as a result of the GDR's ossified power structures. Despite growing discontent among the population, the party leadership was not prepared to abandon its claims to power in favour of political freedom of expression and citizens' right to be involved in decision-making. This did not change even after Mikhail Gorbachev's assumption of office in March 1985, when democratic reforms began to emerge in the Soviet Union. Although Honecker supported Gorbachev's policy of disarmament and détente vis-à-vis the United States, he was not prepared to adopt a change of course in domestic policy. In a high-handed and authoritarian manner reminiscent of his former patron Walter Ulbricht, the General Secretary, together with his ageing cabinet, took all major decisions.

When, in February 1986, Gorbachev called for internal political reforms in order to halt the economic decline of his country and dismantle the Stalinist structures within his party, he also had the neighbouring socialist states in mind. But his initiative met with little resonance at the XI party congress of the SED in April 1986. Although the usual set-piece proclamations of solidarity with the Soviet Union were made, the main focus was on self-congratulation and an emphasis on

Speech by Mikhail Gorbachev at the SED's XI Party Congress in April 1986

independent statehood. The party leadership preferred to close its eyes to the GDR population's hopes, aroused by Gorbachev's policy of perestroika (restructuring) and glasnost (openness). In deliberately distancing itself from the Soviet Union and its new leader, the SED became increasingly cut off from East Germany's domestic problems. The continuing political and economic stagnation, together with the SED's attempts to halt democratization through newspaper bans, and the surveillance and arrest of opposition activists, provoked discontent and protests among the population. The Bloc parties also stuck to their course and proved themselves reliable supporters of the SED regime at their party congresses.

The people's disappointment and growing mistrust of the SED leadership first came to a head during the local elections in May 1989. Opposition peace groups observed that in some districts, up to 20% of electors had voted against the single list of candidates, contradicting the official election results, which claimed that 98.85% of voters had voted for the single-list candidates. These revelations led to protests in various parts of the country, which reflected a growing self-confidence vis-à-vis the all-powerful state and party. Yet the Politburo not only ignored these protests and the reform movements in Hungary and Poland, it even signalled its support for the bloody suppression of the pro-democracy movement in China.

But the response to the SED's rigid stance and the stability it proclaimed was a steady increase in the number of applications for exit permits. In April 1988 alone, the GDR authorities received 112,000 applications for resettlement in the Federal Republic. When Hungary opened its border with Austria in the summer of 1989 and allowed GDR citizens to leave Hungary for Austria, the floodgates finally opened and huge numbers of people wishing to leave the GDR crossed the border. By the end of September 1989, more than 25,000 new resettlers had been registered in the Federal Republic.

For the reformist opposition groups in the GDR, the mass exodus was also a signal that it was time to stand up to the SED more openly. In particular the Churches, which the SED had never been able to integrate fully,

Erich Honecker casting his vote in the local elections in East Berlin on 7 May 1989

developed into forums for critical debate. When a spontaneous demonstration after a peace service in Leipzig on 11 September ended with mass arrests, the discontent spread to ever larger sections of the population. They began to demonstrate every Monday in Leipzig, calling for a say in political decision-making and an end to SED hegemony. The political opposition also gained increasing support and began to organize itself. Both the "New Forum" and the Social Democratic Party, which was re-established in October, called into question the SED's claim to absolute leadership and demanded free elections.

Dismantling of barbed wire fences on the border between Austria and Hungary in the summer of 1989

Not least as a result of the Leipzig "Monday demonstrations", attended by more than 120,000 people by mid-October, as well as the dissatisfaction of party members which had been evident for some time, the Politburo gave way. From the party leadership's perspective, the only way to ensure its own

survival and salvage the regime was to remove Honecker from office. On 18 October, he was stripped of all his functions and Egon Krenz elected as his successor. While the new General Secretary expected the "change of course" which he proclaimed to involve

Demonstration
in Leipzig on
16 October,
attended by
over 120,000
people

little more than a few cosmetic adjustments followed by "business as usual", the opposition demanded a radical overhaul of the political system. The SED's hopes that tensions would ease were dashed. Instead, on 4 November, a mass demonstration initiated by GDR artists' associations took place at Alexanderplatz in Berlin, sending shockwaves even through the SED's own ranks and leading to the removal of the last hardliners from the Politburo. But the real turning point did not come until the evening of 9 November, when the Secretary of the Berlin SED, Günter Schabowski, promised an easing of restrictions on foreign travel at a press conference and the people themselves forced open the border with West Berlin.

Border crossing
at the Born-
holmer Bridge
in Berlin,
10 November
1989

4. The role of the People's Chamber

First session of the People's Chamber in the newly constructed Palace of the Republic on 24 June 1976

According to the Constitution, last amended in 1974, the People's Chamber was formally the "supreme organ of state power of the German Democratic Republic", which, in its plenary sessions, decided the basic questions of state policy (Article 48, para 1), and, "by means of statutes and resolutions which are final and binding on all," set forth "the developmental goals of the German Democratic Republic" (Article 49, para 1). Article 48, paragraph 2 also stipulated that "no one can restrict the rights of the People's Chamber". Its composition was to be determined by the citizens, who, under Article 5 of the constitution, exercised "their political power through democratically elected representative bodies".

In reality, however, the People's Chamber was prevented from taking autonomous or independent action by the SED's claim to

leadership, which had been anchored in the constitution since 1968, but had actually been practised since the founding of the GDR. Combined with "democratic centralism",

Walter Ulbricht giving a speech on the draft Constitution to the People's Chamber, January 1968

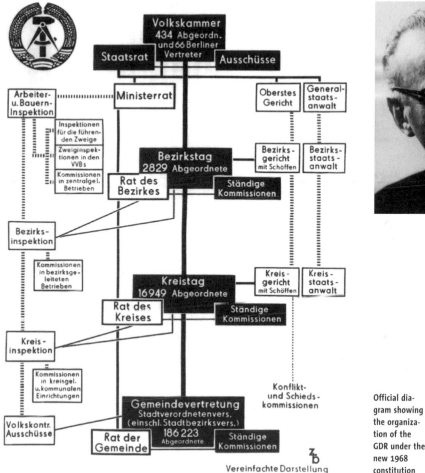

Karl Polak, lecturer on constitutional law and personal advisor to Wilhelm Pieck and Otto Grotewohl on "constitutional matters"

Official diagram showing the organization of the GDR under the new 1968 constitution

which ruled out any separation of powers, this meant that there was no system of checks and balances between the various state institutions. The SED continually emphasized its claim to leadership and used the state organs, the parties and the mass organizations in order to assert its political ideas both within and outside the state. It issued political directives, selected and trained the functionaries for the institutions and monitored the implementation of their decisions. The parliament, and the parties and mass organizations represented in it, were merely intended to serve as a link to the "working population" and legitimize the party's rule. The People's Chamber and the parties did not function as independent institutions, but were fully integrated into the hierarchical system of decision-making headed by the Politburo and the central party apparatus.

The creation and political importance of the People's Chamber

The deliberations on the constitution held by a committee of the SED-dominated People's Council in 1948 focused, inter alia, on the question of the status of the future parliament. From the outset, against the background of the SED's policy on Germany, the People's Council intended to draft a constitution for the whole of Germany. For this

Meeting of the committee drafting the constitution, chaired by Otto Grotewohl, on 27 April 1948

reason, many sections of the draft which was presented contained democratic, rule-of-law and parliamentary principles. As a basis, the Council used the Weimar constitution, the constitutions of the *Länder*, which had already been adopted, and a draft produced in 1946 by the SED, calling for parliamentarism as a constitutive element of the new state order.

In the words of the SED's leading expert on constitutional law, Karl Polak, the parliament

Agitprop for the elections to the Third German People's Congress in May 1949

should assume the "central position of power appropriate to it" and have more extensive powers than the Reichstag in the Weimar Republic. This parliamentary hegemony left no room for a separation of powers in line with the Western notion of constitution and state. The People's Chamber was intended not only to make decisions, but also to scrutinize their implementation. According to socialist thinking, checks or restrictions on the rights of the parliament were superfluous, as it represented the "unanimous will of all working people". As the Marxist Leninist party saw itself as the legitimate representative of all working people, it automatically became the ultimate decision-making body in parliament too. Although the constitution formally assigned all powers to the parliament and its subordinate bodies, the SED's understanding of the function of the state and the political parties meant that in reality they simply remained implementing institutions.

In order to assert its leadership role on a completely legal basis in parliament, the SED rejected the idea of a Western-style party system. Instead, it insisted on a single-list system, where the number of seats to be allocated to the individual parties had already been decided before the actual elections. In the end, the leaders of the bourgeois parties within the SED-dominated "Anti-Fascist Democratic Bloc" agreed to a single list for the elections to the Third People's Congress because they did not yet regard this as the actual parliament. At the People's Congress which emerged from the rigged elections in May 1949, the Second People's Council, consisting of 330 East German and 100 West German delegates, was elected. On 7 October 1949, following the adoption of the constitution, and without any formal involvement of the people, this body then proclaimed itself the "Provisional People's Chamber of the German Democratic Republic". The SED postponed calling elections, however, as the resistance of the CDU and LDPD to the single lists had not been completely broken.

SED members on their way to take part in election campaigning in Brandenburg in October 1950

Meanwhile, the SED, with the support of the mass organizations and its affiliated parties, the DBD and NDPD, with which it was linked in terms of both policies and personnel, used the provisional parliament to expand its own power. Despite objections from several representatives of the CDU and LDPD, who wanted the decision-making powers of the provisional People's Chamber to be limited to day-to-day politics, the SED ultimately succeeded in asserting its will within the Bloc and ensured that the parliament was endowed with all the rights and duties laid down in the constitution. The SED-dominated "Central Bloc Committee", which effectively short-circuited the parliament, was ultimately able to prevent any form of constructive or independent parliamentary work. At the "request" of the Bloc, all the parliamentary groups agreed that they would only table motions in agreement with their party leaderships, in order to prevent the "outdated bourgeois-democratic views and practices of some delegates" and any independent opinion-forming process in advance of parliamentary debates. The code of conduct for the delegates and the rules governing the work of the parliament, as laid down in the rules of procedure adopted on 7 December 1949, were based, according to one SED delegate, on the "awareness of fruitful cooperation, as reflected in the politics of the Bloc", and on the notion that "differences of opinion and divergent views will not be exploited as an opportunity to engage in major rhetorical battles on the floor of the

Walter Ulbricht's speech on the Five Year Plan, adopted retrospectively by the People's Chamber on 1 November 1951

The "supreme organ of the Republic" demonstrated an astonishing level of activity in the run-up to the elections in October 1950. Yet neither regular sessions, nor a genuine exchange of opinions were provided for. Government policy statements and messages of greeting were accepted without opposition and the bills introduced by the government alone were adopted unanimously without any objections being raised or discussions in committees. In 1950, for example, the plenary assembly adopted a law establishing the Ministry of State Security in less than 15 minutes, to general applause.

Finally, the SED exploited its dominance in parliament to have the single-list voting system legitimized by the People's Chamber. In doing so, it created a balance of power favourable to itself, which would remain in place, despite some minor changes later, until the collapse of the GDR. The elections to the People's Chamber held for the first time in October 1950 produced a pattern which was to be repeated again and again until 1989. Voter turnout was close to one hundred percent, with almost all voters voting for the single-list candidates. The formula used only allocated around one quarter of the seats to the SED, yet, together with the SED-infiltrated mass organizations, and the affiliated parties, it had an absolute majority. Since the strongest parliamentary

People's Chamber". This meant that opposing views could no longer be voiced in parliament, which the President of the People's Chamber sought to justify as follows: "We are and were … of the opinion that it is our duty to avoid confusing our people – many of whom are already confused – any further and to an even greater extent; rather, we should offer them a role model for the new society to which we want to lead them all."

The first cabinet, led by Prime Minister Otto Grotewohl (front row, fourth from left), 12 October 1949

the support of the trades- and craftspeople and the self-employed, who were marginalized by socialist economic policy. The NDPD and the DBD, which had been set up under the formative influence of the SED, were to bring former members of the Nazi Party, conservatives, and the rural population closer to the new political and social order. But in view of their repeated declarations of loyalty to the SED, the Bloc parties' delegates in the People's Chamber were not particularly credible as representatives of the interests of other social groups. They fell into virtually the same category as the mass organizations, which the SED used to involve and politically influence all sections of the population.

All the key decisions to be debated by the plenary assembly of the People's Chamber were discussed in advance by the cross-party "Central Democratic Bloc" and approved on the basis of consensus. The informal decisions taken by the Bloc, which in turn received its instructions from the SED leadership, were simply nodded through by the parlia-

Propaganda for the elections to the People's Chamber on 14 June 1981

group was entitled under the constitution to nominate the chairperson of the Council of Ministers, the SED remained the dominant power not only in parliament, but also in the executive – whose members at the same time belonged to the SED's supreme party organ, the Politburo. Throughout the forty years of its existence, the real strength of the People's Chamber was always less than the theoretical powers allocated to it under the constitution. The SED leadership alone decided how much room for manoeuvre should be granted to the People's Chamber and its subordinate state organs.

The parties and members of the People's Chamber

During the 1950s, the Bloc parties, which were dependent on the SED in both financial and organizational terms, not only recognized its leadership role, but were also entrusted by the SED with politically integrating the sections of society which had no natural affinity with the SED itself. The CDU was to win over Christian voters to socialism, while the LDPD had the task of gaining

LDP campaign poster for the local elections in October 1946

Congress of the Democratic Women's League of Germany, one of the largest of the mass organizations represented in the People's Chamber

committees, with a few exceptions, also proved ineffective. In addition, the delegates did not exercise their formal powers to examine legislation in substantive terms, fearing reprimands from the SED and personal and career disadvantages. Only on one single occasion, on 9 March 1972, did a debate take place – on the "Law on the termination of pregnancy" – albeit with the SED's approval. This was the first time that a decision was not taken unanimously: 14 delegates voted against the bill, while eight abstained.

According to one SED member, many delegates thus reacted to the irrelevance and monotony of plenary sessions in the same way as Otto Nuschke (CDU), the Prime Minister's first deputy: "Every time he began to tilt sideways, his neighbour, Dr. Loch, tugged gently on his sleeve, at which Nuschke would glance sleepily into the plenary chamber, sit up straight again and fall back to sleep."

mentary groups in the People's Chamber. Thus discussions between the parties and mass organizations only took place within the Democratic Bloc. The parliamentary groups in parliament were bound by the instructions approved unanimously there, and were unable to take any initiative themselves. In practice, therefore, neither the parliamentary groups nor individual delegates were able to make use of their theoretical right to introduce bills and scrutinize the work of the government. The work of the

Unanimous adoption by the People's Chamber of the Transit Agreement between the German Democratic Republic and the Federal Republic of Germany, 16 October 1972

5. Opposition and resistance in the GDR

Delegates at the SED conference for the East Berlin district of Pankow, held at the Berg-mann-Borsig factory, June 1950

From the beginning of the division of Germany, the SED's dominance of state and society was criticized, and in some instances actively resisted, by a range of opposition forces. This criticism from the opposition was not always aimed at the system itself; sometimes it was directed at individual members of the government, party functionaries or specific political decisions. While opposition during the 1940s and 1950s was mainly a reaction to the SED asserting its rule, in the 1960s, visions of a renewed and reformed socialism gained headway. Later on, there were also calls for the establishment of a parliamentary democracy based on the rule of law.

As the SED believed that there was "no objective or social basis … in socialist states …

for opposition to the prevailing conditions in society and state" either from an ideological or a power-political viewpoint, legal opposition could not exist in the GDR. The main instrument used to suppress opponents of the system was the Ministry of State Security, which was formed in February 1950 and functioned as an independent organization, directly accountable only to the SED Politburo. It ran a network of full-time employees and unofficial informers who subjected all areas of public life to comprehensive and systematic surveillance, in order to quell any activity viewed as "subversive".

The "democratic" opposition

The roots of the opposition movement go back to 1945, when the democratic parties, which were now permitted to exist once again, came under pressure from the communists. Whereas Otto Grotewohl soon became one of the leading proponents within

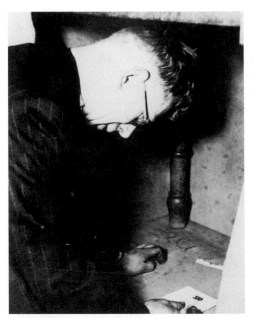

A member of the Berlin SED casting his vote on the merger with the KPD, 3 March 1946

the SPD of a union with the KPD, arguing that only a united socialist party could re-educate the people after the "fascist catastrophe", sections of the Social Democrats did put up resistance. Despite massive intimidation and many arrests, entire local constituency branches spoke out against a merger. Kurt Schumacher, SPD leader in the Western zones, even proposed the formal dissolution of the SPD in the East in order to thwart the communists' plans. But unrelenting pressure from the KPD and the SMAD finally forced the leadership of the Social Democrats to agree to the merger. After the SPD had been deprived of its organizational base at the party conference which sealed the merger, and critics within the SED were increasingly criminalized, resistance continued only in small groups. Previously influential SPD functionaries who continued to voice criticism of the merger were either arrested or pressurized by the Soviet occupying power into leaving East Germany.

Once democratic parties were permitted to exist once more, the bourgeois opposition drew on CDU and LDPD circles for support. Soon after they had been founded, the experiences of the Weimar Republic prompted

Representatives of the "Anti-Fascist Democratic Bloc" in July 1945. From left to right: Grotewohl (SPD), Hermes (CDU), Pieck (KPD), Berlin Mayor Werner (Independent), and Koch (LDP)

the new parties to form the "Unified Front of Anti-Fascist Democratic Parties", which was dominated by the KPD from the outset and served to short-circuit the parliamentary bodies. The communists had thus devised an instrument with which they hoped to use to neutralize the other parties politically. They were supported in this by the SMAD, which

considerable support among the electorate. Their criticism, aimed primarily at the methods used to socialize the economy, repeatedly brought them into conflict with the SMAD, which reacted by removing their leaders from office. In particular, the last freely elected chairman of the CDU, Jakob Kaiser, campaigned vigorously against the establish-

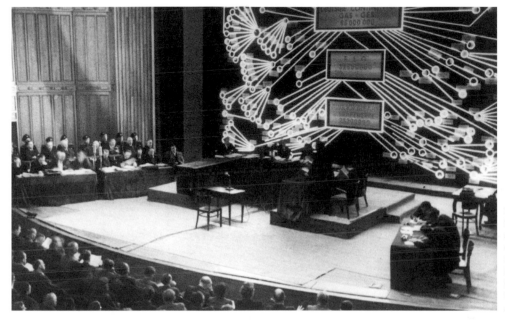

Show trial of Saxony-Anhalt's former employment minister, Leo Herwegen (CDU), in a Dessau theatre, April 1950

ment of a totalitarian and dogmatic form of socialism, which he perceived as being increasingly hostile to the Churches. The SMAD finally put an end to his vision of an economic and social order based on solidarity by removing him from office and "purging" the CDU organs of his supporters. The LDPD leadership, which called for liberal economic policies and criticized in particular the lack of legal certainty, was also subjected to persecution and repression. Only at *Land* and local level were the bourgeois parties able to carry on their opposition, at least in the short term.

Jakob Kaiser and Ernst Lemmer after their expulsion from the East German CDU in December 1947

sabotaged efforts to build up the bourgeois parties, and corrupted, ousted or arrested party members.

Despite all the interference and campaigns against them, the bourgeois parties gained

After the founding of the GDR on 7 October 1949, the SED succeeded in introducing a single-list system of voting, allowing it to more or less eliminate party-political opposition. Although there was some resistance by individual politicians from the bourgeois parties, who were subsequently subjected to show trials and given long prison sentences, the SED had little trouble turning the bourgeois parties into compliant political partners over the next few years.

The 1953 workers' uprising

On 17 June 1953, in the wake of criticism of the government's economic policy, an opposition movement emerged across the GDR within a matter of hours, formed by workers aiming to assert their social and political interests through strikes and protests. When the work norms were raised, workers at two major construction sites in East Berlin downed tools in an effort to achieve social concessions. When the swelling crowd of protesters reached the government building, other more far-reaching demands were also voiced. Finally, some of the workers called for the punishment and resignation of the gov-

17 June 1953: protesters demanding free elections

ernment, which had by this point barricaded itself inside the building and alerted the People's Police. At this stage, the government still believed it could regain control of the situation by reversing the changes to the work norms. But in the morning of 17 June, disturbances took place in around 400 towns and cities throughout the GDR. Hated symbols of the SED, pictures of high-ranking functionaries, banners and slogans were ripped down and destroyed. The demands made in the nine-point list put forward by the Bitterfeld strike committee were broadly representative of the demands being made by the demonstrators across the GDR. They included not only an improvement in living standards and the resignation of the government, but also the formation of a provisional government, the admission of West German parties, and secret and free elections – all of which would ultimately have spelled the end of the centralist system dominated by the SED. However, it proved impossible to coordinate the widespread protest effectively, and by midday on 17 June, the Soviet Union had come to the aid of the SED functionaries and crushed the insurrection. More than 60 people died; around 6000 strikers were arrested, including not only manual workers, but also many farmers, office workers and self-employed people. The members of the strike committees in particular were severely punished. Some were dismissed from their jobs and sent to prison; others were even sentenced to death.

Opposition within the SED

The crushing of the uprising made clear to the people that even an opposition movement supported by the masses had little chance of success at that point against the SED, which had established a monopoly of power with the support of the Soviet Union. This led to a widespread feeling of resignation and an increasing pressure to conform. Within the SED, only a few people interpreted the loss of trust within the population as being a result of the SED's authoritarian and high-handed style of leadership.

Soviet tanks
crushing the
uprising

When SED functionaries Rudolf Herrnstadt
and Wilhelm Zaisser suggested turning the
party leadership into a collective decision-
making body once again, and restructuring
it in terms of personnel, Ulbricht reacted by
immediately relieving them of their posts.

It was not until de-Stalinization was initiated
in February 1956 by the Soviet leader Nikita
Krushchev that new hopes for changes in
Ulbricht's style of leadership were rekindled.
In the cultural field in particular, an increasing number of SED functionaries spoke out,
accusing the party leadership of interpreting
Marxism-Leninism with the sole aim of
securing its own power. Wolfgang Harich, a
philospher and editor at the Berlin *Aufbau-
Verlag* publishing house, became the key
figure in this wave of criticism. In his proposals for "a special German path to socialism"
he called, inter alia, for the SED to be democratized, an end to privileges, legal certainty
and free elections. When he sought support
outside the official party structures, he and
others involved, including the head of *Aufbau-
Verlag*, Walter Janka, were sentenced to long
terms of imprisonment. Harich's initiative
led neither to democratization of the internal
party structures nor to the formation of a

genuine opposition. Rather, following
the failed uprising in Hungary in 1956, it
accelerated the crushing and suppression
of opposition in the Churches and universities.

Rudolf
Herrnstadt,
Editor-in-Chief
of the *Neues
Deutschland*
newspaper,
and Wilhelm
Zaisser,
Minister of
State Security

Wolfgang
Harich giving
a speech, 1955

The "cultural opposition"

Towards the end of the 1950s, people's dissatisfaction with living conditions and the SED's leadership style was primarily evident from the steady flow of refugees westwards, which was not stemmed until the building of the Berlin Wall. Once fleeing as an expression of resistance was no longer possible and Krushchev had begun a new phase of de-Stalinization in 1962, the party relaxed its strict policy of repression.

Intellectuals and academics attempted to exploit this atmosphere, citing the critical impetus of Marxism to underline the discrepancy between power-political reality and socialist ideals. While the author Stefan Heym countered the party's claim to absolute

power with the notion of a socialism which required people to voice doubts, think independently and be willing to take the initiative, Wolf Biermann used his songs and poems to highlight the contradictions between everyday socialist reality and communist utopia. Robert Havemann, a professor of physical chemistry, developed a political ethos based on his scientific-philosophical ideas, according to which "democracy" and "freedom of speech" were basic prerequisites for human progress. These views inevitably called into question the SED's legitimacy and its claims to represent the whole of society, which the party again vehemently defended and reinforced at the eleventh plenary session of the Central Committee in December 1965. The party leadership responded to the political intellectuals' demand for the democratiza-

Robert Havemann holding one of his final lectures at Berlin's Humboldt University, 1964

tion of socialism by declaring that a "socialist community" had been achieved in the
GDR in which common interests and goals
predominated and parliamentary opposition,
as called for by Havemann, was superfluous.
Despite being banned for many years from
exercising their professions, publishing their
work and appearing in public, these prominent regime critics remained true to their

ideas and even defended their opinions
during the "Prague Spring" of 1968, although
its suppression provoked only short-lived
protests in the GDR.

The attempt by the new General Secretary,
Erich Honecker, to weaken the opposition
through a process of controlled cultural liberalization failed, as the most vocal critics

Scene from the film "Trace of Stones", amongst those banned follow-ing the Central Committee's 11th Plenary Session in 1965

POLITIK

Neues Deutschland / 20./21. November 1976 / Seite 3

Wir sind es gewohnt, mitzudenken

Stellungnahmen und Erklärungen von Künstlern und Kulturschaffenden unserer Republik zur Aberkennung der DDR-Staatsbürgerschaft Biermanns

Ernst Busch

Jedermann mag sein eigenes Land kritisch betrachten. Aber wenn er sich mit Text und Stimme an den Klassenfeind verkauft, ist das eine ganz andere Sache. Es macht sein Verhalten fragwürdig und die Maßnahme unserer Regierung verständlich.

Aus „Der Klassenfeind" von Bertolt Brecht:

... und was immer ich auch noch lerne
Das bleibt das Einmaleins
Nichts habe ich jemals gemeinsam
Mit der Sache des Klassenfeinds.
Das Wort wird nicht gefunden
Das uns beide jemals vereint
Der Regen fließt von oben nach unten
Und Du bist mein Klassenfeind"

Ernst Busch

Hermann Kant

Einige meiner Kollegen – darunter solche, denen ich seit langem befreundet bin, und darunter niemand, dessen künstlerischer Leistung ich meinen Respekt versage – haben es für angemessen oder erforderlich gehalten, sich in Sachen Biermann an die Regierung unseres Landes zu wenden, zu protestieren und gleichzeitig um gelassenes Bedenken anzusuchen.

Ich will nicht verhehlen, daß mich zu sagen, daß ich Herrn Biermann ganz gut ausgehalten habe und auch weiterhin ausgehalten hätte, noch brauchte man nicht vor ihm zu schützen.

Meine Sorge geht anders: Wer oder was gewinnt, und wer oder was verliert etwas, wenn sozialistische Künstler, die ihrer sozialistischen Regierung eine Mißteilung zu machen wünschen, sich kapitalistischer Übermittlungs- und Verstärkeranlagen bedienen? Wie behauptet sich Gelassenheit im Medienlärm? Wer kann etwas bedenken in diesem Triumphradau? Woran erkennt man seine Freunde, wenn sie dem Feinde Worte in den Mund legen, die bei nahe schon ausgegangen waren?

Und, übrigens, haben meine Genossen und Kollegen, die solchen Brief zu schreiben wußten, Herrn Biermann um Gelassenheit, Bedenken oder gar Zurückhaltung gebeten? Ist nicht wenigstens dem einen oder anderen von ihnen die Idee gekommen, über Maßnahmen könne sich erst reden lassen, wenn auch der Verursacher dieser Maßnahmen mit reden lasse und gewisse Reden lasse?

Ich glaube nicht, auch dies im Gegensatz zu meinen protestierenden Kollegen, daß die DDR Wolf Biermann zu Zwecken der ständigen Selbstreinigung nötig hat, aber ich glaube sehr, daß sie eine sozialistische und also und also und also kritische Kunst nötig hat. Wollen wir nicht lieber bei dieser Sache bleiben und das, was ihretwegen auszufechten ist, miteinander und untereinander tun? Einer aus unserer Zunft, der besonders scharf wußte, wie man sich im Klassenkampf zu halten hat, schrieb uns die Worte der Viborger Häuslerin auf: Mein Atbin im Gefangenenlager hat einen Fluch und Butter nicht genommen, weil's bei der Gutsherrin gebettelt hab, und er nimmt nichts von denen." Man nimmt nichts von denen – daß man denen nichts gebe, so meine ich. Brecht, brauchte man in dieser Welt nicht mehr zu sagen.

18. November 1976

Hermann Kant

Willi Sitte

Ich bin außerordentlich beunruhigt über die eingetretene Situation durch das Auftreten von Wolf Biermann in der BRD vor einer breiten Öffentlichkeit.

Ich habe Kenntnis erhalten über die Möglichkeit für Wolf Biermann, in einer Reihe von Veranstaltungen in der BRD aufzutreten. Ich war davon überzeugt, daß Wolf Biermann, der sich selbst immer wieder als Kommunist bezeichnet, sich in seinen Auftritten auch als solcher erweisen würde.

Ich war überrascht und tief enttäuscht über die verpaßte Möglichkeit, sich als

sachlich kritischen Atmosphäre zu behandeln.

Ich erkläre in aller Eindeutigkeit, daß wir uns mit allen uns zu Gebote stehenden Mitteln dagegen wehren, daß von irgendwelcher Seite ein Keil in diese Verursacherverhältnis zwischen Partei, Staat und uns Künstlern getrieben wird. Wir haben großes Vertrauen in die zukünftige Gestaltung des weiteren Aufbaus des Sozialismus in unserer Republik und sind sicher, daß wir in dieser Periode mit unserer ganzen Teilnahme verbunden mit unserer Antwortung und unserem ganzen Wil-

Schriftsteller, Bildende Künstler, Schauspieler, Musiker und andere Kulturschaffende nehmen in Erklärungen und Resolutionen zum Beschluß der Regierung der Deutschen Demokratischen Republik Stellung. Wolf Biermann das Recht auf weiteren Aufenthalt in der DDR zu entziehen und ihm die Staatsbürgerschaft der DDR abzuerkennen. Entschieden weisen sie die in diesem Zusammenhang entfaltete Hetzkampagne gegen die DDR zurück.

Wir wählen immer die DDR

Unser Staat hat Biermann ausgebürgert. Das ist sein Recht.

Unser Staat mußte ihn ausbürgern. Das war seine Pflicht, er vollzog nur juristisch nach, was Biermann schon längst getan und in Köln öffentlich demonstriert hatte: seine Trennung von der DDR durch Übertritt in das Lager ihrer halbgefüllten Verleumder.

Die Antikommunisten wollen uns zwingen, zwischen Biermann und der DDR zu wählen. Jeder soll wissen: Wir haben die DDR gewählt und werden immer wieder die DDR wählen!

Karl Georg Egel
Walter Baumert
Irma Münch
Lothar Bellag
Benito Wogatzki

Jürgen Heimlich
Wolf Kaiser
Martin Eckermann
Adam Pöppert
Hans-Georg Ponesky

Albert Hetterle

...In der Kunst gibt es keine konstanten Größen und Begriffe. Es gibt in ihr keine unveränderlichen Kriterien, aber es gibt unveränderliche Forderungen. Die erste von ihnen ist die Forderung nach staatsbürgerlicher Verantwortung", sagt der bedeutende sowjetische Regisseur Georgi Towstonogow.

Und er meint mit staatsbürgerlicher Verantwortung nicht irgendein künstlerisches Schaffensproblem. Er sieht darin (meint damit) die Voraussetzung, das Fundament für jede künstlerische Tätigkeit.

Wer mit seinen künstlerischen Ergebnissen dieser Forderung nicht gerecht wird, bleibt seiner Gesellschaft etwas schuldig.

Wer aber bewußt gegen sie handelt, indem er mit seiner „Kunst" gegen seine Gesellschaft wirkt, macht sich schuldig. Und dies ganz besonders dann, wenn er seine staatsbürgerliche Verantwortung außerhalb der Grenzen seines Landes unter Beweis zu stellen hat.

W. Biermann, der vor einigen Tagen,

Selbst wenn ich ihm seine nur kritische Haltung glauben wollte, ginge die Rechnung nicht auf, denn zur staatsbürgerlichen Verantwortung gehört eben auch zu wissen, wo, wann und in welcher Weise etwas kritisiert wird. Außerdem sollte Kritik immer konstruktiv sein, wie sie uns zum Beispiel bei M. Schatrow in „Wetter für Morgen" oder bei A. Gelmann in „Protokoll einer Sitzung" begegnet. In beiden Stücken werden von einer sozialistisch-kommunistischen Position aus schonungslos Mängel und Fehler aufgedeckt, die der sowjetischen Gesellschaft beim Vorwärtsschreiten zum Kommunismus hemmend im Wege stehen. Diese Art von Kritik regt die Zuschauer an, in eine produktive Richtung weiter zu denken, neue viele Vorstellungen und Foyergespräche bewiesen haben.

Biermanns Auftreten in der BRD war eben kein konstruktiver Beitrag in dem Sinne (eines Sozialisten) für den Sozialismus, sondern im destruktivsten

Erklärung Fritz Cremers

Prof. Fritz Cremer hat sich bereits am Donnerstag von dem Brief einiger DDR-Schriftsteller in der Angelegenheit Biermann distanziert. Er bezeichnete die in der BRD als Protestaktion hochgespielte Erklärung als ein „unglückliches Schreiben über Biermann". Fritz Cremer erklärte, daß sein Name in diesem Zusammenhang mißbraucht wurde. Man habe ihn, der sich im Krankenhaus befindet überfahren.

Erklärung Ekkehard Schalls

Ich möchte betonen, daß ich den Brief einiger Schriftsteller in der Annahme unterschrieben habe, daß er ausschließlich für zuständige Stellen in der DDR bestimmt war. Daß er direkt an westliche Presseagenturen übergeben wurde, halte ich für einen Mißbrauch meiner eingenommenen Haltung. Ich ziehe deshalb meine Unterschrift zurück.

Paul Dessau

Die DDR, in der ich seit ihrer Gründung arbeite, ist eine historische Gesetzmäßigkeit und kein Experiment. Daß wir heute ein weltweit anerkannter, hochentwickelter Staat sind, verdanken wir allen denen, die niemals nachgelassen haben in ihrer unerschütterlichen Überzeugung und ihrem politisch fundierten Kampf für Frieden und Fortschritt. Wissend und mit Stolz kann ich sagen, daß unsere Künstler, jeder auf seine Weise und durch die verständnisvolle Unterstützung seitens unseres Staates zu dieser Entwicklung beigetragen haben. Es ist unsere Pflicht, die bewährten Methoden des Klassenfeinden zu durchschauen und ihnen geschlossen entgegenzutreten.

Paul Dessau

Kunsthochschule Berlin

Wir Angehörigen der Kunsthochschule Berlin verurteilen das feindselige Verhalten Wolf Biermanns gegen unseren sozialistischen Staat und seine Bürger. Wir identifizieren uns voll mit den getroffenen Maßnahmen des Entzuges der net von

Staatsbürgerschaft der DDR und distanzieren uns von jeglichen Versuchen, die Richtigkeit dieser Maßnahme in Zweifel zu ziehen.

Die Stellungnahme wurde unterschrieben.

Prof. Schamel,
amtierender Rektor,

sowie den Professoren und Dozenten

Heuer
Neujahr
Michael
Richter

Seifert
Schals
Hakenbeck
Dutschke

Mrowetz
Schütze
Brüggenkamp
Kuntzsch
Pollaks
Höckler
Schwarz

Flieger
Wicht
Teßmar
Fahlig
Senf
Haider
Rudolph

Günter Reisch

Lenin sagt: „Die Dialektik der Geschichte ist derart, daß der theoretische Sieg des Marxismus seine Feinde zwingt, sich als Marxisten zu verkleiden. Der innerlich verfaulte Liberalismus versucht, sich als sozialistischer Opportunismus als Führerin des Proletariats und konsequente Kommunistin, deren Ausspruch „Dem Feind das Knie auf der Brust" der deutschen Bourgeoisie kein ruhiges Zeitalter verspricht.

[bottom commentary]

Statements by GDR artists in the *Neues Deutschland* newspaper, reacting to the expulsion of Wolf Biermann, 20 November 1976

of the party and state leadership, such as Biermann and Havemann, were not convinced by the shift in course. They used their high profile and contacts in West Germany to continue to publicize their ideas about a democratic form of socialism. The SED now began to resort to more severe measures to rid itself of the two most prominent figures in the intellectual opposition. In 1976, it placed Havemann under house arrest and, following a concert in Cologne, expelled Biermann for alleged agitation against the state. But the SED's hopes that it had struck at the heart of the intellectual opposition, and its political resistance, were dashed. The expulsion of Biermann produced a wave of solidarity within large sections of the population, which was expressed in a protest letter written by Stephan Hermlin, initially signed by eleven authors and artists, and disseminated by the French AFP news agency. Numerous artists who subsequently publicly expressed their solidarity were subjected to

state sanctions, without any discussion about the political reasons for the protest; several were arrested. Only the arrest of the previously unknown Rudolf Bahro, whose work "The Alternative in Eastern Europe" contained a radical analysis of the reality of SED socialism and proposed a communist alternative based on political equality and emancipation, caused a similar shock. The large numbers of people leaving the GDR after this event proved that numerous intellectuals had now also lost their faith in the political system's ability to reform itself.

The peace movement

From 1979 onwards, against the background of the escalating East-West conflict and the arms race, a strong peace movement also emerged in the GDR, becoming a rallying point for what remained of the opposition.

The movement focussed on the Protestant churches, which, despite their leaders' efforts to demonstrate loyalty to the SED, continued to provide a protected space and a forum for debate. It was motivated mainly by Protestant social ethics, with a blend of Marxist ideals. The movement, made up of a wide range of groups driven by different motives, distanced itself from socialist ideology and practice, actively supporting peace education and combating the militarization of society. The "Social Peace Service" and "Swords into Ploughshares" movements in particular attracted a large number of younger people from outside Church circles. Soon, their political demands had gone beyond peace initiatives and included the democratization of society and the recognition of human rights. Despite numerous attempts by the SED to crush the peace movement through bans on demonstrations, arrests and expulsions, it was unable to quell the opposition completely. In the mid-1980s, the foreign and domestic policy reform course being pursued by Gorbachev gave the peace movement fresh impetus. The individual groups expanded both in terms of their social base and the political spectrum they covered. The opposition was soon printing pamphlets and brochures in which it commented on almost all current events and domestic issues. Yet ideological differences prevented the opposition from pooling its forces. It was not until 1989, against the background of the SED's rapidly dwindling power, that several of the groups joined together to form a GDR-wide network.

The citizens' movement, "Monday demonstrations" and the peaceful revolution

The widening scope of the peace movement's political activities led to the establishment of new citizens' groups which sought to air their views independently of Church influence. In light of the reform

Demonstration by the Jena peace movement during the FDJ's Whitsun meeting on 19 May 1983

People's Police grappling with participants in a peace demonstration in Berlin, 1983

Stasi officials outside the Zionskirche in Berlin, where protests are taking place against the raid on the "Environmental Library", 1987

process initiated by the communist parties in Poland and Hungary, they now challenged the SED leadership directly and called for a fundamental democratization of the political system. The opposition movements were given a great boost, both in organizational and political terms, when they proved that the local elections of May 1989 had been rigged. By July, a campaign to re-establish a social democratic party had been launched, which came to fruition on 7 October. The "New Forum", established on 9 September 1989, became the largest and most influential group. Its "Awakening 1989" appeal was signed by more than 200,000 people. Other groups and parties like "Democracy Now" and "Democratic Awakening" soon emerged as well. While the different groups broadly agreed that there should continue to be two German states, they differed widely on how the GDR's political system was to be democratically restructured in practice. Whereas some were in favour of parliamentary democracy, others advocated concepts based on grass-roots democracy or reformed communism.

Meanwhile, from the end of September, a peaceful protest movement had been spreading throughout the GDR. It originated in Leipzig and was boosted by the exodus of GDR citizens via Hungary and Czechoslovakia. The movement finally succeeded in forcing the SED to engage in dialogue and ousting Honecker. The protests culminated in the demonstration organized by GDR artists at Berlin's Alexanderplatz on 4 November 1989, when over 500,000 people protested against the all-encompassing power of the SED and demanded freedom of expression and free elections.

After the opening of the Wall on 9 November, a "central round table" was established at the initiative of the opposition groups, at which the citizens' movement was also represented alongside the SED/PDS, which was still in power, and the Bloc parties. Although the civil rights activists did manage in this forum to roll back the political influence of the SED/PDS and force free parlia-

The "New Forum's" inaugural conference on 28 January 1990 in Berlin. Standing: Jens Reich

Meeting of the *Land* delegates of the "Democracy Now" citizens' movement in Berlin on 21 January 1990

mentary elections, their increased involvement in the work of government led to a further fragmentation of the opposition. As the result of policy differences, organizational weaknesses and the failure to address the issue of German unity, which was becoming increasingly important to people in the GDR, the opposition groups were unable, in the parliamentary elections of 18 March, to hold

Friedrich Schorlemmer and Rainer Eppelmann at "Democratic Awakening's" inaugural conference in Leipzig on 17 December 1989

Over 500,000
people demon-
strate against
the SED regime
at Alexander-
platz in Berlin
on 4 Novem-
ber 1989

their own against the PDS and the parties
which were supported by the West. Following reunification on 3 October, many groups
disbanded or, like Alliance 90, merged with
West German parties.

Representa-
tives from the
SDP and the
United Left at
the "Round
Table" in East
Berlin on
7 December
1989

6. From the opening of the Wall to German unity

In opening the Wall, the SED leadership unleashed a political momentum which soon ended its monopoly of power and ultimately ushered in the demise of the GDR. Within a few days of the fall of the Wall, the Bloc parties announced to the SED the end of their unconditional subservience in the People's Chamber and called for the SED's claim to leadership to be deleted from the constitution and for free elections to be held. As a first step, however, the parliamentarians agreed to elect the SED District Secretary for Dresden, Hans Modrow, regarded as a reformer, as the new head of government. But the SED continued to lose its grip on power. On 1 December, the reference to the party's "leadership role" was finally deleted from the constitution and only a few days later, increasing public pressure and rapidly dwindling support for the SED led to the entire leadership being removed from office and previously influential functionaries being expelled from the party. The SED, renamed the Party of Democratic Socialism (PDS) in

February 1990, attempted to adjust to the new situation by denouncing Stalinist methods of rule and electing the lawyer Gregor Gysi as its new party chairman.

As the parliamentary structures continued to exist, both in practice and in the GDR constitution, the SED/PDS and the Bloc parties initially continued to exercise their functions in the People's Chamber. Thus no

Hans Modrow making his government policy statement to the People's Chamber on 17 November 1989

produktiv • pro DDR

Gregor Gysi and Hans Modrow at the PDS' first party conference in Berlin, 24 February 1990

Helmut Kohl addressing a crowd of tens of thousands in Dresden on 19 December 1989

A scene of devastation in the basement of the Stasi headquarters in Normannenstrasse in Berlin, 15 January 1990

radical restructuring of the political system took place until the elections to the People's Chamber in 1990; as the strongest parliamentary group, the SED/PDS continued to form the government. This situation had a particularly adverse effect on the citizens' movements, which were denied any role in government. But opposition pressure led to the formation of a "round table", which involved the new groups and parties alongside representatives of the Bloc parties and the SED/PDS. This body, which was initially intended to act as a check on the govern-

ment, failed to gain acceptance for the constitution which it had drafted, but was able to press ahead with the dissolution of the Ministry of State Security and to set a date for free and secret elections.

By the beginning of 1990, it was becoming clear that neither the former state party nor the opposition groups, with their vision of a reformed GDR, would win the backing of the people. In view of the impressions which many GDR citizens had gained during their trips to the Federal Republic, and the economic crisis, which was exacerbated by the continuing exodus, the majority of East Germans were pushing for rapid reunification. Chancellor Helmut Kohl exploited the mood in the GDR in order to force the hand of the Modrow government, already under pressure from its own people, with his "10-point programme to overcome the division of Germany and Europe". Modrow, who initially continued to insist on the existence of two German states, also came under pressure from within the government itself, as he continued to try and retain his party's hold on the state institutions. When the ministers belonging to the Bloc parties threatened to walk out of the coalition, the "round table" agreed on a cabinet reshuffle and on early elections to the People's Chamber, which were set for 18 March 1990.

While Modrow was belatedly attempting to gain support for his plan to reunite the two German states, made public on 1 February, most of the other parties were already focussing on the first free elections to the People's Chamber, which was to decide on the further steps towards reunification.

From the end of 1989 onwards, the party system in the GDR had been becoming increasingly similar to that in the Federal Republic. The newly-founded parties like the SDP (from January 1990 onwards, known as the SPD), DSU and FDP were seeking contact with their counterparts in the West, while the former Bloc parties CDU and LDPD were signalling, through their renewal of policies and personnel, their desire to cooperate with their sister parties in the Federal Republic. During the election campaign they received organizational and financial support from their West German partners. From the outset,

Alliance 90's election campaign headquarters in the House of Democracy in Berlin

some of the 33 political groupings standing for election sought to improve their chances of joining the government by forming electoral alliances. Thus the conservative parties (CDU, DSU and Democratic Awakening)

Campaign posters in Berlin-Köpenick for the People's Chamber elections of 18 March 1990

West German CDU politician Norbert Blüm (second from left) at a press conference held by the "Alliance for Germany" on 5 March 1990

failed to achieve an absolute majority on 18 March. The citizens' groups within Alliance 90 received only 2.9% of votes cast. The outcome of the election to the People's Chamber, which was largely confirmed in the local elections in May, demonstrated once and for all that the majority of the GDR population rejected the idea of a reformed socialism and was pushing for the process of reunification to be accelerated.

joined forces in the "Alliance for Germany", which was unequivocally committed to German unity, whereas the SPD decided not to enter into an electoral pact. The liberal parties – the LDPD, the newly-founded FDP and the German Forum Party – formed the Federation of Free Democrats. The citizens'

Despite initial differences between the victors, the Alliance for Germany, the SPD and the liberals formed a coalition, headed by the new Prime Minister Lothar de Maizière. The most important task facing the new government now – besides dissolving the Ministry of State Security – was to deal with the legal and organizational preparations for reunification. The Treaty between the Federal Republic of Germany and the German Democratic Republic

CDU Chairman Lothar de Maizière (right) and his Secretary-General Martin Kirchner on election night

movements – New Forum, Democracy Now and the Initiative for Peace and Human Rights – campaigned as Alliance 90.

Although the opinion polls predicted victory for the SPD, in actual fact, the CDU, together with its conservative partners, only just

establishing a Monetary, Economic and Social Union, signed on 18 May, was a first step in this direction. It was intended to halt the rapid economic decline of the GDR and prepare the ground for the economic and social unification of the two states.

But some foreign policy questions on the road to reunification remained unresolved. These were discussed between the former victorious powers and the two German states in the Two-Plus-Four negotiations. With the recognition of Poland's Western border by the Bundestag and the People's Chamber, one of the most important issues was settled. When Mikhail Gorbachev, as a quid pro quo for certain economic benefits and on the condition that Soviet security interests were taken into account, agreed that the reunified Germany should be accepted into NATO, this accelerated the conclusion of the "Two-Plus-Four" Treaty, which set in place the foreign policy framework for reunification.

After a majority had opposed the drafting of a new constitution in June, the People's Chamber voted on 23 August in favour of the GDR's accession to the Federal Republic

under Article 23 of the Basic Law by 294 to 62 votes. The legal basis for accession was the Treaty between the Federal Republic of Germany and the German Democratic Republic on the Establishment of German Unity, which, as well as providing the necessary legal alignments, also extended the West German political and institutional system to the five new Federal *Länder* and

Federal Finance Minister Theo Waigel presenting a GDR citizen with a deutschmark banknote, valid in the Eastern part of Germany from 1 July 1990

Majority vote in the People's Chamber in favour of the GDR's accession to the Federal Republic, 23 August 1990

Federal Interior Minister Wolfgang Schäuble and GDR State Secretary Günther Krause shaking hands after the signing of the Unification Treaty in East Berlin, 31 August 1990

East Berlin. With the Treaty's entry into force on 3 October 1990, the demise of the GDR, which had existed as a state for just under 41 years, was complete.

The Federal Republic of Germany

1. The Drafting of the Basic Law

Severe bomb damage in a Hamburg street, 1945

Following the collapse of the Nazi regime, the Allies held absolute power over the German territories. Germany's former eastern provinces were now administered by the Soviet Union and Poland, the area between the Elbe and Oder rivers formed the Soviet zone of occupation, and western Germany was divided between the USA, Britain and France. The whole of Germany was governed by an Allied Control Council composed of the four Commanders-in-Chief. Other than this, however, the victorious powers were unable to reach consensus on more than their desire to eliminate all vestiges of the National Socialist regime and prevent Germany from ever waging another war in future. Even the agreements reached at the Potsdam Conference in July and August 1945 on Germany's economic unity and the reconstruction of a democratic system soon proved to be of limited value. The plans to set up German central administrative bodies were vetoed by France, while economic unity fell victim to disputes over reparations, for which the Soviet Union in particular was pressing. As far as the process of political and administrative restructuring was concerned, each occupying power based its approach on its own system of government. In the end, the Allied Control Council was no longer in a position to pursue a unified occupation policy for the whole of Germany. Its responsibilities were increasingly transferred to the Commanders-in-Chief and the military governments in the individual zones of occupation. The development of the

Meeting of the Allied Control Council in Berlin, 11 February 1948

Polling station in Munich during the first Bavarian city and town elections, 26 May 1946

country's political life was correspondingly diverse.

While the Soviet occupying forces began to build up a centralized administration in their zone with the slogan of the "anti-fascist-democratic revolution", using it to lay the foundations of a communist state and social order, institutions of self-government were initially established at local and regional level in the western part of the country. The Western occupying powers relied principally on German politicians known to them from the Weimar period or who were recom-mended to them by senior church figures who had no Nazi past. Only gradually, under strict supervision and accompanied by a programme of denazification conceived as "education for democracy", were the precon-ditions for the resumption of public life put in place with the licensing of mass media and democratic parties.

The first local elections took place in the American Zone as early as January 1946. More than 80 percent of those entitled to vote used this opportunity to decide for themselves who should run their communi-ties. The representatives of the military governments initially installed administra-tions in the *Länder* (federal states) estab-lished by the occupying powers, which – with the exception of south-west Germany – have continued to exist within the borders laid down at the time, but free elections also took place at *Land* level In 1946/47. The *Länder* were given a particularly prominent position in American and French occupation policy, and were soon developed into parliamentary democracies with a wide range of powers. Following an initial phase marked by a more centralized approach, British policy then began to follow this model as well. As a result, these federal structures determined the later political organization of the Federal Republic of Germany.

In January 1947, the British and American zones of occupation amalgamated into a "unified economic area" known as the "Bi-Zone". Its supreme organ was the Economic

Poster promoting the Marshall Plan, around 1949

Council composed of representatives from the parliaments of the eight *Länder* in the Bi-Zone. This body met in Frankfurt am Main for the first time on 25 June 1947 and had the right to initiate legislation.

The anti-Hitler coalition, which had only been held together by the earlier struggle against the Axis powers, now began to break up. In the following decades, the global political climate was dominated by a situa-tion aptly described as the "Cold War". The Soviet Union regarded the protests against its great-power politics and the rejection of its reparations demands as evidence that it was threatened with encirclement by the Western powers, and moved openly to con-solidate its position of supremacy in Eastern Europe. In response, the USA abandoned its previous policy of partial cooperation and its

Currency reform in the Western zones. The first deutschmark banknotes are issued in Munich, 20 June 1948

officially invited to take part in this programme, but it was rejected by the countries subject to Soviet domination. The London Four-Power Conference of November and December 1947 failed primarily on account of conflicting ideas about Germany's long-term restructuring and Soviet opposition to the Marshall Plan.

The steps necessary for the founding of a West German state were now taken in rapid succession. The reshaping of the West German economic administration was initiated at a meeting between the Military Governors, Brian Robertson and Lucius D. Clay, and the minister-presidents of the Bi-Zone in January 1948. A common currency, the deutschmark, was introduced on 20 June 1948 in the western zones of occupation and on 25 June in Berlin. An important building block for the future success of the West German economy had been put in place.

acceptance of separate spheres of interest. On 12 March 1947, the US President proclaimed the "Truman Doctrine", which marked the transition to a policy of containing communism. The new course found its most visible expression in a reconstruction programme that came to be known as the "Marshall Plan". All the states of Europe were

The process of state-building also moved forward rapidly in the administrative field. On 1 July 1948 the minister-presidents of the 11 West German *Länder* were presented with the Frankfurt Documents, which instructed them to convene a constituent assembly charged with preparing for the founding of a federal state. As this would practically seal the division of Germany, the minister-presi-

The three Western Military Governors in Frankfurt am Main, 12 May 1949. From left: Pierre Koenig (France), Brian Robertson (Britain), Lucius D. Clay (USA)

dents insisted that, rather than a constitution, a "basic law" should be drafted as a framework for the parliamentary representation of the *Länder*. Initially, the intention was to build a provisional structure in the West that could later form the "core state" for the gradual unification of Germany.

A preparatory constitutional convention began its discussions at Herrenchiemsee in Bavaria. The work done by this body of experts was to serve as the basis for the deliberations on the constitution in the Parliamentary Council, which was solemnly inaugurated on 1 September 1948 at the Alexander Koenig Museum in Bonn. 65 representatives of the *Länder*, selected on the basis of the *Land* parliament elections, had the task of drawing up a provisional constitution that would form the foundation stone for the future West German state. The Parliamentary Council elected Konrad Adenauer of the Christian Democratic Union (CDU) as its president, while the Social Democrat Carlo

Schmid became the chairman of its Main Committee.

The Basic Law was debated for several months, during which thousands of recommendations and petitions were submitted to the Parliamentary Council from all sections of the population. The men and women charged with drafting it did not repeat the grave errors of the Weimar constitution. The Basic Law does not give the head of state the right to issue emergency decrees, thus ensuring that political power at federal level remains concentrated in the hands of parliament and government. The role of the Federal President, who is elected by a Federal Convention made up of an equal number of representatives from the Bundestag and the *Land* parliaments, is limited for the most part to ceremonial functions. Compared with the Weimar constitution, the Basic Law contains few plebiscitary elements and provides for what is known as the "constructive" vote of no

Road signs near Bonn, where the Parliamentary Council convened on 1 September 1948

The "mothers of the Basic Law". From left: Friederike Nadig (SPD), Elisabeth Selbert (SPD), Helene Weber (CDU), Helene Wessel (Centre, later Federalist Union, then SPD)

confidence, under which parliament can force the Federal Chancellor to stand down only if it simultaneously elects a successor by a majority vote. These provisions were intended to ensure the long-term stability of the country's representative democracy. The lessons of recent German history were also reflected in other areas. A catalogue of fundamental rights, which had already been included in the Weimar constitution, was now placed at the very beginning of the Basic Law, and these rights became directly enforceable in law.

Following the necessary consultations with the three Western Military Governors and the minister-presidents of what had become the Tri-Zone, since it now also included the areas occupied by France, the provisional constitution was adopted by the Parliamentary Council at its third reading on

8 May 1949 as the Basic Law of the "Federal Republic of Germany". 53 delegates voted for its adoption, while the 12 votes against were cast, for widely varying reasons, by six of the eight representatives of the Christian Social Union (CSU), the CDU's Bavarian sister party, and the delegates from the Centre Party, the Communist Party of Germany (KPD) and the Lower Saxon German Party (DP). Two days later the Parliamentary Council voted by 33 to 29 that Bonn should be the future seat of the Federal Government.

Following its approval by the Military Governors of the three Western powers, the Parliamentary Council was able to promulgate the Basic Law on 23 May. All the West German *Land* parliaments – except that of Bavaria – gave the law their assent.

The Basic Law entered into force on the day after its promulgation. The Federal Republic of Germany had officially come into existence. The first elections to the Bundestag were set for 14 August 1949.

The Parliamentary Council's final vote on the Basic Law, 8 May 1949

2. The German Bundestag and the party system of the Federal Republic of Germany

Theodor Heuss
(FDP), Federal
President from
1949 to 1959

The most important constitutional organs at federal level are the Bundesrat, the body representing the *Länder*; the Federal President, the head of state; the Federal Government, the executive; the Federal Constitutional Court, the highest judicial body, which hands down judgements binding on all the country's constitutional organs, courts and authorities; and finally the Bundestag.

The Bundestag elects the Federal Chancellor – formally at the proposal of the Federal President. It is therefore the body primarily responsible for the formation of the government and so indirectly determines the direction of future policy. As the federal parliament, it stands at the centre of the legislative process, and as the only directly elected constitutional organ it represents the German people, a constitutional principle laid down in Article 20, paragraph (2) of the Basic Law: "All state authority derives from the people. It shall be exercised by the people through elections and other votes and through

The election of the Federal Chancellor by the German Bundestag, 22 October 1957

specific legislative, executive, and judicial bodies."

The dualistic relationship between the legislature and the government that dominated German constitutional practice prior to 1919 and continued to influence it until 1933 has become a thing of the past. Parliament is neither, as during the German Empire, excluded from the formation of governments nor – as during the Weimar Republic – easily able to block government action with negative majorities and bring down governing coalitions without proposing any alternative to take their place. Rather, the election of the Chancellor by the Bundestag presupposes a sustainable parliamentary majority. For its part, the government appointed by the Chancellor enjoys greater independence in office than was the case during the Weimar Republic. The long-standing political conflict between parliament and government has finally been transformed into a conflict between the government with its parliamentary majority, on the one hand, and the parliamentary opposition, on the other.

Accordingly, parliament's role of overseeing the government is, in the public sphere, performed primarily by the parliamentary opposition. It carries out this function using the traditional instruments of interpellations and Question Time. In the 1960s, debates on matters of topical interest dealing with issues of particular urgency were also introduced. Where a quarter of the Members of the Bundestag so demand, a parliamentary committee of inquiry entitled to request legal and administrative assistance from other state bodies has to be set up. The investigations carried out by these committees and, above all, their often very detailed reports make a decisive contribution to the transparency of German political life.

View of the press gallery in the plenary chamber of the Bundestag, around 1969

The sittings of the plenary are held in public unless a two-thirds majority of the Members decides otherwise. Legislation is passed by a majority of the votes cast by the Members present, except where a majority of all elected Members or – as for amendments to the Basic Law – a two-thirds majority is required by law. As a rule, a quorum exists when more than half of all the Members are present.

In the early years of the Federal Republic of Germany, the plenary debates were often

Meeting of the Budget Committee, March 1995

marked by an overriding concern for fundamental principles later only apparent when major policy decisions were taken or matters of far-reaching political symbolism were at stake. The traditional high point of the parliamentary year is the annual budget debate, which, since the days of the grand coalition in the late 1960s, has been opened by the

leader of the largest opposition party. These set-piece debates, in which the Federal Government's policies are attacked and defended passionately, demonstrate that the Bundestag truly is the country's central forum for political discussion.

The broader public is often not aware of Members' activities outside the plenary sittings. They consist primarily of their work within the parliamentary groups, in their working groups on specific policy issues and the groups consisting of Members from a given *Land* within each party, on committees and commissions, and in their own constituencies. In particular, the committees, whose membership is determined in accordance with a formula based on the relative strengths of the parliamentary groups, play a central role in the discussion of legislative proposals and prepare motions for adoption in the plenary. As a rule, the media are not allowed to attend committee meetings, but the many hearings of experts and interest group representatives are held in public.

The Bundestag is elected in general, equal, secret and direct elections, in which the voter has two different kinds of vote. The first vote is used to elect a constituency representative. The candidate who gains a simple majority (more votes than any other candidate) is elected with a "direct mandate". The second vote is cast for one of the lists of candidates put forward by the parties in each *Land*. Each party is then allocated a number of seats in parliament proportional to its share of the vote. As the number of direct mandates obtained by a party is then deducted from the number of seats to which it is entitled on the basis of the second votes cast for it, the composition of parliament is determined primarily by the party-list vote. Elections to the Bundestag are held in the last two months before the end of an electoral term, and within 60 days of parliament being dissolved early. At the beginning of the 1st electoral term (1949-1953) the Bundestag consisted of 402 Members and eight representatives from Berlin who did not have full voting rights. Including "overhang mandates"

Elections to the Bundestag, 17 September 1961. Results are recorded at the Federal Electoral Office in Bonn

held by parties that gain more direct constituency seats in a particular *land* than they are entitled to on the basis of the party-list vote, the number of Members of the Bundestag grew to 669 in the 14th electoral term (1998-2002), not least due to the accession of the former GDR to the Federal Republic of Germany, but will go down to 598 in the 15th electoral term commencing in 2002.

A clause in the Federal Electoral Law, tightened up by legislation in 1953 and 1956, reflects the lessons learned from the instability of the Weimar Reichstag, requiring parties to gain a minimum percentage of the popular vote in order to gain representation in the Bundestag. Whereas in the 1st electoral term there were 12 different parties represented in parliament, the five-percent threshold

Left:
Polling station in Bad Godesberg during elections to the Bundestag, 19 November 1972. In 1970 an amendment to the Basic Law lowered the voting age to 18

Elections to the Bundestag, 16 October 1994. A voter with a ballot paper

reduced the chances of smaller parties gaining seats in the Bundestag to such an extent that it operated essentially as a three-party parliament from 1961 to 1983. The extreme right-wing Socialist Reich Party (SRP) and the Communist Party of Germany (KPD), which called for the "revolutionary overthrow of the Adenauer regime", were banned by the Federal Constitutional Court in 1952 and 1956 respectively. In general, the "five-percent clause" has been very effective in preventing extremist groupings from gaining strength, and most of their potential supporters have been absorbed by parties within the democratic spectrum.

A fundamental readiness to make compromises is now regarded in all the parliamentary groups as a basic prerequisite for the functioning of parliamentary democracy, which – despite occasional differences concerning how it should be organized – is supported unreservedly by all the parties represented in parliament. The fundamental ideological conflicts that determined the policies of most parties in the past and did great damage to Germany's polity, particularly during the Weimar Republic, are therefore a thing of the past.

Nevertheless, the links between the parties of the Federal Republic of Germany and the traditions of the Weimar Republic were more than just structural: there were also continuities in terms of personnel and policies. Initially, the post-war parties developed at local and regional level. The Christian Democratic Union (CDU), for example, was not established as a federal organization until October 1950. In the early years, apart from the KPD and the SRP, other small parties that were either regionally based or associated with particular interest groups, such as the Bavarian Party and the Association of Expellees and Disenfranchized, which represented ethnic Germans who had been driven from their homes in Eastern Europe at the end of World War II, were able to exert a certain amount of influence. However, a stable party system made up of the CDU/CSU, the SPD and the Free Democratic Party

The CDU in the British Zone set out its political principles in the 1947 Ahlen Programme

(FDP) was already taking shape and was to constitute the political spectrum represented in the Bundestag and *Land* parliaments for more than three and a half decades. Only in 1983 did a new political force enter the Bundestag in the shape of the Greens, who were mainly concerned with ecological questions and were committed to pacifist principles. A fifth party entered parliament in 1990, namely the Party of Democratic Socialism (PDS), the successor organization to the Socialist Unity Party (SED), the former GDR state party. The PDS had sufficient members to gain the status of a separate parliamentary group for the first time in the 14th Bundestag (1998-2002).

The Christian Democratic Union

Even before the occupying powers licensed parties again in Germany, independent Christian Democrat *Land* associations were formed in some of the larger towns and cities. Though they were often led by politicians from the old Centre Party, they regarded themselves as the nucleus of a "bourgeois

Interzonal meeting of the CDU/CSU Working Group in Frankfurt am Main, 26 April 1948. Centre: Konrad Adenauer

mass party" open to Christians of all denominations. In 1949, in the run-up to the first federal elections, a CDU/CSU working party led by Konrad Adenauer presented the Düsseldorf Principles, in which it supported a social market economy and integration into the Western community of states while emphasizing the goal of German unity. These themes allowed the CDU/CSU to strike a chord with people from all sections of society and denominations. Its success at the polls enabled it to form the first government of the Federal Republic of Germany together with the Free Democrats (FDP) and the German Party. At the founding conference of the federal CDU in Goslar in October 1950, Adenauer was also elected party chairman. He dominated government policy-making

Federal Chancellor Konrad Adenauer (left) with Ludwig Erhard, who would later succeed him, 7 July 1960

until well into the 1960s, and also had a crucial influence on the development of the CDU.

As the economic boom of the reconstruction period slowed down and the CDU/CSU was unable to come up with fresh solutions for domestic and foreign policy issues, the popular Economics Minister Ludwig Erhard replaced Adenauer as Chancellor in 1963, though he was unable to prevent the break-up of the coalition with the FDP in October 1966. His successor, Kurt Georg Kiesinger, formed a grand coalition with the SPD, successfully dealt with the recession and pushed ahead with internal political reforms. In the 1969 federal elections,

Bruno Heck, the first secretary-general of the CDU, in conversation with Federal Chancellor Kurt Georg Kiesinger, May 1967

the CDU/CSU narrowly missed an absolute majority in parliament, but had to content itself with an opposition role for the first time in its history as the SPD and FDP formed a Social-Liberal coalition government.

The CDU used the ensuing period above all to press ahead with the organizational and policy reforms already initiated by its first Secretary-General, Bruno Heck, and later continued primarily by Kurt Biedenkopf and Heiner Geissler. This process was accelerated by changes in the party leadership. As leader of the opposition, Kiesinger's successor Rainer Barzel failed to bring down Brandt's cabinet through a vote of no confidence in April 1972, but the close result initially forced the government to engage in constructive cooperation. In light of the CDU/CSU's poor performance in the elections to the

Bundestag, which had been dissolved before the end of the electoral term, the CDU elected Helmut Kohl, the Minister-President of Rhineland-Palatinate, as its party chairman in 1973. Despite a positive election result, he failed as the CDU/CSU's candidate for the chancellorship in 1976, as did Franz Josef Strauss, the chairman of the CSU, four years later.

The CDU's fortunes only improved in September 1982, when the coalition between the SPD and the FDP broke apart. After a successful vote of no confidence in Helmut Schmidt and the early dissolution of parliament yet again in March 1983, the CDU gained its second-best election result at federal level since 1949 under the new Chancellor Helmut Kohl. However, this victory did not prevent the party losing votes in the *Länder* and its majority in the Bundesrat. Heiner Geissler attempted to stop this trend in the late 1980s by opening the party to the left, triggering a protracted internal debate on party strategy.

Only a few weeks after the fall of the Berlin Wall on 9 November 1989, Kohl seized the opportunity to take a major step towards German reunification with his "ten-point programme". The CDU/CSU-supported Alliance for Germany, consisting of the eastern CDU, Democratic Awakening and the German Social Union (DSU), won the elections to the People's Chamber on 18 March 1990. This result, along with economic, currency and social union, and the approval of the former Allied Powers, paved the way for the signing of the Unification Treaty.

The CDU won the first all-German elections in 1990 with 36.7 percent of the party-list vote, while the CSU polled 7.1 percent. In its first all-German policy programme, the CDU focussed on economic and ecological issues, as well as equal rights for women. Seven months after its electoral defeat in September 1998, the party, now led by its long-standing parliamentary group chairman Wolfgang Schäuble, adopted the Erfurt Principles, in which it further developed its policy positions while remaining firmly committed to

Following the vote of no confidence won by the CDU/CSU and FDP on 1 October 1982, the new Federal Chancellor, Helmut Kohl (centre), accepts the congratulations of his party colleagues

Angela Merkel's election as party chairperson at the CDU conference in Essen, 10 April 2000

its fundamental values and placing great emphasis on the process of European unification. In April 2000, Angela Merkel was the first woman to become the chairperson of a major German political party.

The Christian Social Union

Hanns Seidel, CSU chairman from 1955 to 1961 and Bavarian minister-president from 1957 to 1960

While the state of Prussia disappeared from the map as a result of a decision taken by the Allied Control Council, and completely new *Länder* were created in the north and subsequently in the south-west of the future Federal Republic of Germany, the Free State of Bavaria was re-established by the American occupying forces as early as September 1945. The CSU, which was licensed throughout the *Land* in January 1946, was therefore able to draw on certain continuities typical of Bavaria – whether it was the emphasis on regional independence or a tradition of deeply rooted conservatism.

In the first years of its existence, an inter-denominational grouping around Josef Müller competed with powerful forces that aspired to a Bavarian-Catholic model. In consequence, Minister-President Hans Ehard often found it difficult to reconcile the different factions in the party. Following the party's defeat in the 1954 *Land* elections, the new party chairman,

Hanns Seidel, vigorously pursued the transformation of the CSU into an efficiently organized, highly disciplined mass party, which gradually developed a profile that successfully combined tradition and modernization. It returned to power in Bavaria in 1957 and has governed the Free State alone since 1962.

At federal level, the CSU has cooperated with the CDU since 1949, when the two parties formed a joint parliamentary group in the Bundestag that was subsequently formalized in writing. When there is a conservative or Christian-Liberal governing majority, the CSU is allocated between three and five ministerial portfolios, which enhances its weight in federal politics. During the Adenauer era, the CSU's politicians were essentially loyal followers of the Chancellor. However, under Franz Josef Strauss, who was in charge of various federal ministries early in his career, elected party chairman in 1961 and held office as Minister-President of Bavaria from 1978 to 1988, the CSU pursued a course of cooperative competition with the CDU. After the narrow defeat of Helmut Kohl, the CDU/CSU candidate for the chancellorship in the 1976 elections, the CSU Members of the Bundestag, meeting in Wildbad Kreuth, decided to leave the joint parliamentary group, but soon found themselves forced to back down. Four years later Strauss failed as the CDU/CSU candidate for chancellor after a highly divisive election campaign.

The CSU asserted its strong position in Helmut Kohl's cabinets. For example, Theo Waigel, who was party chairman for many years, headed the key Ministry of Finance from 1989 to 1998, while Max Streibl, a politician with strong regional roots, followed in Strauss's footsteps as Bavarian Minister-President. In the early 1990s, the CSU supported the newly founded German Social Union (DSU) in the former GDR, though the new party soon became irrelevant.

Whereas the CDU/CSU lost the federal elections in September 1998, the CSU secured 48.2 percent of the Bavarian party-list vote. Under the leadership of Edmund Stoiber, its

CSU chairman Franz Josef Strauss (right) with Friedrich Zimmermann, deputy chairman of the CDU/CSU parliamentary group in the German Bundestag, 19 November 1976

Edmund Stoiber, Bavarian minister-president and CSU chairman, at the CDU party conference in Dresden, 4 December 2001

close links with business, targeted policies for small and medium-sized enterprises, liberal-conservative identity and efficient party apparatus, as well as its social commitment, have continued to give it a unique profile.

The Social Democratic Party of Germany

As soon as the war was over, the German Social Democrats began to rebuild their party organization. Drawing on its proletarian tradition and the Weimar Social Democrats' concern for the rule of law, the SPD became the party with the highest membership in

ate aim of Social Democrat policy. With 29.2 percent of the vote in the first Bundestag elections, the SPD emerged as the second strongest party, but lost more and more ground to the governing CDU in the years that followed. Meanwhile, the reformist wing of the SPD around Fritz Erler, Herbert Wehner and Willy Brandt was working on principles for the modernization of the party.

These modernization efforts came to fruition at the Godesberg party conference in November 1959. The policy programme adopted at this conference committed the SPD to national defence and an economic and social

SPD chairman Kurt Schumacher during a party rally on the Römerberg in Frankfurt, 27 June 1946

the three Western zones of occupation, playing a key role in shaping the political structures of the emerging Federal Republic of Germany, particularly in the *Länder* and at local level.

In the early years of the Federal Republic, the SPD's chairman Kurt Schumacher had a crucial influence on the party's policy programme. He categorically rejected cooperation with the communists, encouraged the party to support a combination of the planned economy and the market economy, proclaimed the German people's right to national self-determination and declared German unity to be an immedi-

order based on market economy principles, without ruling out the possibility of state regulation and control. This increased its chances of taking on government responsibility at federal level. Willy Brandt, party chairman since 1964, served as Vice-Chancellor and Minister for Foreign Affairs in the grand coalition formed by the CDU/CSU and the SPD in 1966. In March 1969, Justice Minister Gustav Heinemann became the first Social Democrat to be elected Federal President – thanks in part to the votes of most of the FDP delegates. Shortly before the Bundestag elections in September of the

The SPD's extraordinary party conference in Bad Godesberg, 13-15 November 1959

The second round of coalition talks between the SPD and the FDP in Bonn, 1 October 1969. Foreground: Willy Brandt (left) and Walter Scheel, the chairmen of the two parties

same year, which saw the SPD markedly increase its vote, Walter Scheel, the chairman of the FDP, declared himself in favour of a coalition with the Social Democrats. A month later Chancellor Brandt presented the first Social-Liberal federal government. On 19 November 1972, the majority of the electorate voted in favour of the government's reforms regarding civil rights and social issues, as well as its new *Ostpolitik*, making the SPD the strongest parliamentary group in the Bundestag for the first time.

SPD rally during the 1980 Bundestag election campaign. The poster shows Federal Chancellor Helmut Schmidt

But the initial mood of heady optimism was soon swept away by a global recession that forced the government to resort to crisis management for the time being. The governing coalition led by Chancellor Helmut Schmidt that had been in power since May 1974 was re-elected in 1976 and 1980, but the party was rocked by increasingly strident internal disputes during the 1980s. Many Social Democrats refused to follow their Chancellor over the question of force modernization. Furthermore, with the government facing a complex budgetary and employment policy situation, the arguments within the coalition about the best way to consolidate public finances became increasingly heated. Following the collapse of the Social-Liberal coalition and the federal elections brought forward to March 1983, the SPD was forced to vacate the government benches in parliament.

A phase of policy reorientation now began, accompanied by several leadership changes.

The first tangible results were incorporated into the Berlin Programme of 1989 and the manifesto adopted in 1990 with the newly founded Social Democratic Party of the GDR (SDP) at the party's first conference after reunification. In the run-up to the first all-German national elections, the leading figures around Oskar Lafontaine, the party's candidate for the chancellorship, were concerned to ensure that German reunification took place in an economically sustainable way, which meant that the process had to be gradual. This course was criticized both inside and outside the party, and the Social Democrats suffered a bitter defeat in the elections on 2 December 1990.

Nevertheless, in the following years the SPD was able to strengthen its position in the *Länder* and the Bundesrat. At the same time, in particular following the 1995 Mannheim party conference, its leadership sought in-

From left:
Wolfgang
Thierse, Willy
Brandt and
Oskar Lafon-
taine at the
Berlin Inter-
national Con-
gress Centre
immediately
before the
merger of
the Federal
German SPD
with the newly
founded Social
Democratic
Party of the
GDR, 26 Sep-
tember 1990

The future
Federal Chan-
cellor, Gerhard
Schröder
(centre), at the
Erich Ollen-
hauer Building
in Bonn fol-
lowing the
SPD's election
victory on
27 September
1998

creasingly to project the image of a modern, united party and attract upwardly mobile, technology-friendly voters as it attempted to capture the "new centre". On 27 September 1998, the SPD secured 40.9 percent of the vote, its best election result at federal level for 18 years, with Gerhard Schröder becoming Chancellor in a Social Democrat-Green coalition. This government has concentrated primarily on national and European integration, consolidation of the state budget and reform of the social protection systems.

The Free Democratic Party

Of all the federal parties, the FDP is the one that had been in government for the longest up until the autumn of 1998. With the exception of two electoral terms – 1957 to 1961 and 1966 to 1969 – the party was involved in all the Federal Republic's coalition governments, either with the CDU/CSU or the SPD. For a long time, the party remained divided over whether it should act as a liberal counterweight to the other parties or establish itself as an independent "third power".

After the war, Liberal groupings with varying ideological concerns were active at local and regional level. Meeting in Heppenheim in December 1948, they founded the FDP. The party has been consistently committed to the market economy and to philosophical and religious liberalism. It is not rooted in any particular social group, but – with a high proportion of floating voters – is mainly supported by the professions and self-employed people, senior civil servants and white-collar workers.

FDP poster for the Lower Saxony Land elections on 20 April 1947

In the first elections to the Bundestag, the FDP gained 11.9 percent of the party-list vote under the leadership of Theodor Heuss, who was later to become Federal President. In

Leading FDP politicians at a meeting of their parliamentary group's executive committee, 17 January 1966. From left: Walter Scheel, Erich Mende, Knut von Kühlmann-Stumm, Hans-Dietrich Genscher

Konrad Adenauer's first cabinets, it attempted above all to raise its profile in foreign affairs and policy on Germany. Its support for an all-German option contrasted with Adenauer's unconditional commitment to integration into the West. In consequence, the FDP resigned from the coalition in February 1956 during the 2nd electoral term on account of the "Saar question" and the CDU's plans to introduce a new electoral law. In the 1961 federal elections, the FDP profited from the fact that the electorate was tiring of Adenauer and, with 12.8 percent of the vote, secured its best result ever.

Shifts within the party, above all in connection with policy on Germany, accelerated its gradual change of direction as it moved closer to the Social Democrats. This became very clear at the Freiburg party conference in 1968 with the election of Walter Scheel as party chairman. Although the FDP lost a large proportion of its support among business and the professions in the federal elections the following year, it gained control of two key ministries in Willy Brandt's Social-Liberal government that had always been denied it by the CDU/CSU: the Federal Foreign Office and the Ministry of the Interior. Although sections of the party's national liberal wing defected to the CDU/CSU in protest at the coalition's new *Ostpolitik* and the ideas about

These 1: Liberalismus nimmt Partei für Menschenwürde durch Selbstbestimmung.
Er tritt ein für den Vorrang der Person vor der Institution.

Er setzt sich ein für größtmögliche Freiheit des einzelnen Menschen und Wahrung der menschlichen Würde in jeder gegebenen oder sich verändernden politischen und sozialen Situation.

Behauptung der Menschenwürde und Selbstbestimmung des Einzelnen in Staat und Recht, in Wirtschaft und Gesellschaft gegenüber einer Zerstörung der Person durch die Fremdbestimmung und durch den Anpassungsdruck der politischen und sozialen Institutionen waren und sind die ständige Aufgabe des klassischen wie des modernen Liberalismus.

Oberste Ziele liberaler Gesellschaftspolitik sind daher die Erhaltung und Entfaltung der Individualität persönlichen Daseins und der Pluralität menschlichen Zusammenlebens.

the "reform of capitalism" formulated in the Freiburg Theses of 1971, the governing coalition survived the vote of no confidence tabled by the CDU/CSU parliamentary group in April 1972, allowing the FDP to go on playing its role as a counterweight to the left wing of the SPD within the coalition, particularly on economic policy.

The first of the Freiburg Theses drawn up in 1971

The general crisis in the 1970s prompted the party to place greater emphasis on the market economy. However, this increased its distance from the SPD, which, despite fierce opposition from inside and outside the FDP, ultimately prompted some left-leaning

The newly elected FDP chairman Wolfgang Gerhardt (right) with Guido Westerwelle, who would later succeed him, 14 June 1995

liberals to defect to the Social Democrats. This culminated in a change of coalition in 1982. For the next 16 years the FDP was part of Helmut Kohl's Christian-Liberal government, cultivating its image as a guardian of the rule of law and the principles of the market economy in contrast to groups within the CDU/CSU more committed to the welfare state. Thanks, not least, to the popularity of Hans-Dietrich Genscher, the long-serving Minister of Foreign Affairs, the FDP won 11 percent of the party-list vote in the federal elections and managed to gain seats in the parliaments of all the new federal states in 1990. However, once the euphoria of reunification had faded away, the Christian-Liberal coalition's support among the electorate declined steadily until it was voted out of power in September 1998. Since then, under the leadership of Wolfgang Gerhardt and Guido Westerwelle, the FDP has increasingly sought to sharpen its profile vis-à-vis the CDU/CSU and the Social Democrats, but also Alliance 90/The Greens and the PDS.

Alliance 90/The Greens

The Greens also developed initially at *Land* level. In December 1977, various groups in Lower Saxony opposed to the Gorleben nuclear waste storage facility joined forces with two environmental parties. They caused a stir in the *Land* elections the following year, winning almost four percent of the vote. In October 1979, the Greens in Bremen succeeded for the first time in entering a *Land* parliament. Three months later, the Green party at federal level was founded in Karlsruhe.

The leading figures of the party's founding generation primarily represented the three major political forces outside parliament that were influencing the development of the Federal Republic around 1980. The anti-nuclear movement, formed in response to the increased number of reactors being built after 1975, provided the basis for the new party's ecological outlook. The women's movement fought against the restrictive provisions on abortion in Section 218 of the German Criminal Code, and called for women

An impromptu meeting of the Green parliamentary group, March 1983. Centre: Joschka Fischer

to be given greater opportunities to fulfil their potential. The peace movement burst onto the political scene in Bonn, staging massive demonstrations against NATO's twin-track decision.

At the early federal elections in March 1983, the Greens won sufficient seats to be able to form their own parliamentary group for the first time. Demonstrating their unorthodox approach to politics, they held all their meetings in public as a matter of principle and attracted substantial media attention with their protests against the policies of the Kohl government. The Green view of politics was set out in detail for the first time in the 1980

The Greens' federal conference in Hamburg, 9 December 1984

Members of the Green parliamentary group blocking the entrance to Geilenkirchen Air Base, 5 June 1987

Prominent women candidates for Alliance 90/ The Greens during the 1998 Bundestag election campaign. From left: Marianne Birthler, Andrea Fischer, Gunda Röstel

federal programme, which – besides the party's fundamental commitment to ecology – called for non-violence and grass-roots democracy. Accordingly, the activists in the party's federal assembly exerted a relatively large amount of influence on the course taken by the party leadership, which, in contrast to other parties, was always headed by a man and a woman.

There were protracted struggles between the different wings of the Green Party during the 1980s. While the fundamentalists, whose left-wing, radical ecologist core under Jutta Ditfurth and Rainer Trampert left the party in 1991, called for a "third way" between capitalism and socialism, the increasingly dominant political pragmatists around Joschka Fischer, Krista Sager, Antje Vollmer and Rezzo Schlauch favoured reforms within the existing system. Even if their demands for an ecological restructuring of society, their ideal of a cosmopolitan European civil society and the presence of a majority of women in their parliamentary group assured the Greens sympathy beyond their own core voters, it became clear in the first all-German elections in 1990 that their support had

fallen sharply during the year of German reunification. As the five-percent threshold was applied separately in East and West Germany at the time, Alliance 90, which was made up of citizens' groups, managed to pass the five-percent hurdle in the former GDR and gain seats in the Bundestag. However, it was unable to achieve lasting successes in the new *Länder*.

From the mid-1990s onward, the two parties, which had joined to form Alliance 90/The Greens, succeeded in making a come-back in federal politics with Joschka Fischer, the first member of the party to become a minister in a *Land* government. The decision to relax the strict rules preventing any individual from simultaneously holding a government and party post was indicative of their increasingly professional approach to politics. In the September 1998 elections, the party polled 6.7 percent of the party-list vote. Apart from the Federal Foreign Office headed by Vice-Chancellor Joschka Fischer, Alliance 90/The Greens took over two other ministries in the first Social Democrat-Green coalition at federal level.

The Party of Democratic Socialism

According to its programme and statutes, the PDS is a democratic socialist party seeking to come to terms with the ideological legacy of its predecessor organization, the SED, the former state party of the GDR. "SED/PDS", the double name used by the party from December 1989 to February 1990, therefore accurately reflected the range of ideas – from Marxist-Leninist tradition to leftist reformism – expressed during its protracted policy discussions.

Although the PDS declared itself to be an all-German party on 14 October 1990, at first its impact was largely limited to the former GDR. In the western *Länder*, it primarily attracted veterans of diverse Maoist and Leninist groupings, a few left-wing intellectuals and old DKP sympathizers, but in East Germany it developed very rapidly into an effective protest party representing groups in society who feel they have not benefited from reunification. Although its membership went down from 2.4 million in 1989 to about 100,000 in 1997, it still maintains a tightly knit institutional network in the new *Länder* that offers more than just moral support to many people who

PDS chairman Gregor Gysi speaking at the first sitting of the German Bundestag following reunification, 4 October 1990. Background (from left): Federal Foreign Minister Hans-Dietrich Genscher (FDP), Federal Chancellor Helmut Kohl (CDU), Vice-President of the Bundestag Hans Klein (CSU)

lost out when the GDR system collapsed. While there may appear to be little common ground between the essentially reformist party leadership, radical opponents of the

PDS campaign poster for the Bundestag elections on 2 December 1990

Angela Marquardt, the PDS's deputy chairwoman, with older party members, January 1995

capitalist system and nostalgic old SED cadres, the different wings of the party are united in their insistence on East German self-esteem and strict rejection of liberal economic positions. Furthermore, proposals such as the introduction of a tax on speculative gains and state control of the banking sector were well received beyond the party's core voters. In addition to this, in Lothar Bisky and Gregor Gysi, the PDS had a pair of leaders who, at least for a while, were capable of bridging the differences within the party during the 1990s and giving the reformist line proclaimed by the leadership a degree of credibility in the eyes of the outside world.

Although the party had been pronounced dead by many commentators, it made a remarkable comeback from 1990 on. It gained only 12 percent of the party-list vote in the new *Länder* in the first all-German elections after unification, but in October 1994 it polled 19.8 percent in the former GDR and

won four direct mandates, which made it possible for the PDS to remain in parliament. Four years later it again increased its share of the vote to about 500,000 throughout the Federal Republic of Germany. Though it only narrowly passed the five-percent threshold, it had enough Members in the 14th German Bundestag to form a parliamentary group for the first time. Following the earlier decision to "tolerate" a minority SPD government in Saxony-Anhalt, it concluded its first coalition agreement at *Land* level in autumn 1998, providing the deputy minister-president of the SPD-PDS governing coalition in Mecklenburg-Western Pomerania. Though it is still uncertain whether the party, which has been led by Gabriele Zimmer since early 2001, will consolidate its reformist approach or remain attached to the traditions of the GDR, it is still striving to establish itself permanently as a "left-socialist alternative force" throughout the Federal Republic of Germany.

3. The stabilization of Germany's parliamentary democracy

DIE WELT

Donnerstag, 8. September 1949 — Preis 20 P

Bundestag und Bundesrat am Werk

Westdeutscher Staat konstituiert
Dr. Köhler Präsident des Bundestages
Arnold zum Bundesrats-Präsidenten gewählt

Von unserem Bonner Büro

Bonn, 7. Sept.

Unter einem regenschweren Himmel, aber in der leuchtenden Fülle von Fahnen und Blumen, erlebte die Bundesrepublik Deutschland am Mittwoch in der Beethovenstadt Bonn ihre Geburtsstunde. Die beiden parlamentarischen Institutionen der Bundesrepublik — Bundesrat und Bundestag — traten zu ihren konstituierenden Sitzungen zusammen.

Zum Präsidenten des Bundesrates wurde der Ministerpräsident von Nordrhein-Westfalen, Karl Arnold, zum Präsidenten des Bundestages der bisherige Präsident des Wirtschaftsrates, Dr. Erich Köhler, gewählt.

Zu Vizepräsidenten des Bundesrates wurden Ministerpräsident Kopf (Niedersachsen) und Staatspräsident Dr. Gebhardt Müller (Württemberg-Hohenzollern) bestellt. Zum Vizepräsidenten des Bundestages wurde Prof. Carlo Schmid (SPD), zum Zweiten Vizepräsidenten Dr. Hermann Schäfer (FDP) gewählt.

Die konstituierende Sitzung des Bundestages, zu der sich die 402 Abgeordneten der Bundesrepublik Deutschland und die acht Vertreter Berlins im Plenarsaal des Bundeshauses versammelt hätten, wurde am Mittwochnachmittag um 16.04 Uhr mit der Beethovenschen „Weihe des Hauses" eingeleitet und klang mit dem vom Bonner Orchester vorgetragenen Satz aus der 5. Sinfonie von Beethoven aus.

Die Auffahrt der Wagen begann bereits gegen 9.00 Uhr. Als einer der ersten, die vor dem Portal des Bundeshauses vorfuhren, erlebte die SPD-Vorsitzende Dr. Kurt Schumacher, der, auf seine Sekretärin gestützt, in einem weißen Sporthemd langsam in das Bundeshaus eintrat. Die Wagen der Hohen Kommissare, der westdeutschen Ministerpräsidenten, zahlreicher Abgeordneter, der Vertreter im Bundesrat, vieler Ehrengäste und der Presse schlossen sich an und belebten fast den ganzen Tag in nicht abreißender Kette die An- und Abfahrt.

Das große Viereck des Plenarsaales strahlte aus seinen beiden großen Fensterfronten in die etwas graue Rheinlandschaft. An der Stirnseite des Saales, unmittelbar hinter dem Platz des Präsidiums und hinter der Regierungsbank, trug in weißer Vertäfung die in Gold gestickten Wappen der drei westdeutschen Länder und Berlins. Die neuen Pulte der Abgeordneten — jeweils für zwei — glänzten mit ihren grünbezogenen Politikklapppeltischen ebenso, wie die Reihen der Presseplätze auf der Tribüne.

Außer den Hohen Kommissaren mit ihrer Begleitung und den elf westdeutschen Ministerpräsidenten nahmen auch der Oberbürgermeister von Berlin, die Mitglieder des Frankfurter Verwaltungsrates, hohe kirchliche Würdenträger und viele andere Ehrengäste an der konstituierenden Sitzung des erstmalig nach 17 Jahren frei gewählten deutschen Parlaments teil.

Die Sitzordnung

Die Sitzordnung der Fraktionen im Plenarsaal des Bundestages wurde am Mittwoch durch den Rheinland-Pfälzer Senior noch nicht festgelegt. Es sitzen jetzt von links nach rechts: KPD, SPD, CDU/CSU, FDP, DP, Bayernpartei, Deutsche Reichspartei. Hinter dem Reihen der CDU/CSU, die in der Mitte des Saales sitzen, haben Zentrum und WAV ihre Plätze.

Dem Wunsch der CDU in der konstituierenden Sitzung des Bundestages die 3. Strophe des Deutschlandliedes zu singen, hat sich der Alterspräsident nicht angeschlossen.

Nach der einleitenden Musik eröffnete der frühere Reichstagspräsident und jetzige Berliner Vertreter im Bundestag, Paul Löbe, als ältestes Mitglied des Hauses die Sitzung. Nach seiner Ansprache wurden dann der Präsident des Bundestages und seine Vertreter gewählt. Die Wahl des Bundestages, in der Dr. Köhler mit 346 Stimmen gewählt wurde, dauerte von 16.35 bis 17.18 Uhr. Die KPD hatte an Stelle Dr. Köhlers den SPD-Abgeordneten Hans Böhm vorgeschlagen, der diesen Vorschlag jedoch

ablehnte. Er erhielt 15 Stimmen, 41 Abgeordnete gaben weiße Stimmzettel ab.

Nachdem Bundestagspräsident Dr. Köhler sein Amt übernommen hatte, gab er eine interfraktionelle Vereinbarung bekannt, daß in der Mittwochsitzung nur die beiden ersten Vizepräsidenten gewählt werden sollten. Die Gesamtzahl der Vizepräsidenten soll durch die Geschäftsordnung festgelegt werden.

Durch Zurufe bzw. durch Erheben von den Plätzen wählte das Haus mit großer Mehrheit den sozialdemokratischen Abgeordneten Prof. Carlo Schmid zum Ersten Vizepräsidenten und den FDP-Abgeordneten Dr. Hermann Schäfer zum Zweiten Vizepräsidenten. Auch die KPD stimmte für Prof. Schmid.

Die ersten Anträge

Während die Abgeordneten und Zuhörer nach dem letzten Satz der Fünften Sinfonie von Beethoven den Saal verlassen wollten, beantragte der KPD-Abgeordnete Renner überraschend eine Stellungnahme des Bundestages zum Demontageproblem.

Anschließend brachte der SPD-Abgeordnete Ollenhauer drei Anträge seiner Partei ein, und zwar: eine Entschließung, in der auf den Widerspruch zwischen Demontage und Marshall-Plan hingewiesen wird; eine Erklärung, in der die Verbundenheit mit Berlin ausgedrückt wird, sowie ein Antrag auf Verlegung

Absage an die Machtpolitik

Nach der Übernahme seines Amtes dankte der neugewählte Präsident des Bundestages, Dr. Köhler, den Abgeordneten für seine Wahl. Er hob hervor, daß ein langer Weg bis hierher gewesen sei und allen „daran Beteiligten, die vorbereitenden Arbeiten geleistet haben, größter Dank gebührt". An den Alterspräsidenten Paul Löbe richtete Dr. Köhler ebenfalls Dankesworte für die mit „gewohnter Meisterschaft" geleitete Eröffnung des ersten Bundestages.

Als Pflicht des Präsidenten und des Vizepräsidenten des Bundestages bezeichnete Dr. Köhler die völlig objektive Leitung der Debatten. Das Ausland werde mit Erwartungen auf das erste rechtmäßig gewählte Bundestag blicken. „Wir haben die Verpflichtung, uns der einmaligen geschichtlichen Bedeutung dieses ersten Bundesparlament und des Zusammenbruch Deutschlands in diesem Sinne unserer Arbeit zu führen."

Das Wahlergebnis bezeichnete Dr. Köhler als ein Bekenntnis zur Gemeinschafts-

Für Deutschland und den Weltfrieden

Ratspräsident Arnold über die Aufgabe der Länder im Gesamtstaat

Von unserem Bonner Büro

Bonn, 7. Sept.

Am Mittwochvormittag 11.20 Uhr begann die erste Sitzung des Bundesrates der Bundesrepublik Deutschland in dem

der leitenden Bundesorgane von Bonn nach Frankfurt.

Sämtliche Anträge wurden zur Kenntnis genommen und dem Ältestenrat überwiesen, der am Donnerstag das Datum für den nächsten Zusammentritt des Bundesrats festsetzt und die Tagesordnung

In dieser Ausgabe:

Seite 2
Drei Präsidenten
— drei Repräsentanten

Seite 3
Dieser Tag in Weimar

Seite 6
Für freie ERP-Dollar-Käufe

Erster Staatsempfang

Die drei Hohen Kommissare statteten den Präsidenten des Bundestages und des Bundesrates am Mittwochnachmittag im Bonner Hotel „Königshof" einen ersten offiziellen Staatsbesuch ab. Anschließend gaben Dr. Erich Köhler und Ministerpräsident Arnold eine Cocktailparty für die Hohen Kommissare und ihre Stäbe.

kollegen dafür, daß sie das Land mit der Führung der Präsidialgeschäfte beauftragten, das an schwersten in der Periode der demokratischen verfassungsrechtlichen

Dollarfrage in Arbeit

Verhandlungsbeginn in Washington

Washington, 7. Sept.

Die amerikanisch-britisch-kanadische Finanzkonferenz über die Dollarknappheit des Sterlingblocks begann am Mittwoch im State Department in Washington. Die USA sind durch Finanzminister Snyder, Außenminister Acheson und Marshall-Plan-Administrator Hoffman vertreten. Für Großbritannien sprechen Außenminister Bevin und Schatzkanzler Cripps, Kanadas Vertreter sind Außenminister Pearson und Finanzminister Abbott.

Snyder, der das Vorsitz auf der Konferenz führt, drückte seine Überzeugung aus, daß eine Grundlage für die Lösung

Frage Nr. 1: Wohnungsbau

Frankfurt a. M., 7. Sept. (Eig. Ber.)

Das Wohnungsbauproblem bezeichnete Dr. Adenauer in einem Interview mit der „Mainzer Allgemeinen Zeitung" als Frage Nr. 1, das ihm besonders am Herzen liege. Dr. Adenauer sagte, daß wir uns nirgends vordrängen. Nationalismus werde keinen Raum bei ihm haben.

Als Zentralproblem nannte er die russisch-amerikanischen Beziehungen, „und da wird man auch die Bundesregierung nicht unbeteiligt lassen". Zur Saarfrage meinte Dr. Adenauer, sie könne im Geist der Europäischen Union geregelt und in einem Friedensvertrag bestätigt werden müsse. Zur Frage der Ostgrenze erklärte Dr. Adenauer: „Niemals dürfen wir den Gedanken fallenlassen oder die Überzeugung aufgeben, daß der Osten zu uns zurückkommen wird. Aber die deutsche Regierung darf sich nicht zu unbedachten und voreiligen Schritten verleiten lassen. In so großen politischen Fragen darf man nicht mit kleinen Zeiträumen rechnen."

Auf die Frage, ob er für Berlin als endgültige Hauptstadt sei, erwiderte Dr. Adenauer: „Das kommt darauf an, es wird weit genug von Berlin entfernt ist."

Attlee: Wir kommen als Pa...

Von unserem Londoner Büro

London, 7.

Fast gleichzeitig mit dem Beginn der Dollarbesprechungen in Washington sprach Premierminister Attlee bei dem britischen Gewerkschaftsbund über die britische Wirtschaftslage.

Attlee betonte, daß Lohnerhöhungen nur dann möglich sind, wenn gleichzeitig die Produktivität erhöht und die Produktionskosten gesenkt werden, da britanische auf den Weltmärkten konkurrenzfähig bleiben müsse.

Zur Dollarkrise sagte Attlee, ein völlig falscher Eindruck erweckt werde, daß sich an Großbritannien in einfacher Weise die amerikanische Hilfe Gegenteil. Großbritannien hat Kriegsschulden als Partner der U Mill. Pfund zur Linderung der Kriegsnot in anderen Ländern brachte.

v. Manstein erneut be...

Hamburg, 7. Sept. (Eig.

Im Manstein-Prozeß fuhr die Mittwochvormittag mit der V des Vernehmungsprotokolls des verhörs fort, das der Verteidiger dem ehemaligen SS-Führer Sch Januar 1949 abgenommen hatte. Seitbert erklärte nach diesem daß die Meldungen über die Ers gesandt wurden. Durchschläge Abschriften dieser Tätigkeitsberichte gen an die 11. Armee.

Im Anschluß daran verlas die das Protokoll über die mit dem...

(Siehe auch Seite 6)

Im festlich hergerichteten Plenarsaal des Bonner Bundeshauses eröffnet Alterspräsident Löbe den Deutschen Bundestag. Foto: Die Welt

---

Front page of Die Welt, featuring reports on the founding of the Federal Republic of Germany, 8 September 1949

Ludwig Erhard (CDU), Federal Economics Minister from 1949 to 1963 and Federal Chancellor from 1963 to 1966

gogical Academy in Bonn, which had been converted by the architect Hans Schwippert. Eight days later, Konrad Adenauer was elected the first Chancellor of the Federal Republic by a majority of just one vote. Adenauer formed a centre-right coalition government made up of the CDU/CSU, the FDP and the German Party. The Christian Democrat Ludwig Erhard held the key position of Minister of Economics and the Chancellor himself – following the revision of the Occupation Statute in March 1951 – took over at the Federal Foreign Office. The pioneering achievements of this cabinet, whose policies remained controversial in parliament and among the public for a long time, included establishing a social market economy and preparing the way for the Federal Republic's full integration into the Western community of states.

With a combined 31 percent of the party-list vote, the CDU and CSU won the first elections to the Bundestag while the SPD polled 29.2 percent. On 7 September 1949 the oldest Member of the Bundestag, Paul Löbe, opened its constituent sitting in the former Peda-

The social market economy introduced by Erhard in the Frankfurt-based Economic Council at the same time as the currency reform proved its worth in the early years of the Federal Republic's existence. It was a system that allowed enterprises a great deal of freedom in their production decisions, while assigning the state the task of combating the negative effects of a purely self-

Refugee camp in Schleswig-Holstein, around 1945

Left:
Neon signs in
Frankfurt's
shopping
district, 1954

Right:
Holidaymakers
at Lake Garda,
1955

regulating market economy by means of targeted policies designed to create the right framework for economic activity. Nevertheless, Erhard deliberately accepted short-term social inequalities as his conservative financial policy and, above all, his preferential treatment of the export sector encouraged investment, but initially held down domestic consumption. Growth rates in some areas were already high, but unemployment continued to rise at first and income levels were moderate. It was only thanks to the restraint practised by the newly founded trade unions that the difficulties of this phase were overcome. From about 1952/53 on, the fruits of the economic boom began to benefit wider sections of the population in the form of significant increases in income, which contributed to the internal stabilization of the Federal Republic and the coalition's electoral success in September 1953. The CDU/CSU increased its share of the party-list vote by more than 14 percent, showing that it was capable of integrating voters from across a broad political spectrum.

The struggle over the direction of foreign policy was conducted with great passion. Adenauer sought to secure international equality for the Federal Republic by pursuing integration into Western Europe in close accord with the USA. He believed that the key to achieving this aim was the offer of West German rearmament, in which the Western powers had the strongest interest, given their deep concern about the outbreak of the Korean War in June 1950. The opposition was prepared to support the government over issues of importance to the reconstruction effort and the settlement of Germans expelled from the former eastern territories – for example, in the case of the

Walter Hall-
stein, State
Secretary in
the Federal
Foreign Office
from 1951 to
1957

The Federal Republic of Germany is admitted to NATO in Paris, 9 May 1955

The Federal Armed Forces' first soldiers in training at Andernach, 1956

Housing Ownership Law, which sought to relieve the post-war housing shortage and which was passed unanimously by the Bundestag in January 1951. However, Adenauer's foreign policy was bitterly opposed by the Social Democrats. In essence, the debates centred on the question of whether the

Federal Republic's security could only be guaranteed through integration into the Western community and reunification also achieved over the long term, or whether absolute priority should be given to the goal of German unity, avoiding any step that would deepen the division of Germany. The Treaty on the Establishment of a European Defence Community (EDC), signed in May 1952, was only approved by the Bundestag on 19 March 1953 following a constitutional complaint by the opposition. Following the

ratification on 9 May 1955 of the Paris Agreements signed a year earlier, the Federal Republic joined NATO. The Soviet Union responded to this step in May 1955 with the establishment of the Warsaw Pact, which also included the GDR. This set the seal on the division of Germany and the integration of the two German states into opposing political blocs.

The second half of the 1950s was marked by further economic, social and political consolidation in the Federal Republic. With real annual growth rates of around ten percent, a country that had only recently suffered destruction on a massive scale rose to become the world's third-largest industrial economy. As a result, standards of living increased by leaps and bounds, and it was possible to establish an increasingly comprehensive welfare system. In the 1957 federal elections, which were dominated by the "economic miracle", the CDU/CSU gained an absolute majority and Chancellor Adenauer found himself at the peak of his power. Though the question of whether the Federal Armed Forces, established in 1955, should be equipped with nuclear weapons prompted heated debates, the conflicts over foreign and security policy gradually began to subside. The Federal Republic's integration into the Western alliance was accepted by the Social Democrat opposition from 1959/60 on. On the German question, the Adenauer government was even more determined to assert its claim to be the sole legitimate representative of the German nation, as formulated in the "Hallstein doctrine". Following the failure of the European Defence Community and the plans for the Europeanization of the Saar, which was then administered by France, it was decided to pursue a path of economic integration at European level. Building on the European Coal and Steel Community founded in 1951 by France, Italy, the Benelux states and the Federal Republic, this led to the establishment of the European Economic Community (EEC) in March 1957. Three months later, the integration of the Saarland into the Federal Republic of Germany was sealed when France and the Federal Republic

The signing of the Treaties of Rome establishing the European Economic Community and the European Atomic Energy Community, 25 March 1957

signed the Saar Treaty in Luxembourg. The relationship between France and the Federal Republic of Germany became extremely close, particularly during the presidency of Charles de Gaulle, resulting in the conclusion of the Treaty on Franco-German Cooperation (Elysée Treaty) on 22 January 1963. This partnership has been a cornerstone of European stability ever since.

Yet the "Chancellor democracy" dominated by the central figure of Adenauer was beginning to show signs of stagnation even before 1960. While internal reforms were being implemented by both the SPD, which had finally freed itself from its ideological rigidity at its Godesberg conference, and the FDP, which went into opposition in 1956 and had to cope with a serious internal party crisis, the authority and dominance of the Chancellor, who was now over 80, gradually threatened to paralyse the CDU. Adenauer succeeded in forming another Christian-Liberal government after the 1960 federal elections, when the CDU/CSU lost its absolute majority, but only once he had given an assurance that he would not remain in office for the whole electoral term. A major cabinet reshuffle proved necessary as early as November 1962: Defence Minister Franz Josef Strauss was heavily criticized in the Bundestag for his part in the arrest of a number of staff members on the current affairs magazine *Der Spiegel* who were suspected of high

treason after they had reported on NATO manoeuvres. Ultimately, it was only his decision to step down that made it possible for the coalition to continue. After 14 years in power, Adenauer announced his resignation on 15 October 1963.

Konrad Adenauer (CDU), Federal Chancellor from 1949 to 1963, pictured in 1960

Ludwig Erhard, who had already been nominated as his successor the previous April by the CDU/CSU parliamentary group, took office in what seemed initially to be an unchanged political environment. While this was apparently confirmed when the CDU/CSU won another electoral victory in 1965, it became increasingly evident that Erhard's period in office was to be a difficult transitional phase. Some of the omissions of the Adenauer era, such as the failure to reform the education system, now came to light.

An industrial landscape in Duisburg, around 1960

which had been established in 1964, achieved some surprising electoral successes for a while, prompting considerable doubts – particularly abroad – about the resilience of the Federal Republic's political system in times of crisis.

The economic slump of 1966 was felt above all in the coal industry. The failure to adjust to structural changes in the energy supply sector resulted in many pit closures, particularly in the Ruhr region. This eventually caused conflicts within the Bonn coalition: while Erhard and his economics minister Kurt Schmücker wanted to compensate for the drop in coal production by attracting modern industries to former coal-mining areas and increasing social security benefits for those affected, the FDP rejected all state intervention. In July 1966, the SPD inflicted substantial losses on the governing CDU in the *Land* elections in North Rhine-Westphalia. Three months later, the question of how to offset reduced levels of public revenue finally triggered a government crisis in Bonn, leading to the collapse of the coalition on 27 October. A few days after the resignation of the four FDP ministers, Chancellor Erhard declared that he would not stand in the way of the formation of a new government. There was now a consensus that the country's economic difficulties were so serious they could only be dealt with by a "grand coalition" of the two largest parliamentary groups. On 26 November 1966, the CDU/CSU and the SPD agreed to form a coalition government under Chancellor Kurt Georg Kiesinger and Vice-Chancellor Willy Brandt.

Nor did the extension of the period of limitation for Nazi crimes, voted on by the Bundestag on 25 March 1965, change the fact that there had still been no broad-based public debate about the National Socialist past. Against the background of a general economic downturn, the extreme right-wing National Democratic Party of Germany (NPD),

"Is the Economic Miracle over?" – cover of *Der Spiegel*, 3 January 1966

4. Crises and Change I: The grand coalition and the Social-Liberal alliance

From the outset, the grand coalition between the CDU/CSU and the SPD was intended to be a temporary alliance to resolve specific problems. Initially, the most important task was overcoming the economic crisis. Economics Minister Karl Schiller (SPD) and Franz Josef Strauss (CSU), who took over the Ministry of Finance despite the initial resistance of numerous Social Democrats, worked well together and developed a range of new policy instruments to manage the economy. Following budget cuts, it proved possible to boost growth in a relatively short time and achieve something approaching full employment by means of targeted investment, primarily in the transport and research sectors. In what was known as "concerted action", government officials, the two sides of industry and academic experts met regularly for consultations to coordinate their economic and social policies. The grand coalition also addressed problems which had remained unresolved due to the absence of the parliamentary

majorities required to change the constitution, notably legislation applicable in a state of emergency and the reform of the constitutional rules governing public finances, as well as the restructuring of the relationship between the Federal Government and the *Länder* in the fields of education and health. The comprehensive adaptation of the government apparatus to the requirements of a highly industrialized society must be regarded as the outstanding achievement of this coalition.

However, the coalition between the CDU/CSU and the SPD was widely criticized as well. With 447 seats, the government had a massive majority in parliament, while the FDP, which held 49 seats, formed a small and correspondingly powerless opposition. This was the background to the rise of the mainly student-dominated protest movement known as the Extra-Parliamentary Opposition (APO) in the second half of the 1960s.

The Financial Planning Council chaired by Federal Economics Minister Karl Schiller (SPD; 3rd from left) and Federal Finance Minister Franz Josef Strauss (CSU; 4th from left), 14 March 1968

Demonstration in West Berlin's Kurfürsten-damm against the US war in Vietnam, 18 February 1968

Above all, the members of this movement were opposed to their parents' traditional lifestyle and patterns of behaviour: the focus on the family, the prevailing sexual morality, all forms of authority, the narrow-minded concern with material success and consump-

The Bundestag voting on the emergency constitution and emergen-cy legislation, 30 May 1968

tion, as well as the official anti-communism of the Federal Republic's political leaders and the US war in Vietnam. When the student Benno Ohnesorg was shot by the police on 2 June 1967 following a demonstration against the Shah of Persia's visit to the Federal Republic of Germany, the APO vented its

outrage in a series of protests, some of them violent. After the attempted assassination of the student leader Rudi Dutschke, they culmi-nated in the "Easter disturbances" of April 1968. The emergency legislation passed a month later by the Bundestag, together with constitutional rules applicable in a state of emergency that secured far-reaching powers for parliament in the case of an external "state of defence" or "internal emergency", were based on a government bill dating from March 1967, but were interpreted by the APO as an attack on the very foundations of the liberal democratic order and a reaction to its own activities. The massive protests against the emergency legislation – which has never been invoked to the present day – only died down gradually after the grand coalition was voted out of office in 1969.

The likelihood of a change of government became apparent after tensions within the grand coalition escalated over the election of the Federal President on 5 March 1969. The Social Democrat candidate, Minister of Justice Gustav Heinemann, won the vote thanks to the support of the majority of FDP delegates. The possibility of forming a Social-Liberal government had already been sounded out

The newly sworn-in Brandt cabinet with Federal President Gustav Heinemann (SPD; front row, 3rd from left), 21 October 1969

in the run-up to the federal elections on 28 September 1969. On the night of the election, the chairmen of the SPD and FDP, Willy Brandt and Walter Scheel, reached an understanding on the formation of an alliance based on a tiny lead over the CDU/CSU. On 22 October, having been elected Chancellor by a small majority the previous day, Willy Brandt announced his cabinet, which was made up of 11 Social Democrats, three Liberals and one Independent. This demonstrated that it was possible for a change of government to take place in a democratic fashion in the Federal Republic.

In the field of foreign policy, the Social-Liberal coalition stood for a new *Ostpolitik* – a policy of accommodation with the Federal Republic's Eastern European neighbours. Domestically, it put forward a reform programme that Brandt summed up in his government policy statement with the formula "daring more democracy". At the same time, the Chancellor expressed a readiness to go beyond previous offers on the renunciation of force and accept the status quo in Europe, including the existence of the GDR as a state. Although the first discussions with the GDR government in Erfurt and Kassel failed to

achieve a breakthrough, Brandt's closest foreign policy adviser, State Secretary Egon Bahr, succeeded in paving the way for an agreement with the Soviet Union. The Treaty of Moscow, signed on 12 August 1970, was the keystone of the system of treaties concluded with a number of Eastern European

Willy Brandt (SPD), Federal Chancellor from 1969 to 1974, pictured in 1971

The signing of the Treaty of Moscow, 12 August 1970

countries by the Social-Liberal coalition. The provisions it contained concerning the renunciation of force and the recognition of existing borders anticipated the core elements of the treaties concluded later with Poland, the GDR and Czechoslovakia. The Treaty of Moscow was also relevant to the Four-Power Agreement on Berlin signed in September 1971, which made it considerably easier for traffic to pass through the GDR between Berlin and West Germany.

The image of Chancellor Brandt kneeling before the memorial to those who lost their lives in the Warsaw Ghetto uprising became a symbol of his government's *Ostpolitik* throughout the world. In his own country, however, this policy was highly controversial. The CDU/CSU opposition expressed reservations about it, fearing that it would further entrench the division of Germany. The associations of expellees, representing Germans driven from their homes in Eastern Europe at the end of World War II, were vehemently opposed to it. The conflict over the Eastern

Treaties entered its decisive phase in late 1971 with the beginning of the parliamentary ratification process. The difficulties were aggravated by the defection of a number of Members of the Bundestag from the governing parties to the opposition. Consequently, the government lost its majority in the Bundestag, the result being a deadlock in parliament. However, the attempt by the CDU/CSU to have the leader of their parliamentary group, Rainer Barzel, elected Chancellor in a constructive vote of no confidence on 27 April 1972 failed by a narrow margin. The three parliamentary groups now coordinated their stance on fundamental foreign policy issues in a "joint resolution", in which the Soviet ambassador was also involved. This made it possible for the CDU/CSU to abstain on 17 May 1972 and thus allow the Eastern Treaties to be adopted. On 21 December 1972, one month after early federal elections from which the coalition emerged strengthened, the Treaty on the Basis of Relations between the Federal Republic of Germany and the German Democratic Republic was finally concluded. The

Opposition leader Rainer Barzel (CDU) congratulating Federal Chancellor Brandt after the failure of the vote of no confidence tabled by the CDU/CSU parliamentary group, 27 April 1972

Only now was it possible for the Social-Liberal programme of internal reforms, ranging from the modernization of the legal system and the development of the social welfare system to co-determination rights for workers and the reorganization of the education sector, to be implemented – albeit gradually and at the price of significant concessions. Apart from differences between the SPD and FDP, and the opposition to certain legislative proposals voiced by the Federal Constitutional Court and the CDU/CSU majority in the Bundesrat, the deteriorating economic situation also imposed financial constraints on the government's reformism. Chancellor Brandt resigned as a result of a scandal about a GDR spy in his office, and Helmut Schmidt, who had been Minister of Finance until this point, was elected Chancellor by the Bundestag on 16 May 1974. He faced massive challenges. The cuts in oil supplies to the industrialized Western countries agreed by the Arab states and the subsequent raising of oil prices by OPEC triggered a major economic crisis in 1974/75. Western governments

Fuel prices rise sharply in January 1974 due to the oil crisis

Federal Republic now recognized the GDR as a second state in Germany, but not as foreign territory. Nine months later, the two German states were accepted into the United Nations.

sought to deal with its consequences by coordinating their policies through regular consultations and world economic summits. Schmidt's government tried to cushion the domestic effects of the crisis through programmes to create jobs and boost economic activity. However, high inflation rates and growing levels of public debt, coupled with relatively high unemployment, led to widespread doubts about the effectiveness of gov-

problem of terrorism. Terrorist activities culminated in 1977 when the Red Army Faction (RAF) murdered the Federal Prosecutor General Siegfried Buback, the banker Jürgen Ponto, and Hanns-Martin Schleyer, the president of the Confederation of German Employers' Associations. In the same year, a Lufthansa airliner was hijacked by an Arab-Palestinian group in an incident which was brought to an end on 18 October by GSG 9, a special

Working session during the first world economic summit at Chateau Rambouillet near Paris, 16 November 1975

ernment measures to stimulate the economy. Moreover, with rising awareness of the limits of growth, including its ecological limits, more voices calling for a fundamental rethinking of attitudes were heard in the political debate. The articulation of radical environmental demands gradually led to the emergence of a new force in German politics, the Greens, who gained seats in an increasing number of *Land* parliaments from 1979 onwards.

Starting in the early 1970s, the Federal Republic was confronted with the international

unit of the German Federal Border Guard. The number of attacks went down markedly following the government's firm refusal to let itself be blackmailed by terrorists, combined with legislative changes that introduced measures to curb terrorism, which, however, continued to pose a threat to the Federal Republic's domestic security.

Towards the end of the 1970s, Western governments watched with rising concern as the Soviet Union stepped up its armaments programmes. As a result of a proposal whose initiators included Chancellor Schmidt, in

The scene of the kidnapping of Hanns-Martin Schleyer, president of the Confederation of German Employers' Associations, by members of the Red Army Faction in Cologne, 5 September 1977

December 1979 NATO threatened to station modern medium-range nuclear weapons in Western Europe if the Soviet Union was not prepared to withdraw its new SS-20 missiles. The invasion of Afghanistan by Soviet troops in the same month, the election of the right-wing Republican Ronald Reagan as US president in November 1980 and the imposition of martial law by the Polish government in December 1981 in response to a strong anticommunist union movement signalled conclusively that the phase of international détente was over. Both German states were faced with the task of preserving the progress achieved in bilateral relations in a changed international environment. In addition to this, the new arms race encouraged the growth of a powerful peace movement, particularly in Germany, a favoured location and target for nuclear missiles. Broad sections of the SPD were also opposed to the foreign policy pursued by the Social Democrat Chancellor and his Liberal Foreign Minister, Hans-Dietrich Genscher.

Peace demonstration in Bonn, 10 October 1981

5. Crises and Change II: Return to a Christian Democrat-Liberal Coalition

The collapse of the Social Democrat-Liberal coalition on 17 September 1982. Having resigned, the FDP ministers receive their certificates of discharge

In this situation, the Federal Republic was hit by a new recession, again triggered by rising energy prices. Increasing differences began to emerge within the Social-Liberal coalition, which had been re-elected in 1976 and 1980. 12 September 1982 saw the publication of a "concept for a policy to overcome weak growth and fight unemployment", in which the Liberal Economics Minister, Otto Graf Lambsdorff, called for a budgetary policy oriented towards the economic cycle, cuts in social security, business-oriented economic policies, and the liberalization of tenancy law and the regulations protecting employees against dismissal – demands that, for the most part, were unacceptable to the Social Democrats. As a result, Chancellor Schmidt dissolved the Social-Liberal coalition five days later and formed a minority SPD government. The CDU/CSU and the FDP immedi-

ately entered into negotiations, which were accompanied by sharp internal disagreements among the Liberals. Nevertheless, they reached agreement on the formation of a coalition government, and the Christian Democrat opposition leader Helmut Kohl was elected Chancellor in a constructive vote of no confidence on 1 October 1982. In the early elections held on 6 March 1983, the CDU/CSU narrowly failed to gain an absolute majority, while their coalition partner, the FDP, took seven percent of the party-list vote and the Greens polled 5.6 percent, entering the Bundestag for the first time.

The main challenge facing the new coalition, in which Genscher, Lambsdorff and Minister of Agriculture Josef Ertl retained their previous posts, was overcoming the grave economic crisis. A consolidation of public finances, cuts

Helmut Schmidt
congratulating
Helmut Kohl,
who has just
been elected
Schmidt's
successor in
a vote of no
confidence,
1 October 1982

in welfare spending, a reform of the pension system and tax reductions were intended to revitalize the economy. Supported by extraordinary achievements in the export markets, these measures were successful in bringing about a return to real growth and reductions in the inflation rate. However, the problem of unemployment remained largely unresolved. Though the pace at which it was rising was slowed down, it stabilized at a high level. Economic development thus remained ambivalent in the 1980s, and the opposition and the government clashed frequently over economic policy. Germany's generally buoyant economy was in stark contrast to an enduring crisis in traditional industrial sectors, such as shipbuilding, mining and the steel industry, not least as a result of the structural transformation of the economy associated with advances in computer technology. Despite the fact that wide sections of the population enjoyed significant increases in incomes, there were social problems in many areas of the employment market and structurally weak regions. A few months after the Chernobyl disaster, the Federal Ministry

for the Environment, Nature Conservation and Nuclear Safety was established in June 1986.

As regards policy on foreign affairs and the German question, continuity was the dominant element during the 1980s. For example, on 22 November 1982 the Bundestag ratified NATO's decision on force modernization in the face of stubborn parliamentary and extra-parliamentary opposition. At the same time, however, the Kohl government was con-

Automated
assembly line
at the Opel
factory in
Rüsselsheim,
1987

prepared to dismantle the fragmentation mines along the intra-German border and ease travel restrictions.

However, even the flow of money from the West was no longer sufficient to help the GDR overcome its rapidly increasing economic difficulties. Nevertheless, when the Chairman of the GDR's Council of State, Erich Honecker, visited the Federal Republic of Germany in September 1987, eight months after another electoral victory for the Christian-Liberal coalition, no one could have imagined how far the economic and political erosion of the Eastern bloc states had already advanced. Just over two years later, the opening of the Berlin Wall and the subsequent collapse of the GDR's political system confronted the Federal Government and parliament with new and entirely unexpected challenges.

Hans Mayr, chairman of the Metal-workers' Union, speaking at a German Trade Union Federation rally in Munich against changes to strike law, 6 March 1986

cerned not to endanger the progress achieved in relations between the two German states during the preceding years. Without openly stating that this was a quid pro quo for credits provided by the Federal Republic, the government of the GDR announced that it was

Demonstration in Bonn supporting equal rights for women, Mother's Day 1986

Green parliamentarians protesting against the stationing of US intermediate-range missiles in the Federal Republic of Germany during the Bundestag debate on force modernization, 21 November 1983

Official welcome for Erich Honecker, chairman of the GDR Council of State, in front of the Federal Chancellery, 7 September 1987

6. National Unity and European Integration

The new Glienicke Bridge border crossing between Potsdam and Berlin, 12 November 1989

When the Bundestag was informed of the opening of the Berlin Wall on the evening of 9 November 1989, its Members rose and sang the national anthem, which, just 11 months later, was to become the national anthem of a reunited Germany. It became clear within a few weeks that most of the GDR's citizens were less interested in the reform of their state than in it swiftly becoming part of a larger, democratic and economically prosperous nation. The Federal Government responded to this mood, which was reflected at the first free elections to the People's Chamber in the electoral victory of the "Alliance for Germany" formed under the leadership of the CDU, by promptly introducing a policy for reunification based on comprehensive economic aid, the democratization of the political system and measures to under-

pin human rights. This approach was set out in the *Ten-Point Programme for Overcoming the Division of Germany and Europe* that Chancellor Kohl presented to the public on 28 November 1989.

The intra-German and multilateral negotiations on the re-establishment of German unity and the achievement of full German sovereignty were conducted at a rapid pace. For Helmut Kohl, the signing of the Treaty on Currency, Economic and Social Union on 18 May 1990 represented the "birth of a free and united Germany", while Lothar de Maizière, the last Minister-President of the GDR, felt that the "actual realization of German unity" began with a "compromise". As had been agreed at the first joint meeting of their presidiums, the Bundestag and the

HELMUT KOHL: ZEHN PUNKTE FÜR DEUTSCHLANDS EINHEIT

Ziel der CDU: Einheit und Freiheit für alle Deutschen

1. Sofortmaßnahmen: Humanitäre Hilfe, wo sie benötigt wird, z. B. bei der ärztlichen Versorgung. Devisenhilfe statt Begrüßungsgeld für unsere Landsleute in der DDR. „Wir sind bereit, für eine Übergangszeit einen Beitrag zu einem **Devisenfonds** zu leisten." Voraussetzungen: Mindestumtausch für Reisen in die DDR muß entfallen, Erleichterungen von Einreisen in die DDR, eigener substantieller Beitrag der DDR zu dem Fonds. Letztlich muß die DDR ihre Reisenden selbst mit den nötigen Devisen ausstatten.

2. Ausbau der Zusammenarbeit, die den Menschen auf beiden Seiten unmittelbar zugute kommt, z.B. Umweltschutz, Telefonverbindungen, Verkehrswege.

3. Umfassende Wirtschaftshilfe, wenn ein grundlegender Wandel des politischen und wirtschaftlichen Systems in der DDR verbindlich beschlossen und unumkehrbar in Gang gesetzt wird. Das ist gewährleistet, wenn sich die gegenwärtige DDR-Staatsführung und die Opposition auf eine Verfassungsänderung und ein neues Wahlgesetz verständigt haben. Es müssen neue wirtschaftliche Grundlagen geschaffen werden, damit unsere Hilfe greifen kann. Wir unterstützen die Forderung nach freien, gleichen und geheimen Wahlen, Aufhebung des Machtmonopols der SED, Abschaffung des politischen Strafrechts, sofortige Freilassung aller politischen Gefangenen.

4. Vertragsgemeinschaft: Wir sind dazu bereit. Nähe und besonderer Charakter der Beziehungen zwischen den beiden Staaten in Deutschland erfordern ein immer dichteres Netz der Zusammenarbeit unter voller Einbeziehung Berlins. Gemeinsame Kommissionen für Wirtschaft, Verkehr, Umweltschutz, Kultur.

5. Konföderative Strukturen mit dem Ziel, eine Föderation, d. h. eine bundesstaatliche Ordnung in Deutschland zu schaffen. Voraussetzung: Eine demokratisch legitimierte Regierung in der DDR. Vorstellbare Institutionen: Gemeinsamer Regierungsausschuß zur ständigen Konsultation und politischen Abstimmung, gemeinsame Fachausschüsse, gemeinsames parlamentarisches Gremium u. a.

6. Deutschland als Bestandteil der Architektur Gesamteuropas: Die Entwicklung der innerdeutschen Beziehungen bleibt eingebettet in den gesamteuropäischen Prozeß und in die West-Ost-Beziehungen. Die künftige Architektur Deutschlands muß in eine gerechte europäische Friedensordnung eingefügt sein.

7. Die Europäische Gemeinschaft als Grundlage der gesamteuropäischen Einigung muß gegenüber den reformorientierten Staaten in Mittel-, Ost- und Südosteuropa offen sein. Sie muß auch offen sein für einen baldigen Abschluß eines Handels- und Kooperationsabkommens mit der DDR und angemessene Formen der Assoziierung.

8. Die Verhandlungen der Konferenz über Sicherheit und Zusammenarbeit in Europa (KSZE) müssen energisch vorangetrieben werden, z. B. durch Einrichtung eines gesamteuropäischen Umweltrates und einer Institution zur Koordinierung der Ost-West-Wirtschaftszusammenarbeit.

9. Abrüstung und Rüstungskontrolle müssen mit der politischen Entwickung Schritt halten. Sie müssen vorangetrieben und wenn nötig beschleunigt werden, z. B. beim beiderseitigen Abbau der konventionellen Streitkräfte in Europa, beim weltweiten Verbot der chemischen Waffen, bei der beiderseitigen Verringerung der strategischen Nuklearwaffen.

10. Ein freies und geeintes Deutschland in einem freien und geeinten Europa. Die Wiedervereinigung, d. h. die Wiedergewinnung der staatlichen Einheit Deutschlands bleibt das Ziel der CDU.

»Wie ein wiedervereinigtes Deutschland schließlich aussehen wird, weiß heute niemand. Daß aber die Einheit kommen wird, wenn die Menschen in Deutschland sie wollen – dessen bin ich mir sicher.« Bundeskanzler Helmut Kohl

Helmut Kohl's ten-point programme of 28 November 1989

The special EC summit in Dublin at which the EC member states expressed their support for reunification, 28 April 1990

People's Chamber formed two parliamentary committees on "German Unity" that were intended to guide and help shape the unification process. On 20 June 1990, the two committees passed identical resolutions confirming the recognition of the post-war German-Polish border along the Oder and Neisse rivers, a step that had to be taken before the neighbouring countries would give their support to reunification.

The first round of the Two-Plus-Four talks between the foreign ministers of the two German states and the victorious powers, 5 May 1990

As work began on establishing a democratic system and market economy on the territory of the GDR, and currency, economic and social union entered into force, the principal domestic conditions for the realization of German unity were put in place. On 20 September 1990, the Bundestag adopted, by 440 votes to 47 with three abstentions, the Unification Treaty signed three weeks earlier by Wolfgang Schäuble, the Federal Republic's Interior Minister, and Günther Krause, the Parliamentary State Secretary to the Minister-President of the GDR; the Greens and 13 Members of the CDU/CSU voted against the Treaty. On 3 October 1990, the five newly formed *Länder*, Brandenburg, Mecklenburg-Western Pomerania, Saxony, Saxony-Anhalt and Thuringia, acceded to the territories subject to the Basic Law, and the reunited city of Berlin became the German capital. When it convened at the Reichstag building in Berlin for its constituent sitting on 20 December 1990, the first all-German Bundestag had 662 Members, 140 of them from East Germany.

The rapid pace of reunification was made possible not least by the easing of international tensions resulting largely from the new policy course unexpectedly adopted by the Soviet government and party leadership under Mikhail Gorbachev – a course which was soon pursued by most of the other Eastern bloc states as well. While a crucial step towards an understanding was taken on 13 June 1989 with the signing of the "Bonn Document" by Kohl and Gorbachev, the opening of the border to Austria by the Hungarian government on 27 June prompted a mass exodus from the GDR that accelerated its collapse and put the emerging German-Soviet partnership to the test. On 11 February 1990, two weeks after a high-profile visit to Poland by the Federal German Chancellor, Kohl and Genscher paid a brief visit to Moscow, where they received an undertaking from Gorbachev that it was a matter for the Germans themselves to decide the forms and conditions of their national unity. However, the Soviet President initially opposed a unified Germany with NATO membership. Furthermore, the Soviet Ministry of Foreign Affairs protested

vigorously against any "annexation" of the GDR on the basis of Article 23 of the Basic Law, as this would represent "the usurpation of one German state by the other". However, the Soviet Union gradually retreated from this position. On 22 June 1990, at the second round of the Two-Plus-Four talks, the Soviet delegation was still calling for German sovereignty to be delayed for five years and existing alliances maintained, but three weeks later Chancellor Kohl achieved a crucial breakthrough in personal talks with President Gorbachev in the Caucasus. From this point on, the key foreign policy requirements for a sovereign all-German state to decide freely on its choice of alliance and for the withdrawal of all occupying forces were in place.

German-Soviet negotiations at Arkhyz in the Caucasus, 16 July 1990. Seated from left: German Federal Foreign Minister Genscher, Soviet President Mikhail Gorbachev, Federal Chancellor Kohl

These developments also helped overcome the massive concerns initially harboured by some members of the Western alliance about the process of reunification. The "Two-Plus-Four formula" agreed in Ottawa on 13 February 1990 limited the discussion of "the exter-

The negotiators in the Two-Plus-Four talks after the signing of the Treaty on the Final Settlement with respect to Germany in Moscow, 12 September 1990

Crowds celebrating the accession of the GDR to the Federal Republic of Germany in front of the Reichstag building, 3 October 1990

nal aspects of German unification" to the Federal Republic, the GDR and the four occupying powers, in this way forestalling a dangerous internationalization of the German question, for example through the CSCE. A few days later, at a meeting with Chancellor Kohl, US President George Bush affirmed his support for reunification within the framework of the NATO partnership. In April 1990, a Franco-German initiative on accelerating European political union did a great deal to dispel fears that the changes in Germany could jeopardize or delay the process of European unification. On 7 May, the EC member states abolished the visa requirement for Germans from the GDR. The first international treaty to take account of the imminent reunification of Germany – a supplementary convention to the Schengen Agreement, which had originally been concluded in 1985

to facilitate European internal cross-border traffic – was signed on 19 June. This extended the European information system for the identification of security risks to the new *Länder* as of 1992. German currency, economic and social union came into force on 1 July 1990 at the same time as a customs union between the EC and the GDR, and the first stage of European Economic and Monetary Union, which was intended to facilitate the pursuit of joint economic, budgetary and exchange rate policies by the partners in the Community. The Treaty on the Final Settlement with respect to Germany of 12 September, which has the status of a peace treaty, finally confirmed the full sovereignty of the reunified nation. The Soviet Foreign Minister, Edward Shevardnadze, was not alone in viewing this agreement as the beginning of a "new era".

Certainly, the "unification of Germany under a European roof", as the EC heads of state summed up the events of 1990, represented a significant political achievement on the part of all concerned. However, developments in the ensuing years have demonstrated that national and European integration is a longer, more complicated process than many people hoped in the euphoria of German unification.

The first sitting of the all-German Bundestag in the Reichstag building, 4 October 1990

VI. UNITED GERMANY

The Federal
Republic of
Germany since
1990

The euphoria of unification, which reached its climax in East and West Germany with the official accession of the German Democratic Republic to the Federal Republic of Germany on 3 October 1990, was also reflected in the results of the first all-German elections to the Bundestag on 2 December. While the governing coalition of CDU/CSU and FDP won a clear-cut victory, the other parties saw their share of the vote dwindle in the wake of the rapid reunification process, which they regarded as having been unduly rushed. The enthusiasm of the first few weeks and months, however, soon gave way to a more sober assessment of the challenges arising from unification. It became apparent that the top priority was the narrowing of the social and economic gulf between East and West Germany. Besides the need to pay off substantial inherited debts, to rehabilitate old industries and establish new ones, to create a modern infrastructure and to establish a system of social security, the main task was the establishment of an efficient administration and an independent judiciary.

The comprehensive economic and administrative refurbishment of East Germany took more time and consumed more financial resources than had initially been expected. The social and economic hardships that resulted from this process played a significant part in fostering a sense of embitterment and injustice in East and West, and this was as much of an obstacle to the development of a common identity as the divergent political, social and cultural experiences and perceptions that derived from 40 years of division. These feelings were strongest among the inhabitants of the former GDR, who were disconcerted by the changes in the familiar world in which they had lived and now had to adapt to a new social system. Despite all the material and psychological adjustment problems, it has been observable in recent years that the parliamentary system and the social market economy enjoy widespread public acceptance in the new federal states too. Nor is this appraisal altered in any way by the rise in right-wing extremist violence, although this development reflects an anti-democratic and xenophobic potential that must not be underestimated.

While the accession of the GDR to the Federal Republic of Germany created a new economic and social situation, there was little change in the party landscape. In the run-up to the first free elections to the People's Chamber, or *Volkskammer*, on 18 March 1990, the party system in the GDR had largely aligned itself in line with the West German model. In view of the voters' clearly expressed preference for rapid reunification, virtually all of the East German parties had merged with their sister parties in the West by 3 October 1990, although the merger of the Greens with parts of the East German citizens' action movement was not finally sealed until 1993. Only the Party of Democratic Socialism (*Partei des Demokratischen Sozialismus* – PDS), born of the former state party of the GDR, remained a separate party and now came to represent the far left of the party spectrum in the

Federal Republic. After the 1990 and 1994 Bundestag elections, the balance of power between the parties remained largely stable, in spite of occasional manifestations of disenchantment with politics and perceptible swings in voters' sympathies. A three-party structure of CDU, SPD and PDS has established itself in the parliaments of the five new *Länder*. While the two major parties continue to occupy the conservative and liberal-socialist domains of the political spectrum, making it difficult for the smaller parties to establish a foothold there, the PDS appeals to a traditional socialist constituency and to numerous protest voters, which means that the party polls an above-average share of the vote in elections in East Germany, including Bundestag elections.

At the national level, 27 September 1998 marked a turning point in German politics, because on that day, for the first time in the history of the Federal Republic, a government was voted out of office by the electorate. Every previous change of government had come about because the party with the largest share of the vote changed coalition partners or because the party holding the balance of power switched its allegiance from one of the main parties to the other. Since October 1998, a Social Democrat, Gerhard Schröder, has headed the Government, in which Alliance 90/The Greens are represented for the first time. Since the 1998 election, there have been many signs of a creeping erosion of conventional party loyalties among the electorate, an increase in the percentage of floating voters and a climate of opinion that is more easily swayed by the political issues of the day. All these factors are likely to have an increasing influence on future election results and hence on the composition of the Bundestag.

Since 1990, Germany has also acted as a sovereign nation state once more within the international community. Reunification and the attendant uneasiness of European neighbours at the prospect of a politically and economically dominant Germany have played a significant part in accelerating the European unification process. On 1 November 1993, just over three years after reunification, the Maastricht Treaty entered into force. In the Treaty, the association of states that now called itself the European Union (EU) set itself the aims of establishing a common foreign and security policy, co-operating in the domains of justice and home affairs and creating an economic and monetary union. Four years later, in the Treaty of Amsterdam, these aims were spelled out in greater detail, and a number of priority objectives were added. Thereafter, the transfer of national sovereign powers to the EU institutions, the balance of power between the large and small Member States and eastward enlargement of the Union were to become the main subjects of negotiation within the European integration process. After the dissolution of the Warsaw Pact and the collapse of the Soviet Union, Germany had a special interest in the integration of her eastern neighbours and provided political, economic and financial support for the democratization process in those countries, a process attended by numerous risks.

As a sovereign member of NATO and the UN, united Germany has also been assigned new international tasks and has assumed greater responsibility. Although the end of the East-West conflict has reduced the risk of a global nuclear war, the old stand-off has been replaced by confrontation between Islam and the West as well as by disputes within and between individual states, all of which place world peace in constant jeopardy. Besides an increasing number of diplomatic and humanitarian initiatives, military measures are required time and again to resolve armed conflicts. After heated debates in the Bundestag, the Federal Armed Forces took part in a UN operation outside the NATO area for the first time in 1993; in 1995, the Bundestag authorized the direct involvement of German troops in combat to protect the rapid deployment force in Bosnia-Herzegovina, and in 1999 a contingent from the Federal Armed Forces contributed to a NATO peacekeeping operation in the province of Kosovo to avert the threat of "ethnic cleansing" by Serbian nationalists.

Twelve years after unification, the Bundestag still has to find responses, through constructive debate, to unresolved or new challenges in the realms of economic, social and foreign policy. The challenges on which public attention is most sharply focused are the reduction of unemployment, the reform of the social protection systems and the consolidation of the national budget, along with changes in asylum law and the curbing of right-wing radicalism and global terrorism.

Economic and social challenges

Talks held in
Bonn on
15 September
1994 between
the Federal
Government
and repre-
sentatives
of business
organizations
and trade
unions on the
economic
reconstruction
of the new
Länder

Shortly after the accession of the GDR to
the Federal Republic, the difficulties of the
unification process were already surfacing
very clearly. Besides the establishment of an
efficient administration and the modernization of the infrastructure, including the
transport system, priority also attached to
the narrowing of the economic and social
gap between the older *Länder* of the Federal
Republic and the territory of the former GDR.
At the beginning of the 1990s, the Federal
Government still assumed that initial injec-
tions of funding and the transformation of
the East German economy into a market
economy would enable the eastern *Länder*
to become self-supporting and profitable
within a few years. These hopes faded, not
only because the forecasts had been over-
optimistic but also because of the global
economic slowdown that had been perceptible since 1992, the loss of the Eastern European markets on which the economy of the
GDR had been heavily reliant and the fact
that most production plants in eastern Germany were no longer competitive. In order
to convert the Communist planned economy
into a social market economy, the *Treuhand*
Agency that had been set up in 1990 was

Welding robots
at the Opel
assembly plant
in Eisenach,
which was
opened in 1992
and employs
almost 2,000
people

Rehabilitation work on the site of the Chemie AG at Bitterfeld, April 1993

Dole queue at a Dresden job centre, 1991

given the task of privatizing and modernizing the economic and industrial legacy of the GDR. In the framework of this restructuring process, almost 15,000 former state-owned enterprises were transferred into private or public hands and were modernized, divided up or closed down. Despite the signs of economic recovery that slowly began to appear in the new *Länder*, more than three million East Germans lost their jobs in the first few years after reunification. The tense social situation could only be partly eased by government employment programmes and welfare benefits. Reducing the persistently high level of unemployment in the East therefore remains one of the paramount aims of German economic policy, although it is likely that the two parts of Germany will continue to converge economically and that the gap between their material living standards will gradually close.

Forging a common identity

According to the Federal Government's annual report of 1997 on progress towards full German unity, the unification process will not be completed until legal and institutional unity is accompanied by a sense of unity in the hearts and minds of the German population. Progress towards this aim, however, can scarcely be measured against objective parameters, let alone definitively assessed at the present stage. Besides the material and social imbalances, the divergent political, social and cultural orientations of East and West continue to be reflected in the pace and the state of progress towards a common identity. Another factor that makes it more difficult for East and West to converge without conflict is the view held by many former citizens of the GDR that the full integration of East Germany into the economic,

Rainer Eppelmann (right), chairman of the Bundestag Study Commission on the history and consequences of the SED regime, presenting Roman Herzog (left), President of the Federal Republic, with the Commission's first reports in 1995

Cottbus schoolchildren with the books and certificates presented to them at their initiation ceremony. This event, which culminated in an oath of allegiance to Socialism, was intended to replace the religious ceremony of confirmation in the German Democratic Republic

constitutional and institutional system of the Federal Republic, accompanied as it was by the replacement of large numbers of public employees who were politically "tainted", represented a "sell-out" of the GDR or its "colonization" by the West. One of the reasons underlying the decision adopted by a slim majority of the Bundestag on 20 June 1991 to move the seat of government and parliament from Bonn to Berlin was a desire to forestall an entrenchment of these attitudes.

Unlike the West Germans, the people of East Germany had lost the familiar structures on which their everyday lives had been based and were confronted with a new social and political reality. Although people in both East and West Germany endorse democratic constitutional principles, many former citizens of the GDR still have the impression that their own achievements and values are not sufficiently appreciated in the Federal Republic. Even among the young generation, people in East and West Germany still cherish different political, social and cultural values, although more than ten years have passed since unification, and the gap between these perceptions is only gradually narrowing.

Parliament, parties and elections

With the accession of the GDR under Article 23 of the Basic Law and in accordance with the terms of the Unification Treaty, the Federal Republic, as hitherto constituted in the form of a parliamentary democratic federal state, was extended to include the territory of the former GDR. On 3 October 1990, 144 deputies from the People's Chamber became Members of the Bundestag. Apart from the Members belonging to the PDS and the East German citizens' action movements, the new Bundestag Members represented firmly established West German parties that had merged with their East German counterparts. In the first all-German elections to the Bundestag on 2 December 1990, the parties of the governing coalition were returned to power, while the SPD suffered heavy losses at the polls because of its scepticism about what it perceived as over-hasty unification. For the same reason, the Greens also sustained losses, although these were offset in part by their electoral pact with Alliance 90, an organization formed by a number of East German citizens' action movements with which the Greens merged in 1993. The temporary suspension in the accession territories of the clause whereby parties polling less than 5% of the total vote cannot enter

Election posters in Bonn for the Bundestag elections of 16 October 1994

Posters in Hanover for the 1994 election, featuring the two main parties' candidates for the chancellorship

Parliament also enabled 17 members of the PDS to take their seats in the Bundestag in December 1990. The two main parties, the CDU and SPD, which were less deeply rooted in East Germany, were confronted there with the PDS, a regional party relying on a constituency all of its own and able to command the loyalty of a broad section of the electorate. While the PDS successfully positioned itself as the champion of specifically East German interests, Alliance 90/The Greens and the Free Democratic Party (FDP), which had their own particular political priorities, found it difficult to secure a foothold in the new *Länder*.

The first two all-German legislative terms were largely shaped by the difficulties of the unification process. The restructuring of the largely unprofitable East German industrial plants and the worldwide economic slump that set in during the years 1992 and 1993 not only slowed the pace of economic reconstruction in the East but also led to a rapid rise in unemployment and put heavy pressure on the welfare budget. Mass strikes

Demonstration in front of the Magdeburg tax office against the planned welfare cuts

The negotiating teams from the SPD and Alliance 90/The Greens after the signing of the coalition agreement in Bonn on 20 October 1998

motivated by fear of job losses were a frequent occurrence, as were expressions of discontent in the West about the financial burden of unification.

Faced with these manifold economic and social problems, the Christian Democrat and Liberal Government only just managed to secure a majority in the second pan-German elections on 16 October 1994, while the opposition parties made considerable gains. The continuing high rate of unemployment and the need to subsidize the new *Länder* were proving to be long-term structural problems. These resulted in increased taxes and welfare contributions, which in turn raised labour costs and lowered net incomes, thereby diminishing purchasing power. Even after the "Red-Green" coalition of SPD and Alliance 90/The Greens took office in October 1998, Government and Opposition remained divided on the question whether the cure for economic stagnation lay in a further reduction of working hours, pump-priming measures and limited changes to social legislation or in radical reform of the eco-

nomic order and the welfare system of the Federal Republic.

Germany and the European Union

From the very beginning, the unification of the two states in Germany had a European dimension. The Unification Treaty of 31 August 1990 invalidated Article 23 of the Basic Law, which defined the area of application of the Basic Law pending the reunification of Germany. In its place since 23 September 1990 has been a provision expressing commitment to a united Europe and reflecting the desire of the Federal Republic to participate in the development of the European Union. Despite some initial strains, the European Community had supported the integration of a united Germany since the spring of 1990. While Germany's European neighbours were anxious to ensure that Germany did not pursue a go-it-alone approach and that her economic potential would be committed to common tasks, the interests of the Federal Republic lay in the continuing development of a community based on mutually guaranteed security and common values as well as in closer political cooperation and the creation of a single European market. In view of these complementary objectives and the mutual desire for closer ties, the new federal states were incorporated into the European Community on 3 October 1990. They send 18 Members to the European Parliament; since the 1994 European elections, the Members from eastern Germany have enjoyed the same rights as all other MEPs.

The accession of the united Germany lent perceptible momentum to the quest for deeper European unity, which had been on the political agenda since the mid eighties. These efforts culminated in the signing in February 1992 of the Maastricht Treaty, In which this association of states, known henceforth as the European Union, committed itself not only to a common foreign and security policy and to coordinated policies in the fields of justice and home affairs but also to the establishment of economic and monetary union. The introduction of a common currency, the euro, required a particularly high degree of economic and political coordination among the participating countries. Despite recurring doubts as to whether the economic criteria for entry into the euro

Staff of the "Euro Action Group" informing the public about the impact of the currency change on households

system would be fulfilled in time, Germany did meet the criteria and was able to sign up to economic and monetary union on 1 January 1999. This integration process was accompanied by the establishment of a common European economic area within which people, capital, goods and services could move just as freely as in national domestic markets.

In order to review the progress that had been made and to further develop the agreements enshrined in the Maastricht Treaty, representatives of the national governments and the

Roman Herzog (left), former President of the Federal Republic, presenting the first draft of an EU Charter of Fundamental Rights, as requested by the European Council, in Berlin, 25 August 2000

CONSEIL EUROPÉEN

Présidence française
de l'Union Européenne

NICE 7 - 8 DÉCEMBRE 2000

Summit meeting of the EU Heads of State and Government in Nice in December 2000, which deliberated on reform of the European institutions. In the foreground (left to right) are Nicole Fontaine, President of the European Parliament, Hubert Védrine, Minister of Foreign Affairs of the French Republic, and Romano Prodi, President of the European Commission

EU met in the spring of 1996 for joint deliberations, which led to the signing of the Treaty of Amsterdam on 2 October 1997. While new agreements were sealed in the domains of immigration, employment and common economic policies, the Treaty left the Member States with unanswered questions regarding the criteria for the accession of the applicant countries in Eastern Europe and the institutional reforms necessitated by the enlargement of the EU.

Germany and the new world order

Unification and the demise of the Warsaw Pact and the Soviet Union completely transformed the international framework within which Germany had to operate. As a sovereign nation state, the Federal Republic not only had more freedom to conduct its foreign policy but also greater international responsibility. Not only Germany's allies in NATO and her fellow members of the UN and the OSCE but also the former member States of the Warsaw Pact had great expectations of Germany's contribution regarding the tasks facing the international community.

After the withdrawal of the Soviet Union from the heart of Europe, a key role devolved upon the Federal Republic because of its central geographical situation and its economic weight. Not least because the countries of the former Eastern bloc were her direct neighbours, Germany supported their democratization and economic reconstruction with financial, economic and human resources, hoping thereby to help stabilize the European balance in the East too. The specific aims of this German commitment were the solution of cross-border problems such as migration, crime and environmental pollution as well as the establishment of

Signing of the German-Soviet Partnership Treaty by Mikhail Gorbachev, President of the Soviet Union, and Federal Chancellor Helmut Kohl in Bonn, 9 November 1990

compelitive and sustainable markets in Eastern Europe. Carefully cultivated rapprochement with Russia and the other members of the Commonwealth of Independent States (CIS), which was reflected in friendship treaties and reconstruction aid, was intended as a response to the new geostrategic situation and as an instrument of conflict prevention.

Not only in the East of Europe, however, but throughout the world, the responsibility of the Federal Republic in the realm of security policy increased. The end of the East-West conflict saw numerous disputes resurface between and within individual countries, disputes that could only be settled by means of a multinational approach. Now that Germany was a sovereign member of the United

Russian troops from the Western Army Group on a special train for Moscow after their farewell ceremony in Berlin

Conference of the Organization for Security and Cooperation in Europe (OSCE) in Paris on 20 March 1995, at which the representatives of the 52 participating States concluded a Stability Pact

Nations, NATO and the OSCE, her commitment was expected to go beyond the provision of economic, financial and humanitarian aid and to include participation in military peacemaking and peacekeeping operations conducted on behalf of international organizations. In 1993, when troops from the Federal Armed Forces took part for the first time in a UN military mission outside the NATO area in the civil war in Somalia and

Somali patients being treated by a doctor from the Federal Armed Forces at Belet Huen in July 1993

Special sitting of the German Bundestag on 22 July 1994, at which the deployment of troops from the Federal Armed Forces to international trouble spots was retrospectively approved. At the rostrum is Klaus Kinkel (FDP), Federal Minister for Foreign Affairs

were deployed on surveillance flights over Bosnia-Herzegovina, heated debates ensued in the Bundestag and among the public at large. Whereas one side concluded from the atrocities of the Nazi regime that Germany had a duty to resort to military means if necessary in order to combat genocide and the violation of human rights, the other side concluded that the Nazi atrocities imposed an obligation on Germany to refrain entirely from the use of military force. Without drawing a line under this debate, the Federal Constitutional Court, ruling on an action by the SPD and FDP on 12 July 1994, stated that the deployment of troops from the Federal Armed Forces in the Alliance framework was constitutional if it helped to establish a "peaceful and sustainable order in Europe and between the peoples of the world". Subsequent deployments of German troops in the former Yugoslavia were also the subject of heated discussion, particularly the deployment of troops and aircraft in the peacekeeping operation in Kosovo from March 1999, an operation that was conducted by NATO units without a mandate from the UN Security Council.

Since unification, a mediatory position has been established as a key element of German foreign policy. Germany is increasingly prepared to assume greater responsibility in the framework of clearly defined peace missions and multilaterally legitimized agreements and to develop initiatives of her own, while not neglecting the ties that have bound her to her allies for many years or losing sight of national interests.

Troops from the Federal Armed Forces in the SFOR peacekeeping force manning an armoured infantry fighting vehicle near the centre of Sarajevo, December 1997

PARLIAMENTARY ARCHITECTURE IN GERMANY

Cross section of the "House of the Estates", Karlsruhe

The various parliaments and the parliamentary system were only gradually able to establish their place in the political and social life of Germany alongside the long-dominant institutions of the monarchy. This is also reflected in the somewhat hesitant development of a distinct parliamentary architecture. In the wake of the unrest of 1830, new constitutions were issued in numerous German states providing for a bicameral system in which the second

chamber was the real popular assembly. However, the venues in which they convened were generally small-scale buildings, a far cry from the multi-amenity premises that typify later parliament buildings, with assembly room, lobby, meeting rooms, offices, library, reading rooms, administrative offices and numerous rooms for private consultations. In many cases these chambers met in so-called *hôtels particuliers*, or private hotels. In keeping with their use, such meeting-houses were commonly known as *Ständehäuser*, or houses of the estates, a designation harking back to earlier, pre-absolutist forms of political participation. "Chamber", with its associations of seclusion, was once a term used in connection with officials in charge of a royal household. As the term suggests, public sittings had little role in early parliamentary history.

This, at least, changed with the constituent sitting of the first German national parliament in the *Paulskirche* in Frankfurt. As the National Assembly had been convened in Frankfurt am Main as a result of the revolutionary events of March 1848, there was no time to make longer-term arrangements; the choice of venue was governed primarily by purely practical considerations. Consecrated in 1833, the *Paulskirche* was the largest meeting-hall the city had to offer; by the time the National Assembly opened on 18 May 1848,

Exterior view of the *Paulskirche*, Frankfurt, around 1840

Germania. Painting by Philipp Veit, 1848

as many as 2,000, who followed the proceedings and commented loudly from the gallery. 200 seats were reserved for women, and every one was always taken.

In the end, however, the dream of liberty and unity did not come to fruition. A little over a year after the National Assembly first convened, 130 out of the 585 elected representatives of the people met in the *Paulskirche* for the last time. They resolved to move the so-called "rump parliament" to Stuttgart; there, it was forcibly dissolved three weeks later. In the period that followed, reactionary forces predominated in Germany. It was not until the 1860s, as Berlin gradually emerged as the political centre of a future "Little" German nation state, that the idea of parliament gained new impetus.

Parliamentarism already enjoyed a certain tradition in the future imperial capital around this time. Parliamentary architecture, however, in the stricter sense of the term, failed to

The Berlin *Singakademie*, on the Festungsgraben. First meeting-place of the Prussian National Assembly

the nave of this circular, classicist structure had been converted into a functioning meeting-hall. Space was made for the presidium immediately in front of the altar, which had been covered over; the pulpit became the speakers' lectern, and tables and chairs in front of it were reserved for the shorthand writers. Philipp Veit's painting of "Germania", installed in front of the organ, was intended to symbolize the strength, and the desire for peace, of the free and united German nation-state, the creation of which was the goal of the National Assembly. A seating order for plenary sittings had not yet been established; only in the course of the negotiations did an orientation towards left or right emerge, depending on the deputies' political position. Although the rules of procedure required representatives to exercise discipline, commotions broke out repeatedly. One deputy commented on the first sitting: "There was such a dreadful, insufferable din in the assembly, and such turmoil, that I felt quite sick." Of course, a major contribution to the uproar was made by the visitors, numbering

develop here either. The United Diet convened on 11 April 1847, in the White Hall of the royal palace; the Prussian National Assembly of 1848 initially sat in the *Singakademie*, not far from the Friedrich-Wilhelm University, and then, until it was driven out, in the *Schauspielhaus* on Gendarmenmarkt. Both of these buildings had been designed by Karl Friedrich Schinkel, and were converted in an ad hoc, makeshift fashion by Georg Heinrich

Bürde. It was also Bürde who, in 1849, fitted out the former town palace of Prince Hardenberg at Leipziger Strasse 55, later 75, as the meeting-place of the Lower House of the Prussian Diet, later called the Chamber of Deputies. Although this provided somewhat more spacious facilities – after all, the plenary area comprised reading rooms, dining rooms and administrative offices – it still belonged entirely within the tradition of earlier *Stände-*

Leipziger Strasse 3. Until then, the oddly calm and harmonious conduct of business here had been the butt of local humour in Berlin: the members were assumed to spend more time dozing than debating. For the first all-German Reichstag, however, which included deputies from the southern German states, there was simply not enough space here. So, on 21 March 1871, it convened in the Chamber of Deputies in Berlin. Since space

Left:
The building on Leipziger Strasse where the Prussian Chamber of Deputies met

Right:
The assembly room of the Prussian Chamber of Peers after it was converted in 1874/75

häuser. Moreover, it turned out to have major structural deficiencies: the acoustics in the meeting-chamber were poor, it was draughty, and in summer myriads of midges swarmed in from the nearby *Grüner Graben*. This prompted Rudolf Virchow to remark sarcastically that one needed "to be rather robust and healthy to be an elected representative". Although it was originally intended to be a temporary solution for just a few years, this venue was in fact used right up until 1898.

Even when Berlin became the capital of the North German Confederation and ultimately of the German Reich, for parliamentarians travelling to the city the era of temporary accommodation was far from over. By resolution of the Confederation government, the *Zollparlament*, or Customs Parliament, was accommodated in the Chamber of Deputies, while, rather curiously, the Reichstag of the North German Confederation had to make do with the headquarters of the Prussian aristocratic lobby, the Chamber of Peers at

here too was totally inadequate, a Reichstag Building Commission was set up at once to consider practical alternatives for more acceptable temporary accommodation. As the dilatory and secretive behaviour of the Commission led people to fear the worst, Bismarck intervened. Without further ado, he pushed through plans to alter and roof over a courtyard at the former Royal Porcelain Manufactory at Leipziger Strasse 3, based on

Provisional chamber of the Reichstag in the former Royal Porcelain Manufactory

designs by Friedrich Hitzig. Spurred by the Chancellor's threat to have every last piece of porcelain thrown onto the street in the event of their dallying with the removal, the Manufactory fled to Charlottenburg in what must have been record time. In the summer of 1871, hundreds of excavation workers, builders and joiners were employed on the site so that the Reichstag would be able to convene there on 16 October. The plenary chamber held 400 seats with desks for the deputies, a podium for the representatives of the Bundesrat, and a visitors' gallery comprising 315 seats; the seating was arranged in seven main wedge-shaped blocks, enabling clear and orderly disposition of the parliamentary groups. This was the environment in which the Reichstag met for 23 years.

Paul Wallot, winner of the second architectural design competition

Meanwhile, in December 1871, the first competition was held for a new, purpose-built Reichstag "on the eastern side of the Königsplatz". Among the entries, which were to be judged by a panel comprising members of the Reichstag, the Bundesrat and experts in

building. It was another ten years before the land was expropriated from Raczynski in return for compensation, by dint of a royal decree in favour of the Reich. Plans for a second competition were then able to go ahead. Paul Wallot, the winner, was a former colleague

Ludwig Bohnstedt's prize-winning design for a new Reichstag building, 1872

the field, no fewer than 15 were from England, the cradle of parliamentarism. The prize-winning design by Ludwig Bohnstedt was still to some extent late classicist in appearance; the principal façade of the building featured a portico in the style of a triumphal arch, surrounded by loggias. But it was never built, mainly because Count Raczynski refused to part with his plot of land for the new

of Hitzig and later became professor at the *Kunstakademie* in Dresden. Little did he realize, as he was being fêted in the restaurant of the Zoological Gardens on 8 July 1882, that nearly another two years would elapse before the foundation stone was laid.

The design was twice amended – to lower the level of the meeting-chamber and

increase the height of the edifice as a whole. Nevertheless, the deputies voted in plenary session in favour of appointing Wallot Reichstag architect. He was forced to make still further alterations, however, before the critics were even moderately satisfied. Construction of the new parliament building was launched on 8 June 1884, with a symbolic first blow of the hammer – delivered by Emperor Wilhelm I, rather than the President of the Reichstag. But the building was now to have two large courtyards instead of four smaller ones; the layout of the foyer, the plenary chamber and the corridors was also fundamentally different.

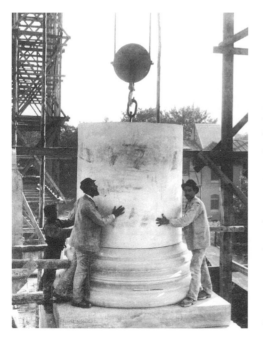

From this point on, work on the building, whose total cost was more than 30 million reichsmarks, proceeded at a relatively brisk pace. Most of the scaffolding was removed from the sandstone façade in the winter of 1891/92; work promptly began on the glazing of the cupola that had been constructed above the plenary chamber. In parliament, there was relentless criticism of the fact that the gold for the external features, including the lantern and crown, came from Belgium. Indeed, debate on Wallot's building persisted right up until its completion, and often concerned matters that were quite trivial, but charged with symbolism. As far as panel member Friedrich von Thiersch was concerned, it was the "most significant building in recent German architectural history"; art historian Karl von Lützow, on the other hand, spoke disparagingly of it as crude, clumsy and hideous, a "thoroughly unsuccessful creation". Emperor Wilhelm II in the end refused to confer on Wallot the Order of the Crown he so coveted, and officiously declared the Reichstag building to be the "height of tastelessness". On 9 December 1894, he wrote smugly to his confidant, Count Eulenberg, that the inauguration of the "Reich ape-house" four days previously had gone off splendidly, with great pomp and ceremony.

Despite all the hostility, the monumental neo-renaissance building, whose structure bore little trace of the Schinkel era that was still discernible in Bohnstedt's designs, soon acquired an appeal all its own. Even though the deputies, always quick to object, still took offence at the décor, and at the shape of the ballot boxes designed by Adolf von Hildebrand, they now rarely complained about the building itself. It says a great deal about the growing presence of the parliament in the public consciousness that from this time on political demonstrations took place increasingly often in front of the Reichstag building rather than in front of the Royal Palace. On 12 December 1916, the inscription bearing the dedication to the German people, "*Dem deutschen Volke*", envisaged by Wallot but long rejected by Wilhelm II and others, was finally put in place above the main

Laying the foundation stone of the Reichstag building, 9 June 1884

Construction work on the Reichstag building. A column drum is put in place for the main entrance

Guard commando in the Reichstag during the Reich Conference of Workers' and Soldiers' Councils, December 1918

entrance. On 9 November 1918, as a vast crowd thronged together between this entrance and the two key architectonic symbols of the German Empire, the victory column and the Bismarck monument, Philipp Scheidemann addressed the masses from a window in the Reichstag building and proclaimed Germany a republic.

Most deputies were well aware of the need to find new architectural symbols to repre-

sent the new – parliamentary – form of government. Naturally enough, however, efforts in this direction were not a priority during the post-war crisis. Nevertheless, in June 1922, a Reichstag committee was assigned the task of "altering or reducing the number of monarchist and militarist symbols, of which the building has a great abundance". A discreet process of removing decorations took its course. In February 1926, the Berlin City Councillors' Assembly passed a motion by the SPD and KPD to rename the square in front of the building *Platz der Republik* instead of Königsplatz. The architectural design competitions of 1927 and 1929, on the other hand, were held owing to the purely practical need to relieve the lack of space that was increasingly making itself felt. Emil Fahrenkamp's prize-winning design of 1929 combined the Wallot building in a rather brusque manner with extensions designed in the pragmatic-functional style of the modern age. The outbreak of the economic crisis that same year, however, prevented progress or more detailed planning on this project.

Plenary chamber with decorations for the Constitution Day ceremony on 11 August 1928

On the evening of 27 February 1933, the Reichstag building went up in flames. Parliament, which, to a large extent, had already undergone *Gleichschaltung*, or coordination, by the National Socialists, had to move to the Kroll Opera house located opposite the Reichstag; the damaged Wallot building was henceforth used mainly for National Socialist propaganda events. Contrary to the ideas of his Chief Architect, Albert Speer, Hitler remained resolute about restoring the Reichstag building. It was nevertheless clear that it would play only a minor role in the scheme for the planned Reich capital, to be called "Germania". The centrepiece of Speer's design for Germania was a "Great Hall of the People" with a dome standing 290 metres high. Up to 100,000 people would be able to gather in this hybrid pantheon to pay homage to the Führer's genius. It was a striking example not only of the overpowering architecture of the National Socialist regime – only a few examples were actually ever built – but also of the regime's endeavours to legitimize its power by pseudo-plebiscitary means. However, the Second World War prevented the implementation of construction plans such as these. In the latter weeks of the war the Reichstag building was turned into a fortress; the central military medical records office, housed in the basement, was moved to make way for a military hospital. On 29 April 1945, the building was shelled by Soviet troops. A day later, the red flag was hoisted on its rooftop.

While the captured Reichstag quickly found a place amongst the national symbols of the Soviet Union, the role it should play in those of Germany remained the subject of much controversy in the years that followed. In the end it was decided to reconstruct the building, but the way in which this was to be done was a compromise that reflected the controversial nature of this issue. Following a unanimous vote by the Presidium of the Bundestag, the Reichstag building was

Left:
The plenary chamber, gutted by fire, 28 February 1933

Right:
Architectural models for the planned Reich capital, "Germania", in the studio of Reich Chief Architect, Albert Speer

Cyrillic graffiti in the Reichstag building following its capture by the Red Army on 30 April 1945

indeed rebuilt between 1961 and 1971, but only its exterior form, and without the cupola, which was demolished using explosives in 1954. In its interior, meanwhile, broad open spaces were created, based primarily on designs by competition winner Paul Baumgarten. These were simple to the point of being stark, in direct and deliberate contrast to the building's pompous façades. A modern

Construction work on the *Pädagogische Akademie* in Bonn, the first seat of the German Bundestag, 1949

plenary chamber was also included. Under the terms of the Four-Power Agreement concluded in 1971, only meetings of parliamentary groups and committees were allowed to take place in the Reichstag building. The permanent exhibition, "Questions on German History" opened there in March of that year.

Meanwhile, in Bonn, another, quite unique parliamentary architecture was developing. In the summer of 1949, the *Pädagogische Akademie*, built 19 years earlier in the Bauhaus style and already used by the Parliamentary Council, was converted to accommodate the *Bundeshaus* under the direction of Hans Schwippert. Even today, the functional design of the edifice, its understated decoration, devoid of all trace of architectonic pathos, and the neon-lit sobriety of the plenary chamber with its walls of glass on the north and south-facing sides, are a gesture of anti-imperialism and a token

of the political modesty of the democratic Germany that returned to the European arena after the disaster of the National Socialist dictatorship. "I wanted to achieve an architecture of openness, of encounter and dialogue. I wanted Germany, as a country, to be a spectator to the work of parliament", recalled Schwippert in 1951. Although people initially dubbed the transparent plenary area the *Bundesaquarium*, or federal aquarium, its popularity quickly grew. The debates that took place against a backdrop displaying the coats of arms of the different *Länder*, and from autumn 1953 under the federal eagle designed by Ludwig Gies, rapidly found their way into the political iconography of the fledgling republic. Gradually the elected representatives became accustomed to the fan-shaped layout of the seating rows, a significant departure from Schwippert's original plans. One feature that did attract repeated criticism, however, was the raised government podium with its central "pulpit", which many critics thought encouraged politicians to indulge in theatrical declamations rather than sober analysis of the issues at hand. In his novel *Das Treibhaus* (The Hothouse) Wolfgang Koeppen played on this association, referring to "the teacher's desk at the front, fittingly elevated". In 1969, the speaker's lectern, along with the government benches and those of the Bundesrat, were lowered to the same level as the Members' seats.

By this time it was already clear that the plenary chamber in fact no longer complied with the building regulations in force. Finally, in July 1983, a study by the Federal Construction Agency (*Bundesbaudirektion*) insisted that its continued use "could no longer be tolerated under building control regulations". In autumn 1986, the plenary chamber was vacated; for 6 years the Members had to make do with somewhat confined temporary accommodation in the pump-house of the former Bonn water works.

On 30 October 1992, the problem of space constraints came to an end with the formal opening of the new plenary facilities in Bonn designed by Günter Behnisch. They had taken

five years to build. Behnisch had won the architectural design competition held in 1972/73, but implementation of his plans had been delayed repeatedly: the plans had to be revised, then they were shelved for a time in favour of compromise solutions, and there was the issue of rising costs. Just when it had been agreed at last that the presidential area was to be included in the plans for the building and that the seating arrangement was to be circular and concave, a spanner was thrown in the works yet again, this time by German reunification: now, space would have to be made to accommodate the Members from the new *Länder* as well!

In the end, however, both the Members and the German public on the whole agreed that the wait had been worthwhile. Behnisch's resolve to turn playfulness into a "metaphor for freedom" is strikingly reflected in the design of the new parliament building in Bonn. The new *Bundeshaus* blends gently into the Rheinaue landscape; the severity of the steel structures is virtually cancelled out by the atmosphere of the entrance hall, which is flooded with light; the foyer, galleries and plenary chamber interconnect harmoniously via glass partitions and on several visual planes. Nevertheless, on the day parliament moved into its new home, it was already clear that it would be using it for only a few years. On 20 June 1991, it had decided by 338 votes to 320 to move to Berlin.

From 1949 up until reunification, the eastern part of Berlin had called itself the capital of the GDR; the parliament of the east German state was domiciled here – although in rather poor conditions, at least until 1976: the People's Chamber met for decades in a converted auditorium of the University clinic, the Charité, in Luisenstrasse, and occasionally in the Congress Chamber of the Finance Ministry or in the Congress Hall on Alexanderplatz.

The *Palast der Republik* during the 9th Congress of the East German trade union organization, FDGB, May 1977

Committees met in the rooms of the parliamentary groups, or in other premises to get out of the way. It was not until the GDR had been in existence for 25 years that the decision was made to provide its parliament with a modern plenary chamber comprising 700 seats in the *Palast der Republik*, or Palace of the Republic, which was under construction at the time. Designed by Heinz Graffunder, this striking, representative building with its dark glass panelling was erected on Marx-Engels-Platz, on the site once occupied by the demolished Royal Palace. However, a great many former citizens of the GDR remember it more as a people's cultural centre than as the meeting-place of their parlia-

ment. After all, the plenary chamber, located somewhat peripherally, was a far cry from the building's Grand Auditorium, which was used for a wide variety of purposes, and was furnished with generously proportioned galleries decked out with monumental panel paintings, a spacious foyer, restaurants and bars. The SED and the east German leadership strove first and foremost to provide space for people to pursue the widest possible range of interests, both communal and personal, in this central venue. For example, the *Theater im Palast* soon acquired artistic renown; meanwhile, a few floors below, East Berlin's bowling fans were able to indulge their passion too. In the last year of the GDR,

The Reichstag building during construction work in Berlin's new parliamentary and government district, January 1999

just before the *Palast der Republik* was closed down because of its asbestos content, public life, and to some extent also political life degenerated into a mild form of anarchy. In this environment, the multi-purpose nature of the building reached its own bizarre climax: as the last People's Chamber debated possible options relating to reunification, a motley group of organizers were making preparations for a punk concert in the next room.

When the Council of Elders of the Bundestag decided on 30 October 1991 that the historical building designed by Wallot should be reinstated as the seat of the united Germany's parliament, the Reichstag building in Berlin suddenly found itself the focus of public interest once again. Following protracted debate, and no little controversy, the results of the competition to rebuild the Reichstag were presented. This did not mean the end of the discussions, however. Sir Norman Foster, the competition winner, in the end gave up his original plan to construct a roof over the building; instead, there was to be a cupola made of glass with walkways around the inside, but it was to be built in the architectural style of the outgoing twentieth century, rather than the way it was originally designed. In other respects too, Foster's revised design was completely in line with the concept of "critical reconstruction" adopted by Berlin's city planners: it neither pays homage to one-dimensional architectonic historicism, nor tries to deny history in the fashion of the modern era or melt it down into fanciful post-modern reminiscences. Instead, it endeavours to sustain an ongoing dialogue with history using an interplay of architectural elements, some reconstructed and some that are new departures.

In November 1994, massive reconstruction operations commenced in the interior of the Reichstag building, briefly interrupted by the spectacular "wrapping" of the old-new seat of parliament by Christo and Jeanne-Claude. Rebuilding and rehabilitation work proceeded briskly; in the process, layer upon layer of historical imprints were revealed which the Bundestag, as the client, wanted to preserve. The whole building was systematically stripped to its shell and preparatory work undertaken for the construction of the new plenary chamber, complete with seating, which was now to be arranged in elliptical form. The federal eagle, affectionately dubbed the "fat hen", now has a new, slimmer image, created by Norman Foster.

On 19 April 1999, it was ready, and the building where the German Bundestag was to meet from the following autumn was officially opened. And already it has become an emblem of Germany's capital city and German parliamentary democracy.

Inauguration of the reconstructed Reichstag building as the seat of the Bundestag, 19 April 1999

CHRONOLOGY

Chronology

1776	4.7.	Declaration of Independence by North American colonies
1786	17.8.	Death of Frederick II of Prussia; accession of Frederick William II
1789	5.5.	Meeting of the Estates General at Versailles
	17.6.	The third estate proclaims itself the Assemblée Nationale
	20.6.	Tennis Court Oath
	14.7.	Storming of the Bastille
1791/94		Development of Common Law *(Allgemeines Landrecht)* for the Prussian states
1792	20.4.	France declares war on Austria and Prussia
	21.9.	First meeting of the National Convention, abolition of the monarchy, and proclamation of the "one and indivisible French Republic"
	21.10.	Occupation of Mainz by French troops
1793	21.1.	Execution of French King Louis XVI
	18.3.	Proclamation of the Mainz Republic
	31.5.–2.6.	Uprising by the *sans-culottes* in Paris, start of Jacobin rule under Maximilien de Robespierre
1794	10.6.	Introduction of new law intensifying the *Grande Terreur*
	27./28.7.	Fall and execution of Robespierre
1795-99		Government by the Directory in France
1797	16.11.	Death of Frederick William II of Prussia; accession of Frederick William III
1799	9.11.	*Coup d'état* by Napoleon, establishment of a consular government under his leadership
1803	25.2.	Principal Resolution of the Imperial Deputation (secularization of ecclesiastical lands and property)
1804	24.3.	Publication of Napoleon's Civil Code *(Code Napoléon)*
	2.12.	Napoleon I is crowned Emperor
1806	12.7.	Founding of the Confederation of the Rhine
	6.8.	Abdication of Emperor Francis II
	14.10.	Battles of Jena and Auerstedt
	27.10.	Napoleon enters Berlin
1807	7.7.	Peace of Tilsit (Prussia loses all territories west of the Elbe)
	30.9.	Appointment of Baron Karl vom und zum Stein as chief minister in Prussia, start of Prussian reforms
1809	12.10.	Appointment of Count Klemens von Metternich as chief minister in Austria
1810	4.6.	Appointment of Baron Karl August von Hardenberg as chancellor of Prussia
1813	28.2.	Prussian-Russian military pact signed at Kalisch
	15.3.	Prussia declares war on France
	16.–19.10.	Battle of the Nations at Leipzig
	4.11.	Collapse of the Confederation of the Rhine
1814	30.3.	Allied troops enter Paris, Napoleon exiled to Elba
	18.9.	Opening of the Congress of Vienna
1815	1.3.	Napoleon returns to France
	8.6.	Signing of the Federal Act, founding of German Confederation
	18.6./7.8.	Napoleon defeated at Waterloo, exiled to St. Helena
	29.6.	Signing of Holy Alliance between Russia, Prussia and Austria

1816	6.11.	Opening of Federal Assembly in Frankfurt am Main
1817	18.10.	Patriotic student fraternities hold Wartburg Festival
1818	26.5.	Adoption of a constitution in the kingdom of Bavaria
	22.8.	Adoption of a constitution in the Grand Duchy of Baden
1819	23.3.	The conservative writer August von Kotzebue is murdered by the student Karl Ludwig Sand
	6.–31.8.	Karlsbad Conference (suppression of the liberal and national movement, censorship)
	25.9.	Adoption of a constitution in the kingdom of Württemberg
1820	24.5.	Signing of Final Act of Congress of Vienna, extension of the Federal Act of 1815
	17.12.	Adoption of revised constitution in the Grand Duchy of Hesse-Darmstadt
1830	27.–29.7.	July Revolution in France, unrest spills over to Brunswick, Hanover, Kurhessen and Saxony
1832	27.–30.5.	Hambach Festival
1833	3.4.	Storming of Frankfurt's main guard house by students
1834	1.1.	Entry into force of the treaty establishing the German Customs Union
1837	1.11.	Hanover's constitution is repealed by King Ernst August, protest and dismissal of seven Göttingen professors
1840	7.6.	Accession of Frederick William IV of Prussia
1844	4.–6.	Uprising by Silesian weavers
1846/47		Crop failures, rise of pauperism in Germany
1847	3.2.	Convocation of United Diet in Prussia
	June	Founding of Communist League in London by Karl Marx and Friedrich Engels
	12.9.	Adoption of Offenburg Programme by south and west German democrats
	10.10.	Adoption of Heppenheim Programme by south and west German liberals
1848	February	Publication of Communist Manifesto by Karl Marx and Friedrich Engels
	22.–24.2.	Revolutionary unrest in Paris, overthrow of King Louis Philippe, proclamation of a republic
	27.2.	Drafting of the first "March Demands" by a popular assembly in Mannheim (start of March Revolution)
	Early March	Establishment of liberal "March ministries" in many German states
	5.3.	Heidelberg Assembly calls for the election of a national parliament, formation of preparatory "Committee of Seven"
	12.3.	Committee of Seven invites former or present members of the estates and legislative assemblies in all German states to Frankfurt for discussions on a National Assembly.
	13.–15.3.	Uprising in Vienna, Metternich flees to England
	18.3.	Riots and street fighting in Berlin
	21.3.	Proclamation by King Frederick William IV of Prussia: "To My People and the German Nation"
	29.3.	Appointment of the liberal ministers Ludolf Camphausen and David Hansemann in Prussia
	31.3.–3.4.	Meeting of the pre-parliament in St Paul's Church in Frankfurt; decision taken to establish a German National Assembly
	12.–27.4.	Republican uprising in Baden, led by Friedrich Hecker and Gustav von Struve
	1.5.	Start of the elections to the German National Assembly in Frankfurt am Main and the Prussian National Assembly in Berlin
	15.5.	Democratic uprising in Vienna, convening of a Reichstag based on general and equal elections
	18.5.	Meeting of the German National Assembly in St. Paul's Church, Frankfurt

	22.5.	Opening of the Prussian National Assembly
	14.6.	Storming of the arsenal in Berlin (clashes between striking workers and the civil guard)
	29.6.	Creation of a provisional central government, election of Archduke John of Austria to the post of Imperial Administrator
	12.7.	Transfer of the Federal Diet's powers to the Imperial Administrator
	15.7.	Formation of a provisional Imperial Ministry
	20.7.	Start of General Workers' Congress in Frankfurt am Main
	26.8.–16.9.	Under pressure from the great powers, Prussia signs the armistice of Malmö which settles the conflict with Denmark over Schleswig and Holstein; the National Assembly in Frankfurt initially rejects the armistice but is eventually forced to accept it
	18.9.	Uprising in Frankfurt am Main, fighting on the barricades ends with victory for the established powers
	21.–24.9.	Proclamation of the German Republic by Gustav von Struve in Lörrach, crushing of the second uprising in Baden
	6./7.10.	Unrest in Vienna, murder of War Minister Latour, Austrian Emperor Ferdinand I and his court flee to Olmütz
	16.10.	Clashes between the civil guard and striking workers in Berlin (Spandau)
	31.10.	Recapture of Vienna by imperial troops, victory of the counter-revolutionary forces
	1.11.	Appointment of a conservative ministry under Count Friedrich of Brandenburg in Prussia
	9.11.	Summary execution of Robert Blum, a member of the National Assembly, in Vienna
	21.11.	Appointment of Prince Felix zu Schwarzenberg as Austrian minister-president and Foreign Affairs Minister
	2.12.	Abdication of Austrian Emperor Ferdinand I in favour of his 18-year-old nephew, Franz Joseph I
	5.12.	Dissolution of the Prussian National Assembly; imposition of a constitution; victory of counter-revolutionary forces in Prussia
	20.12.	Adoption of the chapter of the constitution setting out the fundamental rights of the German people by the Frankfurt National Assembly
	28.12.	Rejection by Austria of Heinrich von Gagern's "little German" solution
1849	4.3.	Dissolution of the Austrian Reichstag; imposition of a constitution
	27./28.3.	Adoption of the German imperial constitution by the Frankfurt National Assembly; election of Frederick William IV of Prussia as German Emperor
	28.4.	Rejection of the imperial crown and constitution by Frederick William IV
	4.5.	Resolution by the National Assembly in Frankfurt calling for the recognition and enforcement of the imperial constitution
	6.5.	The Central March Association calls on German troops to fight for the imperial constitution
	May–July	Campaign for the German imperial constitution (brutal crushing of uprisings in Saxony, Breslau, the Rhineland, Westphalia, the Palatinate and Baden)
	26.5.	Three Kings' Alliance between Prussia, Saxony and Hanover (formation of a union of states led by Prussia); call by the Frankfurt National Assembly for the deployment of armed civil guards
	30.5.	Introduction of three-class voting system in Prussia
	6.–18.6.	Meeting of the "rump parliament" at Stuttgart, forcible dispersal by Württemberg troops
	23.7.	Surrender of besieged revolutionary troops at Rastatt
	Early August	Military courts mete out summary justice to German revolutionaries
	20.12.	Resignation of the Imperial Administrator, Archduke John

1850	31.1.	Entry into force of the Prussian constitution, which was imposed from above
	1.9.	Reopening of the Imperial Diet in Frankfurt
	29.11.	Signing of the Treaty of Olmütz, end of Prussia's policy of union
1851	23.8.	Adoption of Federal Resolution on Reaction (repeal of the fundamental rights adopted by the National Assembly); the Federal Diet becomes the supreme body overseeing the individual state constitutions
1854/56		Crimean War between Britain, France and Russia; Prussia and Austria declare their neutrality
1858	7.10.	William I becomes regent on behalf of his mentally ill brother, Frederick William IV; start of the *New Era* (appointment of liberal ministers in Prussia)
1859	16.9.	Founding of the German National Association
1861	2.1.	Death of Frederick William IV of Prussia; coronation of William I.
	14.3.	Victor Emmanuel II of Piemonte proclaimed King of Italy; founding of the Kingdom of Italy
	6.6.	Founding of the German Progress Party
1862	24.9.	Bismarck appointed Prime Minister of Prussia; the constitutional conflict over military reform intensifies
	28.10.	Founding of the Reform Association
1863	23.5.	Founding of the General Association of German Workers in Leipzig under the leadership of Ferdinand Lassalle
	16.8.–1.9.	In the absence of the Prussian King, the debate in the Congress of Princes in Frankfurt on plans for reform of the Confederation fails to reach a conclusion
1864	16.2.–1.8.	Austria and Prussia at war with Denmark
	18.4.	Prussian victory over Danish troops at the Dybbøl (Düppel) fortifications
	30.10.	Peace of Vienna, in which Denmark cedes Schleswig, Holstein and Lauenburg to Austria and Prussia
1865	14.8.	Convention of Gastein, in which Austria and Prussia establish arrangements for the administration of Schleswig, Holstein and Lauenburg
1866	21.6.–26.7.	Austro-Prussian war for hegemony in Germany
	3.7.	Prussian victory at Sadowa *(Königgrätz)*; elections to the Prussian Chamber of Deputies result in defeat for the Progress Party
	23.8.	Treaty of Prague (dissolution of the German Confederation); recognition of Prussia as the leading power in Germany
	3.9.	The Prussian Chamber of Deputies approves the Bill of Indemnity, ending the constitutional crisis in Prussia
	20.9.	Prussia annexes Hanover, the Electorate of Hesse, Nassau and Frankfurt am Main
1867	12.2.	Elections to the constituent Reichstag of the North German Confederation
	6.6.	Founding programme of the *National Liberal Party*
	12.6.	Austro-Hungarian settlement, in which Austria consents to the institution of the Dual Monarchy
	14.7.	Otto von Bismarck appointed chancellor of the North German Confederation
	21.12.	The *December laws* in Austria mark the start of a liberal era
1869	7.–9.8.	*Social Democratic Workers' Party* founded in Eisenach under the leadership of August Bebel and Wilhelm Liebknecht
1870	13.7.	*Ems telegram*
	18.7.	The First Vatican Council proclaims the dogma of papal infallibility
	19.7.	France declares war on Prussia
	2.9.	The French army capitulates at Sedan, and the Emperor Napoleon III is taken prisoner
	19.9.	Start of the siege of Paris

1871	18.1.	Proclamation of the German Empire in the Hall of Mirrors in the Palace of Versailles
	3.3.	First elections to the Reichstag of the German Empire, from which the National Liberals emerge as the largest party
	16.4.	Entry into force of the German imperial constitution
	18.3.–28.5.	Insurrection of the Paris Commune
	10.5.	Peace of Frankfurt, in which Alsace and Lorraine are ceded to Germany and France is compelled to pay five billion francs in reparations
	8.7.	Dissolution of the Catholic Department in the Prussian Ministry of Education and Cultural Affairs, heralding the start of the *Kulturkampf* in Prussia and in the German Empire as a whole
	10.12.	Adoption of the "pulpit clause", the first legislative measure of the *Kulturkampf*
1872	11.3.	School inspections become the sole responsibility of the state in Prussia
	4.7.	The Jesuit order is banned
1873	20./21.3.	Adoption of the *May laws* by the Prussian Chamber of Deputies in an attempt to introduce state supervision of the church in Prussia
	9.5.	Stock-exchange crash in Vienna, triggering an economic crisis
	22.10.	League of the Three Emperors *(Dreikaiserbund)* concluded by Austria-Hungary, Russia and the German Empire
1874	10.1.	Reichstag elections: the number of votes cast for the Centre Party doubles
	20.4.	Adoption of the first *Septennat*, a military-appropriations bill in which the effective strength of the armed forces is laid down for the next seven years
	7.5.	Entry into force of the *Imperial Press Act*
1875	March–May	*War scare* as hostilities threaten to break out between Berlin on the one side and London, Paris and Saint Petersburg on the other
	22.-27.5.	Lassalle's *General German Workingmen's Association* and the Marxist *Social Democratic Workers' Party* unite in Gotha to form the *Socialist Workers' Party*
1876	15.2.	Founding of the *Central Association of German Industrialists*
	7.7.	Founding of the *German Conservative Party*
1877	10.1.	Reichstag elections: the Social Democrats poll almost half a million votes
1878	11.5./2.6.	Attempts to assassinate William I
	11.6.	Dissolution of the Reichstag
	13.6.–13.7.	Congress of Berlin
	30.6.	Reichstag elections: substantial gains for the Conservatives
	18.10.	*Anti-Socialist laws* adopted by the Reichstag
1879	12.7.	*Tariff laws* adopted by the Reichstag
	7.10.	Conclusion of the Treaty of Vienna creating the Dual Alliance between the German Empire and Austria-Hungary
1880	4.5.	First prolongation of the *anti-Socialist laws*
	14.7.	First relaxation of the *Kulturkampf* legislation
	30.8.	The Secessionists break away from the National Liberals
1881	27.10.	Reichstag elections: defeat for the Conservatives and National Liberals
1883	15.6.	Adoption of the *Sickness Insurance Act* by the Reichstag
1884		Acquisition of German colonies in South West Africa, Cameroon and Togo
	5.3.	Founding of the German Liberal Party *(Deutsch-Freisinnige Partei)*
	12.5.	Second prolongation of the *anti-Socialist laws*
	6.7.	Adoption of the *Accident Insurance Act* by the Reichstag
1886	2.4.	Third prolongation of the *anti-Socialist laws*
	21.5.	Adoption of the first pacification act designed to end the *Kulturkampf*
1887	14.1.	Presentation of the three-year military-appropriations bill and dissolution of the Reichstag

	21./28.2.	Reichstag elections: the Conservatives and National Liberals, who have formed an electoral pact (the "cartel"), secure a majority of seats in the Reichstag
	29.4.	The second pacification act finally puts an end to the *Kulturkampf*
	18.6.	The Reinsurance Treaty, a secret neutrality agreement, is concluded between Russia and the German Empire
1888	17.2.	Fourth prolongation of the *anti-Socialist laws*
	9.3.	William I dies and is succeeded by his terminally ill son, Frederick III
	15.6.	Death of Frederick III and succession of his eldest son, William II
1889	22.6.	Adoption of the *Old-Age and Invalidity Insurance Act*
1890	25.1.	The Reichstag rejects a further prolongation of the *anti-Socialist laws*
	20.2.	Reichstag elections: heavy losses for the "cartel" parties. The Social Democrats poll the largest share of the vote for the first time
	20.3.	Bismarck is dismissed as Imperial Chancellor and Prime Minister of Prussia; General Count Leo von Caprivi succeeds him, and a *new course* is pursued in the realms of social and tariff policy
	27.3.	The Reinsurance Treaty between Germany and Russia is not renewed
	1.7.	Zanzibar is exchanged by treaty for the British colony of Heligoland in an accommodation between British and German colonial interests
	30.9.	Termination of the *anti-Socialist laws*
1891	1.7.	Founding of the *Pan-German Association*
1893	18.2.	Founding of the *Farmers' League*
	6.5.	The Reichstag rejects a bill to increase the strength of the army and is dissolved
	15.6.	Reichstag elections: victory for the parties of the "cartel"; the new Reichstag approves the bill to increase the strength of the army
1894	26./29.10.	Caprivi is dismissed as Imperial Chancellor, and Chlodwig, Prince of Hohenlohe-Schillingsfürst, is appointed Imperial Chancellor and Prime Minister of Prussia
1895	11.5.	The Reichstag rejects the *Sedition Bill*
1896	1.7.	The German Civil Code is adopted by the Reichstag
1897	18.6.	Admiral Alfred von Tirpitz is appointed Secretary of State in the Imperial Naval Department and oversees the expansion of the German fleet
1898	28.3.	Adoption of the first *Navy Act*
	30.4.	Founding of the *German Navy League*
1899	20.11.	The Reichstag rejects the *Prisons Bill*
1900	1.1.	The German Civil Code enters into force
	17./18.10.	Resignation of Hohenlohe-Schillingfürst and appointment of Prince Bernhard von Bülow as Imperial Chancellor
1903		Construction work begins on the Berlin-Baghdad railway
1904	8.4.	The *Entente Cordiale* is concluded between France and Britain
1905/06		First Moroccan crisis between France and the German Empire; start of the Anglo-German naval arms race
1906	21.5.	Repeal of the constitutional provision prohibiting the remuneration of members of the Reichstag
	13.12.	Dissolution of the Reichstag
1907	25.1.	Reichstag elections: the election campaign is dominated by colonial issues and is dubbed the *Hottentot election*
	31.8.	Signing of the Anglo-Russian convention
1908	Oct./Nov.	The *Daily Telegraph* affair
1909	14.7.	Resignation of Bülow and appointment of Theobald von Bethmann Hollweg as the new Imperial Chancellor and Prime Minister of Prussia
1910	March	The Liberal parties of the Left unite to form the *Progressive People's Party*

1911		Second Moroccan crisis; Alsace-Lorraine is accorded the same constitutional status as the German federal states
1912	12.1.	Reichstag elections: for the first time, the SPD emerges with the largest number of votes and seats
	21.5.	The Reichstag adopts the amended Navy Act
1913	Nov./Dec.	The *Zabern affair*
1914	28.6.	Assassination of the Austro-Hungarian crown prince, Archduke Franz Ferdinand, by a Serb nationalist in Sarajevo
	28.7.	Austria-Hungary declares war on Serbia
	30.7.	Russia mobilizes her armed forces
	1.8.	Germany mobilizes her forces and declares war on Russia
	3.8.	Germany declares war on France
	4.8.	German troops invade neutral Belgium, and Britain declares war on the German Empire; all the parties in the Reichstag approve the war credits, including the SPD *(parliamentary truce)*
	26.–31.8.	Annihilation of the Second Russian Army at the Battle of Tannenberg
	10.9.	German advance grinds to a halt at the River Marne
1916	21.2.–9.7.	Battle of Verdun
	29.8.	Field Marshal General Paul von Hindenburg and Major General Erich Ludendorff are entrusted with supreme control of the Army High Command
1917	9.1.	Decision to engage in unrestricted submarine warfare
	14.3.	*February Revolution* in Russia. Czar Nicholas II abdicates
	6.4.	The United States declares war on the German Empire
	7.4.	William II, in his *Easter message*, announces plans to reform the Prussian three-class voting system
	9.–11.4.	Founding of the *Independent Social Democratic Party* (USPD)
	13./14.7.	Dismissal of Bethmann Hollweg and appointment of Georg Michaelis as Imperial Chancellor
	19.7.	The Reichstag adopts a peace resolution, and a Cross-Party Committee is formed by Social Democrats, Centrists and Liberals
	2.9.	Founding of the *German Fatherland Party*
	1.11.	Dismissal of Michaelis and appointment of Georg von Hertlings as Imperial Chancellor
	7.11.	*October Revolution* in Russia (Bolshevik coup)
	15.12.	Ceasefire between Russia and the German Empire
1918	8.1.	Publication of US President Woodrow Wilson's 14-point programme
	28.1.	Mass strikes in Berlin and other major German cities
	3.3.	Signing of the Treaty of Brest-Litovsk with the Soviet Union
	8.8.	Collapse of the German positions at Amiens
	29.9.	Call by the Military High Command for a ceasefire to be offered
	30.9.	Dismissal of Reich Chancellor Hertling; signing of the Parliamentarization Decree by William II
	3.10.	Appointment of Prince Max of Baden as Reich Chancellor, involvement of the SPD, Centre Party and Liberals in the government
	24.–28.10.	Constitutional reform approved by the Reichstag, Federal Diet and Emperor, parliamentarization of the Reich Executive
	26.10.	Dismissal of Ludendorff, appointment of Wilhelm Groener as his successor
	28.10.	Beginning of the mutiny in the German High Seas Fleet
	3./4.11.	Sailors' uprising in Kiel, formation of workers' and soldiers' councils
	6.11.	Spread of the revolutionary movement to Hamburg, Lübeck and Bremen
	7.11.	Revolution in Munich, fall of the Wittelsbach dynasty

	9.11.	Transfer of the office of Reich Chancellor to Friedrich Ebert (SPD) by Prince Max of Baden; proclamation of the Republic by Philipp Scheidemann (SPD); proclamation of a socialist republic by Karl Liebknecht from the Berlin City Palace
	10.11.	Formation of the Council of People's Representatives made up of politicians from the SPD and USPD; alliance between Ebert and Groener; flight of William II to the neutral Netherlands
	11.11.	Signing of the Armistice at Compiègne
	15.11.	Founding of the Central Working Group as a forum for collective bargaining between employers (heavy industry) and workers (the trade unions)
	20.11.	Founding of the German Democratic Party (DDP)
	24.11.	Founding of the German National People's Party (DNVP)
	28.11.	Abdication of William II
	15.12.	Founding of the German People's Party (DVP)
	16.-20.12.	Reich Congress of Workers' and Soldiers' Councils in Berlin
	23.12.	Mutiny of the People's Naval Division in Berlin, unrest and fighting around the Berlin City Palace
	29.12.	Resignation of the USPD members from the Council of People's Representatives
1919	1.1.	Founding of the Communist Party of Germany (KPD)
	5.1.	Founding of the German Workers' Party (later NSDAP)
	5.–12.1.	Spartacus Uprising in Berlin
	15.1.	Murder of Rosa Luxemburg and Karl Liebknecht by Free Corps soldiers
	18.1.	Opening of the peace conference in Paris
	19.1.	Elections to the constituent National Assembly
	6.2.	Opening of the National Assembly at the Weimar National Theatre
	11.2.	Election of Friedrich Ebert as Reich President
	13.2.	Formation of the Weimar Coalition (SPD, Centre Party and DDP) under Reich Minister-President Philipp Scheidemann
	March/ April	Communist uprisings in Berlin, the Ruhr region and central Germany
	7.4.–2.5.	Munich soviet republic
	7.5.	Presentation of the peace conditions to the German delegation at Versailles
	16.6.	Presentation of ultimatum to the German government on the acceptance of the peace treaty
	20.6.	Resignation of Scheidemann's government
	23.6.	Acceptance of the peace treaty by the National Assembly
	28.6.	Signing of the peace treaty (Versailles Treaty)
	11.8.	Entry into force of the Weimar Reich Constitution
	18.11.	Confirmation of the "stab-in-the-back" legend by Hindenburg
1920	13.–17.3.	Kapp-Lüttwitz Putsch in Berlin
	March/ April	Communist uprisings in the Ruhr and central Germany
	6.6.	Reichstag elections: severe losses for the Weimar Coalition, formation of a minority cabinet (Centre Party, DDP, DVP) under Reich Chancellor Konstantin Fehrenbach (Centre Party)
	16.10.	Split of the USPD
	4.–7.12.	Merger of the left wing of the USPD with the KPD
1921	20.3.	Plebiscite in Upper Silesia
	26.8.	Murder of Matthias Erzberger (Centre Party) by right-wing extremists
1922	16.4.	Treaty of Rapallo between the Soviet Union and the German Reich
	24.6.	Murder of Reich Minister for Foreign Affairs Walther Rathenau (DDP) by right-wing extremists

	18.7.	Adoption of the Act for the Protection of the Republic
	24.9.	Amalgamation of the remainder of the USPD with the SPD
	22.11.	Formation of a minority cabinet (DDP, Centre Party, DVP, BVP) under Reich Chancellor Wilhelm Cuno (Independent)
1923	11.1.	Occupation of the Ruhr by French and Belgian troops
	13.1.	Call for passive resistance by Reich Chancellor Cuno
	12./13.8.	Resignation of the Cuno cabinet, formation of "grand coalition" (SPD, DVP, Centre, DDP), led by Reich Chancellor Gustav Stresemann (DVP)
	26.9.	Abandonment of the struggle in the Ruhr by the Stresemann government; imposition of a state of emergency in Bavaria, leading the Reich government to impose a state of emergency throughout Germany
	October/ November	Separatist unrest in the Rhineland and the Palatinate
	19.10.– 18.2.1924	Conflict between Bavaria and the Reich
	22.–24.10.	Attempted Communist uprising in Hamburg
	29.10.	Invocation of Article 48 of the constitution against the SPD/KPD government in Saxony
	8./9.11.	Hitler's putsch in Munich
	15.11.	Introduction of the rentenmark aimed at halting inflation
	23.11.	Collapse of the Stresemann government, formation of a minority cabinet (Centre, DDP, DVP, BVP), led by Reich Chancellor Wilhelm Marx (Centre)
1924	13.2.	Lifting of the state of emergency across the Reich
	1.4.	Sentencing of Adolf Hitler (NSDAP) to five years imprisonment
	4.5.	Reichstag elections: losses for the governing parties
	29.8.	Acceptance of the Dawes Plan in the Reichstag
	7.12.	Reichstag elections: gains for the SPD and the middle-class liberal parties, beginning of a period of relative stability in the Weimar Republic
1925	15.1.	Formation of a "Citizens Bloc" government (Centre, BVP, DVP, DNVP), led by Reich Chancellor Hans Luther (independent)
	27.2.	Re-establishment of the NSDAP
	28.2.	Death of Reich President Friedrich Ebert
	26.4.	Election of Paul von Hindenburg as Reich President
	14.7.	Beginning of withdrawal from the Ruhr by French and Belgian troops
	27.11.	Vote in the Reichstag approving the *Locarno* Treaties
1926	24.4.	Signing of the Treaty of Berlin with the Soviet Union ("Treaty of Friendship and Neutrality")
	5.5.	Entry into force of the Flags Regulation
	12.5.	Resignation of the Luther cabinet triggered by the Flags Regulation
	20.6.	Referendum on the expropriation of the princes' assets
	8.9.	Admission of Germany to the League of Nations
1928	20.5.	Reichstag elections: gains for the SPD and KPD, losses for the conservatives and liberals
	28.6.	Formation of a grand coalition (SPD, Centre, DDP and DVP), led by Reich Chancellor Hermann Müller (SPD)
	October	Lockout of metalworkers in the Ruhr
	20.10.	Election of Alfred Hugenberg as Chairman of the DNVP
	16.11.	Vote in the Reichstag on the building of Armoured Cruiser A
	8.12.	Election of Ludwig Kaas as Chairman of the Centre Party
1929	7.6.	Signing of the Young Plan
	3.10.	Death of Reich Foreign Minister Gustav Stresemann

	25.10.	Black Friday on Wall Street, beginning of the world economic crisis
	22.12.	Rejection of the Young Plan in a referendum
1930	12.3.	Approval of the Young Plan by the Reichstag
	27.3.	Resignation of the Müller government
	29./30.3	Appointment of Heinrich Brüning (Centre) as Reich Chancellor, formation of the first presidential cabinet
	30.6.	Withdrawal from the Ruhr ahead of schedule
	16.7.	Dissolution of the Reichstag. Issuance of first emergency decree by the Reich President to "safeguard the economy and finances"
	14.9.	Reichstag elections, emergence of the NSDAP as the second-strongest parliamentary group
	1.12.	Continuation of anti-inflationary policy, with further emergency decrees
1931	13.7.	Banking crisis in Germany
	9.10.	Reshuffle of Reich Chancellor Brüning's presidential cabinet
	11.10.	Rally by the NSDAP, DNVP and *Stahlhelm* in Bad Harzburg *(Harzburger Front)*
	16.12.	Formation of the "Iron Front" (SPD, General German Trade Union Federation, workers' sports federations and the *Reichsbanner Schwarz-Rot-Gold* organization)
1932	February	Peak in the number of unemployed (over 6 million)
	10.4.	Re-election of Reich President Hindenburg
	13.4.	Ban on the SA and SS
	30.5.	Resignation of the Brüning government
	1.6.	Formation of a rightwing conservative cabinet led by Reich Chancellor Franz von Papen (independent, formerly Centre)
	4.6.	Dissolution of the Reichstag
	16.6.	Lifting of the ban on the SA and SS
	16.6.–9.7.	Lausanne Conference (end to reparations payments)
	20.7.	Use of emergency decree against Prussia, ousting of the acting *Land* government led by Otto Braun (SPD), Papen takes over government duties
	31.7.	Reichstag elections: emergence of the NSDAP as the strongest parliamentary group
	12.9.	Vote of no confidence in Papen, dissolution of the Reichstag
	6.11.	Reichstag elections: despite suffering losses, the NSDAP remains the strongest parliamentary group
	17.11.	Resignation of the Papen cabinet
	3.12.	Appointment of General Kurt von Schleicher (independent) as Reich Chancellor
	8.12.	Resignation of Gregor Strasser (NSDAP) from his party functions
1933	4.1.	Meeting between Papen and Hitler, preparations made to oust Reich Chancellor Schleicher
	28.1.	Reich Chancellor Schleicher resigns
	30.1.	Adolf Hitler appointed Reich Chancellor
	27/28.2.	Reichstag fire
	28.2.	Reich President's Decree "to protect the people and the State"
	5.3.	Reichstag elections: a majority for the NSDAP and its coalition partner, the DNVP
	23.3.	The Enabling Act is approved by the Reichstag, despite the opposition of the SPD
	31.3.	First "law to coordinate the *Länder* with the Reich"
	1.4.	Organized boycott of Jewish businesses begins
	7.4.	Second "coordination law" and the "Act on the Re-establishment of the Permanent Civil Service"
	2.5.	Smashing of the trade unions
	10.5.	"Burning of un-German literature" on the Opernplatz in Berlin
	June/July	Disbanding of all parties with the exception of the NSDAP

	14.7.	"Law for the Prevention of Progeny with Hereditary Diseases"
	20.7.	Concordat between the German Reich and the Vatican
	14.10.	Germany withdraws from the League of Nations
	12.11.	First Reichstag elections on the basis of unified lists
1934	31.1.	Abolition of the *Länder* parliaments
	24.4.	The *Volksgerichtshof*, or "People's Court" established to prosecute those accused of high treason or treason
	30.6./1.7.	*Röhm Putsch*, elimination of the SA as a power factor
	2.8.	Death of Hindenburg; the offices of Reich President and Reich Chancellor are merged
1935	21.5.	Reintroduction of conscription
	15.9.	*Nuremberg Laws*; beginning of process depriving the Jewish population systematically of their rights
1936	7.3.	German troops march into the demilitarized Rhineland
	17.7.	Spanish Civil War begins
	1.8.	Olympic Games open in Berlin
	25.10.	German-Italian treaty, *Berlin-Rome Axis*
	25.11.	*Anti-Comintern Pact* between Germany and Japan
1938	12.3.	German troops march into Austria
	10.4.	Last elections to the – now renamed – *Reichstag of Greater Germany*, in conjunction with a plebiscite on the annexation of Austria
	29.9.	Munich Agreement on the ceding of the Sudetenland to the German Reich
	9.11.	*Reichskristallnacht* (organized pogrom against German Jews)
1939	30.1.	Constituent sitting of the Reichstag of Greater Germany; Enabling Act extended
	15.3.	German troops invade Czechoslovakia; Reich Protectorate of Bohemia and Moravia established
	23.8.	German-Soviet non-aggression pact concluded
	1.9.	Germany attacks Poland
	3.9.	Great Britain and France declare war on the German Reich
1940	9.4.	German occupation of Denmark; invasion of Norway
	10.5.	Germany attacks Belgium, the Netherlands, Luxembourg and France
	22.6.	Signing of the Franco-German ceasefire in Compiègne
1941	24.3.	The Wehrmacht advances on the Libyan-Egyptian border
	17.4.	Yugoslavia surrenders; German operations against Greece are intensified
	27.4.	Athens captured
	22.6.	Germany attacks the Soviet Union
	11.12.	Germany declares war on the USA
1942	20.1.	*Wannsee Conference* (announcement of the "final solution to the Jewish question")
	26.4.	Last sitting of the Reichstag (the will of the Führer declared absolute by decision of the Reichstag)
1943	14.–25.1.	Casablanca Conference between Churchill and Roosevelt (demand for unconditional surrender of the enemy)
	31.1./2.2.	Surrender of the German 6th Army at Stalingrad
	13.5.	Surrender of German troops in North Africa
	24.7./3.9.	Mussolini ousted from power; Italy's new government calls a cease-fire following negotiations with the western Allies
1944	6.6.	Landing of the western Allies in north-western France
	20.7.	Attack on Hitler by Stauffenberg, attempted *coup d'état* fails
1945	4.–11.2.	Yalta Conference (basic outline of future occupation policy laid down)
	25.4.	American and Soviet troops meet at Torgau
	30.4.	Hitler commits suicide

	7./8.5.	Total surrender of the Wehrmacht in Reims and Berlin-Karlshorst
	10.6.	Command No. 2 of the Soviet military administration (SMAD): licensing of political parties and trade unions
	1.–4.7.	Withdrawal of British and American troops from Saxony, Thuringia and Mecklenburg; occupation of the western sectors of Berlin
	14.7.	Founding of the *United Front of Anti-Fascist Democratic Parties* in Berlin
	17.7.–2.8.	Potsdam Conference
	August/ September	Licensing of political parties begins in the western zones of occupation
	10.10.	Prohibition of the NSDAP
1946	20./27.1.	First municipal elections in the American zone
	5.3.	Churchill's Fulton speech on the emerging division of Europe
	21./22.4.	Merger of the KPD and SPD to form the SED in the Soviet Zone and East Berlin
	30.6.	Referendum in Saxony on expropriating the property of "war criminals and Nazi activists"
	29.7.– 15.10.	Paris peace conference
	30.9./1.10.	Delivery of judgements in the trial of main war criminals at Nuremburg
	20.10.	*Land* parliament elections in the Soviet Zone of Occupation (SBZ)
	2.12.	Anglo-American agreement on the merger of the British and American zones signed in Washington
1947	25.2.	Formal dissolution of Prussia by the Allied Control Council
	12.3.	Proclamation of the Truman Doctrine
	5.6.	Announcement of a European reconstruction programme by US Secretary of State Marshall
	6./7.6.	Conference of German minister-presidents in Munich
	14.6.	Formation of the German Economic Commission in the Soviet Zone
	25.6.	Constitution of the Frankfurt-based Economic Council
	25.11.– 2.12.	London conference of the foreign ministers of the four victorious powers
1948	23.2.–6.3./ 20.4.–7.6.	Six-power conference in London (adoption of the London Recommendations on the establishment of a West German state)
	17./18.3.	II German People's Congress in the Soviet Zone
	20.3.	Last meeting of the Allied Control Council
	20./21.6.	Currency reform in the Western zones
	23.6.	Currency reform in the Soviet Zone
	24.6.	Beginning of the Berlin Blockade
	1.7.	Presentation of the Frankfurt Documents to the minister-presidents of the West German *Länder*
	10.–23.8.	Constitutional convention on Herrenchiemsee
	1.9.	Constitution of the Parliamentary Council in Bonn
1949	4.4.	Founding of NATO
	4.5.	Jessup-Malik Agreement on the lifting of the Berlin Blockade on 12 May
	15./16.5.	Elections to the III German People's Congress in the Soviet Zone with a single list of candidates
	23.5.	Promulgation of the Basic Law of the Federal Republic of Germany
	14.8.	Elections to the 1st German Bundestag
	7.9.	Constituent sitting of the German Bundestag
	12.9.	Election of Theodor Heuss (FDP) as first President of the Federal Republic by the Federal Assembly
	15.9.	Election of Konrad Adenauer (CDU) as first Federal Chancellor by the Bundestag

	20.9.	Swearing-in of the first Federal Government made up of the CDU/CSU, FDP and German Party
	21.9.	Entry into force of the Occupation Statute
	7.10.	Constitution of the Provisional People's Chamber, founding of the GDR
	11./12.10.	Election of Wilhelm Pieck (SED) as President of the GDR by the Provisional People's Chamber; formation of the first GDR government under Minister-President Otto Grotewohl (SED)
	22.11.	Petersberg Agreement to end the dismantling of industrial facilities in the Federal Republic
1950	8.2.	Vote by the People's Chamber on the establishment of the National Defence Council and the creation of a Ministry for State Security in the GDR
	15.6.	Vote in the Bundestag on the accession of the Federal Republic to the Council of Europe
	25.6.	Outbreak of the Korean War
	20.–24.7.	III Party Conference of the SED, election of Walter Ulbricht as Secretary-General
	29.9.	Accession of the GDR to the Council for Mutual Economic Assistance (COMECON)
	15.10.	First elections to the People's Chamber
1951	15.3.	Entry into force of the Housing Ownership Law in the Federal Republic
	10.4.	Adoption of the Law on Co-determination in the Coal, Iron and Steel Industry by the Bundestag
	18.4.	Signing of the Treaty of Paris establishing the European Coal and Steel Community
1952	27.5.	Signing of the Treaty on the Establishment of a European Defence Community (EDC) in Paris
	9.–12.7.	2nd SED Party Conference, vote on the "construction of the foundations of socialism in the GDR"
	23.7.	Division of the GDR into 14 districts and 217 counties
1953	5.3.	Death of Joseph Stalin
	7.–19.4.	Federal Chancellor Adenauer's first visit to the USA
	17.6.	Anti-Communist workers' uprising in East Berlin and the GDR
	25.6.	Adoption of the electoral law for the 2nd Bundestag (introduction of the second vote, tightening of the clause on the percentage of the vote required to win seats in parliament)
	27.7.	Ceasefire in Korea
1954	25.3.	Recognition of the GDR as a sovereign state by the Soviet Union
	23.10.	Signing of the Paris Agreements on the Federal Republic's accession to NATO and West German rearmament following the rejection of the EDC Treaty by the French National Assembly
1955	5.5.	Entry into force of the Paris Agreements, expiry of the Occupation Statute
	14.5.	Founding of the Warsaw Pact with the GDR as a member
	9.–13.9.	Visit by Chancellor Adenauer to the Soviet Union
	23.10.	Referendum in the Saarland (rejection of a Europeanization of the Saar)
	12.11.	Founding of the Federal Armed Forces
	8./9.12.	Hallstein Doctrine (threat of sanctions by the Federal Government against states that granted diplomatic recognition to the GDR)
1956	18.1.	Vote by the People's Chamber on the establishment of the National People's Army
	14.–25.2.	XX CPSU Party Congress, beginning of de-Stalinization in the Soviet Union
	20./23.2.	Collapse of the Arnold government in North Rhine-Westphalia triggered by the FDP, coalition crisis, withdrawal of the FDP from the Federal Government
	4.6.	Saar Treaty on the incorporation of the Saarland into the Federal Republic signed in Luxembourg
1957	21.1.	Adoption of the Pension Reform Law by the Bundestag

	25.3.	Signing of the Treaty of Rome establishing the European Economic Community (EEC)
	15.9.	Bundestag elections: absolute majority for the CDU/CSU
1958	19.3.	Constituent sitting of the European Parliamentary Assembly in Strasbourg
	20.–25.3.	Bundestag debate on the arming of the Federal Armed Forces with nuclear weapons
1959	13.–15.11.	SPD Federal Party Conference at Godesberg (adoption of a new party programme)
1960	30.6.	Herbert Wehner's speech in the Bundestag: SPD's declaration of support for rearmament and integration into the Western community
	7./12.9.	Death of Wilhelm Pieck; formation of the State Council of the GDR chaired by Walter Ulbricht
1961	4.5.	Adoption of the Federal Insurance Contribution Act by the Bundestag
	13.8.	Construction of the Berlin Wall
	17.9.	Bundestag elections: CDU and CSU lose their absolute majority
1962	27.11./ 14.12.	Federal Government reshuffle following the *Spiegel* affair
1963	22.1.	Signing of the Treaty on Franco-German Cooperation in Paris
	24./25.6.	Conference of the SED and the Council of Ministers of the GDR to discuss the New Economic System of Planning and Management
	26.6.	Visit by US President Kennedy to West Berlin
	15./16.10.	Resignation of Federal Chancellor Adenauer, election of Federal Economic Minister Ludwig Erhard (CDU) as his successor
	17.12.	First agreement between the GDR and the West Berlin Senate on the issue of passes to West Berliners for visits to East Berlin
1964	21./24.9.	Death of Otto Grotewohl; confirmation of Willi Stoph (SED) as new Chairman of the Council of Ministers by the People's Chamber
1965	25.3.	Vote by the Bundestag on the extension of the period of limitation for Nazi crimes
	15.–18.12.	11th Meeting of the Central Committee of the SED (implementation of a restrictive cultural policy)
1966	27.10.	Resignation of FDP ministers from the Federal Government
	1.12.	Formation of a Grand Coalition between the CDU/CSU and the SPD under Federal Chancellor Kurt Georg Kiesinger (CDU)
1967	31.1.	Establishment of diplomatic relations between the Federal Republic and Romania (relaxation of the *Hallstein* doctrine)
	14.2.	Establishment of the "concerted action" group, led by Federal Minister of Economics Karl Schiller
	20.2.	Introduction of GDR citizenship
	1.7.	Merger of the EEC, ECSC and Euratom into the European Community (EC)
1968	6.4.	Referendum on the new GDR constitution, legitimizing the SED's claim to political leadership
	11.–17.4.	"Easter disturbances" in West Berlin and several cities in the Federal Republic, following the attempted assassination of student leader Rudi Dutschke
	30.5.	Passing of constitutional rules applicable in a state of emergency and several items of emergency legislation by the Bundestag
	21.8.	Invasion of Czechoslovakia by Warsaw Pact troops, suppression of the *Prague Spring*
1969	5.3.	Election of Gustav Heinemann (SPD) as Federal President
	12.5.	Promulgation of amendments to the Basic Law, introducing financial reform (changes to the distribution of tax revenue between the Federation, the *Länder* and the municipalities)

	28.9.	Bundestag elections: significant increase in votes for the SPD
	21./22.10.	Election of SPD Chairman Willy Brandt as Federal Chancellor, formation of a government by the SPD and FDP
	28.11.	Signing of the Treaty on the Non-Proliferation of Nuclear Weapons by the Federal Republic
1970	19.3.	Meeting between Stoph and Brandt in Erfurt
	21.5.	Return visit by Stoph to Kassel
	12.8.	Signing of the Treaty of Moscow between the Federal Republic and the Soviet Union
	7.12.	Signing of the Warsaw Treaty between the Federal Republic and Poland
1971	3.5.	XVI Plenary of the SED Central Committee: replacement of First Secretary Ulbricht by Erich Honecker
	3.9.	Signing of the Four-Power Agreement on Berlin
	10.12.	Award of the Nobel Peace Prize to Federal Chancellor Brandt
1972	9.3.	Debate in the People's Chamber on the "Law on the termination of pregnancy", adoption of the bill with 14 votes against and 8 abstentions.
	27.4.	Failure of the vote of no confidence in Federal Chancellor Brandt tabled by the CDU/CSU
	17.5.	Ratification of the Treaty of Moscow and the Warsaw Treaty by the Bundestag
	19.11.	Bundestag elections: clear victory for the Social Democrat-Liberal coalition
	21.12.	Signing of the Basic Treaty between the Federal Republic and the GDR in East Berlin
1973	18.9.	Accession of the Federal Republic and the GDR to the United Nations
	October	Beginning of a world oil crisis, imposition of export restrictions by the Arab producers and introduction of price increases by OPEC
	11.12.	Signing of the Treaty of Prague between the Federal Republic and Czechoslovakia
1974	6.5.	Resignation of Federal Chancellor Brandt
	16./17.5.	Election of Finance Minister Helmut Schmidt (SPD) as Federal Chancellor, renewal of the Social Democrat-Liberal coalition
	4.9.	Establishment of diplomatic relations between the GDR and the USA
1975	1.8.	Signing of the CSCE Final Act in Helsinki
1976	18.–22.5.	IX SED party conference (proclamation of the "unity of economic and social policy"
	3.10.	Bundestag elections: narrow victory for the ruling Social Democrat-Liberal coalition
	16.11.	Expulsion of singer and poet Wolf Biermann from the GDR
1977	5.9.–15.10.	Climax of a wave of terrorist attacks in the Federal Republic: kidnapping and murder of the president of the Confederation of German Employers' Associations, Hanns-Martin Schleyer, hijacking of a Lufthansa plane en route to Mogadishu in Somalia, liberation of the hostages by GSG 9, suicide of the terrorists Baader, Ensslin and Raspe in custody
1978	16./17.7.	G7 summit in Bonn
1979	31.3.	Mass demonstrations against the planned nuclear waste disposal site in Gorleben
	7.–10.6.	First direct elections to the European Parliament
	12.12.	Decision on force modernization by NATO Council of Ministers
	27.12.	Soviet intervention in Afghanistan
1980	5.10.	Bundestag elections: strengthening of the Social Democrat-Liberal majority
1981	10.10.	Demonstration in Bonn against NATO's policy of force modernization
	11.-13.12.	Visit to the GDR by Federal Chancellor Schmidt
	13.12.	Imposition of martial law in Poland
1982	17.9.	Collapse of the Social-Democrat Liberal coalition, dismissal of the FDP ministers

	1.10.	Vote of no confidence: replacement of Federal Chancellor Schmidt and his minority SPD government by a Christian Democrat-Liberal coalition led by Federal Chancellor Kohl (CDU)
1983	6.3.	Bundestag elections: absolute majority for the Christian Democrat-Liberal coalition; entry of the Greens into the Bundestag
	29.3.	Confirmation in office of Helmut Kohl as Federal Chancellor
	21./22.11.	Bundestag debate on NATO's decision on force modernization
1985	11.3.	Beginning of Mikhail Gorbachev's term in office as General Secretary of the Communist Party of the Soviet Union
1986	3.6.	Establishment of a Federal Ministry for the Environment, Nature Conservation and Nuclear Safety
1987	25.1.	Bundestag elections: retention of majority by the CDU/CSU and FDP, who once again form the Federal Government
	7.–11.9.	Visit to the Federal Republic by the Chairman of the Council of State, Erich Honecker
1988	27./28.6.	EC summit meeting in Hanover (decision on the establishment of a European single market)
1989	7.5.	Local elections in the GDR, protests against blatant vote-rigging
	11.6	Opening of the Hungarian border with Austria, beginning of a mass exodus of GDR citizens to the Federal Republic
	4.9.	First of the Leipzig *Monday demonstrations*, in support of political reforms and democracy
	9.9.	Founding of the New Forum opposition movement in the GDR
	7.10.	Celebrations marking the 40th anniversary of the foundation of the GDR, stepping-up of action against protest demonstrations by the security forces
	18.10.	Replacement of Erich Honecker as SED General Secretary by Egon Krenz
	9.11.	Opening of the Berlin Wall, lifting of travel restrictions on GDR citizens
1990	18.3.	First democratic elections to the People's Chamber: victory for the "Alliance for Germany", formed under the leadership of the GDR-CDU
	1.7.	Entry into force of Monetary, Economic and Social Union between the Federal Republic and the GDR, and the first stage of European Economic and Monetary Union
	23.8.	People's Chamber resolution on the accession of the GDR to the territories subject to the Basic Law
	31.8.	Signing of the Reunification Treaty by Federal Minister of the Interior Wolfgang Schäuble and GDR State Secretary Günther Krause
	12.9.	Signing of the Treaty on the Final Settlement with respect to Germany (confirming full sovereignty and the freedom of the united Germany to belong to alliances)
	3.10.	Accession of the five new *Länder* and East Berlin to the Federal Republic of Germany
	2.12.	First Bundestag elections for the whole of Germany: clear confirmation of support for the CDU/CSU/FDP coalition, entry into the Bundestag by the PDS and the East German citizens' rights party Alliance 90 for the first time
1991	17.1.–3.3.	War of the USA and its allies against Iraq to free Kuwait
	20.6.	Vote by the Bundestag to transfer the seat of parliament and government to the capital, Berlin
	20./28.6.	Declaration of independence by Slovenia and Croatia, beginning of sustained armed conflicts in many areas of the former Yugoslavia
	8.12.	Dissolution of the Soviet Union; founding of the "Commonwealth of Independent States" (CIS) in Minsk

	9./10.12.	EC summit meeting in Maastricht, signing of the Treaties on Economic and Monetary Union and on political union
1992	3.6.	Earth Summit in Rio de Janeiro
	6.12.	Agreement between the coalition partners, the CDU/CSU and the FDP, and the social-democratic opposition on an amendment to the article on asylum law in the Basic Law and a reorganization of asylum procedures
1993	1.1.	Entry into force of the EC single market
	14.–16.5.	Merger of the Greens with the civil rights party Alliance 90
	26.5.	Ratification of the change to asylum law
	22.7.	First participation of German soldiers in a UN peace-keeping mission, in Belet Huen, Somalia
	29.10.	Agreement by the EC heads of government on Frankfurt am Main as the seat of the future European Central Bank
	1.11.	Entry into force of the Maastricht Treaty, conversion of the EC into the European Union (EU)
1994	29.5.	Death of Honecker in Chile
	12.7.	Rejection by the Federal Constitutional Court of a constitutional complaint by the SPD and FDP opposing the participation of the Federal Armed Forces in out-of-area missions
	16.10.	Bundestag elections: retention of narrow majority by the CDU/CSU and the FDP; success for the PDS in the new federal states
1995	30.6.	Resolution by the Bundestag on sending units of the Federal Armed Forces to protect the international rapid reaction force in Bosnia-Herzegovina
	15./16.12.	Meeting of the European Council in Madrid, decision on the introduction of the euro for cashless transactions on 1 January 1999
1998	27.9.	Bundestag elections: victory for the SPD, which becomes the largest parliamentary group
	27.10.	Election of Gerhard Schröder (SPD) as Federal Chancellor by a governing coalition of the SPD and Alliance 90/Greens
1999	1.1.	Launch of the euro as a single currency in eleven EU Member States
	24.3.	Beginning of NATO air strikes against Yugoslavia, with German participation, to contain the repression of the Albanian population in the Serbian province of Kosovo
	12.6.	Stationing of German KFOR troops in the south-west of Kosovo
	23.6.	Adoption by the Federal Government of an austerity programme, set forth in greater detail in the following months, to limit national debt
2000	11.1.	Ruling by the European Court of Justice in favour of the acceptance of women in the Federal Armed Forces
	4.2.	Entry into force of EU sanctions against Austria because of the inclusion in government of the Freedom Party of Austria (FPÖ)
	25.2.	Adoption of the law on the "Promotion of electricity produced from renewable energy sources"
	18.5.	Adoption of the Social-Democrat-Green tax reform in the Bundestag (reduction of the basic and top tax rates, taxation of gains from the sale of shares, increase in tax allowances for the sale of companies)
	1.8.	Entry into force of the *Green Card* regulations aimed at tackling the shortage of IT specialists

Acknowledgements for photographs

Agentur Joker, Bonn
341 bottom

Archiv der sozialen Demokratie der Friedrich-Ebert-Stiftung, Bonn
162, 334

Archiv des Deutschen Liberalismus der Friedrich-Naumann-Stiftung, Gummersbach
104 top right and bottom, 338 top

Archiv für Christlich-Demokratische Politik der Konrad-Adenauer-Stiftung, St. Augustin
113, 115, 328, 330, 363

Archiv für Kunst und Geschichte, Berlin
52/53, 80, 90 bottom, 95, 97 bottom, 100 top, 112, 119, 124/125, 127 bottom, 135 top, 141, 142, 146, 147, 160 bottom, 161 bottom right, 168 top, 172 top, 173 bottom, 178 top, 180 top, 181, 186, 194 bottom, 196 top, 196 bottom, 201, 204 top, 213 bottom right, 218 bottom left, 220 bottom, 227, 230 bottom, 244 top, 248 top, 261, 263 bottom, 265 bottom, 268 top, 274 bottom, 275 top, 283, 297 top, 298 top, 300 top

Archiv Gerstenberg, Wietze
91

Bayerische Staatsbibliothek, München
248 bottom

Berliner Verlag (Gruner & Jahr), Berlin
116/117, 143 top, 144, 148 bottom, 271 bottom

Bildarchiv Preußischer Kulturbesitz, Berlin
23, 26, 27, 28, 30, 31, 32, 33, 34, 35 bottom, 36, 37, 39, 42, 43, 44, 45, 46 bottom, 47, 48, 49, 50, 51, 55, 58, 59, 60, 61, 62, 65, 66 top, 67, 68, 69, 70, 71, 72, 74, 75, 76, 77, 78, 79, 81, 82, 83, 89, 90 top, 92, 93, 94, 96, 99, 100 bottom, 101, 102, 103, 104 top left, 105, 106, 107, 108, 109, 110, 111, 114, 118 top, 120, 121, 122, 123, 127 top right, 128, 129, 130, 131, 132, 133, 134 top, 138, 139, 140, 143 bottom, 149, 150, 151, 163, 164, 165, 166, 167, 169, 170, 171, 172 bottom, 174 bottom, 176 top, 178 bottom, 179, 180 bottom, 183, 185, 188, 189 bottom, 190, 191, 192, 193 bottom, 194 top, 197, 198, 199, 200, 202 top, 203, 211, 212, 213 bottom left, 214 top, 215 bottom, 216, 217 top, 221, 222, 223 top, 224, 226, 228, 229 bottom, 230 top, 232 top, 233 bottom, 234 bottom, 235, 236, 238, 241 top, 244 bottom, 245, 246, 247, 251 top, 253, 254, 266 bottom, 267, 268 bottom, 269, 270 top right and bottom, 272 bottom, 273 bottom, 276, 279 top, 280 bottom, 286, 294 bottom, 295, 296, 299, 318, 320 top, 327 top, 347 top right, 386 bottom, 387 top, 388 top, 391

Siegfried Büker, Berlin
14 bottom, 15

Bundesarchiv Koblenz
159, 173 top, 174 top, 175, 177 bottom, 189 top, 273 top, 270 top left, 280 top, 293 left, 301 top, 311 bottom, 312 top, 313 top, 314 top, 394

Michael S. Cullen, Berlin
387 bottom, 388 bottom, 389, 390

Deutsche Presse-Agentur, Frankfurt am Main
288 bottom, 298 bottom, 314 bottom, 315, 320 bottom, 323, 335, 340, 343 top, 346 bottom, 357 top, 359 bottom, 365 bottom, 372 bottom, 375, 377, 379 bottom, 381 top, 382

Deutscher Bundestag, Berlin
24 bottom, 25, 35 top, 38 top, 46 top, 57, 63, 64, 66 bottom, 97 top, 98, 127 top left, 134 bottom, 135 bottom, 136/137, 145, 176 bottom, 214 bottom, 217 bottom, 223 bottom, 231 middle, 297 bottom, 300 bottom, 331 top, 332, 339 top, 345, 346 top, 350 top, 357 bottom, 385 top, 386 top

Deutsches Historisches Museum, Berlin
56, 73, 218 bottom right, 237

Generallandesarchiv Karlsruhe
38 bottom

Germanisches National-museum, Nürnberg
40

Reinhard Görner, Berlin
14 top

Historisches Museum der Stadt Frankfurt am Main
54, 385 bottom

Jürgens Ost+Europa-Photo, Berlin
312 bottom

Landesarchiv Berlin
352 top

Landesmuseum Mainz
24 top

Matthias-Domaschk-Archiv in der Robert-Havemann-Gesellschaft, Berlin
307

Presse- und Informationsamt der Bundesregierung, Berlin/Bonn
310 top, 316, 321, 322, 324, 325, 327 bottom left, 329 bottom, 333 top, 337 bottom, 343 bottom, 347 bottom, 348, 349, 351, 352 bottom, 353 top, 354, 359 top, 361 top, 364, 367, 372 top, 373, 374, 376, 378, 379 top, 380, 381 bottom, 383, 396

Progress Film-Verleih, Berlin
305 bottom

Der Spiegel, Hamburg
350 bottom

Staatliche und Städtische Kunstsammlung Kassel
41

Stadtarchiv München
215 top

Stiftung Archiv der Parteien und Massenorganisationen in der DDR, Berlin
262 top, 263 top, 264 top left, 264 bottom, 265 top, 266 top, 281 top, 294 top

Stiftung Stadtmuseum, Berlin
29

Süddeutscher Verlag (Bilderdienst), München
160 top, 161 bottom left, 168 bottom, 177 top, 182, 187, 193 top, 195, 202 bottom, 204 bottom, 225 top, 231 top, 239 left, 241 bottom, 250 bottom, 251 bottom, 252

Ullstein Bilderdienst, Berlin
118 bottom, 148 top, 152, 161 top, 184, 205, 213 top, 219, 220 top, 225 bottom, 229 top, 231 bottom, 232 middle and bottom, 233 top, 234 top, 239 right, 240, 242, 243, 249, 250 top, 255, 262 bottom, 264 top right, 271 top, 272 top, 274 top, 275 bottom, 277, 278, 279 bottom, 281 bottom, 282, 284, 285, 287, 288 top, 289, 290/291, 292, 293 right, 301 bottom, 302, 303, 304, 305 top, 306, 308, 309, 310 bottom, 311 top, 313 bottom, 317, 319, 326, 327 bottom right, 329 top, 331 bottom, 333 bottom, 336, 337 top, 338, 358, 360, 361 bottom, 362, 365 top, 366, 392, 393, 395

Acknowledgements for loans

Arbeiter-Wohlfahrt Hamburg

Archiv der sozialen Demokratie der Friedrich-Ebert-Stiftung, Bonn

Archiv des Deutschen Liberalismus der Friedrich-Naumann-Stiftung, Gummersbach

Archiv für Christlich-Demokratische Politik der Konrad-Adenauer-Stiftung, St. Augustin

Archiv für Christlich-Soziale Politik der Hanns-Seidel-Stiftung, München

Archiv für Kunst und Geschichte, Berlin

Archiv Gerstenberg, Wietze

Archiv Grünes Gedächtnis der Heinrich-Böll-Stiftung, Berlin

Badisches Landesmuseum, Karlsruhe

Bayerische Staatsbibliothek, München

Berliner Verlag (Gruner & Jahr), Berlin

Bildarchiv Preußischer Kulturbesitz, Berlin

Bundesamt für Bauwesen und Raumordnung, Bonn

Bundesarchiv (Filmarchiv), Berlin

Bundesarchiv Koblenz

Thomas Busch, Frankfurt am Main

Chronos-Film, Berlin

Michael S. Cullen, Berlin

Renate Dabrowski, Frankfurt am Main

Jupp Darchinger, Bonn

Deutsche Presse-Agentur, Frankfurt am Main

Deutsche Wochenschau, Hamburg

Deutsches Architekturmuseum, Frankfurt am Main

Deutsches Historisches Museum, Berlin

Deutsches Rundfunkarchiv, Frankfurt am Main/Berlin

Horst Dühring, Herford

Erich Schmidt Verlag, Berlin

Europäische Kommission (Vertretung in der Bundesrepublik Deutschland), Berlin

Europäisches Parlament, Straßburg

Galerie Brumme, Frankfurt am Main

Generallandesarchiv Karlsruhe

Germanisches Nationalmuseum, Nürnberg

Haus der Geschichte, Bonn

Rudolf Herz, München

Historisches Museum, Frankfurt am Main

Historisches Museum der Pfalz, Speyer

Wolfgang Hochbruck, Stuttgart

Jutta Hofmann, Neu-Isenburg

Institut für Stadtgeschichte, Frankfurt am Main

Interfoto, Hamburg

Jürgens Ost+Europa-Photo, Berlin

KEYSTONE Pressedienst, Hamburg

Lutz Kleinhans, Frankfurt am Main

Kruschke Film- und Fernsehproduktion, Berlin

Kunstarchiv Beeskow

Landesarchiv Berlin

Landesbildstelle Rheinland, Düsseldorf

Landesdenkmalamt Berlin

Landesmedienzentrum Hamburg

Landesmuseum Mainz

Matthias-Domaschk-Archiv in der Robert-Havemann-Gesellschaft, Berlin

Klaus Meier-Ude, Frankfurt am Main

Militärhistorisches Museum der Bundeswehr, Dresden

Museum der Stadt Butzbach

Neues Deutschland, Berlin

NDR, Hamburg

Axel Oleniczak, Neu-Isenburg

Polizeitechnische Untersuchungsstelle, Berlin

Georg Prager, Neu-Isenburg

Presse- und Informationsamt der Bundesregierung, Berlin/Bonn

Progress Film-Verleih, Berlin

Emma Rempfer, Frankfurt am Main

Kurt Röhrig, Braunfels

SFB, Berlin

Signum Fotografie, Hamburg

Der Spiegel, Hamburg

Staatliche Museen zu Berlin, Kunstbibliothek

Staatliche Museen Kassel

Staatsbibliothek zu Berlin Preußischer Kulturbesitz

Stadtarchiv München

Stiftung Archiv der Parteien und Massenorganisationen der DDR im Bundesarchiv, Berlin

Stiftung Stadtmuseum, Berlin

Süddeutscher Verlag (Bilderdienst), München

SWR, Baden-Baden

Transit-Film, München

Twentieth Century Fox of Germany, Frankfurt am Main

Ullstein Bilderdienst, Berlin

U.S. Embassy (Press Office), Berlin

VdK Landesverband Bayern, München

WDR, Köln

Dr. Paul Wolff & Tritschler, Offenburg

ZDF, Mainz

The publisher has endeavoured to establish the holders of the rights to the photographs in this catalogue, and is willing to compensate any holders of rights with substantiated claims who are not named here.